HOW IT WORKS

# HOW IT WORKS

## Recovering Citizens in
## Post-Welfare Philadelphia

ROBERT P. FAIRBANKS II

The University of Chicago Press | Chicago & London

ROBERT P. FAIRBANKS II is an assistant professor in the School of Social Service Administration at the University of Chicago.

The University of Chicago Press, Chicago 60637
The University of Chicago Press, Ltd., London
© 2009 by The University of Chicago
All rights reserved. Published 2009
Printed in the United States of America

18  17  16  15  14  13  12  11  10  09      1  2  3  4  5

ISBN-13: 978-0-226-23408-3    (cloth)
ISBN-13: 978-0-226-23409-0    (paper)

ISBN-10: 0-226-23408-8    (cloth)
ISBN-10: 0-226-23409-6    (paper)

Library of Congress Cataloging-in-Publication Data

Fairbanks, Robert P., II, 1968–
    How it works : recovering citizens in post-welfare Philadelphia / Robert P. Fairbanks II.
        p.  cm.
    Includes bibliographical references and index.
    ISBN-13: 978-0-226-23408-3 (hardcover : alk. paper)
    ISBN-13: 978-0-226-23409-0 (hardcover : alk. paper)
    ISBN-10: 0-226-23408-8 (pbk. : alk. paper)
    ISBN-10: 0-226-23409-6 (pbk. : alk. paper)   1. Self-help housing—Pennsylvania—Philadelphia.   2. Self-help housing—Political aspects—Pennsylvania—Philadelphia. 3. Recovery movement—Political aspects—Pennsylvania—Philadelphia.   4. Social settlements—Pennsylvania—Philadelphia.   5. Kensington (Philadelphia, Pa.)—Social conditions—21st century.   6. Welfare recipients—Housing—Pennsylvania—Philadelphia. 7. Alcoholics—Rehabilitation—Pennsylvania—Philadelphia.   8. Substance abuse treatment facilities—Government policy—Pennsylvania—Philadelphia.   9. Informal sector (Economics)—Political aspects—Pennsylvania—Philadelphia.   I. Title.
HV4196.P5F347   2009
362.29'1850974811—dc22

2008054100

♾ The paper used in this publication meets the minimum requirements of the American National Standard for Information Sciences—Permanence of Paper for Printed Library Materials, ANSI Z39.48-1992.

*To Krista, and her mother Patsy*

# Contents

Acknowledgments      *ix*

Introduction      *1*

1   The Making of AHAD      *27*

2   "How It Works":
The Basic Architecture of the Kensington Recovery House System      *65*

3   The Art of Building Programmatic Space      *99*

4   The Persistent Failures of the Recovery House System:
Low-Wage Labor, Relapse, and "the Wreckage of the Past"      *147*

5   Unruly Spaces of Managed Persistence      *189*

6   Statecraft/Self-Craft:
Policy Transfer in the Recovery House Movement      *231*

Conclusion      *261*

Notes   *271*
Bibliography   *287*
Index   *293*

# Acknowledgments

Several scholars at the University of Pennsylvania were influential to this study. Among the most notable, Ritty Lukose served as a quarterback for the project during its conceptual, fieldwork, and initial write-up stages. Mark Stern's patience, foresight, and leadership provided the necessary space for me to stretch out intellectually. Allan Irving altered the conditions of possibility by forging a path for theoretical explorations in social welfare, while Ram Cnaan played a central role in establishing my disciplinary foundation in the history and philosophy of the welfare state. In addition to reading multiple drafts after I moved to Chicago, Todd Wolfson was a consistently lucid sparring partner during the fieldwork phase. I also thank Julia Paley's seminar on urban social theory for introducing me to the literature that this book seeks to unsettle.

Since my arrival at Chicago, my colleagues at the University of Chicago's School of Social Service Administration have provided a congenial space to write this book. Of particular note, Bill Sites has been an exceptional colleague and mentor—first by reading the entire manuscript and then by way of his tireless efforts to make a stronger final product. Summerson Carr provided useful comments on earlier excerpts, and Virginia Parks has been an invaluable source of support. I was fortunate to have had two careful readers in Barbara Cruikshank and Marianna Valverde, both of whom helped to recast and fortify the book's central arguments. Jamie Peck also read and sharpened the analysis in multiple chapters. Other readers and supporters include Mark Bostic, Ralph Cintron, Richardson Dilworth, Bobbie Iversen, Stephanie Kaza, Fabian Kessl, Richard Lloyd, Davis TeSelle, Nik Theodore, Gregory Wolmart, and Steven Ziliak.

On the editorial front at the University of Chicago Press, Doug Mitchell shepherded this project through from A to Z, from what seemed like a courtesy cup-of-coffee-cum-three-hour acquisition conversation to the final page proofs. Tim McGovern has also been a stalwart throughout the process, and Sandy Hazel has been a meticulous copy editor in the final stages. In the early stages, freelance editor Laura Helper-Ferris cleaned up the book considerably through the art of developmental editing. I also acknowledge my photographer friends Geoff DeVertueuil and Renee Wagoner, as well as my brother Bruce Fairbanks, for contributing their images to the book.

This book would have been impossible were it not for Malik's unequivocal willingness to share his daily struggles and his penetrating insights on the recovery house scene. The same is true for Bilal, the consummate recovery house philosopher who had a healthy suspicion not only of his own immediate surroundings, but also of academic research. I owe a debt of gratitude to the men in each of their houses, as well as to the many recovery house operators and residents in other programs who opened their doors to an ethnographer from Center City. The man I call Billings deserves special mention for introducing me to the formal treatment sector in Philadelphia. I also wish to thank city officials from Philadelphia's Department of Licenses and Inspections, Department of Public Welfare, and Coordinating Office for Drug and Alcohol Programs for their willingness to participate in the research process.

To my young son Davis, I send thanks for the gifts of endless inspiration and the capacity to be present when I get home each night. And to Krista, and her mother Patsy, this book is dedicated to each of you for supporting me since day one.

# Introduction

After forty-plus years of hard drinking and drugging, Malik "finally surrendered." He had spent the better part of the 1970s and '80s in and out of prison (including a ten-year sentence for armed robbery at a federal penitentiary), and the better part of the '90s either unemployed, hustling, or in dead-end jobs. Threatened with living on the streets for the first time in 2001, Malik was desperate enough to follow a tip from a friend. He left his beloved city of Newark, New Jersey, to take refuge in a Christian retreat center in the Catskill Mountains of Upstate New York. He stayed "clean" in the bucolic setting for three months, and it was here, with the help of others, that he gradually came to contemplate a life of "recovery" from drugs and alcohol:

> MALIK: I wanted help because I was tired. I was fifty-one years
> old, and during the time up there on the mountain, I just kept
> thinking. It was the first time that I had a chance to open up and
> look at my life, and I said wow, everything just went, the wife, the
> house, all this stuff. I just became a different person. I had never had
> a chance to sit down and [realize that I didn't like myself]. So now I
> don't like me, and I'm like, "how did this happen?" So many things

were going in my mind, and what I had just left wasn't worth going back to. I was ready for recovery, I had made up my mind, and I was ready.

As many addicts put it, Malik had "run out of good ideas" and burned out all his options in Newark. Because he needed to make a move as his discharge date approached, retreat workers suggested that he consider Philadelphia, known among social service providers in the Northeast Corridor[1] to have relatively accessible, if loosely defined, drug and alcohol recovery networks. To actualize the plan, Malik reached out in desperation to a woman from his past, the mother of one of his seven children who lived in Chester, Pennsylvania. She agreed to help him by purchasing a one-way bus ticket to Philadelphia. Malik eventually found his way to Temple University Hospital in North Philly, a beachhead for the city's expansive recovery scene. He quickly learned that without insurance or proper identification, the hospital would not admit him unless he was intoxicated. Although he had been sober for ninety days, Malik was happy to comply with the "admission policy." He returned to the hospital drunk and, after being admitted, waited an entire weekend to speak with a social worker.

On Monday morning, a hospital social worker put him in a cab with nothing but a trash bag full of clothes and an address for a "recovery house" called Positive Attitudes. His arrival at the house in the Kensington neighborhood redefined his understanding of help and social service in the postindustrial city:

> MALIK: Now when the cab pulled up, remember I had come from this place [in the Catskill Mountains] called Mountain of Miracles, where they have all kinds of statues up the entrance walkway, you know, it's a retreat, a holy retreat, and you can't even spit on the ground. So I come from there, which is beautiful, and I go to Temple, which is a hospital. Now when they take me out, they sending me to a "recovery house." I've never been in a recovery house before, so I'm looking for [some type of] sign out front, or somebody with a white jacket to meet me and all this. So they take me to this house and I pull up in the cab, and the driver says, "You here." [starts laughing] I'm looking around, he says, "Get out, man, 3248, it's right there!" So I get out and I'm looking around and he drove off. I'm looking for a goddamned facility or an institution. I said, "What the fuck is this shit!"

The crumbling "intake house" for the Positive Attitudes program gave Malik pause. It was located on a crowded block of row houses on Frankford

A typical street corner depicting row house abandonment in the Kensington neighborhood of Philadelphia. Photograph by Renee Wagoner. Used by permission.

Avenue, several of which looked either abandoned or in extreme disrepair. What was less visible, but what Malik would soon discover, was that many such row houses had become the physical infrastructure for a new kind of recovery system.

The Kensington row house, formerly a proud symbol of working-class home ownership, has become the architectural testament to the structural violence of Philadelphia's postindustrial decline. The city is home to some thirty thousand abandoned row houses and just as many vacant lots, many of which are jarringly visible yet quickly left behind by I-95 commuters speeding past the distant landscape of Kensington. A closer look reveals the ways in which street-level recovery house operators have strategically reconfigured the row house as a site for collective poverty survival. Taken together, their efforts have produced the Philadelphia *recovery house movement*—an informal housing strategy for drug addicts and alcoholics located in the city's poorest and most heavily blighted zones.

The widespread transformation of dilapidated row houses into unlicensed, unregulated recovery houses has taken place primarily in the city's West Philadelphia, North Philadelphia, and Kensington neighborhoods since the early 1980s, with estimates ranging between four hundred and five hundred such houses citywide.[2] In Kensington alone, the estimate exceeds two hundred—with as many as sixty per square mile in the blocks surrounding the intersection of Kensington and Allegheny, or "K&A," as it is known affectionately by locals. Philadelphia's recovery houses are similar to addiction halfway houses found in other cities, yet unique given the magnitude of their numbers, the geographical scope of their constituencies, and their tendency to proliferate almost exclusively in areas of extreme poverty. Recovery houses in Pennsylvania have no official licensure or regulatory board, and they are run almost entirely by nonprofessional recovering addicts. As such, there have been widespread concerns throughout the movement's history that the houses have developed outside the realm of formal regulation.

Like so many other impoverished addicts in the Northeast Corridor, Malik found his way to Kensington by way of an intricate yet decidedly makeshift referral system. Facilitated mainly by word of mouth through family, friends, and treatment providers, the system has grown in conjunction with the recovery house movement to draw thousands of addicts and alcoholics from as far away as New Jersey, New York City, Baltimore, and even Puerto Rico. Newark's hospital and detox workers transport addicts to Philadelphia via one-way tickets on Greyhound buses or New Jersey Transit trains, establishing what many refer to as the "NJ/PA pipeline." Recovery house operators have similar networks in Baltimore, with some even traveling to the same street corners there every Saturday morning in order to haul addicts back to Philly by the vanload. More recently, town governments and churches in Puerto Rico have started purchasing one-way airline tickets to ship addicts to Philly. Whether by bus, train, plane, or car, many of these addicts land in Kensington. Some are motivated by their aspirations for a new life in recovery; others face external pressures from family members, the criminal justice system, or the hard realities of living on the street. All are driven to a perhaps most unlikely setting for rehabilitation by common forces of poverty, insecurity, and the vagaries of public welfare.

## Kensington as Recovery Capital: The Unworthy Civil Society

A world apart from the pastoral treatment settings of old, the Kensington recovery house is in many respects a manifestation of urban decay. With the loss of 75% of its manufacturing jobs between 1955 and 1980, and a decline in population from 2.1 million in 1950 to fewer than 1.5 million in 2004, Philadelphia has been especially hard hit by postindustrial decline. The vis-

An abandoned factory in Kensington, just two blocks from the intersection of Kensington and Allegheny avenues. Photograph by Bruce Fairbanks. Used by permission.

ible fallout is evident in the presence of some sixty thousand vacant properties located overwhelmingly in the city's racially segregated and formerly blue-collar factory neighborhoods. As a prime example of the latter, the neighborhood of Kensington has been transformed from a relatively stable textile manufacturing community to one of the most heavily blighted pockets of spatially concentrated poverty in the United States. At the 2000 census, 53.7% of the Kensington population lived below the official poverty line, and 40% of its properties were classified as vacant.[3] Over half (53%) of the population was classified as detached from the labor force, with over 50% receiving public assistance. Originally a predominantly white working-class neighborhood, Kensington is now, ironically, a remarkable instance of racial diversity, comprising roughly 30% whites; 25% African Americans; and 40% Latinos.[4]

The persistent migration of drug addicts and alcoholics to Kensington entails a "sobriety pilgrimage" to an area that for years has carried the dubious moniker of "the badlands" based on its allegedly having the highest per-capita cocaine and heroin sales in the country. For many, the pilgrimage ends at K&A, a renowned landmark that in many ways symbolizes

Street scene at K&A, one block from the actual intersection of Kensington and Allegheny avenues. Photograph by Bruce Fairbanks. Used by permission.

postindustrial dissolution in Philadelphia. Once a glorious streetscape and marketplace for Kensington's blue-collar families, K&A is now most commonly known for its open-air drug markets, prostitution, and countless other untaxed economies. It has also become ground zero for the neighborhood's burgeoning recovery house scene.

The presence of one of the nation's most advanced open-air drug markets alongside one of the most vibrant recovery networks in the Northeast is just one of many contradictory threads woven into the recovery house phenomenon. Depending on who's asked, Kensington recovery houses are described as either illegal flophouses or admirable self-help collectives. Politicians and community groups have labeled the houses a rogue economy rife with exploitation and fraud. Operators, however, tout them as heroic agents of civil society, "spaces of hope" in areas of spatially concentrated poverty. Through their persistent efforts to transform down-and-out addicts into "productive members of society," operators claim to reduce drug addiction, homelessness, and crime. They celebrate their almost exclusive reliance on traditions of self-help, 12-step recovery, and voluntarism, arguing that their continued service without formal state or city funding bodes favorably in an era of fiscal austerity. Recovery houses have survived by pooling the meager resources of impoverished addicts, which derive primarily from General Assistance (hereafter GA) in the form of cash aid and food stamps. Using these resources, the operators generate sustainable economies that combine food and shelter with a street-level brand of self-help recovery.

While seemingly an improvement over the abundant crack houses and "shooting galleries" dotting the Kensington landscape, the inexorable spread of recovery houses has engendered periodic hostilities from community groups and politicians. State Representative John Taylor has disparaged recovery houses as Kensington's newest and most prominent form of "industry," crowning his home district as "the absolute drug and alcohol rehabilitation capital of the world."[5] Taylor is one of the most qualified public officials to speak on the issue, as he has witnessed firsthand the growth of the recovery house industry in Kensington as well as in nearby Port Richmond and Frankford. Yet his comments belie his own reliance on recovery houses for electioneering labor as well as his reputed role in the community as a "sometimes" advocate for the movement. He has offered conditional political support for recovery house operators, based in part on their provision of cheap campaign labor as well as their occasional willingness to crowd residents into buses headed for Harrisburg for lobbying purposes. Other politicians such as Mayor John Street, Chaka Fattah, Arlen Specter, and even New Jersey governor John Corzine have either openly acknowledged their use of recovery house labor as a component of their GOTV (get out the vote) machines, or been widely reputed to have done so.[6]

Even so, most politicians are unwilling to endorse recovery houses publicly. Invoking common themes in a key informant interview, Philadelphia City Councilman James Kenney described the houses as a "misery industry" composed of little more than modern-day flophouses:

KENNEY: What happened [in the 1980s] was, there were these kind of flophouses that were being set up all over, being run by some corporation with no real credentials, no real background, no certification, no licensing, and no insurance. They were basically setting up a house where twenty to thirty people would live, where drugs were going on inside and outside. The environment they were in was not conducive to recovery, because the bad activity was going on all around them. These recovery houses, along with other types of operations, when they are good they are fine, when they are bad they become part of what I call the *misery industry*, where people who have problems—substance abuse problems, mental problems, other problems—are taken advantage of doubly. The [recovery house owners] take their welfare checks and social security checks without offering any real treatment. [The result] is just recidivism.

As Kenney's comments suggest, it is the drive for profits in this "misery industry" that is believed by critics across a range of groups (city officials, neighborhood residents, recovery house clients, and even some operators) to have fueled the spread of unlicensed recovery houses to epidemic proportions. The recurring question of profitability puts the movement's moral legitimacy under constant public scrutiny. Kenney observed that even in the best of circumstances, few among the city's politicians, city employees, social workers, or even formal treatment providers would stick their neck out publicly on behalf of a recovery house:

RF: In the best-case scenario, consider a house that really is about recovery—
   does the city look at least somewhat favorably upon the house?
KENNEY: I don't know if they would do that in any formal way. I mean,
   [to make a point], when you have people who have either a religious or a
   social mission, and they are about more than just profit, you always have
   a better operation. There are church-sponsored kinds of social services,
   people who aren't just in it for the profit, who really do care about these
   people. It's the guys that come in trying to make a fast buck, they say, "I
   can make money [running recovery houses]." They pick up two or three
   houses and stuff 'em full of people. They are the bad actors—and guess
   what? They're not the majority, but they give the majority a bad name.
   It's a small group of people tapping into other people's misery for money.

The question of welfare profiteering becomes even more potent when racial tensions enter the picture. In the case of Kensington, recovery houses have relocated hundreds of blacks and Latinos from distant locales into a once predominantly white working-class neighborhood. In the 1980s and early '90s, community groups seethed at the influx of drug addicts and criminals from neighboring states, almost all of whom were said to have applied for public assistance on the day of their arrival. At the height of racial tensions in 1994, a Port Richmond recovery house containing twelve African-American women was burned down in what authorities classified as a "racially motivated incident."[7] Fueling the controversy, the media has documented incidences of not only substandard housing and overcrowding, but also welfare fraud, financial/sexual exploitation, and the dissolution of certain recovery houses into crack houses or brothels. In so doing, the Philadelphia press has effectively slandered Kensington's "newest form of industry" as a highly exploitative form of welfare economy.[8]

Yet while the allegations of moral depravity are varied and abundant, critics consistently harp on the absence of government oversight as the most significant factor explaining the movement's troubled history and unchecked proliferation. During times of crisis such as house fires or fraud investigations, community groups and politicians have decried the spread of "illegal" houses operating in an increasingly conspicuous yet regrettably "unmonitored industry." Indeed, critics and operators alike attribute the persistence of recovery houses to the city's notoriously lax regulatory climate. This is often attributed to Philadelphia's broader political culture, which has long been said to have enabled illicit activity to persist in a wash of incompetence, patronage, benign neglect, and tolerance by default.[9] Along these lines, Malik attributed recovery house "mass production" to the city's long history of vice and corruption:

> MALIK: Philadelphia has been crooked since I was a kid, man. I've seen the worst dope fiend shit that you could ever see in your life in Philadelphia. That's why they let these houses go up . . . this recovery house shit is mass production down here—I mean, everybody doing it and it's just accepted! You know damn well the governor would have been in on this shit and shut us down, but the City of Philadelphia and the State of Pennsylvania said this is so goddamned big, they say, "Yo, man, let them guys do what they want, some of those guys are doing good."

Malik's general indictment of lax enforcement targets both the city and the state. But the notable sense of abstraction in his charge is quite typical. Despite the fact that critics have periodically threatened crackdowns and the advent of stringent regulations from some unknown entity, most observers—whether on the street or from loftier perches—are unclear about what recovery house "regulation" would actually look like in Philadelphia. So what can be said of the recovery house movement's "unregulated" and "unmonitored" status at the outset? One obvious reality warrants immediate attention: the simple absence of a specific recovery house licensure or regulatory board in Pennsylvania. As a result, questions of licensure default to the Department of Licenses and Inspections (L&I), the only city entity with the power to grant recovery houses "legal" status through zoning approvals and boardinghouse licensure.[10] Yet L&I is an unlikely candidate for stemming recovery house proliferation, especially because its notoriously uneven enforcement strategies have only grown more ineffectual in regulating sixty thousand vacant properties during an era of fiscal austerity. The consummate Kensington recovery house philosopher, my key informant Bilal, noted that the solitary oversight of L&I has all but ensured the recovery house industry's persistence, and its shady reputation:

BILAL: For the most part, these places aren't regulated. Right now the only way the city can find out about a house is if someone calls L&I. But if someone doesn't call and complain, the chances of L&I finding out are slim and none. This is unfortunate, because profit carries the day. We need to have more actively involved recovery houses instead of a house that is just warehousing people. Of course there's going to be money made, you can't help but have money made because you got to pay the bills, you know, gas, electric, food, that's a necessity. But in some ways [the profit motive] has led this thing to really mushroom into a gigantic snowball. In some parts of the city, it is gigantic in terms of being out of control.

In Bilal's rendition, L&I's reactive enforcement strategies enable widespread corruption among operators. We can see how panic ensues from the "warehousing" of welfare bodies in a cheap and degraded housing stock. The struggle for subsistence, when combined with the stigma of "unregulation," stands as something of a curse for the recovery house movement. In an age that purports to nurture an ostensibly waning civil society, we might expect politicians to celebrate them as models of voluntarism to be replicated in other cities. But the geographical location of recovery houses, combined with the racial and class composition of their inhabitants, puts them in a position that few would outwardly embrace. And yet, the houses persist.

## Research Scene, Data, and Methods

The dominant public perceptions of the Kensington recovery house movement, then, offer a murky view of a supposed pariah. As is often the case when a researcher begins to examine an object of study, however, the popular discourse on the houses left me wholly dissatisfied. What seemed immediately more interesting than the torrid past and supposed shunning of these houses was the more complicated attitude of tolerance, indifference, and even courtship that had been directed toward the recovery house movement by a host of state entities and community groups. Quite unlike other gray markets or underground economies that function by virtue of their invisibility, it was readily apparent that recovery houses operated conspicuously on the periphery of Philadelphia's formal social service sector. Hospital social workers had cultivated intimate referral networks with informal recovery house operators, and it was quite typical to see probation and parole officers delivering addicts to the doorsteps of Kensington's decayed row houses, often in handcuffs. These initial findings suggested that perhaps the most interesting question concerning recovery houses was how and why they have managed not only to survive, but to proliferate—in their own fashion—and even to thrive in a seemingly inhospitable landscape over the course of twenty-five years.

To pursue this guiding analytical question, I conducted two years of ethnographic fieldwork (from January 2002 to December 2003) in Kensington and other parts of Philadelphia. To explore the internal operations of recovery houses, I conducted fieldwork in a Kensington recovery house program that will be referred to in this study by the acronym AHAD, an abbreviated reference to the pseudonym Always Have a Dream.[11] I came to know about AHAD from Bilal, a fifty-eight-year-old African-American drug and alcohol counselor and recovery house operator. It was Bilal who connected me with Malik just as he was launching out "to reach a dream," as he often said, by moving into an abandoned Kensington row house in order to convert it to a recovery house. As the self-described owner-director of AHAD, the fifty-two-year-old Malik (also an African American) allowed me to follow his program during its first eighteen months of operation. I came to know more than thirty men in Malik's house who would become, in varying degrees, the subjects of this book.[12]

During the course of my fieldwork at AHAD as well as at Bilal's Positive Attitudes program, I participated in and observed numerous house meetings, 12-step meetings, chore sessions, grocery shopping trips, chess games, television sessions, and countless hours of informal activity with recovery house residents. I accompanied many men to their appointments in the formal treatment sector, the welfare office, and the probation/parole office. I shadowed several men as they pursued enterprising activities in the day labor markets of Kensington and in other sectors of the informal economy. Through my connections to Bilal and Malik, I came to know other recovery house operators, and expanded my analytical purview to assess the consistency of recovery house systems in Kensington. This led to participant observation activities in over ten separate recovery house programs, including multiple, in-depth interviews with over twenty-five additional recovery house operators and residents.

Across these research activities, I began to see that much more was at stake in the process of recovery, and in the Kensington recovery house itself, than simply abstinence from drugs and alcohol. It is true that within the Kensington recovery house scene and in the 12-step rooms that operators and clients frequent, recovery entails coming to believe that alcohol and drugs are the single most controlling force in one's life. In both contexts, the essence of addiction is defined and framed by the crucial proclamation of the First Step in Alcoholics Anonymous: "I am powerless over alcohol, my life has become unmanageable." The process of recovery entails a transformation of identity and a reinterpretation of one's past, present, and future.[13] It is here that the addict comes to believe—through Kensington recovery house practices, 12-step meetings, formal outpatient treatment, and other sites in the vast assemblage of competing recovery industries—that continued use of substances results in the continued loss of jobs, freedom, autonomy, family, friends, health, economic security, and housing. An essential part of recovery is to channel this knowledge and the consonant willingness to change that it generates into a broad array of activities, known collectively as "working a program." In turn, the subject becomes capable of reclaiming (that is, recovering) what has been lost. This quintessential if often elusive loss to be recovered, reclaimed, and reinstated is the capacity for self-governance.

And yet despite—or perhaps because of—all of its emphasis on the *self*, the problem of addiction and recovery must be explored as a symptom of our contemporary urban condition. The recovery house movement has taken shape amid political and economic upheaval as late twentieth-century transformations in employment markets and social welfare provision have created a surge in informal poverty survival strategies. Economic restructurings in tandem with changes in welfare policy have incited an active response among recovery house entrepreneurs, resulting in the organization of a movement that has become an informal but essential part of Philadelphia's social service sector. A central purpose of this book, therefore, is to understand something more broadly about the relationship between techniques of self-governance—as embodied in recovery—and systems of power that converge on the neighborhood of Kensington.

Toward this end, this book explores the relationship between recovery house systems and the City of Philadelphia. While its early chapters focus primarily on the activity of recovery house operators and residents, the research for the later chapters is based on key informant interviews with elected officials, public welfare officials, drug and alcohol treatment providers, inspectors at the Department of Licenses and Inspection, and officials from the city's Coordinating Office for Drug and Alcohol Programs (hereafter CODAAP). I also conducted participant observation in CODAAP's ten-week recovery house training series, as well as fieldwork in Philadelphia's Treatment Court. My explorations are augmented by archival data from newspaper accounts to gain historical perspective. Numerous documents procured from L&I, Treatment Court, and the CODAAP training series also contribute to my findings and analyses. Taken together, these research activities illustrate how the recovery house movement has become a decidedly political as well as an economic and spiritual movement.

## Utopian Visions

Malik was an outspoken philosopher on the dire poverty in Kensington. It was quite common for him to hold court on a range of issues such as education and teen pregnancy, along with the cyclical nature of what he often called "the project syndrome." On one of our routine walks around the neighborhood, for example, he offered his views on the connections between personal responsibility, family planning, and social advancement:

> MALIK: People around here need to go school and get a job, because first of all, you got to be educated, so that starts where? It starts with the parents. I'm talking about just *basic* education, man, that we don't have, like graduating from high school. How the motherfuckers going to have basic education when they knocked up in the eighth grade? I mean, you got people twenty-two years old with six fucking kids, tell me what happened there? I wish you could see how many people we have, grown men, in recovery, that can't write their name, man . . . I'm serious!
>
> RF: Yeah, but there are also other factors too, right? I mean, these communities were left behind to die by people who control the city . . .
>
> MALIK: I disagree, I disagree . . . that's a bunch of crap, take your ass and get a job, man, go to school.

At other times, Malik seemed to be meditating on the structural violence of American racism and class inequality, albeit in a very particular way. His ongoing diatribes on responsibility and participation articulated not only with social movements in the African-American community, but also with contemporary welfare politics:

> MALIK: You see, this recovery thing, this shit bigger than Nino Brown, man [reference to a dope dealer in the film *New Jack City*; the public face of a much broader cartel]. I'm getting in touch with a lot of shit since I've been in recovery, things that I used to listen to Farrakhan tell us, that we shouldn't blame all our problems on corporate America and white America in general. Because even though white America plays a part in holding you down, you keep yourself down, man. And once you know the truth, once you have been taught to do certain things in this recovery thing, then you need to do it. I shared last night at the meetin' about

everybody getting help in this process because it is our *job*. We got all this help and all these people willing to lend a hand. But that doesn't mean shit if we don't participate.

Malik believed that once he and his counterparts had knowledge of addiction and American racism, it was their responsibility, if not their "job," to rise above it through personal transformation and heroic displays of self-will. He often said that the current failings of the black community can be linked to a breakdown in past generations. And while these sentiments are certainly familiar enough, perhaps less so was his assertion that a broadly conceived "recovery program"—as opposed to, for example, civil rights or Black nationalism—provides a way out:

> MALIK: It's time for this shit to stop, you understand what I'm saying? Why do we work the recovery program, and why do we pass this thing on? Because we want this thing to be here if our grandsons, sons, or nephews need it. See, I'm trying to think like the people before me thought, because somewhere between [them and] these [later] generations it got real selfish, and they said fuck the motherfucker behind me. That's why we caught up in this bind now, in this fucking ghetto.

Like several operators, Malik had come to believe that recovery houses represent the most hopeful social movement in poor communities. Far from serving as a program for abstinence alone, recovery houses were viewed by them as tools to instill self-responsibility, as well as to foster notions of "good citizenship" and social mobility. Herein lies the strategic vision of the recovery entrepreneur, who champions the recovery house as a panacea for the innumerable social ills that popular figures and policy pundits alike (from Bill Cosby and Louis Farrakhan to Robert Putnam) have long attributed to a decline in personal values and civic participation.

Malik was not alone in his vision of the recovery house as clearinghouse for moral, personal, vocational, and economic revitalization. Clarence, co-owner and operator of a program consisting of several houses, echoed Malik's broadly transformational themes:

> CLARENCE: You are not going to come in one of my houses just to collect $102.50 [GA's bimonthly welfare payment] and just sit around here, you have to *do* something. We have GED classes, we also have school that we send you to that do job fairs and help you get job ready. These guys go down to Market Street, I think it is through the urban coalition, and they

do all different kinds of stuff. It's like a social skills course, and they learn how to prepare a resume, how to dress for an interview, how to prepare themselves to go into a professional environment.

Clarence spoke to the centrality of workfare discourses that operate within recovery houses. He insisted that his program worked with other service providers to reclaim productivity:

> CLARENCE: We have a lot of people that have skills. At one point these
> people were productive and actually living life on life's terms. Some have
> been office managers, contractors, salespeople . . . we have all types of
> people like that. But then the drugs came in and we lost jobs, homes, all
> of that stuff. That space in between jobs got greater and greater apart, and
> people got away from what they was actually doing.

While my fieldwork with the men and women of Kensington recovery houses introduced me to few, if any, former white-collar or management employees, Clarence's rhetoric is significant in and of itself. The linkage of addiction to an inexorable decline in life outcomes, followed by the suggestion of recovery as a mechanism of employment restoration, is what's at stake here. It should also be noted that Clarence's lofty employment goals surpass the nonexistent work and training requirements of GA for the "needy substance abuser" in Pennsylvania. These objectives are also beyond the stated goals of 12-step groups, which require only "the desire to stop drinking" as grounds for membership.

Billings, a self-proclaimed CEO of a formal outpatient treatment center who worked extensively with recovery houses as feeder sources, further illustrated the type of ambitious agenda that becomes possible under the recovery rubric. He envisioned a $3 million complex in North Philadelphia (which he also saw as part of Mayor John Street's Neighborhood Transformation Initiative, since the project would utilize vacant property) that would offer a "holistic" revitalization strategy. It would be a public-private venture in the war on dependency, working in collaboration with job training programs and recovery houses.

> BILLINGS: [As it stands now], people enter recovery and they stay on wel-
> fare, that's really what is happening. And not only that, they are going
> from welfare to SSI [Supplemental Security Income], so we want to break
> that cycle. I think the state would help us, because the people that we are
> dealing with are wards of the state, that's who pays for their treatment,

you see. With a holistic training center like [what we are proposing] in this community, with doctors, a psychiatrist, with the acupuncture, with another doctor who will come in and do holistic healing, and with job training and maybe even ESL, the cost of the treatment is not going to be any more expensive than what they are paying now, but they get a bigger bang for their dollar.

Billings's vision brought together previously compartmentalized entities such as mental health services, social welfare, immigration services, community revitalization, and criminal justice.

And Bilal had even more ambitious hopes for the local recovery movement as a whole. He claimed that it could be "a catalyst that would lift Kensington up and start it forward for the new millennium." On several occasions while hanging out at his 42 House, he would launch into his vision of a "total recovering community" to be interspersed along what he called "the eastern corridor, from Fishtown all the way up to Frankford." In the heart of this corridor, at the intersection of K&A, he envisioned a recovering community that would "break the back of drugs and poverty" in the postindustrial wastelands of Kensington. This would consist initially of a three- or four-block radius of recovery houses and "recovery-owned businesses." Recovering people would reach out to the broader community by helping to revitalize vacant and abandoned properties for use as recovery houses and small businesses, which would allow people to develop careers and entrepreneurial ambition through recovery networks and apprenticeships.

Bilal imagined Philadelphia's Center City business district—a public-private venture that controlled cleaning contracts for segments of retail districts in Center City and University City—as a model for recovery house labor. His ideas included for-profit contracting of recovery house workers to clean office buildings, and nonprofit work in community service areas such as block cleanups and neighborhood watch. He envisioned a Kensington recovery house council, where operators would work with the city and the police force to identify issues for community revitalization. The council would bring the Kensington recovery community together for award dinners, picnics, and even basketball and chess tournaments. Bilal acknowledged that his vision of a "recovering" civil society was idealistic, if not utopian, and he readily pointed to greed and market competition among operators as the primary obstacles to its realization. Nonetheless, he had great faith in the recovery house as a full-scale mechanism of reform. In many ways, he felt that it was already operating in this fashion.

*utopian imaginary of operators*
*vs.*

The utopian imaginary of recovery entrepreneurs gives a very different picture from that of routine public perceptions. It also suggests how recovery discourse infiltrates many forms of the "do-it-yourself" welfare state.[14] These operators do not take up the formal criteria of addiction as a treatment science per se, but rather suggest how a certain type of poverty management system[15] becomes possible, across a range of institutional and quasi-institutional contexts, through an expansion of recovery discourse and practices. As Marianna Valverde illustrates in *Diseases of the Will*,[16] addiction is a compelling and important site of regulatory richness due to the multiple ways in which it is governed and used to govern several things at a single site. This contention alters conventional analyses of topics such as treatment, diagnosis, and even shelter. The contours of possibility become evident in the visions of recovery house operators, who have capitalized on their relative invisibility and the hybridity of the recovery project to advance a new form of poverty politics, a burgeoning informal housing market, and a new model of citizenship. In this light, recovery houses can be scrutinized as microtechnologies that put into play certain assumptions and objectives concerning the selves that inhabit them; additionally, they can be explored based on their relationship to wider political, economic, and social forces.

## Post-Welfare Urban Poverty Studies

In an era of globalization, welfare state transformation is a central topic of debate. Increasingly seen as harbingers of pathology and impediments to progress, welfare states have become objects of recurring political campaigns seeking to abolish and transform their last vestiges.[17] While we have not yet seen the "end of the welfare state," consensus holds that the Keynesian welfare state appropriate to the Fordist mode of growth has been under attack since the early 1970s. Keynesian doctrine, originally introduced as a modicum of state intervention designed to stabilize the postwar economy through a mix of welfare statism, wage controls, and rising standards of living,[18] has given way to political economic regimes more suited in form and function to an "ambient neoliberalism."[19] Our present historical conjuncture has only now been referred to as a "post-welfare" moment, described by Sandra Morgen and Jeff Maskovsky[20] as a period of intensely coordinated activity to dismantle the liberal welfare state in accordance with the new ideological and political imperatives of market liberalism. Many commentators have charted the ascendancy of what has been variously referred to as a post-Fordist, post-Keynesian, or "Schumpeterian workfare" state.[21] Historian Michael Katz has more prosaically referred to the contemporary state of welfare politics as the trifold victory of three great forces in modern history: the war on dependence, the devolution of public authority, and the dominance of market models for public policy.[22]

Policy critics have most often characterized these trends as a retrenchment, withdrawal, or rollback of the state in order to liberate markets. This book contends, however, that we would do well to problematize totalizing descriptions of welfare state restructure. To the extent that the political economic underpinnings of the welfare state have been destabilized and unsettled, it is important to note that welfarism has been displaced not solely by markets, but also by new forms of statecraft. As Jamie Peck contends, the rollback of the state has entailed a rollout of new institutions and new modes of regulation that are being constructed out of the vestiges of earlier regimes.[23] In this vein, old and relatively obscure welfare formations such as Pennsylvania General Assistance—which in some form preceded the buildup of state capacity in the New Deal and survived its eventual retrenchment—may be providing the foundations, once again, for new urban poverty survival strategies.

Taking this approach seriously requires a shift from the popular obsession with "unregulated" recovery houses as reflecting state indifference or nonintervention. This book is equally concerned with a careful mapping of emergent street-level and state-level forms of welfare resettlement, to show and to ask what the state might actually be *doing* to transform and extend its regulatory power. These considerations call on us to detach research from the normative questions of "what should be" that frame the ever-venerable "policy implications" of urban and welfare research. The post-welfare age calls on us to map questions of the *how*—such as how policy is *done* (that is, lived); how welfare restructurings are facilitated through the value systems, aspirations, and volitions of the poor; how notions of autonomy, freedom, choice, and responsibility are presupposed in contemporary policy formulation; and how urban citizens are *made* en route to taking up their place in the new urban order. Such an approach leads us to the *doings* of the formal and informal apparatuses of the welfare state; the technologies which facilitate its restructurings; and the effects, meanings, experiences, and subjectivities which derive from these restructurings.[24] It also calls us to consider how the do-it-yourself welfare state might rely on the state's own appropriation and reinterpretation of the informal poverty survival mechanisms of the street. It is in this spirit that the book's analytical arc and trajectory draw momentum from a phrase made famous in the title of chapter 5 in the Big Book of

Alcoholics Anonymous: "How It Works."[25] Through various iterations of ethnographic data, my study attempts to explain how recovery houses work, as well as how their operators have all but institutionalized their informal programs through a confluence of street-level and socio-historical forces. Such an orientation requires a suspension of the question, "what works?" and a replacement of the common search for social policy and practice "success" with an investigation into the effective workings of social failure.

The purpose of this book is to explore, ethnographically, the ways in which informal, street-level poverty survival mechanisms in the Kensington recovery house movement articulate with the restructuring of the contemporary welfare state and the broader political economy of Philadelphia. Focusing primarily on the ways recovery houses refashion poor subjects into recovering citizens, and secondarily on the ways that the houses take their position in a *shadow welfare state*,[26] my analysis illustrates how recovering subjects have become able partners in a larger regulatory process. I argue that Kensington recovery houses have become viable and sustainable informal economies by promulgating systems of knowledge/power that are attuned to the contingencies of the social, economic, and welfare politics of the contemporary age. In so doing, the book recasts conventional arguments about informal poverty survival strategies that focus on re-moralizing the poor or eradicating their malfeasance. It does so by establishing reconstitutive links between state restructuring, the production of poverty, the production and regulation of recovering subjects, and the rescaling of urban governance. In this sense, I will argue that the variegated functions of the Kensington recovery house movement have broader implications for contemporary welfare provision and the political economy of cities.

At first glance, ethnography seems an ideal methodology for combing through this particular minefield, to the extent that it has the capacity to focus on the role of human agency in the production and negotiation of post-welfare regulatory projects. But the specific task of forging *ethnographic* conceptual linkages between recovery houses and the structural forces that explain their existence and survival is a complex matter. Novel approaches are elusive, but imperative.

## Governmentality, Welfare-State Regulation Theory, and Urban Ethnography

Ethnographic poverty studies have had an impact on popular and political discussions of urban poverty for decades, particularly in relation to welfare policy.[27] Critiques of this body of work have shown us that the task of writing experience-near accounts of urban poverty in ways that are not pathologizing, romanticizing, or overly celebratory of resistance is equally as challenging as the effort to situate experience within the broader context of structural forces. The issues at stake are well mapped out by the culture-of-poverty debates stemming from the 1960s;[28] the crisis-in-representation debates in anthropology across the 1980s;[29] and the more recent polemics concerning the complicity of urban ethnography with the policies of neoliberal state-building across the "regressive 1990s."[30] The debates of each period have enumerated representational traps that continue to have a stronghold on urban ethnographers, particularly in terms of the longstanding search for the moral subject.[31] Yet however hackneyed these debates may seem, the challenges confronting ethnographic poverty studies continue to hold great importance—in fact, perhaps now more than ever.

At the same time that we are witnessing a burgeoning of survival strategies in urban cores that are new and in urgent need of study,[32] the close relationship between the social sciences and the dominant discourse on urban poverty has only become more complicated in the age of late capitalism. The challenges at stake are a product of transformations in urban policy and urban landscapes alike. New urban realities call on us to analyze the ways in which knowledge forges links between the projects of the retrenching welfare state and the value systems of poor subjects. These developments elevate the debate to a new plane, one that can accommodate the capillary systems of consent that operate within informal street-level poverty survival mechanisms. To advance this agenda and to confront the problems of urban ethnography that long preceded it, this book integrates two approaches to welfare and urban analysis that have developed in relative isolation from each other: studies in governmentality and welfare state regulation theory.[33]

Taken in turn, Foucault's late concept of governmentality describes the techniques that govern the self as well as society via a set of apparatuses operating across distances of time and space. For Foucault, it is the tactics of government at the level of individual conduct that make possible the continual definition and redefinition of what is within the competence of the state and what is not. The state, as such, can only be understood in its survival and its limits on the basis of the general tactics of governmentality, which shift perpetually based on the nature of its agents.[34] A governmentality approach has the potential to address the traditional pitfalls of moralizing or pathologizing the poor that have long plagued urban ethnography, precisely by opening us up to the ways in which liberal governance, often operating through the apparatus of social policy, presupposes rather than annuls the agency of poor subjects.[35] In this vein, this book takes the agency and morality of recovery house subjects quite seriously. I explore how the recovery house movement has been induced by the operations of welfare state restructure, while simultaneously being configured as a form of resistance to these trends. Such a move allows me to place human practices at the center of discussions on neoliberal reform, by examining how street-level addicts have become foundational actors in an incipient and an informal welfare regime.

While the concept of governmentality has not been monopolized by a single methodological approach, the analytical tradition is best known for mapping discursive shifts in governmental rationalities, primarily under the auspices of political theory and philosophy. Despite the conceptual advances in these areas, the empirical payoffs have been questionable for scholars in social welfare and urban studies. This book is forged on the assertion that there are real contributions to be made through an ethnographic approach to governmentality. I will consider how devolution, retrenchment, and the withdrawal of the state do not merely constitute a retreat from public space, but rather enact a set of finely grained, interrelated strategies designed to redistribute the disciplines of governance throughout the interstices of the social body.[36] It is along similar lines that a growing number of anthropologists have argued that the reemergence of notions such as voluntarism, participation, and self-help are linked to a more broadly based set of political imperatives to reconfigure the relationship between citizen and state.[37] This work suggests how "rolling back the state" entails a series of projects that have become very inventive for positive techniques of government in the post-welfare age.

The politics of poverty in the Kensington recovery house movement is broad and complex. It requires us to think beyond the politics of elites and Marxist revolutionaries alike, toward the more mundane politics of poverty survival via informal welfare administration.[38] Under the aegis of governmentality, the concepts of self-help and recovery take on new political meanings. Barbara Cruikshank envisages self-help as a "technology of citizenship," a participatory and democratic scheme for correcting the deficiencies that preside within the hearts and souls of poor subjects. This book considers how self-help in the Philadelphia recovery house movement may be operating as a technique for solving social problems such as addiction and poverty, along with political problems such as devolution and retrenchment. It may therefore enact the inner logic of welfare policy mechanisms designed to provide, simultaneously, the means for individual autonomy, minimal security, and risk management in the post-welfare age.

This book uses the recovery house, as well as the concept of recovery, to analyze how impoverished alcoholics and addicts are governed in postindustrial Philadelphia. I will explore the extent to which recovery, as a complex site of moral and social regulation, enables the state to achieve multiple regulatory objectives at a single site, even as the state keeps its hands off the recovery *house* proper.[39] To explore this question, the recovery house needs to be discerned in its complicity and collaboration with other regulatory projects. Following Aihwa Ong's premise that technologies of subject making are dependent on material processes of capital accumulation, my approach foregrounds the co-constitutive nature of human agency and political economy in the shaping of Kensington recovery house markets.[40] What's at stake is the prospect of producing analytical inroads not only to the immanently human configurations that play out in poor neighborhoods, but also to the many ways in which these transformations have actively reshaped both subjectivity *and* the regulatory strategies of state and local governance. It is in the latter regard that the insights of welfare state regulation theory become crucial.

In his seminal text *The Great Transformation,* Karl Polanyi elucidated the role of social protection in altering, slowing, or regulating the rate of change in market societies. Nineteenth-century mechanisms of protection materialized into contemporary welfare states, which enabled the state to manage the shifting demand for workers either by expanding relief (*decommodifying* labor) or by disembedding social protections through a greater reliance on the self-regulating market. Subsequent welfare texts in the political economy tradition have shown how welfare regime types manifest historically, variously classifying the U.S. welfare state as a liberal regime, a residual welfare state, a divided or private welfare state, a bifurcated or semiwelfare state, or a poor relief state.[41] This book is particularly concerned with the historical extension of the poor relief tradition at the urban scale, via outdoor relief mechanisms such as General Assistance. As a quintessentially informal regime type, urban poverty survival strategies deriving from local poor relief render ethnographic methods as particularly germane. Indeed, grasping welfare state restructure at this scale requires particular analytical precision, due to the ways in which GA inevitably seeds flexible and informal local economies of subsistence—the rules of which must be constantly made and remade by street-level actors.

Accordingly, a central purpose of this book is to trace the interconnections between the microfoundations of regulation (in the constitution of new modes of urban subjectivity) and the institutional forms and regularities of the postindustrial city.[42] While governmentality theorists have taken up the former, state regulation theorists have taken up the latter by mapping the modalities, prototypes, and zigzagging pathways of regulatory transfer. For these scholars, particularly the critical geographers among them, the local exigencies of institutionally inherited landscapes are the key to understanding—in sufficiently spatial terms—the inherently uneven rescaling and activation tendencies of regulatory change.[43] We are led to consider a careful mapping of how macroeconomic steering—that is, capital accumulation and its associated regulatory problems—is always articulated in territory and place, as well as how unevenness is woven into processes of institutional change (in part to intensify institutional differentiation).

Mobilizing these insights in an ethnographic project holds great promise. At the outset, however, it is important to address the dangers of abstraction that both plague and enable the visions of recovery house operators, much like the governmentality and welfare-state regulation theory literature more generally. Indeed, after a roughly coincidental twenty-five-year run, the literature on governmentality and welfare-state regulation theory remain, in Clifford Geertz's words, theoretically muscle-bound yet empirically anemic. In a similar vein, the logic of recovery discourse is potently abstract, as can be recognized by its appeals to humanism and its numerous permutations throughout the history of liberal governance.[44] As such, there would be vast limitations if we were to merely sketch "how it works" in the utopian imaginary of recovery entrepreneurs. Their musings become visible as overdetermined scripts that draw authority from a timely and particularly salient metanarrative. To mitigate against the reification that accompanies these scripts—both in the field and in the analytical realm—it is important to treat recovery houses ethnographically, as historically and spatially embedded technologies. This must be done, however, without obscuring the very real ways in which recovery discourse culls its authority by appealing to abstractions. My intention is to explore the ways that authority is constituted, or how abstraction "works," while ultimately recognizing that it must always forge alliances on the ground (the point at which governmentality so often breaks down). This strategy enables us to appreciate—as Neil Brenner and Nik Theodore's framework for urban analysis insists[45]—the path-dependent and contextual embeddedness of street-level post-welfare reform projects, and the role of recovery house operators in re-regulating urban subjectivity and remaking postindustrial space.

## An Overview of the Chapters

The findings of the book are presented across the span of six chapters. In chapter 1, I explore the making of AHAD by tracking the initial months of operation in Malik's fledgling recovery house. The chapter grounds the utopian visions of recovery entrepreneurs by joining Malik and his men just

as they moved into a previously abandoned row house. I explore the original partnership and founding members of AHAD, as well as the incessant
struggles and forced illegalities associated with recovery house operation.
The chapter also introduces the players who make the recovery house system work, from the absentee property owner, to the director-manager, to
the assistant manager, the chore monitor, and the "house watcher." To gain
a more systematic understanding of Malik's struggles, chapter 2 begins with
a brief policy history of welfare reform legislation in Pennsylvania, the perhaps unintended wellspring of the recovery house movement. This is followed by an exploration of the informal categories of recovery houses that
have developed—however inadvertently—from the Pennsylvania Welfare
Reform Act of 1982. In the aftermath of welfare reform, street-level entrepreneurs have achieved economic sustainability through the advent of informal administrative techniques in welfare provision. I sketch how welfare
entrepreneurialism has produced an informal social service delivery system
that operates simultaneously as a predatory and an informal rental market.

This analysis leads directly into chapter 3, which explores how recovery
house operators envisage and construct "programmatic space" as a mechanism of governmentality. I explore the operator's capacity to *constitute* the
addict—first as pathological subject, then as modern citizen. To explain
the various technologies pertinent to this project, I analyze the regimented
daily schedule and the informal yet rigorous "program" that sets the recovery house apart from the flophouse. I also explore some of the more
free-floating practices in the recovery house experience, such as the telling
of war stories, intake rituals, the confrontation of "old behaviors," daily
participation in domestic labor, and informal case management.

The remaining chapters analyze the complex relationships between recovery houses and the city. Chapter 4 illustrates how the transformative
promises of recovery are undermined and reshaped by the vicissitudes of
spatially concentrated poverty. By exploring the persistent failures of the
recovery house, the chapter reveals how the depredations of subsistence and
the impoverishment of recovering technologies force operators to transmute
risk, vulnerability, and further suffering onto recovering subjects. Through
the lived experiences of the men and women inhabiting recovery houses,
my analysis reveals how the actual recovery house regimen is characterized
by relentless backsliding. The chapter delves into relapse, recidivism, health
failures, and the constant return to hustling activities and contingent day
labor jobs. Chapter 5 sketches an elaborate ecology of *managed persistence* to
explain the proliferation of unregulated, illegal recovery houses in Philadelphia. This concept, introduced by the anthropologist Alan Smart, explains

how illegal forms of housing settlement are selectively tolerated due to the benefits that governments enjoy from their survival. To illustrate how managed persistence works in Philadelphia, I begin by showing how the recovery house movement has taken shape at the vortex of several factors—among them a degraded postindustrial landscape, modest pump-priming dollars from a declining welfare state, the absence of recovery house licensure, and the role of the houses in providing affordable housing options. The chapter then complicates and builds on the notion of managed persistence through ethnographic analysis of recovery house practices, as well as key informant interviews with L&I inspectors and public welfare officials.

Finally, chapter 6 analyzes how recovery houses have become integrated with formal state systems. I explore the relationship between recovery houses, Philadelphia's CODAAP programs, and the formal treatment sector. The chapter then explores the criminal justice system's encroachment into recovery house networks through the Forensic Intensive Recovery program and the Treatment Court system. Ultimately, the chapter exposes the sophisticated networks of policy transfer operating between informal recovery houses and legitimate state systems. Taken together, I argue that these networks facilitate the small-scale governmental restructurings of the postindustrial city.

Throughout the book, I will argue that the question of recovery house persistence reveals a culture of tolerance, strategic indifference, nonintervention, and direct intervention that operates in concert with the economic restructurings of the post-welfare state. From a position inside the dilapidated Kensington row house, we are opened up to the ways in which the political mandates and regulatory strategies of the postindustrial city take spatial and discursive form.

# The Making of AHAD

1

## A Partnership and a House on Genoa Street

When I first met Malik in the fall of 2002, he was the assistant manager of Bilal's house, a Positive Attitudes program commonly referred to as the "42 House." Bilal worked full time as a counselor in the formal treatment sector during most of Malik's eighteen-month tenure, and thus was able to augment his formal paycheck with the in-kind manager's "salary" of free room and board while allowing his able assistant to run the house. While the setup worked well for mentor and apprentice, neither Bilal nor Malik were the owners of the 42 House. They were limited not only in terms of the money they could make, but also in the autonomy they had in designing, implementing, and running their own program. Accordingly, the two men began to dream of opening a house together, and Bilal began to devise strategies to bank capital while looking for vacant houses at sheriff's auctions and on the street.

But as time went on in the 42 House, Malik grew impatient. He could see that Bilal's situation was "too cushy" to give up: he had free room and board, a full-time job with "a hustle on the side" selling

Muslim oils to vendors in Kensington and North Philly (these are typically sold on the street as body oils, aromatherapies, fragrances, or supplements to lotions), and an assistant manager to run the house. Bilal also sold recovery memorabilia (framed pictures of AA founders Bill W and Doctor Bob, tapes of speaker meetings, the AA Big Book and NA "Basic Text"[1]) out of the front room of the 42 House. Given the relative comforts of the setup, Malik suspected that Bilal was scared to make a move, a sign of weakness that he saw as contrary to the basic principles of both recovery and entrepreneurial ambition. What made him even more unforgiving was that Bilal ought to have had the financial resources to make it happen.

> MALIK: You see a lot of shit Bilal had, or could have got, or could have had, [he slept on it]. I mean, we could have taken Kensington by storm, but check this out, you know how shit happens, you just can't get comfortable, and you don't have to be [getting high] to get lazy. I told him, "You the one that sold me the dream of running a recovery house, but you just sat there too long. What you going to do when they kick you out one day?" I mean, there's gonna come a time when he got to pack his shit up.

Malik's harsh assessment reflected his developing entrepreneurial spirit and increasing faith in personal initiative, both of which grew ever more prominent during the time that I knew him. Eventually, he made his move without Bilal, in partnership with two men from the Kensington Avenue AA Clubhouse (affectionately dubbed "the Avenue").[2]

The first of these partners was his sponsor, Frank, a middle-aged man of Irish-Polish descent who grew up in nearby Port Richmond as the son of factory workers. After quitting high school, Frank got a job in a Kensington textile factory, where he worked for over fifteen years until he lost his right leg in a conveyor belt accident. Always a heavy drinker, he became a "full-fledged alcoholic, drug addict, and gambling addict" after the accident. He received disability insurance for the loss of his leg, but, no longer bound by the rhythms of steady employment, he proceeded to launch "full force" into addiction. According to the recovery narrative that he shared often, he lost his marriage, home, and family and ultimately became embroiled in the K&A underworld of drug dealers, bookies, and loan sharks. Frank got another job as an orderly at a local hospital, but he continued to spend virtually all of his waking hours in the drug subculture. Finally, in the early 1990s, he sought help. After checking into an inpatient rehab, he completely devoted himself to Alcoholics and Gamblers Anonymous. Frank was able to compile nine years of sobriety, "by the grace of God," as he often said, by the time that I met him.

Frank eventually married a woman that he met in AA, and their blended family comprised eight children between the ages of six and nineteen. This did not include Frank's two older sons from a previous marriage who were in their thirties, or another of his wife's daughters who had died the year before of a heroin overdose (according to Frank, her body was found under the El tracks near K&A). Frank and his wife somehow supported their large family on his Supplemental Security Disability Insurance (SSDI) check and her survivor's insurance check from the loss of her first husband (also to a drug overdose). Despite their many years of sobriety, the couple was still deeply committed to the Avenue AA Club, and in many ways they were pillars of the rough-and-tumble, gritty recovering community of Kensington. While he lived in the Greater Northeast,[3] Frank often said that his heart would never truly leave K&A. It was here that he came within inches of his life, bottomed out, and lived to be born again in recovery. His devotion to his sponsees was entirely rough, domineering, and inelegant by the class standards of more affluent AA groups, but he had an enormous heart and a capacity for unyielding loyalty. Recovery even offset his racist upbringing—he sponsored many African Americans, including Malik.

Throughout their "sponsor-sponsee" relationship, Malik told Frank about his dreams to open a house. Frank had learned about recovery houses during his many years of service in the Avenue Club, as Kensington houses sent most of the people attending its meetings. He knew that recovery houses can help suffering addicts, and he also knew that they can yield modest financial gains on relatively small investments. Both Frank and Malik knew the basic elements for starting a house: site acquisition and a small amount of cash for furniture and bunk beds. The biggest hurdle was to acquire the house itself.

Frank approached his friend Milton, also in recovery and a former longtime resident of Kensington. Milton had raised his four children in a two-story, two-bedroom row home on Genoa Street, located just three blocks from K&A, the so-called heart of Kensington. Like many of his white neighbors who had the means to depart, Milton had moved out of the neighborhood in the late 1980s, partly in response to an influx of African Americans and Puerto Ricans. Kensington also had been ravaged by crack cocaine during the decade, furthering the white exodus to nearby Port Richmond and the Greater Northeast. Despite his many years of active addiction, Milton had managed to pay off the mortgage on his Genoa Street home, in part by renting it out after he moved his family to the Torresdale neighborhood. He was able to maintain it with some degree of stability throughout the '90s, until his tenant fell prey to a cocaine addiction and stopped paying his rent and utility bills. Eventually, the gas, electric, and water were shut off at the property.

Milton was forced to evict his tenant, only to find that the man had let the house fall into extreme disrepair. He had great difficulty renting or selling the house due to the neighborhood's troubled reputation, not to mention its failed housing market. Making matters worse, Milton's own relapses with cocaine and alcohol sidelined his efforts to make the house attractive to new renters. Consequently, it fell into the official category of vacant property, joining the rest of Genoa Street's inexorably decaying housing stock. A microcosm of Kensington as a whole, the street (which covers just one city block) had upwards of twenty-five abandoned row houses during the course of my fieldwork.

Milton's house had sat vacant for over two years by the time Frank approached him with the idea to open a recovery house. With Milton in agreement, Frank contacted Malik to get his opinion on whether the structure could work. Malik recounted the event as a launching point of his career in "the industry":

> MALIK: I was home at the 42 House one day and Frank called me, and he says, "Come down to the Avenue Club, I'm going to take you to look at this house." He drove me around here, he took me in, and we seen all these holes in the walls, but he looked at me and he said, "What can you do with this?" I walked upstairs to the two bedrooms and I said [*pointing one arm in each direction*], "Five here, five here! Yeah, I can do something with this." I mean, the house was in bad shape, but I seen the potential. There was no doors, none of that shit, it was fucked-up, man, but I seen the potential.

As the broker of the new deal, Frank proposed a simple partnership. He would borrow ten thousand dollars from his eldest son, a tavern owner in Port Richmond reputed to be involved in numbers-running rackets. With this money, Frank would pay for materials to make the necessary "minor" repairs that would make Milton's house livable again: fixing the roof, cleaning the carpets, rebuilding a set of stairs, and replacing ceiling tiles and doors. He would also pay for furniture, including a full living and dining room set, big-screen TV, bunk beds, and dressers. Malik would be the director and acting manager, making executive decisions on a range of issues

*3-way Founder partnership* [handwritten note]

pertaining to program development and operational oversight. With Frank bringing the capital, Milton putting up his house, and Malik bringing the expertise and the labor to run it, a three-way partnership was born. While we inspected the ailing hot-water tank in the basement during one of my initial visits, Frank explained how the deal—which they all agreed was the first stage in an entrepreneurial venture—would work:

> FRANK: I ended up putting about seven thousand dollars into the place, roughly, but I'm not getting that back . . . that was my contribution. The return is, once the place starts making money, we intend to buy the house across the street and the one next door. [Eventually] we're going to get a loan for thirty thousand dollars. I owe my son ten thousand, so when we get thirty grand, we only need fifteen grand to buy two other houses, and I'm taking ten thousand of that and paying him off. That covers everything. We're going to split the responsibility three ways, but the payments will come out of the house profits.

Frank, Milton, and Malik never formalized their arrangement, however, and consequently there was always confusion about the specifics—particularly the way that Frank's initial investment was to be repaid as well as the plan for a bank loan. In fact, after Frank left that day, Malik asked me to explain what I understood Frank to be saying, suggesting that this was the first time he had heard it spelled out. Malik confided to me that he preferred to keep his name out of any official documentation that might bind him to a formal contract. He preferred to operate as a freelance entrepreneur with a flexible commodity in the form of recovery house expertise, which he could recreate and deploy in any space that could house at least eight bodies. This strategy minimized risk, but it also did not yield any type of capital in the form of equity.

*informality of partnership ↓ Malik minimize risk but yield no capital in equity* [handwritten margin note]

In this sense, the AHAD partnership was typical. White real estate owners—formerly from the Kensington-Port Richmond area who now lived in the Northeast—put up the house and the start-up capital, while black men like Malik put up their recovery house expertise and large amounts of unpaid labor to make it run. As Bilal saw it, the system operates like a modern-day urban form of sharecropping. Indeed, many recovery houses have absentee landlords who have little to do with recovery or the day-to-day operations of the house, beyond initial investment and monthly rent collection. Property owners have discovered recovery houses as entrepreneurial opportunities, often after their properties have languished in vacancy and disrepair for years at a time. Some may be familiar with, and

*typical partnership ↓ urban sharecropping?* [handwritten margin note] even committed to, the process of recovery. For others, the recovery house concept merely provides access to an otherwise invisible rental population. They rely on directors to broker connections with social service providers in order to get residents, and in some instances this allows them to open up multiple recovery houses under one program name. Clarence, director of a recovery program called We Stood at the Turning Point, described how a successful alliance between director and property owner works:

> CLARENCE: I know a lot of people in this business, and people call me all
> day every day—you know, missions, shelters, churches, rehabs. They call
> from all over, Allentown, New York, Puerto Rico. So what happened
> was, I had an *overabundance* of people. I started showing my partner the
> letters and phone interviews to tell him I didn't have enough room. He
> had an apartment building with five apartment units in it. We opened up
> that building, with twenty-five beds, and that worked out pretty good.
> We opened up another building that he had, with twenty-five beds, and
> that worked out pretty good. We were facilitating mainly men, but I was
> getting a lot of calls for women. So I opened a house for women at Hope
> and Allegheny. That got overwhelming, and I started to not have enough
> beds for women, so I opened up another [women's] house. Now mind
> you, this is in a period of two years, so now I have one, two, three, I have
> four buildings. Then there was a real need for the Latino community,
> because they always felt alienated, so I open up a house for Latinos with
> thirty-two beds. And finally, I opened up another house for methadone
> clients. So right now I have six houses.

As Clarence's comments suggest, an ambitious and savvy director can quickly produce a larger and more diversified client base. The key is to have access to space, which is readily available in Kensington. Directors normally work through existing property owners, or by foraging and pitching potential sites to real estate investors. In either case, they need only have the skills to retrofit what is in many cases a previously vacant or abandoned row house. In the best of circumstances, a director might become a partial owner of recovery house property, perhaps even under relatively sound contractual arrangements.

But the inner workings of the AHAD partnership were invisible to most who were involved with the house, and the new program generally had an air of enthusiasm and hope. And change happened quickly. On the first day that Malik took me to the Genoa Street house, he had a crew of women—volunteer labor recruited from his fiancée Blanche's recovery house—paint-

ing the walls and cleaning out fallen ceiling tiles and chunks of plaster from
the decayed walls. Separate teams of men from the 42 House were clear-
ing chipped slate from the roof and bagging random pieces of heavy refuse
from the backyard, as both areas had become illegal dumping sites during
the two years that the house lay vacant. Lopez, a Puerto Rican sponsee of
Malik's from the 42 House, was the only man being paid, based on his status
as a semiskilled laborer. He had been a carpenter and construction worker
in the past, so he had the power tools to rebuild the house's basement and
second-floor stairways and the skills to fix the many holes in the wall (where
it was rumored that the former tenant had hidden his cocaine stashes). Lopez
also replaced two doors in the house and equipped them with new locks,
all for a nominal fee of $150 cash. Malik's original crew fixed the roof's
many leaks (and would need to do so periodically thereafter) by retarring it
themselves. All told, the AHAD partnership occupied and reappropriated
the vacant structure essentially for the price of cleaning materials, ceiling
tiles, paint, and roofing tar.

For the director, as we have seen with Malik, site acquisition entails not
only securing a house but also overseeing baseline renovations to make
the house livable. As the public ambassador of the program, the director
also deals with the fallout of occasional L&I inspections. This may include
bringing a house up to code for boardinghouse licensure and proper zoning,
or weighing out the cost/benefit of abandoning the structure for another
location. Some directors spend time cultivating relationships with politicians to manage community relations. They also deal with more immediate
public relations, such as relationships with local residents. In Malik's case,
he was able to establish the recovery house on Genoa Street without any
friction from neighbors or community groups; in fact, his efforts went virtually unnoticed by the other residents on his block. The only person to
say anything was an elderly white woman from across the street that Milton knew from years back, and she only commented because the partners
offered to buy her home in order to convert it to a recovery house (they
offered $8,000, but she was holding out for $10,000). She wondered how
Malik, Frank, and Milton could turn her home into a recovery house, as
multiple-occupancy homes in the city needed to have one bathroom for
every five residents. Knowing that the layout of Milton's house was identi-
cal to hers, she pointedly asked how they would get around this issue over
there. Malik had met this kind of inquiry in the Kensington community
before, and he identified it as a strategy for neighbors to assert—without
being explicit—their own suspicions about recovery houses. He and other
directors heard such unsolicited interest as a subtle message that if a house

becomes a problem on the block, neighbors had the ability to "drop a dime" on its operator by calling the city.

For precisely these reasons, Bilal had "hired" Lopez to add a toilet stall in the 42 House, literally a small closet containing only a toilet—no sink or tub. Malik and Frank planned to have Lopez build a similar stall at AHAD, and they told the elderly neighbor as much (but they never built it). Other than this small speed bump, the AHAD partnership slipped their recovery house program onto the block without a hitch. They did not need a license for a recovery house, since no such thing existed, and while they had every intention of getting a boardinghouse license they never got around to applying for one. Nor did they approach community groups, block captains, or the city councilman. Indeed, in just two weeks' time, Malik and his men occupied the previously abandoned space almost seamlessly.

## The Original Staff Members of AHAD

MALIK: I don't know how to say this without sounding soft, but it's always been my intention to have a unique house. Anybody that's been around here knows I've always said the 42 House was the ultimate house of the Positive Attitudes program. Well, this house stands far apart from even that house, because you know, *the men make the house*. It is hard to get a good crew together, we got a good crew here, man, and I'm happy to know that I have something to do with it, because I have the choice to say whether you are in or out, and I'm glad I'm making good choices.

Staff recruitment is a central task for the recovery house director. Having climbed the ladder from entry-level positions in early recovery, directors like Malik are generally committed to the concept of recovery as both a career and a personal path of spiritual transformation. They know the industry inside and out, and they work hard to recruit, mentor, and groom new clients in informal apprenticeships that afford status, authority, and privilege in exchange for the performance of role-specific tasks. Recovery house labor is divided into a hierarchical management system, with a chain of command that descends from the director, to the manager/assistant manager, to the "housefather" or chore monitor. Under ideal circumstances, recovery house directors are able to take a consulting role with the manager, devising efficient strategies of operation while delegating the bulk of daily operational tasks to staff. A reliable staff not only unburdens the director from the day-to-day, but also sets optimal conditions for recovery and builds a solid house reputation.

For these reasons, Malik took staff recruitment seriously. He handpicked his original staff from the 42 House—four African-American men, ranging in age from thirty-eight to fifty-two—to assume management titles on Genoa Street. Malik gave himself the title of director and cofounder, and installed Infinite as manager. However, given his penchant for perfectionism and the labor-intensive nature of opening the program, Malik assumed the bulk of managerial duties in the initial months. The true weight of the recovery house labor system rests on the shoulders of the manager, whose long hours of toil and commitment should not be understated. Consider the following list of responsibilities, all of which fall under the manager's watchful gaze: monitoring curfews; ensuring meeting attendance; overseeing chore operations; budgeting and maintaining food supply; composing a weekly menu and cooking schedule; paying bills; recruiting new clientele; performing intake interviews; instituting and enforcing rules; conducting urinalysis; facilitating daily morning meditation and weekly house meetings; dispensing medications; collecting rent; and documenting the house finances. Managers also maintain contact with parole officers, outpatient counselors, welfare case managers, and Supplemental Security Income (SSI)/SSDI payees. They must be skilled at completing paperwork whenever necessary to ensure prompt and consistent payment from public welfare. In addition, they "walk the walk" by attending to their own sobriety at daily 12-step meetings and, in some cases, continued outpatient counseling.

Assuming they are lucky enough to have one, managers are also responsible for the oversight of their staff, which usually consists of an assistant manager and a chore monitor. In Malik's case, he designated Albert as his assistant manager and Delmar as chore monitor. As the assistant manager, Albert would help with any and all managerial tasks. He would also be deployed to strengthen the manager's authority by shoring up support for house policies and raising morale more generally. Albert was a tall, lanky man in his late forties who had formerly dealt crack to support his own addiction and alcoholism. By the time he left the 42 House to join Malik at AHAD, he had been clean almost a year. He also had a thriving business selling Muslim oils at K&A—a trade that he had learned under the auspices of Bilal and Malik as a contracted salesman before striking out on his own as an "independent businessman." As I stepped off the El each day at K&A, Albert could always be found at the corner yelling "Oils, oils, got your oils ready!" Oftentimes he would come running in to the house to "bag up" more oils, causing Malik to chide him for acting "just like a dope man, only thing new is, now he don't be saying 'Ready-rock, ready-rock!' Now it's just 'Oils! Oils!'" But Albert took pride in his business, just as he took pride in the recovery time he had built over the course of a year in the 42 House.

As chore monitor, Delmar was responsible for checking that all the men followed through on their daily cleaning assignments, which are completed each day before morning meditation as well as after meals. Because of his sedentary nature and affinity for "chilling at home," he doubled as a "house watcher," the person posted on the premises at all times for intake and security reasons (as keys are usually designated only to staff, a house watcher is required to let residents in at approved times of the day). Delmar's quiet demeanor and tendency to fall asleep on the couch where he spent most of his time earned him the nickname "Steady D" and the informal role of house mascot. During the first few months of my fieldwork, I could almost always count on finding him at the house watching daytime television. I even started to time my appearances so that I could catch *Walker, Texas Ranger* with him while we waited for others to roll in from their day. Generally, the supportive roles of assistant manager and chore monitor are relatively short-lived, as they are undesirable unless taken as stepping-stones toward the manager position. This group is prone to high levels of turnover due to relapse, transience, and the allure of quick-cash opportunities in Kensington's many competing untaxed economies. Even so, their contributions are essential in rounding out the basic labor system of the house.

Professionally and personally, Malik was most invested in the fourth member of his founding crew. Infinite, a strident young "roughneck" in his late thirties, had grown up on the streets of North Philadelphia as a self-proclaimed "gangbanger, street fighter, and ladies' man." He had seen a great deal in his relatively short life, having traveled throughout Germany and Eastern Europe while serving in the Army during his twenties. He had also spent many years incarcerated—first in reform schools as an adolescent and later in the Pennsylvania state prison system. Infinite had fathered eight children with several different women by the time he reached twenty-five, and had been "rippin' and runnin'" as a heavy drinker since the age of twelve. He was known to be a brawler around North Philly, and when I met him he was just two years out of prison after having served eight years for manslaughter. (He had been in a bar brawl with a man and beaten him so badly that he was hospitalized. Infinite learned a week later that the man had died of his injuries, an outcome that locked him first into prison and then into the probation and parole system throughout the course of my fieldwork.) Despite his violent reputation, Infinite was an exceptionally bright and endearing man who was full of optimism, hope, and leadership quality. He often explained that the rough road of his past made him feel older than his years:

> INFINITE: I just had a birthday, I'm only thirty-eight but I'm hitting forty hard. You know what I mean? I'm hitting forty *hard*. The alcohol wears and tears on your body, and I can't do the things I used to do. I been shot numerous times, stabbed numerous times, and as I get older I feel it now. Sometimes when I get up in the morning I hurt so bad, my knees, my back, my fingers . . . [*showing me his hand*] look at my fingers, they all crooked! I done broke almost every knuckle punching people's faces. I'm tore up, and I feel all this now, and sometimes I hurt so bad. Sometimes I dwell on a lot of things, and I say my life could be this or it could be that. But there is no gratitude in that [type of thinking], and really I'm just grateful to be standing after all of this.

Malik and Infinite had become good friends during a full year together at the 42 House. Malik not only worked to train Infinite as a manager, he also planned to purchase a house with him, where the two of them would live with their respective partners—Malik's fiancée, Blanche, and Infinite's wife, Lucia. This would not be a recovery house, but rather an independent space for living "life on life's terms," in the recovery house vernacular. Malik and Infinite envisioned this as a starter house for both couples, their first foray into financial security in the form of real estate equity. Malik also saw the house as an offsite sanctuary from which he could run his "recovery house empire" without having to put up with the daily travails of living with ten or more men.

In line with their vision, Malik carefully selected his original crew at AHAD to form a solid core. He trusted these men, and felt as if they had all grown up together in sobriety. He was certain that their collective experience forged a strong foundation not only for the clients who would eventually come into AHAD, but also for the original four to continue in recovery. Malik was poised to build his recovery program from the ground up.

## The Intake as Arrival Scene

Just a year and a half after his own first encounter as a client with the manager of a recovery house, Malik would become responsible for facilitating the "intake" for his own clients. It was not uncommon to see him in action, indoctrinating new arrivals into his program with the style and grace of a

recovering addict as well as the academic demeanor of a functionary bu-
reaucrat. One rainy day while I hung out at AHAD, Malik had me answer
the door. I opened it to find a man carrying three trash bags full of clothes.
As I grabbed one of the man's trash bags and followed along, Malik directed
him to a bedroom upstairs that he would share with four other men. The
man stopped at the top of the stairs to assess the two small bedrooms, each
approximately 220 square feet and equipped with two sets of faux-wood
bunk beds. Each bunk had a plastic-wrapped mattress that displayed prints
of boys and girls playing soccer, football, tennis, and baseball. In addition
to the two sets of bunk beds in each room, there was a twin bed, strategically placed in the bay window in the front room and in the rear window
in the back. The man's assigned room was littered with the belongings of
the original AHAD staff: bags full of shoes, clothes, and compact disks, a
framed photo of Janet Jackson, portable radios, stacked baseball caps, and
framed photos of friends and family members.

While the new man settled in upstairs, Malik prepared for the intake
interview, pulling from separate manila file folders the numerous forms he
had created on a friend's computer. The man came back downstairs and
asked if he could smoke in the house. Malik placed an ashtray at the dining
room table, where the intake procedure was to take place. The man, who
was black and appeared to be in his midforties, had arrived with his life in
trash bags to live in a two-bedroom Kensington row house with as many as
ten other adult men. Most of these men had fathered children, worked hard
to survive, and been active participants in their communities. In this space,
however, they were all strangers brought together by common forces of
insecurity: poverty, addiction, incarceration, and welfare.

We sat in silence while Malik shuffled around like an office worker getting ready for an appointment. Finally seated at the table, he gathered his
papers and began the intake interview. He asked for a photo ID and a social
security number, and wrote down the man's date of birth, emergency contact information, and medications. Malik then learned that the man held a
job as a tree trimmer and landscaper. He told him that his status as a worker
meant that he would be charged $260 in rent, as opposed to the set fee of
$200 for "welfare clients." He ascertained that the man was in counseling,
and asked for the name of the agency and counselor. "What about a primary doctor?" No, he didn't have one. "And who were you referred by?"
Malik laughed and answered his own question ("Me, I guess"), as he had
recruited him from the Kensington Avenue AA meeting. When the man
said he had a son and a daughter, Malik explained the visitation policy. He
then went over the daily schedule, explaining that every morning a resi-

dent was expected for breakfast, morning meditation, and then chores. To accommodate the 12-step meeting schedule, and to prevent men from lying around during the day, the house was closed down from 10:00 a.m. to 3:00 p.m. After 3 p.m., residents were allowed to watch TV, but not before. Dinner would be served promptly at 6:00 p.m., but Malik informed the man that if he was going be late for dinner, he simply needed to call ahead for them to hold a plate.

As a worker, the man would also need to coordinate his job's hours with the manager of the house as well as with his outpatient caseworker. As an aside, Malik told him that he expected employed clients to contribute by occasionally buying four or five dollars' worth of "foil, spray (disinfectant), or pine (floor cleaner)," as these items cannot be paid for with food stamps. Clients also would be expected to attend at least four mandatory 12-step meetings per week, although the recommendation was for seven. As Malik explained, "Four meetings per week belong to this program here, and the other three are yours." This essentially meant that the man should take it upon himself to hit a meeting every day. The mandatory meetings were located in what Malik referred to as the "box," an area ranging from the Northeast Club to Orleans and Frankford, and from Frankford Avenue to 5th Street. Next, Malik laid down the power hierarchy of the house, letting his new client know that while the house manager could help with just about anything, Malik had the final say in all matters. Malik told him this place was his home, and started to modify that sentence by adding "this ain't no"—only to have the man interrupt to finish his sentence with *flophouse.* Malik said that while indeed it was not a flophouse, "it ain't no facility either." This was a place where the new client would come each night to receive the support that he needed to stay clean and sober. In essence, this was a space of daily restoration, with a built-in recovery network.

Malik explained that the rules were mostly common sense, and that trust and communication were essential. "If you do what you are supposed to do in here, I won't deny you anything," he promised, "but this is an advanced recovery house, with no intake house to send people back to if they screw up." This meant that Malik expected a high level of commitment to the rules, and a higher degree of responsibility in absence of the disciplinary options that existed in most programs. Returning to bureaucracy, he asked his new client "where your card at," meaning his Medicaid access card. The man reported that he needed to retrieve this from the house manager at his last program. Finally, Malik had him sign a "referral form," invoking a fictitious "state law" that "requires we do a referral to another program in the event that the arrangement here fails." Malik said he hoped this wouldn't happen, but made it clear that he reserved the right to terminate the man's housing at his discretion.

With the intake interview officially over, the new man walked over to the couch to have a celebratory cigarette. He had just come from another recovery house, he said, which did not work out: someone in the leadership had relapsed, starting a "domino effect of destruction" throughout the program. He described himself as a relatively functional or "binge" crack addict who had recently spent time in an inpatient treatment center before moving into his former recovery house. As part of his introductory offering to AHAD, he also began to tell us about his employment problems. A company at the Navy Yard had recruited black and Latino men, many of whom tested at the eighth-grade education level or below (as per criteria for inclusion), into a journeyman's program. It promised $16 an hour, with a future in the union that might bring as much as $21 an hour. However, after the men had worked for months, carrying the heaviest burden of the workload on the docks, the company was acquired by a new firm that refused to honor the original program contract. The men were forced to either quit or stay on doing the bulk of the work at a significantly lower wage than originally promised.

Malik would later tell me that as a man with a work history, the new prospect was something of an ideal client: "He'll pay his rent and stay busy [that is, out of the house] most of the time." Malik also felt that this man was "motivated" for recovery, given the relatively "fresh" dissolution of his employment and relationship. Yet despite his promising profile, within just a week the man would fail to come home one night. As was often the case in this scenario, Malik would hear from him two days later when he telephoned, asking to come and pick up his clothes after yet another crack binge. After he retrieved his belongings the next day, Malik would not see him again. In short order, Malik was learning and experiencing the contradictory tensions between collective self-help, informal welfare administration, a transient client population plagued by economic insecurity, and an informal rental economy.

## The Dilemma of the Well-Intentioned Recovery House Operator

Programmatic aspirations and empty bunk beds alike put extra pressure on Malik to find new residents in the early days of AHAD. Initially, he set out to do so with recovery principles in mind, following the AA adage "attraction rather than promotion." Yet as a savvy recovery entrepreneur, he also recognized that he needed to recruit people actively—a reality made even

more acute by his low head count and poor retention rate in the early going.
Malik soon felt torn between his programmatic idealism and his economic
pragmatism, but remained certain that he could succeed where he had seen
many others fail in finding a balance between the two. He was wary of the
dangerous temptation to put money above recovery, but at the same time
sought to make some "honest" money for the first time in a long time.

> MALIK: I know I gotta be careful, because I assume that some people started
> out like I started out, being for real about it and getting caught up in the
> dollar. They might have made some money right, but it's getting real
> shitty with them right now. It's going to be a struggle for me. But I know
> I'm not going to get caught up in the sauce, and I know just by doing that
> God is going to see that I have what I need, and I'm going to open an-
> other program and have some things. I'm not going be up in this process
> for five years just to be living rent free somewhere. I was telling Blanche,
> it's time for us to have something for ourselves.

In the fall of 2002 Malik outlined his vision to me again, using my fieldwork
timeline opportunistically as a measure of accountability for his challenge:

> MALIK: See, you'll be around to see how my thing works, because like I
> told you between June and July, I'm going to have three recovery houses
> operating . . . with the three recovery houses I'll have the money for our
> own house by June or July. And this will also kick-start Blanche's [career],
> 'cause she can run one of the houses. Boy, you talk about what a relief
> that will be, because now she'll have something that will be independent
> from me.

Like many recovering addicts who had come before him, Malik saw an
opportunity in the recovery house industry not just for subsistence but also
for social mobility and capital accumulation. His candid and confident articulation of his plans to acquire real estate stemmed from his genuine belief in the process of recovery itself. In his eyes, this belief eliminated any
contradictions between "giving back" and "gettin' mine." He consistently
expressed, first and foremost, his commitment to God; and second his commitment to be true to himself. With this solid foundation in place, a keen
business sense and an adherence to a set of calculated, enterprising tactics
to fill his beds were merely secondary tools to help him manifest a noble
vision. In this sense, Malik expressed something perhaps unique: a sense
of entitlement to the basic elements of security (income, home ownership,

something beyond "living rent free") in exchange for doing the "right thing" in the recovery house industry. Put another way, the recovery house setup offered a form of citizenship—at the vortex of service, subsistence, and security—that was contingent on his ethical comportment.

But the tension between the two poles of "being for real about it and getting caught up in the dollar," between recovery principles and profits, didn't go away just because Malik was confident that he could negotiate it. Indeed, a crucial component of his confidence, so it seemed, was to frequently and perhaps dutifully raise it as an issue. This is perhaps the most pervasive ethical dualism in the recovery house industry. As the general wisdom goes—as articulated by operators, clients, the media, and politicians alike—the vagaries of an unfettered, unregulated free market located in the "ghetto" actually foster the incipient greed of recovery entrepreneurs. Whether the operator sees the recovery house as accumulation or subsistence strategy, and no matter how well intentioned he might be, profit potential looms as an omnipotent threat to the integrity of the recovery project.

The threat appears seductively, in the siren song of market incentives. Consider Clarence's calculations:

RF: I don't know how profitable the recovery houses are, but it seems most of them fall pretty quick and go under.

CLARENCE: They can be [extremely] profitable.

RF: Extremely? or . . .

CLARENCE: Extremely. You can take a small house and make $2,500–3,500 a month. And if you outright buy the house for anywhere from ten to nineteen thousand, and you making $3,500 a month, you can recoup that easily. I mean you figure $3,500 a month before bills, and you only need about $600 for bills. And that's just one, house, one *small* house. With a bigger house you can make maybe five grand a month, that's around sixty grand a year. Now say you got three of those, at sixty or seventy grand each, and you can see where I'm going with this. It is very profitable, and people that's not in it, don't know it. But by me sitting in the office, and writing up receipts, I see the amount of money. This is why over the years I've seen places constantly pop up all over, because you can make six figures in this thing. It is a very profitable situation, provided we doing the right thing.

Clarence was one of the most forthcoming and perhaps hyperbolic recovery house operators that I knew, and he also tended to be one of the most ostentatious in terms of his tastes in jewelry and automobiles. He claimed to have a hundred "clients" at any given time in his six recovery houses, a number that many in the community confirmed. Yet even holding his claims under suspicion, we can see how the promise of a lucrative career path spurs operators into action. And even if exorbitant gains are rare and difficult to achieve, what mattered to Malik and many others was that profits are within the realm of *possibility*.

> MALIK: Look, man, dude at Miracle of Recovery makes twenty-seven grand a month or more, add it up. Let's say he averages 100 people in all of his houses, per month. Even at $200 per person, you add that up and tell me how much you get per month.
>
> RF: That's $20,000.
>
> MALIK: OK, now we just did the $200, then do the $380 for SSI, we just did it for a flat rate for welfare clients. Last time I talked to him, in one house alone, the intake house, he told me he had twenty SSI clients, you see what I'm saying? That's SSI clients, at $380 a pop. So we going to give you the benefit of the doubt and get in there and say $25,000 a month. It might only cost him $5,000 a month to operate all of them houses; you understand what I'm saying? [*Malik gets something to write on and continues to work on the math.*] It's only going to cost $5,000 to man the houses and keep 'em operating, that easily covers operating costs and that's paying off every bill in the house. So that's $20,000 profit per month total for the five houses, so how much is that a year?
>
> RF: That's $240,000 per year.
>
> MALIK: [*dropping his pencil and stepping back from the table*] There it go, right there . . . [*pauses, and then reacts to my skeptical expression*] I'm just saying, it's *possible!*
>
> RF: It's possible to do it, yeah, but how many people do it? It's possible to win the lottery too. And can that program last? I mean, is it offering a good product?
>
> MALIK: No, they ain't offering a good product, they full of shit. But they stay *full!*

Bilal countered these claims, saying that the most he ever knew a recovery house operator to make was $45,000 per year, though he also noted that this man's profits came after splitting program revenues with two partners.

However, while the issue of profits is in fact a very real part of the Kensington imaginary, my fieldwork revealed that recovery houses very rarely

generate sustainable profit structures. The simple fact is that most struggle
merely to survive. Chronic insecurity, unevenness, and informality are endemic to the recovery house industry. In this respect, the houses are more
accurately described as "subsistence niches,"[4] not modes of capital accumulation. But $45,000 is far from trivial in this kind of neighborhood, and
even the possibility of gaining subsistence counted as upward mobility. The
depredations of subsistence create considerable market competition—and
ironically, a persistent downward pressure on costs that has vast implications
for stability (for example, substandard housing, overcrowding, high client
and staff turnover). Moreover, driven by a highly moralized discourse, recovery operators fight pitched battles with one another over market share,
program legitimacy, and, perhaps most of all, clients.

### "Bodies is what makes it work": Filling the Beds, Constituting the Census

> MALIK: Bodies is what makes it work. When you got your nine or ten men
> in there right, the men will pay for the phone, and then you get forty
> toward the cable, and everything is covered, the gas, rent, and the electric
> too. On the flipside, you take a beating when your count go low, man . . .

As Malik pointed out in his deceptively simple phrase, the body is the economic unit of analysis in the recovery house industry. It follows that the
volume of bodies, which I will refer to as the client *census*, determines the
economic viability of the house. This basic truth sets a fluid web of relationships and a fledgling economy in motion. Whether for boom, bust,
or merely subsistence, the pump-priming dollars of GA set the recovery
house operator out as an enterprising subject, driven to maximize advantage by any means possible. Market competition puts great pressure on directors and managers to recruit and maintain a stable census as a matter of
survival.

There are as many ways to traffic bodies as there are recovery house operators. We can map them generally by adapting Jamie Peck and Nik Theodore's
concepts of "restructuring up" and "restructuring down" in temporary-
labor markets to what I will call the low road and high road to census recruitment.[5] The low road entails a "warm-bodies" approach characterized
by minimal screening; a quantitative, "warehousing" strategy emphasizing
high volume regardless of capacity to serve; and a "one-size-fits-all" mode
of indoctrination. Recruits garnered along the low road typically come
from word-of-mouth contacts on the streets and in 12-step meetings. On
a more primitive level, operators sometimes engage in "turf wars." When

the management or leadership of a house has a relapse or when it becomes clear that a house is doomed to financial ruin, designated recruiters from other houses will "raid" the program in attempts to salvage residents. (In my experience, this scenario operated more in the realm of lore than reality, although Malik insisted that it happened quite frequently.) In response, the larger programs will engage in retaliatory tactics to avenge houses that have "stolen" their clients.

Ideally, low-road or street-level contacts (also referred to as "walk-ins") are supplemented by a stable, high-road referral source from the formal treatment sector. The latter connection pertains to imports, as recovery houses recruit bodies from the inpatient treatment sector (hospitals, detoxes, residential centers); and exports, as virtually all recovery houses serve as feeder sources to formal outpatient treatment settings.

The high-road approach toward recruitment is characterized by qualitative criteria such as the appropriateness and "motivation" of the client. The recovery house operator deploys softer administrative tactics, appealing to the self-interests of the recovering subject. Screening is more intense here, and designed to assess a fit between the client's hopes (especially his desire for change) and the services offered by the recovery house. The advantage of the high road is access to professional documentation (for example, a "psych-social" history), which the operator can use to assess the "quality" of the client. Professional documentation, in particular that which contains appropriate diagnosis, is also crucial for the task of initiating and maintaining welfare eligibility.

At first, Malik had to operate without formal referral sources. By default, his initial tactics entailed low-road recruitment strategies. He began by drawing on the expertise developed during his tenure as manager of the 42 House. For example, he was savvy about the implications of the fixed $205 per month received by addicts and alcoholics on GA. GA benefits set a price floor that limited his options for making the house more attractive to "consumers," and it kept him from negotiating rent to recruit clients. This price floor also constricts other operators, except in those rare instances when they try to undersell competitors. I observed this strategy in action only once, when Malik lost a client who had come to him disgruntled from another house.

> MALIK: Check this out: this guy came to me 'cause he was having a problem around his other recovery house, like not being able to eat right and all this other shit. He told me they were stealing, and he couldn't get along with this person and that person. So I had a bed for him but he didn't

move in, because the guy talked him into staying, like, "Hold on, man, what do you want, I'll drop a couple of dollars." He pulled the old drop-a-couple-of-dollars trick! So then he comes back to me saying, "The man said he going to come down on my rent," like I'm supposed to say, "Well, I can give you the same." Motherfucker, this ain't no fucking Monty Hall let's-make-a-deal shit!

Faced with fixed price points, operators find other strategies to add value. Some advertise their programs with business cards and flyers, most of which combine 12-step recovery nostrums with catch phrases to denote a superior clean-and-sober living environment. Malik kicked off his project with a flyer distributed mainly in 12-step rooms:

Recovery House "AHAD, Inc." will be holding around the clock interviews at its location in the Kensington area for qualified clients. You've tried the rest, now try the best.

Another strategy is to advertise amenities, as in the case of a card from a Frankford Avenue house that read as follows: "TV in every room, satellite system, fully functional kitchen on each floor, full bathrooms on each floor, free telephone." Provision of central air conditioning and heat are also common sales pitches.

While advertising is fairly common, the more typical recruitment strategy is to draw clients away from other houses. The basic scenario is to listen for disgruntled clients at 12-step meetings and group treatment sessions speaking freely and woefully about the rules in their current recovery house. Recruiters will deride overly strict recovery houses for their suppression of freedom and heavy reliance on regimented rule structures. Legend holds that when a person relapses in a house, or if there is a theft that goes unresolved, a high turnover is imminent. This is because the house staff often puts the entire house under strict rules of conduct (known as "blackout" or "lockdown"). Knowing that other options await them on the market, many "consumers" opt to go elsewhere in search of more lenient conditions. Smaller operators like Malik recognize a market advantage in the less disciplinary, "family-like" atmosphere of their programs. Many offer a rejection of rigid paternalism in favor of concepts such as compassion, brotherhood, and an ostensibly more "lax" environment.

It was along these lines that, even when recruiting at street level, Malik found ways to think quantitatively while introducing qualitative selection criteria. His slogan "You've tried the rest, now try the best" suggested this type of two-pronged marketing strategy. While seeking merely to draw bodies on the one hand (notice the message seems to target "frequent flyers," perhaps inadvertently, by assuming "you've tried the rest"), it also spoke to less tangible factors that Malik took quite seriously in terms of what constitutes a "qualified" client. He often suggested that "honesty and willingness" were prerequisites for his program, and he used what might be called his admissions criteria to represent the integrity of his recovery house, trying to set his program apart from the "flophouses and money mills" in the area.

> MALIK: I keep telling Milton and Frank, I could fill this house up tonight
> . . . *tonight.* But it won't be the caliber of people that need to be here.
> If I didn't live here and I was just like, "I want the money," I'd throw
> anybody in this motherfucker. But this is my livelihood, it's part of my
> dream. I want quality in here, so I ain't got to worry about my TV going
> out the door when I take a piss. I'm not going to go in the bathroom asking people "Make noise, clap your hands!" So I know the TV is not going
> out the door. Do you understand what I'm saying? I'm an addict and
> alcoholic, I done seen it all.

To emphasize the notion of quality, and to sell notions of brotherhood and camaraderie, Malik would often boast about the accrued recovery time among his senior staff members. He challenged anyone who maligned his program to match their combined recovery prowess:

> MALIK: [*pointing around at Albert, himself, and Infinite, respectively*] 12 months,
> 20 months, 9 months—Delmar, how much time you got, 6 months?
> Who can step to that? Come on, man, you don't know *us.*

Malik encouraged all of his men to carry themselves well in the community to indicate the quality of their sobriety, which in turn would advertise the stability and integrity of his program.

> MALIK: See, man, everybody knows you in Kensington, that's the reason
> I don't take just anyone in my program, because I don't want nobody
> [representing AHAD poorly]. You know I ask every man, when you
> get out of this house, act like you are in this program, you understand
> what I'm saying? Carry yourself like you know what's up. Because in this
> recovery community, when shit happens it spreads like a fucking bonfire.
> It's bad when you don't even know a house and somebody brings it up

and you say, "I don't want to go there," or even worse, "I *want* to go there because you can do whatever the fuck you want." That's what it is about, protecting the integrity *now*, because every program that is not protecting their integrity, everybody is talking about it. If you don't start from the beginning, it's going to get out of hand.

But he considered the "public face" of his program important for reasons beyond reputation. It was his desire to provide the optimal conditions for personal transformation within the house, and he knew that he would need the "right" men to accomplish this. He often said that the strength of the program depends on the strength of its men, as each member of the house is integral to the constitution of quality across the population as a whole. For Malik, a solid core is perhaps the most important component of the program, as it can clarify motivations throughout the census and even draw in the potential fence-sitter.

> MALIK: If you got a solid core of people, they are the people you can depend on. That way we know the people that's going to be with us and who ain't. And if you got a solid core, it might just be that a newcomer come in here and latch on to being a part of where we going, and that's a beautiful thing.

Yet even with his solid core, Malik would need to recruit heavily at the street level to reach program solvency. To resist the "warm-bodies" approach, he was proactive in learning all he could about the motivations of prospective clients. Initially, he kept his eyes and ears on the recovery scene by attending 12-step meetings to hear people share—and to assess risk.

> ALBERT: I heard a guy in there today share that he just relapsed last Saturday, and now he claiming he got a week from three months [clean time]. Ooh that made me hot.
>
> MALIK: Which one?
>
> ALBERT: The big boy with the scars, big fat dude with the dark skin, just shared about relapse a couple days ago, now he a week from three months. I said listen, when I came in here they told me to be open-minded, willing, and honest most of all.[6] If you coming in here and you sharing, watch what you sharing, because nobody don't miss nothing.
>
> MALIK: That's right, we hear you, we hear that shit, this is a small community. Man, I'd-a told the motherfucker, "You just said you used! Make up your fucking mind!" See, you need to be in there [so you can] hear who

fucking who in so-and-so house, and then you don't let them in your
house.

Similarly, Malik immediately instituted an informal policy on walk-ins.
A walk-in client is someone who comes in off the street, sight unseen, running from drug dealers, the cops, the harsh elements of winter, or some
combination of these. Malik would often contend that these men are
"locked and loaded," simply taking a rest before their next crack mission:

> MALIK: I don't do walk-ins; I only do referrals from people I know. Mother-
> fuckers come in here like . . . [*starts to mock an emaciated addict by shaking and
> dragging one foot on the floor*] "Unnnh, unnh, I don't got no fucking money,
> oh shit I can't go home and it ain't my fault." Some guys like that go in a
> recovery house, and dude say "C'mon, man, we'll hook you up." Then
> the manager goes upstairs to the bathroom, the guy's running out with
> the goddam TV. See, he want one more hit, he locked and loaded, right
> [*primed for another run on crack*], he come in here like, "I'm taking this
> shit, I'm takin' it!" I ain't got to worry about nobody stealing in here, I
> want everybody to be comfortable, and that's what I'm doing, making
> them comfortable. When it's all over I'm going to have a quality group of
> guys that I'm going to have to *put* out before they leave.

Malik's policy was a screening/deterrence strategy meant to limit losses and
ensure quality. AHAD also had an initial policy of refusing anyone not already "plugged in," a term used by operators to signal that an addict is connected to the welfare system. He felt this too would limit financial risk (and
enhance quality, as these men were presumably already in some form of
treatment). Moreover, he was weary of testing the waters with his newly
unlicensed program—hesitant, in other words, to engage public welfare.

Malik's connection to the 12-step rooms offered a start-up channel for
learning about and acquiring clients, but it soon became evident that this
was inadequate in and of itself. Worse, his admissions criteria, restrictions
on walk-ins, and insistence on plugged-in clients were good in principle,
but they quickly began to appear impractical. After failing to fill any beds
(beyond the original crew) in his first three weeks, Malik started to feel
anxious. Clarence tried to comfort him, saying, "There are plenty of dope
fiends to go around in Kensington, just you wait." But Malik gradually
came to terms with the fact that to survive he would need to confront the
formal sector and cultivate a good referral source, a relationship with public
welfare, and a relationship with an outpatient treatment center.

### Early Days of Struggle: The Travails of Reappropriating Blighted Space

The low census was Malik's first major problem in opening AHAD, and his
addressing it revealed cracks in his program's foundation: early signs of an
unstable and incompetent partnership, substandard levels of participation
among the residents in the house, and the difficulties associated with occupying a row house that had been vacant for two years. Further struggles
illustrated how the operator's moves to reappropriate blighted space and the
welfare apparatus introduce market competition and regulatory forces to
the landscape. In Malik's case, it all began with obtaining telephone service
in the first month of AHAD's operation. The landline telephone is crucial
to the success of any recovery house program, as Malik made abundantly
clear after he first learned that getting service was going to be a complicated
matter:

> MALIK: We want to let people know that we are in business, we'll call the
> outpatient places, and the inpatient places, people like Kirk Bride [a local
> inpatient treatment center]. The phone is the program, and I need it, man.
> Without it, I'm like a taxicab driver without a cab.
>
> RF: But at the same time, this house is about recovery and sobriety, and you
> don't need a phone for that.
>
> MALIK: [*snaps back at me*] Yes, you do! This is the twenty-first century, we
> need a fucking phone, man. We ain't knocking on the floorboards like,
> "Yo!" You need to have a phone to run the business, this shit ain't shake
> and bake!

He explained that the phone is essential for formal referrals and—perhaps
more important—for dealing with welfare. Malik had already acknowledged that he would not be able to turn away clients who were not already
plugged in. Too many potential clients had burned out their benefits and/or
come to the recovery house after extended periods of living on the streets.
So the landline was vital for plugging in and verifying addresses for new
welfare clients. It was also vital for keeping Malik's original crew eligible
after they had transferred over from the 42 House, as they would need to
change their addresses with their welfare caseworkers.

But, as Malik had discovered, there were seemingly endless problems
with getting the phone turned on. To begin, no one wanted the responsibility and visibility of having his name on the account. After some discord
among the partners, Frank reluctantly agreed to put his name on it. They
soon learned from the phone company, however, that Milton's property

already carried a number of delinquent accounts. Accordingly, the "house owner" would need to set up the first account in order to settle problems with the line. Milton claimed to have taken care of this.

Meanwhile, Delmar had submitted a change-of-address form (at Malik's behest) to his welfare caseworker with two phone numbers for verification—the number for the as-yet-to-be-turned-on house phone, and Malik's cell phone number. Malik had been diligent in telling all of the guys in the house that they would always need to answer the phone with "Always Have a Dream," just in case it was a caseworker calling. But when Delmar's caseworker could not get a working number at AHAD, she instead phoned Malik on his cell number. Not knowing who was calling, Malik had unwittingly answered with an informal "Hello?" This mistake would lead to the termination of Delmar's benefits—not only because cell phones are unacceptable for verification of address, but also because it appeared as though Delmar had been lying to his caseworker.

Irate over this development, Malik called the phone company, only to learn that Milton had waited two weeks to place the actual phone order. Malik began to question his partnership with Milton. His growing distrust even led him to consider formalizing their handshake deal.

MALIK: I don't trust the guy, and that's why I want to hurry up and try to finalize to get these papers drawn up together, because he acting like a dope fiend and he might be the first guy to use [relapse] between the three of us, and we need something to protect ourselves from him, or from each other.

RF: What happens if he relapses?

MALIK: He got to get out of here, I guess like until we finalize and get an agreement that he just can't come around until he either sell out or we buy him out. But the point I'm trying to make is, I don't want him to use [relapse] and then be talking about "this is my house," see what I'm saying? He could do that, because he owns the house. I mean *I* would do it, shit! I'd be like, "What the fuck you guys talking about? This is my house, get the fuck out." He got a history of relapsing too, so we gotta be careful.

RF: Well, it doesn't sound to me like Frank was thinking of getting anything on paper until you all get a loan, right? So right now you are relying on verbal contracts?

MALIK: Yeah. Well, right now is not bad, because right now I could bail the fuck out, but I'm talking about down the line. If I get a loan, I have to protect myself.

In fact, early on in our relationship Malik showed me one of his secret documents of protection: a one-way bus ticket to Newark. He kept this in his
dictionary as a method of escape, "just in case the shit goes down" (in this
same dictionary, he taped a Polaroid of himself next to the definition of the
word *alcoholic*, "to remind me of who I am").

But on the more immediate front, the issue of the phone remained a
pressing problem. When I arrived at the house one morning, Delmar and
Infinite were engaged in a series of trial-and-error tactics in the basement
to get the phone lines to work. Malik had summoned Frank and Milton to
the house, and they were arguing with one another over the situation while
remaining on hold on their cell phones to see who could get ahold of a
service representative. Milton insisted that the line should be good, since he
had wired the house himself. He considered the possibility that the previous
tenant had somehow damaged the wiring, but was hesitant to pay for a service call without trying everything else first. While waiting to resolve the
issue with the phone company, Malik explained to his partners the crucial
significance of the telephone:

> MALIK: You need a phone to work with a referral source like Kirk Bride. I
> done turned down ten clients because they are walk-ins, you can't take a
> walk-in because if he just come off a crack run I gotta watch him with all
> this shit in here. The clients I got in here now are the best I can have, and
> I want to get the best I can get.
>
> FRANK: That's your end; fixing this shit is our end.
>
> MALIK: My end is going to be all right, I'm not worried about that, but I
> can't have these headaches. I already got to the point now where I *look* for
> something to go wrong, I'm tired of it.
>
> FRANK: I just said to Milton I'd be surprised if something goes *right*. What
> you're dealing with, it's not just Milton, a lot of things weren't paid here,
> and now we have to turn around and square that away.

In the absence of a phone, and quite apart from his exaggerations with
Milton and Frank concerning how he had "turned away ten clients," Malik
implored his staff to actively recruit new members in meetings and on the
streets. Even though they agreed to do so, they consistently disappointed
him by failing to "step up." He also had to push them incessantly about
delivering a change-of-address form to their welfare caseworkers to prevent
being cut off, but Delmar and Albert procrastinated nonetheless. Following
the bad news about Delmar's benefits, Albert soon learned that he too had
been suddenly terminated following his move from the 42 House.

ALBERT: Positive Attitudes cut me off, welfare told me they called and said I
didn't live there no more, that I had left the program. Three days before I
left I paid the rent, so I figured it wouldn't be a problem, but it was. It was
like taking money out of their pocket, and they had an attitude about it.

DELMAR: They had you cut off, that's what they do [when you leave].

ALBERT: Yeah, they made a problem for me, it's a lot of unnecessary headaches.

Malik had fallen victim to a common retaliatory strategy between com- *retaliation*
peting operators. In this move, house managers and owners sabotage de- *among*
parting men by informing the welfare office that their former client no *competing*
longer has an address. Operators often justify this move by saying it is their *operators*
"duty" to report to the welfare office when a client leaves their program.
Indeed, the welfare system relies on the informal and voluntary documentation practices of the recovery house industry, deploying "eyes and ears
on the street" to ensure the location of the GA population. On one occasion, Malik explained how he had heard on the street of a new requirement
among recovery house operators to help on this account:

MALIK: I just got a whiff of this, that we need to let them know, because
that fraud shit, the [welfare office] coming right hard on us about fraud.
So if somebody is no longer in your program, then they got to be noti-
fied. Normally I just do the call, but now they want the social security
numbers. I learned [how to keep all that information] from Bilal, he's
always kept his own records in the 42 House.

However, the reporting strategy can also be used as a weapon. In this
sense, Albert's termination was a product of market rivalry. When Malik
left Positive Attitudes to start his own program, he had taken four paying
clients with him (Albert, Delmar, Infinite, and himself). This produced tension between AHAD and Positive Attitudes. In addition to Albert's cut-off,
the director of Positive Attitudes confiscated Infinite's and Malik's "Wheels"
checks,[7] forcing them to have the originals cancelled and reissued to their
new address. Malik and his men were convinced that these were venge-
ful acts. Their case became even more convincing when Malik's partner,
Blanche, was unaccountably ejected from the woman's house at Positive
Attitudes, a move that Malik read as a direct attempt to hurt him.

If this was actually the case, the strategy had worked. Just weeks into operation, Malik found himself with two of his three original crew members
terminated from welfare. The financial situation was made even more acute

by the fact that Malik did not pay rent as the manager, in addition to the fact that Infinite was ineligible for GA due to his past felony charges. On top of this, Malik could not take action to reinstate Delmar or Albert (nor could he work to plug in anyone new) for the first month of operation, since he still did not have a phone.

Moreover, his problems with address verification resulted in his first direct regulatory encounter with the state, a relatively inconsequential but nonetheless anxiety-provoking affair. Infinite, Delmar, Malik, and I had been sitting on the living room floor assembling newly arrived dining room chairs. All of us were telling stories and laughing while we worked, when suddenly there was a knock on the door. Delmar answered to find a white man displaying a badge and stating that he worked as an investigator for the attorney general's office. The man asked for Malik Bronson, and when Malik stepped up to greet him the investigator inquired, "Is this facility like a rehab?" I found the man's choice of terminology to be quite strange, given the decidedly domestic air of this modest two-floor house located on a block composed of nothing but residential (and mostly abandoned) row houses. Thinking on his feet as he always did, Malik replied, "It's a recovery house." When the inspector asked if this was a facility or a rehab, he knew to say no. Yet by responding that the location was a recovery house, Malik might have left himself open to scrutiny if the man was an L&I inspector (although his low census at the time might have saved him, since a boardinghouse license is required only for a home with six or more unrelated persons).

The inspector appeared to brush off Malik's rephrasing, as if it mattered little to him what he chose to call the dwelling. He informed Malik that his purpose was to verify whether Albert James lived in the house, to which Malik answered yes. The man then made a mark on his clipboard and declared that this was all he needed to know. Malik breathed a sigh of relief.

> MALIK: Damn, I seen a badge and that kind of threw me off, man, they came
> out fast. Anyhow, so now that's straight with Albert, Albert is straight
> now.
>
> RF: Do you think he might not have to go apply and redo all his paperwork
> now? That's all he needs to do is see you in here, that's it?
>
> MALIK: Proof of residence, that's it. At first I thought it was Positive Atti-
> tudes sending L&I out, so I had to be careful about what I said, this is not
> a rehab, you see what I'm saying? I'm not slow.

Malik was never slow in these types of situations, and his inscrutable demeanor and agile mind often impressed me across a host of challenging scenarios. This time, the visitor was a welfare inspector, and—although perhaps suspicious—seemed unaware (or unconcerned) of the difference between a recovery house, a facility, and a rehab. His stated purpose, rather, was to affix geographical locations to subjects receiving welfare. Malik relaxed into a more confident posture. As the man turned to depart, Malik asked if he needed verification for any of his other guys so as to prevent any interruption to their benefits, since they had all just moved and were therefore undergoing address changes in the system.

Malik would not hear from this inspector again for months, and he noted that we probably would have never even seen him if the phone had been in working order. In most cases, verification takes place from a caseworker's desk in the welfare office, and the bureaucrats responsible for verifying eligibility are rarely (if ever) in a position to actually inspect the recovery houses in which their clients live. At first, Malik suspected retaliation from Positive Attitudes for having taken three paying clients. While he had been wrong in this instance, the situation between Malik and the director of his former program grew increasingly acrimonious during the first few months of AHAD. Ultimately, Infinite had a physical altercation—a rather nasty, clothes-ripping fistfight—with the director of Positive Attitudes over withheld funds. Additionally, alleged threats from the director circulated throughout the recovering community, causing Malik to counter by puffing up his chest in AA meetings and on the street. In the end, little would come of this situation beyond a certain "neighborhood rivalry" or "turf war" between the two houses.

Malik's initial experiences reflect the more general trends of market competition for bodies in the recovery house industry, as well as how market forces work in concert with welfare administration. In essence, the constant rhythms of connect, disconnect, and reconnect through address verification become a game of quasi citizenship, oddly mapped onto the recovery house movement's own quasi-legitimate status.

## Establishing Stability

During AHAD's second month of operation, a phone company serviceman finally came out to check the line from the external pole box on Genoa Street. I arrived on that day to find Infinite scrambling around in the basement trying different things and, with each wire he repositioned, yelling for someone upstairs to check the line. I sat making small talk with the tall, dreadlocked African-American phone man, an amicable character who seemed to balance his official role with some sense of sympathy for (if not solidarity toward) the men of AHAD. Infinite emerged from the basement in defeat, and the phone man began to apologize, telling us he had done everything in his power. He had been ordered only to check the external line, which was fine, meaning that the owner of the house would need to resolve the problem by settling past accounts. No sooner than he had said this, the man took us outside to the transformer box on the side of the house and started to show Infinite how to run a phone line out the window to make a connection. It was clear that he was demonstrating a way to rig the line— something he was unwilling to do himself but willing to discreetly explain. When Infinite went in to check the line he came out elated. The phone finally worked![8]

Now that he had a reliable phone, Malik landed a fairly consistent referral source: a woman from Kirk Bride, the formal inpatient treatment center he had targeted early on. She sent him Jack, one of his first two clients outside the original crew. Malik's first white client, Jack was considered a "good catch," since he came complete with a psycho-social history. He was also a prized SSI recipient, valued in the industry for paying higher rent and having a more stable income. At the same time that Jack came in, Malik met Rufus, a black man who was unhappy in another house and had approached Malik after reading his flyer at the Avenue meeting. Rufus's job downtown as a parking lot attendant made him an attractive client as well, since he fell into the higher-paying (and ostensibly more stable) ranks of the "worker" client. With these two additions, plus a new man named Brilliante that the guys knew from their 42 House days, Malik had filled six of his ten beds halfway through AHAD's second month.

Malik went on to use three channels rather effectively to fill the remainder of his beds in fairly short order: the Avenue AA Club meeting, his referral source at Kirk Bride, and informal contacts from recovering friends who knew other disgruntled clients looking for a change. In this respect, Clarence's consoling advice about "plenty of dope fiends to go around" seemed to hold at least some degree of truth. Malik argued that he had not given in entirely to "the dollar," and that he still believed his selection criteria were shaped above all by the connection of his programmatic principles to the goals and objectives of each resident:

> MALIK: I am making choices not on the strength of who you are or what you are, but on what you going to do for yourself. That's how I make choices, and it has to be based on that, because that's basing it *on the program*. Hell, if it was just up to me I would say, "I ain't letting you in, look how you wearing your pants," or "I ain't letting that guy in, he

got a fucking rebel rag around his head." That's what a program in this process does for you—it allows you to make those kind of decisions based on what a person has to offer you in this house, and what they want for themselves.

Here Malik identified the junction between the working of the house and the clients' maximization of self-interest. He sought not to institute an authoritarian model based on his own personal discretion, but rather to work on programmatic principles that secure the welfare of the population as a whole. But ongoing economic pressures kept compromising—if not eclipsing—his visions in these early days and beyond. As AHAD entered its first winter, Malik experienced a high degree of turnover caused by relapse and chronic levels of census instability more generally. Just as his initial turf wars had illustrated, the tenuous nature of the client population and the vagaries of market competition in a subsistence economy produced a constant state of insecurity.

## The Informality of AHAD's Infrastructure

Weeks after the phone incident, Malik had problems with the house's gas and the electricity, both of which seemed to operate, at least for a time, on some type of pirated configuration. I learned about the rigged gas hookup after we began to smell the unmistakable odor of a leak, which became enough of a presence that it could no longer be ignored. Infinite thought that he might have caused a problem in one of the hoses behind the stove by going after a dead mouse that was stuck on a glue trap underneath. The new man, Brilliante, had some experience working on gas ranges, since his brother owned an appliance repair shop. I watched as Brilliante and Infinite pulled the stove away from the wall to look for kinks and leaks by running a lighter over the hoses (both men insisted this was a safe and surefire method).

They thought they had solved the problem by duct-taping a couple of leaks in the hose, but soon thereafter they began to smell gas again. Finally, the smell grew so bad that Infinite called the gas company at 1:00 a.m. for emergency service. The serviceman came out and checked all the lines, only to proclaim that there were too many leaks to leave the service on. Consequently, he put a padlock on the gas valve, and the men were left without any service despite the fact that it was November and evening temperatures were dropping into the thirties. Malik would later explain that the gas man was making excuses that night (by framing his course of action in the name of safety rather than piracy), as he did not want to face an altercation with a group of men in the middle of Kensington at two o'clock in the morning.

Up until that point, the men had somehow been able to get gas without an account, but Infinite's call had alerted the gas company and triggered a shutoff. Without gas, the men were forced to make adjustments. They scrambled to get three kerosene space heaters—one bought by Albert, one received from Infinite's mother, and one purchased by Malik from the thrift shop. They were unable to shower for a week, and relied on the women from a recovery house down the street to bring them food, as they were without a working stove. Although it was a hairy situation, they explained that they all pulled together and stayed afloat. Malik eventually resolved the gas problem by putting the account in his name, even though he was loath to do so. He had Milton type up a bogus lease that he was required to show to the gas company. The fictitious lease claimed that Malik was renting the property for $350 per month, and that he had paid a $1,000 deposit.

On the heels of that crisis came another fiasco the same month with the electricity. Malik suspected at first that the electricity had been running on some type of pirated connection based on the insufficient wattage that made their lights flicker and blink. He checked into this and again learned that the house had no account for electricity. He was told that he would need to get an account within a matter of days to avoid a shutoff. Milton was required to pay a $75 inspection fee to be considered for service, which he did grudgingly. Malik explained the situation with some degree of humor, referring vaguely to the ways they had been able to get service to that point:

MALIK: The electricity was not registered in nobody's name, and the meter's not reading. So we have until the twelfth to do something about it. I mean, I'm not going to be sitting around here going, [*gesticulating to mock flickering lights*] "blink . . . blink . . ." Check this out, you talk about being poor, right [*stealing a bit from a comedian on Black Entertainment Television*]? Well, poor is when the motherfucker comes to your house at night, right, and you sitting there with the fucking candles and the motherfucker says, "Didn't I tell you? I said *no* lights!" [*laughter from all of us*] That's poor! Motherfucker come blow your candle out, "We said *no* lights!"

RF: Well, how are the lights on in here right now?

MALIK: They hooked up some shit, and the electric has been on, but there is only sixty-six currents or something, because [Milton] got it hooked up all dope-fiend style, and it is not on the main [grid]. But I'm not trying to be all illegal or nothing, you know what I mean? I already learned that lesson when a motherfucker put a padlock on the gas [*laughs*].

RF: But when you moved in here, you had electric and gas without setting
up any accounts?

MALIK: Yeah. Ain't nothing in this house registered, but now it's going to be
registered.

RF: Is it easy to get away with that?

MALIK: Listen, in this kind of house it ain't worth it, because the day that
they come get you and shut your ass off you going to hurt [*laughing
with Infinite*], you going to *hurt*! That's some more shit Milton did, man,
because I went and took care of that right away. Milton's name [credit] is
so fucked up, everything he do you got to pay, you see what I'm saying?
Now I got two bills in this house in my name, and I ain't going no further
than that, that's the gas, and the cable. The electric is going in Milton's
name.

The situation revealed not only the instability of basic utilities at AHAD,
but also the precariousness of their tenure on Milton's property. The
men—including Malik—had not even so much as a rental agreement to
protect them from whatever contingencies might arise. If nothing else, the
utilities crises made Malik realize that he had no security in the space, and in
this regard he found some sense of comfort in the lease that he and Milton
devised, even if it was just for show.

Problems persisted as the temperatures continued to drop in AHAD's
initial months of operation. The house's poor heat-circulation system led
clients to complain about the unbearably cold bedrooms on winter nights.
The house was a sieve, with the heating bill exceeding $300 in January—an
increase of $100 from the December bill, suggesting that Malik had been
gouged by the new rates that took effect in 2003. Even Malik ranted about
the terrible heat ducts and the horrendous drafts that could be felt in every
room. On these occasions, he would curse Milton (who had promised to fix
the problems but never did) while speaking about the house in disembodied
terms. He distanced himself from its structural failings, indicating that he
had no ownership rights and that Milton was the one to blame. He believed
his capital lay in his "program," which he could relocate to any available
space in Kensington.

Making matters worse, while it seemed Malik had dodged a bullet
with the electric company in November, he was still not receiving a bill
as late as January. He grew suspicious and even began to wonder if Milton
actually sent a friend under the guise of being a meter reader and then collected money each month for pirated electricity. While Malik would later
concede that these suspicions were far-fetched, his worst fears about the

bill were realized one day in mid-January when he found a shutoff notice
attached to the door. He was furious with Milton, who had again claimed
to have taken care of the situation; and at his houseman, Delmar, who had
literally fallen asleep on the job and not heard the serviceman knocking
at the door because he was upstairs napping. Consequently, Malik had to
postpone a planned trip to Newark. He lamented that he was doing everything by himself due to the failings of both his partners and his staff: ·

> MALIK: I'm throwing good money behind bad money, you know what that
> means?
> RF: You're always cleaning up somebody else's garbage?
> MALIK: Yeah, and this is shit that don't make sense, man, I'm starting to get
> a headache behind it. It's a lot of shit, and if I'm not here to take care of
> everything it falls apart. I mean the boy [Delmar] sat here this morning
> doing house, and the man knocked on the fucking door with a notice.
> When he couldn't get in, he left a notice saying your shit will be cut off
> in seventy-two hours, and today's Friday! So come Monday [it might be
> off], because it says seventy-two hours [reading the notice], "after 8 a.m.
> your service may be cut off." So now if my service is cut off, right, I gotta
> rip and run all day to get the lights on, and then they might not come
> on until late night, and then I'm fucked with the food, and I'm fucked
> period. You can't be messing around like that.

Malik once again took matters into his own hands by going to the Philadelphia Electric Company (PECO)[9] billing office before leaving town. But
as time progressed he would have more and more difficulty getting a response from his partner Milton. Frank was somewhat more responsive, but
his busy family life prevented him from much involvement. This left Malik
to fend for himself, and he became increasingly stressed with what truly
became a twenty-four-hour-a-day job. He grew resentful of Milton, particularly since he felt that at the very least he deserved something in return
for making Milton's house livable again:

> MALIK: Milton better not ask for any money right now, because what we
> doing here, we did his house over! I mean, if we move out of here right
> now, he can put a tenant right in here, you see what I'm saying? This
> wasn't livable, I didn't bring you around here at first, but it wasn't livable
> at all, it had like feces [all over] and everything!
> RF: Feces?

MALIK: Yeah, man, all kinds of shit, it wasn't livable. Every wall in here was knocked out. All this shit right here [*pointing to the new ceiling tiles*], all this was knocked out. This wasn't here [*pointing to a door frame*], we put all this in here. The new staircase we put in, we did all this shit!

Although the men had done a great job in making the place "livable," many of Malik's ongoing stressors were nonetheless caused by the dilapidated and underfinanced state of the house. In the initial months of the program, its roof continued to leak, its hot-water tank was faulty, and its plumbing system was quirky. On top of this, the house had fairly severe cockroach and vermin problems. Once while sitting around the living room, we heard sounds of rather heavy scratching and scurrying coming from behind the ceiling tiles—the unmistakable noises of an unexpected visitor that indicated further structural problems.

MALIK: [*looking up incredulously*] Did you hear that?
RF: [*scared*] Yeah, what the fuck was that?
MALIK: That's a squirrel.
RF: [*thinking it was a rat*] You better *hope* it's a squirrel! How'd a squirrel get in there?
MALIK: Probably through the crack, I don't know . . . Man, I'd die if one of those motherfuckers fall on me, I'd die.
RF: Can you look up there and check him out?
MALIK: Man, I ain't looking up there . . . [*smiling cautiously*] oh my *God*.

As was quite typical among recovery house operators, Malik relied on his men to act as roofers, appliance repairmen, and utilities servicemen, applying their ad-hoc skills to structural crises. Similarly, they had to rely on the informal support of other recovery houses when forced to go without heat, electricity, and cooking appliances. All of these tasks required a response from each man of AHAD, but active participation fluctuated between sufficient responses in times of crisis to passive absences and substandard participation more generally, forcing Malik to carry the burden of the workload. As Malik struggled with these types of issues throughout his tenure as the program's director and cofounder, he became increasingly concerned about their effects on other aspects of keeping AHAD afloat. One was his own mental health, for it is commonly known in the recovery house community that many directors and managers burn out within a year or two, often falling victim to relapse brought on by the great pressure of their work. Further, he knew that most programs fail due to the kinds of financial and structural instabilities he was facing. (I knew of several houses closing down after going weeks without heat, electricity, and in some cases even water, simply because they could not acquire legitimate accounts or dig themselves out of the hole they had gotten into with back payments.) His third and perhaps most important concern was his program itself, for he felt strongly that the quality of sobriety at AHAD was directly connected to the house's living conditions.

When Malik was most frustrated, he would travel over to the 42 House seeking Bilal's advice. Bilal empathized and pointed out that the industry's continuous neglect of its property due to tight profit margins almost always comes at the expense of recovery. In his jeremiad, he made vague references to Milton and Frank while addressing the many absentee owners and directors across the neighborhood:

> BILAL: A lot of people in this thing ain't really got any intentions of *helping* anybody. They see it as just an easy way to make some money. I call it the quick fix. I mean, I get to visit a lot of these places, and I don't like what I see. I been here five years, and for the amount of money that some of these guys are pulling in, I'm not seeing improvements in their houses. I keep telling them, you making the money to fix your places up, but [apparently they think] that's not being business-minded, so they ain't looking towards reinvesting in their houses. Basically they just saying, "You know them motherfuckers will live anywhere you want them to live, just give them a little shelter and a little food."

In Bilal's assessment, the allure of the "quick fix" operates in a zero-sum relationship with the programmatic infrastructure necessary to truly help people. One the one hand, he was comfortable with what being "business-minded" ought to look like in this context. His ethical axe to grind had more to do with the "quick fix" than with an inherent compromise to the recovery principle of "giving back" in recovery house markets. In this sense, Bilal contended that the capacity to neglect overhead costs—or indeed even the absence of these—results in a short-run perspective that limits or eliminates reinvestment. In his eyes, most operators are corrupted by the profit motive, which leads them to simply "warehouse" addicted bodies in substandard shelter for the extraction of capital. By extension, this introduces chronic instability into the market,[10] as short-term commitments to both place and client prevent investment in a stable infrastructure.

Bilal's biggest wish was to have the financial backing to renovate his own dilapidated recovery house. He too saw a strong link between the structure of the house and the quality of recovery inside it:

> BILAL: I've found over my years [in this business] that one of the biggest distractions for clients is complaining about where they living, and how they living, how they being treated. This detracts from their efforts to put their energies into working on themselves, and understanding how to work on themselves, which translates into their personal recovery. So if all they are thinking about and talking about is how the recovery house is mistreating them, then there is no insight into their own self and their own defects. There is no ability to look at what it is you really want in recovery, like what it is you want to do with your life in terms of, like, getting a GED, going to college, or career planning. There is none of that, because they haven't become stable enough, they still acting out on anger and resentment, so in effect there is no growth, and there is no change.

Bilal suggested that a stable living environment provides the best conditions for clients to "work on themselves." By speaking of the structure in this way, he posited the house itself as vitally important to the efficacy of programmatic technologies for personal recovery—not only in its role as spatial container but also in terms of the effects that its quality can have on personal transformation.

The grinding and corrosive impact of spatially concentrated poverty greatly transforms the utopian visions of the recovery house operator as well as the effects of recovering technologies. To fight back, Malik soon realized he would need to deploy his own expertise to counterbalance incompetent partners, substandard levels of participation in the house, intense market pressures, and a dilapidated recovery house. Faced with the ongoing challenges presented on all fronts, he would need to focus on the actual *program* that his recovery house on Genoa Street contained. Before departing Bilal's house that day, he declared his intentions to institute his program as a way to change the otherwise lax "recovery atmosphere" that defined the opening month at AHAD:

> MALIK: Man, these fools in my house, they got it made right now, but I'm getting ready to change all this shit, it's not working, I even want to have meetings here, like group meetings. I mean, this shit got to go to the next step. I'm moving slowly right now, because I'm hindered [by the phone

and utilities], and it's not my doing. I'm just trying to make everybody comfortable right now, with no sudden changes, but I'm about to make this shit fucking tight.

It is important to note that Malik did not simply rely on his clients' pre-existing qualities of active involvement or meritorious conduct. Rather, he expected that they would acquire these attributes under recovery house tutelage.

In chapter 3, I will explore the concept of program development as an integral process in the making of AHAD. Malik's efforts to build his program in some ways instantiated an attempt to transcend the chronic insecurity and debilitating poverty of the Kensington recovery house setup. But to gain a more systemic understanding of his struggles, we must pause to consider the conditions of possibility for the recovery house industry as a whole. The following chapter explores how welfare reform in Pennsylvania, in conjunction with the broader policy climate of the 1980s, created an inadvertent wellspring for street-level operators like Malik. These historical conditions would ultimately produce an elaborate framework of informal welfare administration in Philadelphia's most notorious areas of spatially concentrated poverty.

# "How It Works" 2

## The Basic Architecture of the Kensington Recovery House System

MALIK: A person is always gonna need a place to live, you understand what I'm saying? Ain't like you shutting the money down and we going home. And in this game here, you don't have to be intelligent or smart to know the next action to take once you cut off. There'll be a guy right there to tell you, "Oh, man, fuck that, this is what we doin' now, you just go down and you see Dr. So-and-So, and you go in there like this" [*making a lunatic pose, walking hunched over*]. There is always someone there to direct you.

As long as we can get the welfare part right, and they can *always* find a way to get the welfare part, we going to be here. If you close the door on D&A [drug and alcohol], then you gonna open the door for mental health, and we be like, "I'm crazy as a motherfucker." Because if you an alcoholic or addict, if you sticking coke in one arm and dope in the other, you gotta be fucking crazy! There always got to be an avenue. It may take some people longer than others to figure it out, but eventually when one door closes, another one has to open.

The specificity of Malik's utopian and entrepreneurial visions of the AHAD program, along with the program's many challenges explored in chapter 1, must be considered against a backdrop of key historical developments in social policy and urban political economy. Malik's experiences are emblematic of a broader recovery house *network*, which has been forged in a very particular time and place as part of a broader conjuncture of history and politics. As the network's history and the policy history of welfare reform in Pennsylvania will show, the recovery house phenomenon lends credence to Malik's claim that "when one door closes, another one has to open." Another way to view Malik's faith in the ingenuity and agency of street-level actors is to consider how destabilization and the partial rollback of the state in Pennsylvania bred not only risk and vulnerability but also convenient instruments for the administration of welfare.[1] This chapter considers how former *welfare settlements*—described by John Clarke as temporary alignments of social forces, interests, and demands in social policy—were *unsettled* in Pennsylvania's Welfare Reform Act of 1982.[2] As evidenced by the consequent street-level formation of a broad, elaborate, and informal network of poverty survival and welfare administration, the chapter also considers how contradictory, contestable, and conjunctural forces created *new* welfare settlements in the Kensington recovery house movement.

While the Pennsylvania welfare reform story is perhaps less dramatic than the "hollowing out"[3] or "root and branch"[4] narratives of most welfare critics, it provides an inroad to the types of small-scale transformations that are in urgent need of study. Pennsylvania's Welfare Reform Act of 1982, which restructured the state's GA program, was the inadvertent fountainhead of the recovery house movement. It was a distinctive corollary of Ronald Reagan's ideological commitments to welfare reform, and it illustrates not only how reform played out at the state level, but also how street-level actors reshaped the reform process itself by building a multifaceted antipoverty system in Philadelphia's shadow welfare state. The history of the recovery house movement illustrates how official policy makers must forge alliances—whether directly or indirectly—on the ground in poor neighborhoods. Since the bill's passage, street-level actors have attempted to institutionalize (or at least systematize) new approaches to welfare provision, in part by organizing an informal spectrum of recovery house categories and a series of administrative innovations. It is precisely in this sense that the vagaries of welfare "reform" are based on the contingencies of local geographies and moral codes, and the reembedding of regulatory logics.[5]

## The Pennsylvania Welfare Reform Act of 1982

Pennsylvania's Welfare Reform Act of 1982 (Public Act 1982-75, or "Act 75") was launched in accordance with Reagan's national agenda to encourage "attachment to the labor force and self-support [while reducing] the public assistance rolls."[6] A central objective of Act 75 was to restructure GA, an often-overlooked but important target in the broader assault on America's oldest forms of outdoor relief. Defined simply as public assistance given to individuals residing outside institutions, and better known as "welfare" in common parlance, outdoor relief has consisted historically of "public aid in the form of food, fuel, and small amounts of cash."[7] Originally administered to "needy people" by towns, counties, and parishes, outdoor relief first took national form during Franklin Roosevelt's New Deal, with the advent of Aid to Families with Dependent Children (AFDC), and Supplemental Security Income (SSI consolidated New Deal–era benefits to the blind, aged, and disabled in 1974). At the state level, low-income individuals and families fell under the broad and highly variegated rubric of General Assistance.[8]

With a lineage tracing all the way back to the colonial era, outdoor relief has earned its title as the "bedrock" of America's "semi-welfare" state.[9] It has survived centuries of attack, even in the face of radical retrenchment, in part because voluntarism and private charity have failed so consistently to address the structural inequalities of capitalism. It survives too because so many legislative attempts to link welfare to work in social policy have failed. But late twentieth-century rounds of neoliberal retrenchment and devolution have altered the landscape of outdoor relief in compelling ways. To the extent to which reform measures have entailed, as Gøsta Esping-Andersen puts it, "stripping society of the institutional layers that guaranteed social reproduction outside of the labor contract,"[10] reform has also necessarily entailed the remaking of the local rules, standards, eligibility requirements, and restrictions of outdoor relief.

President Reagan's 1981 Omnibus Reconciliation Act (OBRA) emboldened conservative governors by switching the momentum of reform from the federal to the state level. Clear parameters set by Washington granted states the freedom to explore new combinations of punitive sanctions and supportive services, which had the effect (in some states) of resuscitating workfare programs that had gone to seed back in the mid-1970s.[11] The devolution of authority in welfare policy from the federal to the state level set the stage for locally administered forms of *statecraft*, designed in the main to purge the able-bodied from the welfare rolls.

As the "last strand of the safety net," GA was already a "residual program in decline" as early as 1980, even before Reagan-era reforms accelerated its retrenchment.[12] Across the '80s and '90s, most governors moved to simply eliminate GA entirely. But a select number of states opted instead to reduce grant levels, introduce time limits, and restructure categories of eligibility. Led by Governor Richard Thornberg, the Commonwealth of Pennsylvania was at the vanguard of such efforts to "reform" GA.[13] The collective efforts of the Thornberg administration, known to students of the local welfare state as "Thornfare," mobilized three primary objectives: (1) to encourage "self-reliance" through workfare programs; (2) to reallocate resources to the "most needy"; and (3) to eliminate fraud and abuse among the recipient population.[14]

Building in part on the Pennsylvania legislature's earlier retrenchment efforts (Act 202 of 1976 had already required able-bodied GA recipients to seek employment), Thornberg—now fortified by OBRA—prepared for more comprehensive reform. He began by advancing a striking claim: the GA rolls for single individuals, representing 92% of the GA caseload, had increased by 77,000 from 1969 to 1980. The surge had more than tripled the program's cost, from $82 million to $291 million.[15] His outrage over such expenditure was an effective rhetorical move, making the case that the state should retrench its welfare costs while also setting a simple metric for success. But it was in the restructuring of rules and standards, not merely in the reduction of expenditure alone, that we begin to see the bloodlines of welfare resettlement in Kensington.

Restructuring under Act 75 began with the administrative division of welfare recipients into two distinct categories. Legislators classified the first group as the transitionally needy, able-bodied individuals between the ages of eighteen and forty-five. This group would be authorized to receive benefits only once per calendar year, and not for more than ninety days in a twelve-month period. The law required recipients (along with individuals receiving AFDC) to register for employment, job training, and manpower services. The second group was the chronically needy: (1) children under the age of six; (2) persons aged 19 years or under attending full-time secondary or vocational school; (3) chronically unemployed persons over the age of forty-five; (4) persons employed full time for forty-eight months out of the previous eight years (meant primarily to aid displaced coal workers and steelworkers); (5) disaster victims; (6) persons with a physical or mental disability; and, for the first time, (7) needy substance abusers involved in licensed or certified treatment programs.[16]

With the inclusion of the needy substance abuser, addiction and alcoholism became Pennsylvania's newest category of destitution. Act 75 stipulated that recovering persons were eligible to receive cash assistance, food stamps, and limited medical assistance (for formal outpatient substance abuse treatment) for nine months over the course of a lifetime. Procurement of benefits required recipients to secure a physician's diagnosis of drug and alcohol dependency, which was (and still is) tantamount to an official declaration of the client's temporary unemployability. Thus, Act 75 exempted substance abusers from employment or training requirements, provided that they enrolled in treatment with a certified drug and alcohol treatment center. Consequently, as a measure of last resort, GA was down but not out in Pennsylvania. Perhaps more important for our purposes, the pump-priming dollars for the recovery house movement were firmly set in place.

## A Basic Economic Formula: A New Form of Partnership

Under PL 1982-75, qualified recipients receive monthly benefits of $205 per month in cash assistance and $139 in food stamps.[17] Clearly, these provisions are inadequate for individuals trying to make it on their own. But in a neighborhood with a cheap and degraded housing stock, street-level actors can channel welfare dollars rather effectively into a sustainable economy. In this sense, an "unintended consequence" of PL 1982-75 can be recognized in the proliferation of recovery house settlements across Kensington, West Philadelphia, and North Philadelphia. In many ways like early "mutual aid" fraternal societies during the Progressive era, recovery house operators networked effectively to combine outdoor relief subsidies with self-help recovery, affordable housing, and an informal brand of risk pooling.[18]

Meager benefit allotments force cities to rely on partnerships with informal poverty survival networks at street level. In Philadelphia's case, recovery house operators have responded to such allotments through a simple economic formula. Operators can rent a typical two- or three-bedroom Kensington row house for $350–$500, or purchase one for roughly $5,000–$20,000 depending on condition. Directors collect $180–$200 per month from each client, in addition to half their food stamps. These benefits are provided via the access card, public welfare's version of an ATM card that clients forfeit to the recovery house operator to ensure monthly payment. In this manner, even a small recovery house of eight to ten persons is potentially sustainable owing to minimal overhead costs. Operators have mastered and replicated this economic formula since the early 1980s. It forms

A Kensington side street comprising two-bedroom row houses typically used by smaller recovery house operators. Photograph by the author.

the basis of a highly localized welfare economy by incentivizing recovery entrepreneurs to generate affordable housing options for addicts. In this sense, the recovery house is historically contiguous with earlier forms of mutual aid and contracting out.[19] It differs, perhaps, in its precariousness as well as its informal and, in most cases, extralegal nature.

The city's reliance on a particular brand of partnership is also unique. Treatment operations under PL 1982-75 depend on an economic, regulatory, and technological partnership between the welfare department, the formal treatment sector, and the informal recovery house matrix (I use the latter term synonymously with *network*). In economic terms, addicts' inability to live independently crystallizes the relationship between receipt of benefits, treatment, and the recovery house. In regulatory terms, state expenditure of welfare dollars provides a temporary form of "decommodification,"[20] or relief for the addict: a respite, albeit time limited, from participation in the labor market. Operators see it as a symbiotic relationship.

> BILAL: [An addict can get] welfare for a temporary period of time, which is usually nine months to a year. It can be just for alcohol dependence

too, because this is a mental incapacity. It is a reasonable expectation for society to help you, because after all this is what welfare was set up for, to help indigent people more or less survive for a period of time until they are able to help themselves survive. This is what the department of welfare is actually doing, they are providing the means for you to be able to pay rent in the recovery house, get in off the street, clean yourself up with a shower and a bath and put on some clean clothes, and to get some food into your stomach. Once you begin to clean up your mind and your body, you are able to process the information that's being given to you about what recovery is all about.

Bilal and others believed that the fit between the goals of a residual welfare state and those of the recovering community was not only functional but in many ways ideal.[21] But the partnership must be rounded out by the formal outpatient treatment sector, which provides technological, expert knowledge on the eligibility and "health" of the client.

BILAL: For the most part, the recovery houses will get the client plugged in with the Department of Public Welfare [DPW]. But the recovery house program itself is just a stable structure, the living environment, and that's not sufficient for the person to maintain welfare, because they have to be getting treatment. So a person's eligibility has to be connected to health, and health comes in the form of the therapeutic diagnosis. There has to be a doctor in play here, giving the diagnosis in terms of what this person is temporarily suffering from.

Bilal voiced the common operator position that the partnership between the welfare department, the formal treatment sector, and the informal recovery house produces positive dividends for society. Indeed, the recovery house plays a very specific role.

BILAL: We need to use the welfare system to get as many of these people out of harm's way as possible. If we don't help, we will create an epidemic bigger than what it is now. And, we will be at risk of being overrun by what we sometimes term as the rat population, which is drug-infested people. This is where the recovery house comes in; we can take people in off the street and get them connected to systems of help, so that ultimately they can become *productive members of society*. That is one of the things that welfare was created for, to help people who are less fortunate than themselves get a toehold back into the system of workability and acceptability in society. That way they can become a taxpayer, and give back what was freely given to them.

Bilal believed that addicts can use their nine months appropriately and efficiently, provided that they are living in a "good" recovery house (a qualification that he felt is hard to come by in practice). He also believed that the ultimate objectives of the GA provisions go beyond mere abstinence from drugs and alcohol, as evidenced by his additional statement: "The goal is to stabilize you so you well enough for the workforce."

The effect of PL 1982-75 exceeded its mandate by catalyzing a new form of partnership for the delivery of welfare services. On one side of the relationship stands a declining welfare state beleaguered by the economic pressures of neoliberal reform; on another, a formalized treatment apparatus; and on the third, the recovery house network, a marketized, informal poverty survival strategy operating as a core mechanism of Philadelphia's shadow welfare state.

## An Unlikely Survival?

Despite the preponderance of liberal dogma in the nineteenth century, chronic displacements (of land, labor, and communal traditions) associated with market liberalism forced politicians to seek recourse in precapitalist institutions of social aid.[22] So too did the neoliberal dogma of the late twentieth century force a reliance on informal poverty survival mechanisms. (To the extent that liberal dogma contradicted itself by relying on precapitalist institutions unable to play the market game due to the burdens of social responsibility, recovery houses overcome this contradiction, in part by remaking the idea of social responsibility vis-à-vis the commodity logic.)[23] Political attacks on outdoor relief in both periods were chronically uneven and only somewhat successful, in part because citizens were left with no way to survive outside the "cash nexus."[24] In a similar vein, while GA is one of the most politically vulnerable and stigmatized forms of relief, its curiously uneven resiliency suggests that it has ongoing utility in contemporary social policy. GA has survived as a program of last resort, with minimal budget outlays, decentralized administration, relatively small or insignificant caseloads (mostly "single" individuals), and unapologetically punitive benefit levels. Several states' refusal to increase benefits over the last two decades suggests how the program accommodates, facilitates, and even accelerates policy logics of austerity and "less eligibility."[25] Moreover, GA's local administration (mostly at the county level) continues to articulate with the regulatory unevenness of labor markets and welfare geographies more generally.[26]

After weathering the retrenchment storms of the early 1980s, GA endures today as one of the welfare state's last vestiges in Pennsylvania. Its survival across the 1980s is no small matter. This was an era in which cities scoured the landscape for new sources of revenue. Trimming labor expenses, retrenching services, privatizing city responsibilities, and assimilating city government to the market were standard urban policy fare.[27] It was also an era in which homelessness, alcoholism, heroin addiction, and the onset of both AIDS and a crack epidemic were putting massive strains on social service systems. A new sociological concept, the "urban underclass,"[28] had emerged to capture the plight of growing populations caught up in these social forces. For mayors and governors alike, balancing the objectives of retrenchment with the increasing fiscal and health crises in cities was more than arduous. In this political climate, Pennsylvania lawmakers fared better than most in preserving aid categories—indeed, simply by maintaining GA, Pennsylvania outpaced many states.

This is perhaps because GA, as a local strong arm of welfare restructure, is able to work in concert with reform measures on a variety of scales. For example, just as Reagan's OBRA devolved an ideology through the state scale in Pennsylvania's Act 75, subsequent rounds of national retrenchment enjoyed certain elective affinities with the state's GA programs. As the underclass debates fueled welfare reform across the 1980s and '90s, policy makers at the national level questioned the appropriateness and rationale of providing SSI for alcoholics and addicts.[29] Critics began to question not only whether alcoholics on SSI were receiving any treatment, but also the discretionary nature of cash assistance for addicts and the worthiness of those suffering from a "self-inflicted" disease.[30] These debates culminated in the Contract with America Advancement Act of 1996, which eliminated provisions for alcoholism and addiction under SSI. The reform rationalities at play once again included fiscal austerity, roll purging, and the devolution of authority to the local scale.

Concurrently, lawmakers across the country generated controversy about substance abuse and state-level relief. Critics argued that alcoholics and addicts were not only flooding the relief rolls, but also abusing the system while stymieing official attempts to help them make the transition to employment.[31] As lawmakers continued to frame addiction as a set of deviant behaviors rather than a disease per se, substance abusers were increasingly targeted by reform measures oriented toward self-sufficiency and caseload reduction.[32] In the case of Pennsylvania, these debates would have direct implications for GA. Lawmakers eliminated the previously legitimated transitionally needy category in 1995, in part as a way to force those recipients suspected of substance abuse (although not previously classified as such) into the chronically needy category.[33] Act 75's needy substance abuser category would prove to be something of a watershed. It not only provided a ready-made solution to the question of treatment in exchange for work and training requirements, but also allowed policy officials to go after the as-of-yet-unidentified alcoholics thought to be abusing the system. A more substantial part of the GA population would now be required to submit to treatment as a condition of temporary eligibility.

Effectively, lawmakers constricted the scope of outdoor relief across the 1980s and '90s at the federal, state, and local levels. No longer was SSI an option for the substance abuser; no longer was GA an option for the able bodied in Pennsylvania. In this sense, federal reform worked in conjunction with Pennsylvania reform on two levels: (1) it purged alcoholics and addicts from the federal rolls and into state-level GA programs that were far cheaper[34] and more closely monitored at the county level—even as (2) state-level elimination of the transitionally needy category limited options for the totally destitute, pushing them into the "chronically needy" channels of either physical disability or mandatory substance abuse treatment.

Just as the workhouse model and the welfare model represent two historically and institutionally specific responses to America's enduring regulatory dilemmas,[35] Pennsylvania GA represents yet another response. It is beholden to two age-old criteria for the state's exemption of workers from labor markets, as per Claus Offe's formulation[36]: (1) exemptions may not be freely chosen individually; and (2) the exempted population must be selected in such a way that it will not be in a position to place excessive demands and politically effective expectations about its need for subsistence on the production and occupation system.[37] Pennsylvania GA is also consistent with earlier "hierarchical" models of mutual aid, as it offers state and local governments an opportunity to indirectly subsidize or "incentivize" self-help poverty survival networks with cash and in-kind assistance.[38] Yet as Jamie Peck contends, "history may be filled with echoes, (but) it is never repeated." The recovery house movement represents a "concrete expression of regulatory imperatives" that is "always and necessarily conditioned by temporal and spatial contexts."[39] Indeed, Kensington street-level actors *make* recovery markets happen, and they do so in a very specific time and place.

## The Categories of the Recovery House System

In the aftermath of Pennsylvania's Welfare Reform Act, the recovery house movement has produced new geographies of informal social service provision within the "skin" or "casing"[40] of the welfare state's last vestiges. The semi-inadvertent outsourcing of governmental functions over the last twenty-five years has enabled recovery house operators to appropriate an increasingly significant portion of Philadelphia's GA and SSI welfare apparatus. Operators achieved a form of welfare resettlement in their industry through a series of innovations in administrative practice. Two street-level imperatives shape these developments: first, operators must establish and maintain some semblance of legitimacy by distancing themselves—programmatically, discursively, materially—from the ever-looming and unscrupulous "flophouse"; and second, they must establish protocols, linguistic devices, and circulatory channels in order to negotiate between the formal treatment sector and the extralegal arrangements of the recovery house. In part to accomplish the ends of each imperative, operators have produced a set of recovery house categories and administrative techniques designed to channel bodies through the recovery house experience.

## The CODAAP House

There is only one form of recovery house that the City of Philadelphia officially recognizes and sanctions: the *CODAAP house*. The name stems from the CODAAP Housing Initiative (CHI), a competitive city-funded program that subcontracts a new brand of residential case management to an elite subset of recovery houses. The purpose of this initiative is to standardize, monitor, and therefore regulate a small number of recovery houses at a distance.

Philadelphia has long recognized recovery houses as important players in the realm of informal social service provision. Its use of subcontracting reflects the city's extension into, and reliance on, recovery houses to compensate for the inadequacies of state-funded institutions. Those operators most aggressive in navigating the continuum between formal and informal sectors have been able to secure contracts with the city, the state, and the criminal justice system since the mid-1990s, most notably with the city's

FIR (Forensic Intensive Recovery) and Treatment Court programs (these programs, along with CHI, will be explored in chapter 6). Some recovery houses also provide beds for the city's "code blue" program, an initiative designed to get homeless persons off the street when temperatures drop below freezing. As the only true channel of recovery house legitimacy in Philadelphia, CODAAP funding represents the apex of formality for operators. In most instances, houses that qualify for CHI are the most structured and well-heeled programs in the city (for example, Fresh Start). As a result, they are referred to on the street as the "Cadillac" programs of the recovery house system.

Evidence from my fieldwork suggests that the city restricted contracts to the more organized and "legitimate" CODAAP programs inconsistently. In many instances, police officers, social workers, and judges placed addicts in houses at the informal end of the spectrum for probation/parole and "code blue" purposes. Moreover, as of 2004, the CHI was funding just 23 houses out of the estimated 400 to 500 that exist in Philadelphia. Accordingly, the vast majority of recovery houses continue to languish in the zones of relative informality.

## The Friendly User and the Meth House

Long before the city formalized the CODAAP house, street-level operators organized the recovery house industry into a field of informal subcategories. The first that I will discuss here are what the operators call *friendly user houses*. Operators disparage this subset of houses so consistently that it forms a baseline for their claims of legitimacy and moral superiority.

Also referred to as a flophouse, the friendly user gets its name by violating the cardinal rule known as "you use, you lose," the near-universal stipulation across the industry that any use of drugs or alcohol results in immediate eviction. In contrast to industry practice, friendly users provide a space of exception by penalizing "users" or "relapsers" only with fines. Operators and clients alike consistently malign these houses for "tarnishing the name of the industry," as one informant put it, by selling a façade of clean and sober living without any type of "real disciplinary or programmatic structure." Critics contend that these houses are little more than nightly lodging spaces in which to "fall out" after a hard day of drinking and drugging. Worse, operators like Malik refer to the houses as "cancers," and accuse them of enabling active addiction and undermining the principles of "true" (that is, abstinence-based) sobriety. As one director from an ostensibly more rigorous program put it, managers of friendly users are also guilty of "siphoning off" clients into a kind of parasitic rental market.

Operator hostility toward the friendly user fuels an ideological warfare over public space in Kensington. Several operators deploy the frequent refrain, "This ain't no flophouse!" as a rhetorical weapon. Malik, for example, consistently pointed out flophouses on our walks around Kensington, primarily to show me what his program was not:

> MALIK: See, those are the programs . . . like I am trying to tell you, right, where people just constantly use and drink and do any fucking thing, man, they *ain't* no fucking programs. What they really are is fucking shelters, or flophouses . . . for real for real.

A close cousin to the friendly user in the minds of most operators and clients is the *meth house*, also sometimes known as a *wethouse*. This subset of houses specializes in serving addicts on methadone maintenance, a controversial treatment modality in the Kensington recovering community. Recovery purists (operators, 12-step members, and treatment providers committed to the abstinence model) argue that methadone users are still getting high and are therefore incapable of achieving personal transformation. They stigmatize meth users for exhibiting "dope fiend behaviors" and for "nodding off"[41] in the presence of others who are "really" trying to kick the use of heroin. Early on in my fieldwork, Blanche complained of feeling "triggered" by the women on methadone in her house, or as Malik described it:

> MALIK: First there was two women there [on meth], and now she sitting around with five fucking girls nodding off, and it's bothering her. That's what they call a *wethouse* really. It's bothering her that somebody is doing something right in front of her that she wants to do.

Most recovery house operators turn away clients known or suspected of methadone maintenance as a matter of policy.[42] This was one of Malik's most rigid screening tools.

> MALIK: They tried to give me two of them people, but I don't want to be around them. You also don't want to get the reputation of taking just anyone in your house.

In fact, he rejected meth users on several occasions, even when his count was low.

Municipalities such as Seattle, Washington, and Hamilton, Ontario, have recently experimented with *formal* wethouses for alcoholics, the rationale being that the programs save public money by reducing arrests and ER visits.[43] In contrast, Philadelphia has a hands-off policy, and Kensington operators build legitimacy on the street-level gold standard of abstinence. Street debates over wethouses and methadone maintenance partially echo the harm-reduction debates in the formal sector, yet Kensington's fierce commitment to abstinence is inflected by, and contingent on, local moral codes. Lurking in the backdrop is the gravitational pull of spatially concentrated poverty, which inextricably shapes the ethical path of all recovery house operators, to one degree or another.

## Slouching toward the Money Mill

Countless stories circulate in Kensington (and in the media) about the fraudulent practices and scandalous activities that have gone down over the years. Among some of the more prominent are allegations of illegal food stamp rings (whereby corner store owners use debit card machines to swipe thousands of dollars more than the actual grocery bills and then split the profits with the recovery house operators); stories of house operators' continued collection of SSI checks on deceased clients; accusations of rampant drug and alcohol use among the house staff; and tales of the dissolution of certain houses into crack houses and/or brothels. Stories get around about raids carried out by the Department of Licenses and Inspections on programs housing as many as thirty men without beds, furniture, food, heat, or electricity. Residents at Malik's house also spoke of violence among residents, some of whom were rumored to carry guns. Other informants told of the comings and goings of prostitutes and heroin/crack addicts at certain recovery houses to cop drugs.

Whether we call it lore, mythology, or history, this circulation of scandalous stories plays a role in shaping operators' practices regarding the reputation and legitimacy of their house. Operators have a great deal invested in distancing themselves not only from friendly users and meth houses, but also from rogue actors whose recovery houses have degenerated into predation on the very people they are supposed to be helping. The circulation of scandals prompts them to stake claims for their program along a spectrum of formality and legitimacy. Perhaps most important, the street-level dis-

tinction between *nonprofit* and *for-profit* houses signals the ubiquitous tensions between profits and recovery. The distinction is unrelated, at least in
technical terms, to a house's acquisition of 501 [c] (3) status.[44] Rather, operators use the terms to distinguish the more recovery-oriented programs
from what they often call *money mills*. Douglas, a seasoned veteran of Bilal's
house, explained the vagaries of the latter term:

> DOUGLAS: They aren't programs that are about helping addicts recover. You
> see now there is recovery in our house, because we make it be based in
> recovery, and Bilal is about recovery. But most of these houses are money
> mills—man, they just want your dough. Because if they were about
> recovery, [you would have an answer to the question] where do you go to
> when it is time to leave? First and foremost they would have you tapped
> into other programs like Section 8.[45] [But] they don't give you that kind
> of information; if you know about it, it is because you find it out on your
> own. They don't want you to know, because you are no longer a client
> if you are moving on. So why would I try to tell you how to take your
> money out of my pocket, you understand what I'm saying?

The common accusation is that profit-driven operators simply "warehouse" recovering addicts in extralegal rental markets. It should be noted,
however, that there is a range of acceptability on the question of monetary
incentive. Even recovery purists do not take issue with the notion of a for-
profit recovery house program. Both Malik and Bilal, for example, had con-
sulted and advised potential investors on how to pursue this option. Neither of them had illusions about the prospect of making money in recovery
houses, and they often referred to the system as an industry or a business.
Organizing a for-profit house is simply a way of foregrounding the profit
motive for an independent investor, the dangers of which can be ostensibly
offset by the "right" manager who inculcates a solid recovery ethos. But an
overbearing commitment to profits is said to contaminate the project and
principles of recovery. For these reasons, Bilal often asserted that he was
interested solely in starting a nonprofit house. Malik made similar claims
as a way of seeking the moral high ground afforded to the loosely defined
nonprofit status.

Tensions between profit and relief are as old as Speenhamland in the early
nineteenth century and the English poor laws in the early seventeenth,[46] long
plaguing any number of social welfare practices driven by subcontracting
and market incentives. The recovery house operator's quasi-legal status in

the informal sector only exaggerates these tensions. But as an ethical litmus test, the profit fixation alone obscures more than it reveals. As nongovernmental actors integral to new models of urban governance and social service provision, the operators' posturing around the false binary of recovery versus profits is a way for some of them to expand their domain of access to the formal welfare and treatment apparatuses. Left behind are those who willingly occupy the more humble and informal rental market niches for the friendly user or flophouse. In other words, operators capitalize on the antagonism between recovery house categories, making these tensions functional and marketable in promoting morally superior recovery programming. Alternatively, some operators sell a form of shelter that more closely resembles a boardinghouse while holding out the guise of recovery for the appearance of legitimacy in the eyes of public welfare. Unevenness is a virtue here, in the sense that both positions have great utility in taking up surplus: in the realm of labor, by absorbing the "jobless" and the "permanently" detached labor force;[47] in the realm of space, by reappropriating blighted row homes.

## Gender, Race, and Religion

Beyond the immediate question of profit, operators have divided recovery houses along gender, racial, and religious lines. To begin, while the bulk of my fieldwork took place in "men's houses," the market for "women's houses" is particularly strong, rivaling if not exceeding men's houses in number. A small subset of women's houses operates in close contact with the child welfare system. These more formalized houses, most located in or closer to Center City, are designed for Temporary Assistance for Needy Families (TANF) women living with young children. But the majority of women's houses operate informally and serve either the childless or those permanently or temporarily separated from their children.

   I knew of only one house that was "coed" at the time of my fieldwork. It carried a negative reputation, as several informants said that its operator condoned (or at the very least failed to control) the formation of sexual liaisons that the informants felt were highly detrimental to the recovery process. Certainly the practice of dividing houses along gender lines accords with wider cultural presumptions of heterosexuality, an errant maxim that afforded one lesbian client whom I knew the opportunity to enjoy a lasting relationship within a recovery house. The division along gender lines also mirrors wider cultural assumptions about the inner city poor, whose "hypersexuality" is viewed as a causal factor impeding social mobility.[48] This assumption stands in accordance with culture-of-poverty theories, which in many respects constitute the moral and ideological fiber on which most programmatic structures are built.

Some operators segregate Kensington recovery houses by race as well. While overt classifications of "black" and "white" houses are atypical, residents often use these titles to denote a de-facto pattern of racial segregation. One of the houses in Positive Attitudes was known to admit only white clients. According to legend, the program owner's mother lived across the street and implored her son to refuse black clients on her Kensington block. More typically, programs segregate along race and class lines less formally, through a gradual process of operator disinvestment and "dumping." "Black" houses are often underresourced and structurally unsound relative to their "white" counterparts. Rufus, a long-term resident at Malik's program, moved out of a black house before moving into AHAD. According to Rufus, that earlier house—in addition to being frequented by people "tricking" and stealing—lacked furniture and was falling down around him. The white house operating under the same program name was decidedly more stable, both structurally and programmatically.

Another categorical distinction is the *Spanish house.* While one program called Fresh Start named one of its houses Casa de Latina, operators are more likely to use the category of Spanish house abstractly to describe a house's primary spoken language (this also reflects the Kensington practice of conflating multiple ethnicities into the monolithic referent *Spanish*). Several of the "Spanish" houses overlap with the category of *Christian recovery houses.* These typically eschew the 12-step model in favor of intensive Bible study and prayer. Partly as a result, they carry a reputation for rigid rule structures and insularity. Residents and operators alike associate their regimentation, which goes so far as to prevent cigarette smoking, with their high attrition rates. Mario, a short-term bilingual resident of AHAD, put it like this:

> MARIO: The problem I had with [the Christian recovery house] was when they took my cigarettes; I said, "Hold up, man, whoa, whoa, whoa." I went in there for one night and that was it. You can't smoke, and everything is prayer, prayer, prayer . . . like Christ is going to save you. It was just too much.

Although a number of Christian programs are open to whites and African Americans, they are known to house mostly Puerto Ricans. The growth of the Puerto Rican recovery house market is attributed to recently developed programs on the island. Town government and church officials in Puerto Rico have started to subsidize migration to Philadelphia for alcoholics and

drug addicts. They provide funds for one-way travel under the condition
that the person seeks refuge in a recovery house. As Billings, the director of
a formal outpatient treatment center, averred, the connections between the
two locales are mutually beneficial:

> BILLINGS: It is no problem [for them to come here because] Puerto Rico is
> a part of the United States. They go to the churches there and the church
> sends them here. What they're trying to do is recycle the guy: after they
> are here, finish the program and do well, they want to send them back to
> Puerto Rico.

Consequently, hundreds of Puerto Ricans are now making the "sobriety
pilgrimage" directly to Kensington as their first trip to the mainland. Several
operators in the recovery house community noted the irony of this, given
that Kensington also boasts the highest per capita heroin and cocaine sales
in the country. (Actually, the presence of one of the most vibrant recovery networks on the eastern seaboard alongside one of the most advanced
open-air drug markets seems to keep both economies robust.) Operators
also described the bizarreness of meeting these new "clients" at the airport,
oftentimes with little description or knowledge of the person beyond the
color of the baseball cap he would be wearing.

The isolation of Spanish-speaking clients tends to track these addicts into
Christian programs against their will while restricting their access to the
broader Philadelphia economy. I knew of several Puerto Rican men who
felt that their government was trying to "cleanse the island" of undesirables
by purchasing one-way plane tickets to Philadelphia. These men also told
stories of feeling betrayed on arrival at a Kensington recovery house, after
having been told they were heading to a more "lavish" institutional setting equipped with amenities like swimming pools. In addition, many had
friends who had disappeared from recovery houses after relapses, with no
way to get home and few, if any, ties to their new surroundings.

Clearly, the operator practice of separating populations along ethnic
and racial lines further differentiates the recovery house population. Several
addicts from a variety of ethnic backgrounds told me that they preferred
to be with their "own people." Moreover, for those coming from Puerto
Rico, the Christian houses play an incorporation role by at least helping
non-English speakers connect to social services and informal employment
opportunities. But perhaps most important, this form of operator categorization begins to suggest how race, class, and gender markers are continu-

ously salient. It also suggests how these categories are made and remade in conjunction with informal restructuring of the welfare state.

## Administrative Categories: Intake, Recovery, and Three-Quarter Houses

Operators differentiate their programs from the money mill and the friendly user houses not only along ideological lines, but also by way of administrative techniques designed to organize and rationalize their recovery house both spatially and temporally. The basic road map of the addict's recovery house experience unfolds in stages, from *intake/blackout house*, to *recovery house*, to *three-quarter* or *worker house*. Operators deploy a specific form of street-level administrative expertise within each stage, from the welfare "plug-in" in the intake house, to a form of ancillary case management during formal treatment in the recovery house, to the welfare extension for longer-term clients in three-quarter houses or recovery houses. It should be noted, however, that operator deployment of these categories and administrative techniques is quite variegated in practice, simply because smaller operators lack the resources (that is, the multiple houses) for the kind of specialization that these categories imply. Nonetheless, even smaller operators aspire to this basic template for the most part, adapting these administrative practices into their own version of the one-stop-shop recovery house experience.

### Administrative Practice in the Intake House: Blackout, the Welfare Plug-In, and the Local Address

Larger programs (those with six to twelve houses) typically designate one house as the *intake house*, a strategic space that operators use to streamline the welfare plug-in. The intake house is also where addicts undergo a more general process of indoctrination in the probationary phase known as *blackout*. During the blackout period, operators restrict the addict's travel outside the house unless accompanied by an escort (someone with an established length of sobriety). Moreover, operators restrict outings to "taking care of business" with welfare case managers, probation officers, doctors, treatment providers, and sponsors at 12-step meetings. Addicts are typically placed on blackout during their entire stay in the intake house, which usually lasts two to four weeks.

Although most intake house operators encourage clients to undergo full detoxification before arrival, they are often forced to deal with heroin, alcohol, and cocaine withdrawal. While some help addicts detox with informal methods, others simply push them through the early paces. Operators typically see detoxification as an obstacle to the process of getting connected to welfare in a timely manner. When Malik's partner, Blanche, came to Philadelphia, for example, she was still actively using heroin and in dire need of detoxification. Blanche had been living on the streets of Newark for seven years and did not have any identification or insurance. She was denied admission to detox centers in Philadelphia and Camden, but Malik finally got her into a women's intake house at Positive Attitudes. The program took Blanche in when no one else would, but the staff had little sympathy for her dope sickness. Blanche reflected on her own arrival with resentment, as the house staff was more concerned about her ability to become a paying client than about her physical suffering:

> BLANCHE: When I got there they sent me to the welfare office right away, and it was pouring down rain outside. I was real weak, and I had to walk. Then the next day I had to get up when everybody else got up, I had a chore I had to do, I had to go to the meetings they went to, and I couldn't lay down. Matter of fact, one time I went upstairs and laid down [for] like five minutes, and I ended up getting put on restriction for two days. I couldn't lay down until after the last meeting at 9:00 p.m. They knew I was dope sick, [but they told me] to just stick it out.

Blanche's story illustrates how operators coordinate the steady processing flows of the intake house with the administrative channels and protocols of the formal welfare bureaucracy. Indeed, as we have seen in Malik's case, the prospective financial solvency of addicted bodies renders verification, documentation, and procurement of their eligibility essential administrative practices for *all* recovery house operators. For this reason, all operators have some form of intake procedure, even if they cannot afford to designate a house exclusively for intake purposes. Innovative processes for procuring GA (and, to a lesser extent, SSI), known in recovery house vernacular as "getting plugged in," have risen to the level of a widely recognized system.

As a point of pride, several operators claimed they could get an addict plugged in and "turned on" with the Philadelphia Department of Public Welfare in just two weeks, regardless of his/her state of origin. One of their typical strategies for plugging in clients from out of state is to register them to vote, often the first order of "taking care of business" in the initial days of the blackout period. Intake house managers have formulated special procedures (emulated by managers and directors industrywide) to ensure that

referred clients come equipped with at least the bare essentials of identification: a driver's license, birth certificate, or voter registration card from
neighboring states. Houses frequently turn away people who lack these documents, as they present a financial risk.

Under Philadelphia welfare regulations, proof of address is the only legal
channel to benefits and social services in the formal sector. For this reason,
operators must also provide a letter for proof of address for the addict walking in off the street. This is an essential document that the addict must present to a welfare caseworker. Equally important, as we have seen in the case
of AHAD, is the change-of-address form, a crucial document that prevents
welfare benefits from being terminated when a person leaves one recovery
house en route to another. Address verification is one of the primary regulatory interests that the state welfare department pursues with respect to the
recovery house population. Public Welfare Unit Manager Jeff Blumberg
spoke of this requirement as one that could invite a visit from the welfare
inspector:

> JB: They do have to verify the address . . . they usually just bring us a note,
> or a rental agreement. I'm sure the people that run the houses have
> worked through that. Hopefully it's on some form of stationery; if it's
> just written on a little piece of paper, that would be a red flag. If there is
> a question about living arrangements, then they have inspectors that will
> go out and verify the addresses and make sure it is there. Because some
> people use bogus addresses, that's very common.

Recovery house operators create makeshift letterhead as a tactic of legitimacy for their program, usually by typing the name of the house in boldface
using a word-processing program on a borrowed, hired, or house computer
(not all houses are equipped with computers, but an informal market does
exist for these types of word-processing tasks). While the incentives on the
side of the recovery houses may be separate from those of the welfare office, policy-driven imperatives for address verification generate a mutually
beneficial form of street-level administrative expertise.

In part to mitigate the kind of risk endemic to taking people in off the
streets, operators also use the intake house to reach an economy of scale.
The practice, known in recovery house vernacular as "carrying," or subsi-
dizing an addict on the backs of paying clients until he or she is "plugged
in" or "hooked up" to welfare, highlights what's at stake in terms of welfare
administration, market share, and volume disparities between houses. For
a smaller program like Malik's, the pressure to get people "plugged in" is

intense, and the risks associated with carrying people were part of the cal-
culus of whether his house would take a loss, break even, or come out ahead
on any given month. During an especially desperate time when his census
was low in the winter of 2003, Malik took a risk on two new intakes.

> MALIK: Listen, if the first guy stays, it is okay; but if he leaves, I done took
> my other guys' food to feed him. He ain't got shit for money, and I'm car-
> rying him, you understand what I am saying? I'm carrying another new
> guy too, but at least his girlfriend gave me money for him coming in the
> door. That is basically what I am feeding him with, the intake fee, but he
> is going to have to pay me for what he owe me for carrying his rent come
> the third. Now I already took that gamble with the first guy, so suppose
> one of them go back out [i.e., relapses]? See, when I had a lot of clients
> I had a lot of food, plus I was getting stamps too. It is not there no more
> and I can't afford that, man, I can't afford to have nobody here that I can't
> trust. If a guy comes with a risk factor, man, you can't always mess with
> him.

Like most operators, Malik charged a fifty-dollar intake fee, a nominal sum
typically deployed as a stopgap measure or security deposit, and often applied toward the first month's rent. But in many instances, he was forced to
waive the intake fee, simply because men were destitute and he needed to
fill beds. The small scale of his program made him especially vulnerable to
the inevitable losses, particularly when compared with larger programs that
were equipped with an intake house, as in the case of Positive Attitudes.

> MALIK: Positive attitudes will take that shit, man, they take so much money
> from them motherfuckers going in and out, like if ten people go into
> Positive Attitudes [intake house] and they only get money for two, that
> is good [enough] for them, you see what I am saying? The [established]
> programs with more than one house can do that, because the losses they
> take are nothing since they get more in than they lose. So they can carry
> guys with the other men's food until they got hooked up a lot easier.
> They take beatings too, but look where they are at; they are not taking no
> *big* beatings. It's the same way with Miracle of Recovery; those programs
> can take that shit because they got the volume and the size. Even if they
> just get the emergency stamps from the guys and they go out [relapse],
> they still keep all that food money, you see what I am saying?[49] They call
> that one meal one check, you know, a guy come in we hook him up real

fast we get him an emergency jointy, and they think, "You know, maybe we at least can get that."

Malik pointed out that larger programs may be able to reach an economy of scale by taking in larger volumes of clients off the street, as they know that enough will become paying customers and that others—at the very least—will be able to contribute food stamps to the house coffers. Another advantage of larger programs is that operators can use the blackout period in the intake house as a disciplinary tool for more "advanced" clients who may have "graduated" to the recovery house yet subsequently relapsed. In this instance, the intake house revokes privileges and relegates the addict to the starting point of the process. Thus, apart from its disciplinary attributes, the intake house affords the operator the option of recycling relapsed clients, rather than losing them to the streets.

Moreover, the large operator's ability to establish volume disparities distributes risk unevenly between larger and smaller programs. This type of advantage engenders bitterness among smaller operators, often resulting in allegations of monopolization. But quite independent of these squabbles, the practice of carrying is one of the most functional provisions of the recovery house industry. The chance to ride free, even temporarily, is especially attractive to addicts and alcoholics seeking shelter after destructive runs on heroin or crack. Carrying also marks a point of pride for operators, who rightfully boast that their houses shelter "those that no one else in the city will," even without formal state or city funding. And it is the operator—large or small—who bears the risk in terms of whether or not the addict will become a paying client. The intake house helps to mitigate this risk, acting first as a kind of holding pen until the addict is "plugged in," and then as a triage mechanism for the next phase.

## Connecting to Formal Treatment in the Recovery House Phase

Completion of detoxification, welfare processing, and the blackout period entails moving the addict to a separate location known simply as the *recovery house*. The recovery house is where an addict lives while attending several months of Intensive Outpatient Treatment (IOP).[50] While the tactics of recovery house operators are essential in this transition, the state has preconfigured the circuitry for the welfare plug-in not only in its welfare offices, but also within the formal treatment sector. The origins of this circuitry can be found in Pennsylvania's original Welfare Reform Act of 1982, which stipulates that all persons receiving GA for drug or alcohol dependency are required to attend treatment. Philadelphia's Public Welfare Department determines eligibility upon receipt of what is typically known as the "medical form," which contains the treatment provider's diagnosis of chemical dependency and effectively declares a person unfit for employment for nine months.

Recovery house operators rely on the treatment centers' resources, such as computers, physicians, and credentialed professionals, for documenting eligibility in the medical form. As a matter of economic survival, then, they must establish an intimate relationship with at least one outpatient treatment provider. This relationship enables operators to convert addicted bodies to solvent bodies at the outset, and to *keep* these bodies plugged in to the welfare system by maintaining their eligibility throughout the treatment process. As Malik put it, "Without treatment there is no money, period. There is no welfare, no nothing. You have to go to treatment."

Proximity to the bureaucracies of social welfare and professionalized treatment furthers the evolution of recovery houses as quasi-institutional frameworks. Operators hone their administrative techniques while "cutting their teeth" as managers and assistant managers. Consider, for example, Malik's learned expertise in navigating paperwork and using his connections to the formal treatment sector to plug in a new recruit.

> MALIK: [*shuffling through the man's paperwork*] This form will register you at New Horizons, I called Tammy [receptionist at New Horizons treatment center] this morning to get a slot for you. Now, this employment form right here [is for welfare], it explains why you can't work, because you are presently seeking drug and alcohol treatment, right, that's one of the primaries. See, your first time [on welfare you need] your primary, which the doctor going to give you right here. [*pointing at the form*] The doctor does the diagnosis right here, primary/secondary. And the doctor will say you are temporarily disabled for twelve months or six months, whichever it is.

The strategic merits of the partnership between the state and the recovery house operator are twofold. First, the partnership enables the operator to use channels for obtaining welfare funds that are established, at least partially, on the operator's terms. Second, it enables the state to transfer and convert poverty survival strategies to mechanisms of social policy. Sustained by a market logic that furthers the interests of both parties, the matrix provides recovery house entrepreneurs with the means to appropriate the welfare apparatus, and the foundation for a new form of poverty management system driven largely by street-level addicts; the state, in turn, is provided with a mechanism to extend its regulatory reach into areas of spatially concentrated poverty. The motivations of subsistence drive the imperative for welfare documentation. So too does the emerging importance of informal social service administration as a matter of governance.[51]

## Welfare Extension in the Three-Quarter or Worker House

Welfare requirements stipulate that IOP is followed by a period of Outpatient Treatment (OP), which entails a "step down" to just one or two appointments per week (usually one group and one individual counseling session) for several months. Accordingly, an addict might expect to stay nine to twelve months in the recovery house, although most stays are much shorter and often people end up living there for several years. Malik tried to follow the credo "Nine plus three will put you where you need to be." He explained his position on how the addict should utilize the year to achieve optimal results:

> MALIK: You should do nine months in the recovery house; I'm talking about
> with IOP and OP. The OP stage should take you to a job and transitional
> living, and if you living right, after three months you should be able to
> move into your own place.

In Malik's ideal scenario, completion of IOP and OP should enable the addict to "graduate" to the next phase, known as either the *transitional house*, the *worker house*, or the *three-quarter house*. Transitional houses offer less programmatic structure while still providing a collective and thus affordable residence with housemates committed to a clean and sober living space. Or, as a recovery house operator named Murphy put it, three-quarter houses are "for people with time who really just can't afford to live alone, so together they all pay the bills." These spaces are designed for addicts to learn how to "live life on life's terms"—the assumption being that the addict is "almost capable" of managing daily life.

Yet despite their claims to sever welfare dependency and return people to the workforce, it is in the interests of recovery house operators to extend the longevity of their clients' welfare eligibility. Several operators use the transitional house to this end. Operators lacking a three-quarter house proper simply use the normal recovery house by default to keep clients long term, often well beyond the first year. While to most of the city officials I interviewed this seemed impossible due to the nine-month time limit, the lived experience of addicts suggested otherwise. In fact, as Clarence informed me, to assume that welfare is limited to nine months is simply naïve:

> RF: What about guys on welfare for drug and alcohol—you can only stay on for nine months, right?
>
> CLARENCE: Wrong information. You can get that for five years.
>
> RF: Do you have to change your diagnosis somehow, or get reclassified? How do guys keep staying on all these years?
>
> CLARENCE: You can go to outpatient for nine months, that will keep that going. After you get out of intensive outpatient, or IOP, you can go down to OP [Outpatient] for nine months. And then you can pick it up on the medical, now we can start to go and see a psychiatrist over at Comhar or some other place for polysubstance, that's another nine months. Then you can go for [co-occurring disorder], extension, another nine months. You can keep that up for like five years.

In some cases operators try to extend welfare in the interests of recovery, so that addicts engage longer with the recovery project. But economics is an equally if not a more important motive: extending a client's time on welfare can help an operator to stay open or even make money. Malik echoed Clarence's general sentiment, suggesting that there are always ways to extend in the state of Pennsylvania:

> MALIK: In some states, like Virginia, for example, your leg gotta be shot off to get welfare. But here in Philadelphia it's pretty easy.
>
> RF: They say nine months lifetime, though, so how come guys are living in the house for, like, three to five years?
>
> MALIK: Well, you can keep living in the house, and some people stay for years. But they only going to do nine months of treatment for D&A [drug and alcohol], you understand what I am saying? If you still homeless you still homeless, and as long as you can go to the doctor and get a thing that says you are not eligible to work, you are entitled to the welfare for five years, basically, until they tired of you.

Information on welfare policy varied considerably in the Kensington recovering community, but operators and clients alike boasted that their anecdotal accounts and lived experiences trumped formal knowledge of regulations. As a recovery house manager and a past recipient of welfare,

Bilal was familiar with several ways in which the resourceful addict can stay afloat:

> BILAL: Even when you are eligible, welfare don't tell you . . . they are
> designed to make it difficult for you to get benefits. The way the thing
> works is, you get on initially for six to nine months, and then you get a
> review, you get another six to nine months. You can stay on drug addic-
> tion therapy up to two years, then you get another two years on medical
> disability. Then you can do a fifth year on job search, job training, school,
> whatever. But once you do that five years, you can't get back on welfare
> for another five years, even if you relapse. The only thing you can get is
> medical assistance and the food stamps. They can't deny you for that.

Bilal was notorious for maintaining a cadre of "old-timers" in his house,
many of whom had multiple years of sobriety and had been able to stay
connected to benefits under his guidance. Other operators were opposed
keeping people on welfare, as they felt the practice encouraged people to
"warehouse" clients and thus was counterproductive to the recovery goals
of self-sufficiency, autonomy, and self-responsibility. Malik, for example,
believed that operators should encourage people to move off welfare into independent living situations. However, he also respected the power of addiction and the realities of poverty, which legitimate using the welfare subsidy
for however long it takes, "provided, of course, we doin' the right thing."

All of these men articulate a common set of faiths among operators
concerning the recovery house experience. First, they expressed a certain
faith in the ability of the participants—both recovery house operators like
themselves, and addicts—to remain solvent in the process of recovery. Second, they indicated their faith in the recovery process as a dynamic through
which citizens can take their lives into their own hands, thus facilitating the
objectives of time-limited welfare policy. Third, they attached no shame or
stigma to the operator's or client's use of welfare funds. In many respects,
operators take pride in their capacity to navigate the complexities of welfare bureaucracies as active entrepreneurs rather than welfare dependents.
Their comments reveal that they act as a new form of market-driven social
worker, operating in the shadow welfare state.

The widespread emphasis among operators and clients alike on making the transition to independence through the recovery house experience
articulates with long-standing regulatory objectives of the residual welfare
state. Operators extol the potential of the recovery house matrix to operate

as an effective milieu for this purpose. But typical lengths of stay, both short and long, also suggest that the recovery house stands as an important form of low-income, informal rental market that combines risk pooling with collective poverty survival and poverty management. Utopian visions of self-transformation coexist with, and in some ways are coconstitutive of, dystopian strategies of warehousing and predatory subsistence.

## The Food Club

Hailed by operators as one of the greatest successes of the recovery house industry, the food club illustrates how questions of volume, discipline, and strategic calculation work within an economy of shared risk. Briefly, the food club allows operators to maximize returns on modest food stamp allotments while setting out a structured meal schedule and a division of labor to handle cooking and cleaning responsibilities. Recovery house operators' widespread establishment of mandatory food clubs naturalizes clients' consensual surrender of food stamps. GA clients are required to contribute roughly half of their monthly food stamp allotment ($60–$70, depending on program size) to the house. They are allowed to keep the remaining $70 for discretionary spending, which is most typically used for cigarettes and laundry. Workers in the house (that is, clients not on GA) are required to pay $60 a month in cash for the food club, since they generally don't receive food stamps. In return, operators provide all residents with breakfast and dinner at a cost of just over two dollars a day (larger programs and CODAAP-funded programs typically provide lunch as well). As Malik would boast: "Where else could you get breakfast for $2.50 a day? If you go to the place around the corner, you only get a bowl of cereal for that, and you sure as hell don't get dinner!"

Operators replicated the basic elements of the food club in all of the houses that I studied. Like other sections of the industry, the system depends on informal apprenticeships in which addicts trade their work for recovery. More specifically in this case, the food club fuses the informal labor of poverty survival with therapeutic projects geared toward responsibility, self-sufficiency, and plain old good eating habits. A well-run food club enables all members of the house to eat consistently and heartily. Indeed, weight gain is one of the most common indicators of health and sobriety in Kensington, as most addicts enter the recovery house in an emaciated state after months or years of heavy crack and heroin use.

At the most basic level, operators believe that addicts cannot be trusted to be responsible with their own funds. Mandatory membership prevents frivolous spending (men would often sell their stamps for cigarettes or presents for girlfriends, for example). In this sense, the food club reinforces the underlying logic of the "in-kind" benefit—described by Vivianna Zelizer as a special kind of currency echoing the centuries-old suspicion that poor people are incompetent at managing cash.[52] It does so by acting as an ancillary, informal street mechanism to prevent profligacy and resale in the black market. Moreover, pooling resources in the mandatory food club allows recovery houses to "carry" men and women who come in off the streets until their benefits are "turned on." On another level, the club serves as a peacemaking force by leveling the field in the houses and reducing the threat of "food wars." Malik told stories about infighting over scarce resources at houses lacking mandatory food clubs. This often resulted in operators locking refrigerators due to rampant theft among the client population. In other cases where a food club was absent, two or three clients within a house formed alliances to pool resources, only to have the informal agreement dissolve in a betrayal of some sort (sometimes leading to violence). An established food club eliminates these threats, as it renders the matter of subsistence for everyone in the house self-sustaining and automatic.

Managing the food club is a skilled practice, and people usually learn it as apprentices. Malik experienced the trials and tribulations of keeping a house stocked and maximizing the food budget while managing the Positive Attitudes 42 House, then replicated this system when starting his own program. It was his responsibility to make sure that he purchased everything in accordance with his carefully planned menu. Purchasing and planning are much easier at larger programs, because their larger censuses help the food club manager reach economies of scale (Malik typically had sixteen men to fund his budget at the 42 House, whereas his own program struggled to keep six to ten). At a smaller program like AHAD, coordination of the food club is much more complex. It was quite common for me to find Malik scheming in his head to come up with efficient subsistence strategies with a much smaller client base. He would launch into a detailed and harried analysis of how he would get through the month, proud that he kept his well-equipped kitchen fully stocked:

MALIK: [beaming in his kitchen] We learn how to live good in here, man, go get any gadget you want, put a blender over here and throw some fucking bananas in there. Everything is good, the oven kicks, and this motherfucker here is my baby [pointing to the refrigerator].

RF: So the food is all on target?

MALIK: Yeah, I got two cards ready to go now, I might spend $100 this
Saturday. Infinite's card is spent, I still got $25 on my card. I'm going to
spend Delmar's card, and Albert's . . . One of those cards I'm going to
have to get all canned goods, because Delmar's card will take me with the
meat for the whole month. If I spend $60 to $70 with the meat I'm good.
With Albert's card I can get cans and spaghetti and stuff like that, so I got
two cards that will take me out for the month, not counting if someone
comes in. Oh, and I got $60 coming from Rufus.

Malik explained to me that Rufus, as a worker, could contribute cash that
he allocated for nonfood items that could not be purchased with stamps:

MALIK: I use it for supplies for the house, stuff like aluminum foil, toilet paper, garbage bags, disinfect, pine (floor cleaner), you know, shit like that.

Again, larger programs with multiple houses enjoy significant advantages
in purchasing power. At programs on the scale of Benito's Fresh Start or
Clarence's We Stood at the Turning Point, directors would distribute bags
of toilet paper, garbage bags, and cleaning supplies to all of the managers
at weekly "community meetings," where all the houses of each program
would convene. Directors purchase these nonfood items in bulk out of general revenues, or using earmarked funds from worker contributions.

As an independent operator, Malik had to be more resourceful in stretch-
ing his budget. He preached about the virtues of rational planning and the
completion of reproductive tasks, pointing out how his "well-oiled machine" operated in contrast to his old "dope fiend ways." His mastery of
food club management was evident not only in an immaculate kitchen
(where he also cooked on most nights), but also at the grocery stores. I took
several trips with Malik and Rufus, the only man in Malik's house with a
car, out to Aramingo Avenue for what he called the Supermarket Sweep.
Knowing exactly how much he had to spend from the multiple access cards
in his possession, Malik would move through the aisles at a feverish pace,
collecting in his cart all the items he needed for the weekly menu. On more
than one occasion, Rufus and I stood back in awe as Malik hit the final sum
perfectly at the register. He hoped to teach his "proven system" to men like
Garvey, his latest manager prospect.

MALIK: I hit the sucker right on when we came up out of there, the object
was to come out within a dollar, and I came within forty-something

cents—*and* I got everything on the list. Garvey asked, "How did you do that?" I said twenty-three months as a recovery house manager has taught me this, you understand what I am saying? There is a system behind this, tried and true, and that's what I'm trying to tell him, you know what I mean? So I said (it might seem like I'm fucking up by not grabbing this?), but I try to tell him my system works, it's proven, and you gotta learn it. I'm keeping him with me because I'm teaching him.

Apart from its economic advantages, the food club allows recovering clients to contribute to their community while learning independent living skills. Benito explained the therapeutic merits of his food club during a tour of his Fresh Start house:

> BENITO: Once a month we take one of the company vans and we go to Sam's Club. I'll just give you a rough idea, man, let me get the key [*leads me to a large reach-in freezer that is fully stocked with frozen food items*]. See, these guys eat good, they won't go hungry. And the clients cook for themselves, we use it like a therapeutic tool because they are expected to work together and build self-esteem. Plus, you gotta learn how to cook, because you're going to be living on your own, unless you're going to be pulling down a crazy salary.

Benito's CODAAP-funded system was more organized than most (not to mention uniquely endowed with the luxury of a "company van"), but otherwise typical. Effectively, their purpose was to combine collective principles of poverty survival with therapeutic technology.

## Conclusion

As Malik's story in chapter 1 has shown, and this chapter has further contextualized, recovery house operators have assembled, or re-embedded, a series of welfare practices that are strongly conditioned by exigencies at the local scale.[53] In the aftermath of Pennsylvania's Welfare Reform Act of 1982, the operators have learned, transferred, and fused policy and practice abstractions (personal responsibility, treatment milieu, 12-step aphorisms) with local moral codes and informal administrative practices. Through the adaptive reuse of working-class row houses (and some warehouses and former sites of light industry), operators make it all work by embedding an informal economy within an inherited geographical landscape. They do so by inventing, emulating, and retrofitting social service administrative practices—many of which the operators themselves learned as clients—to a decayed and heavily urbanized milieu.

The result is a complex recovery house *system* that accommodates fluid, if contradictory, sets of cross-purposes. On one level, recovery houses operate as an ancillary mode of urban governance, jumping scales from the conduct of local operators to the state regulatory powers of criminal justice and public welfare. On another, the movement parallels a transnational proliferation of nongovernmental organizations seeking to advance new visions of emancipation, self-transformation, and citizenship.[54] And at the most basic level, recovery houses operate as collective poverty survival strategies (or "subsistence niches") that have become highly competitive, extralegal, and informal low-income rental markets.[55]

The constellation of possible forms in the many categories of the recovery house system has evolved into a highly variegated poverty management system. Categories and tactics of differentiation operate as more than simply efficient containers for the specialization of services. Informal categorization and active differentiation perform a number of more elusive functions, many of which map onto, and derive from, the contradictory purposes I've just articulated. First, differentiation sets out a moral field, or a spectrum of formality, around which recovery house operators position themselves to make claims of legitimacy to the state. Thus, most operators castigate the friendly user, while larger owners denigrate smaller ones (and vice versa); and Christian recovery houses malign secular houses due to their lax disciplinary structures. Second, administrative categories operate as organizational and linguistic devices that allow recovery houses to appropriate a broader expanse of the formal welfare apparatus. And yet not all recovery house operators are so inclined, which leads to a third function of differentiation and administrative *un*-rationality: many operators are compelled to push further into the realm of invisibility and informality, capitalizing on the recovery house concept—very loosely defined—to capture greater control of a low-income/invisible rental market.

Herein lies the true significance of variegation in the recovery house movement. Operators' differentiation and posturing ultimately rescales (and remakes) urban governance, risk management, and welfare administration. The full spectrum of the addiction experience, from transforming the self, to being warehoused, to undergoing plain old wethousing, is accommodated here. In this respect, informal categorization is consistent with Esping-Andersen's claim that despite their role in providing services and security, welfare institutions are inherently stratifying institutions.[56] Across the wide spectrum of the "unregulated" recovery house, operators facilitate a reshuffling, restratification, or churning of addicted bodies in the lower-class strata. Forged at least in part on social grounds—race, gender, and (under)class markers—these sorting and channeling practices stand very much in contrast to neoclassical and neoliberal tenets of laissez-faire, rational choice, and freedom from coercion.[57] Taken together, they amount to a new, informally *planned* and multifaceted system of poverty management that transfers and adapts vestigial welfare practices to a highly localized geography of social service provision.

# The Art of Building Programmatic Space    3

Self-help provides a political solution to political problems that do not
require state action, conformity to society, or the repression of dissent. . . .
Self-help is a technique that works to limit the need for state action–not by
"depoliticizing" class relations or excluding the poor from politics but by
getting them to act.
—BARBARA CRUIKSHANK, *THE WILL TO EMPOWER* (1999)

The visions of recovery house entrepreneurs and the history of welfare reform policy in Pennsylvania begin to suggest how recovery
houses have rescaled the landscapes of poverty management and urban
governance in areas of spatially concentrated poverty. Operators have
come to imagine recovery house space as a crucible for the transformation of selves and the communities within which they are situated.
The pursuit of stated goals—nothing short of molding down-and-
out suffering addicts into upstanding, rational, "productive members
of society"—has mobilized a very particular form of poverty politics.
Recovery houses operate as nodal points situated within complex and
unpredictable networks of regulatory power. At one scalar level we
find the deeply complicated relationship between the state and the

recovery house industry. At a second scalar level stands the interface between recovery house *technologies of the self* and *technologies of power*. This
chapter will focus on the latter scale, in particular by analyzing the ways in
which recovery house operators envisage and construct programmatic space
for the constitution, transformation, and regulation of recovering subjects.

Recovery houses are one among many proliferating forms of governance
in poor neighborhoods. The knowledge, discourse, and practices that unfold
within them act as complex sites of moral, social, and political-economic
regulation. We have seen how welfare administration loses direct spatial
association with the state, as street-level actors increasingly seek to accu-
mulate addicted bodies in elaborate census-building projects. But to gain a
more comprehensive picture of the full ramifications of the recovery house,
it is necessary to move beyond the functions of economic subsistence.

Under Foucault's guidance, the term *government* encompasses the multiple ways in which the self has become related to fragmented and decentralized configurations of power in the age of devolution and welfare retrenchment.[1] He examined transformational ethical fields using the term
*technologies of the self*, which he defined as follows:

> Technologies of the self permit individuals to effect by their own means or
> with the help of others a certain number of operations on their own bodies
> and souls, thoughts, conduct and way of being, so as to transform themselves
> in order to attain a certain state of happiness, purity, wisdom, perfection, or
> immortality.[2]

Foucault described *technologies of power* as those mechanisms "which determine the conduct of individuals and submit them to certain ends or
domination, (to effect) an objectivizing of the subject."[3] Taken together,
Foucault's agonist conception of government moves beyond programs conducted solely by the state to encompass, as Barbara Cruikshank's work so
provocatively makes imperative, "any program, discourse, or strategy that
attempts to alter or shape the actions of others."[4] This includes recovery
discourse itself, and the voluntary and internal relations of rule set forth by
recovery house operators, to the extent that their "programs" are concerned
with "managing and administering social and personal existence to introduce economy, order, and virtue."[5]

In this chapter I will consider how recovery knowledge takes shape in the
form of technologies of the self. I will explore how addicts are first actively
constituted as subjects who suffer from a particular "lack,"[6] and then incited to become productive members of society—or *ethical beings*. I will also

consider how the constituent mechanisms of "the program"—for example, daily schedules, rule structures, intake rituals, informal case management, and divisions of labor—operate as technologies of power in the recovery house setting. My primary purpose is to connect recovering subjects to the programmatic practices bearing down on (and *through*) them in Kensington recovery houses. It is at the intersection of two forces—programmatic technologies of power, and technologies of self-regulation—that Foucault locates the proverbial encounter of *governmentality*.

The sections that follow explore the programmatic strategies deployed in Malik's recovery house as they were developed in context. In particular, I focus on the designation of the "diseased" will under the auspices of recovery house practices, a process that is crucial for the manufacture of consent which underlies the general efficacy of recovering technologies. My intention is to explore the ways this authority is constituted, while ultimately recognizing that it must always forge alliances in contextually specific sites. I am also concerned here with the ways in which the self, no matter how much caught up in larger structures of power, comes to be seen as the only political solution to poverty.

## Giving Back, Participation, and "the Program"

> MALIK: I put it to you like this: a lot of these guys don't know how to keep house, because they never had one and they never had the responsibility, or they just don't fucking know how, or don't care. In here it's like this: if you the chore monitor and I explain to you that your job is to make sure everybody do their chores . . . and if the chore is not done, you gotta do it, *you* gotta get it done. You know, it's basic shit that we learn in here, man. We learn how to *live* in here.

I begin my analysis of the program at the most fundamental level: the requirement that the men *participate* in the daily maintenance of the house. The job of the recovery house director and the manager is to enroll recovering subjects as participants in the house's operating structure. During one of his initial intake interviews, for example, Malik enlisted the participation of a new client by way of a particular rationality known as "giving back."

> MALIK: What I'm basically trying to say here is like this: we don't want a jail-type setting in here, we want a setting where you can *just about be free*, but this house has to be taken care of just like if you living in your own house. It's a simple program, and I want it to be a program that you

would be able to have some freedom for yourself. But the freedom [re-quires] that we give back to this house, and this house must always come first.

Like many operational concepts of the recovery house industry, the notion of "giving back" derives from the 12-step discourse of recovery (as the old AA adage puts it, "In order to keep it we must give it away"). Within the informal rental/subsistence niche, giving back amounts to a peculiar form of voluntarism. Residents "freely give" their labor, that is, performing daily chores like cooking meals, cleaning, watching the house, and other role-specific tasks. Operators pitch this not simply as a form of labor unto itself, but rather as reciprocity, giving back that which is freely given to them in the form of recovery and salvation. They present this process as healing and transformative, a form of daily *practice* that is synonymous, in Malik's perspective, with learning "how to live."

Malik believed in the transformational capacities of doing "basic shit" in the recovery house, particularly those activities that inculcated personal responsibility for the collective as a whole. Active participation was para-mount, for as Malik claimed incessantly, one could get a "free ride" for only so long:

> MALIK: There is a part of this program that will give you a free ride, and
> you can enjoy some of the spoils without doing shit, and that's what a
> lot of people do, they go along for the ride. I mean, there is a part of this
> program that will let you stay clean, but are you *sober*, that's the question.
> You know, you get people around here saying, "I got twelve months . . ."
> but you gotta ask back, "You got twelve months of what?" It's like this:
> you can stay around a barbershop and get good conversation every day,
> [in fact] some of your most intelligent conversation comes out of a
> barbershop. If you go every day you get the rap, but when you going to
> get the haircut? You can be on the outskirts getting the kibbles and bits,
> wanting all the fucking rewards that those people inside got, but the real
> meat is on the inside, and you gotta work for that.

Appeals to active participation are pervasive in the recovery house indus-try—perhaps best exemplified by another co-opted 12-step aphorism, "It works if you work it." So it is essential that client and recovery house op-erator cooperate. The point at which a client goes beyond the pale marked the point of anxiety for Malik's fledgling recovery house:

MALIK: The whole thing in making this thing work, and being successful in making this living situation work, is cooperation. Once you have the cooperation of each one of the men, you don't have a problem. It's just when somebody has to go on their own, that's when we have problems. If we don't have some harmony, or some type of cooperation in the house, it can get miserable.

Malik felt strongly that desire and willingness were crucial elements of the recovery practice, and it was for this reason that he established an "advanced" recovery house that would "practically run itself." But as we have seen, it became apparent soon after AHAD's opening that active participation in the house was sorely lacking. Malik increasingly found himself overworking as a result, and it was typical to find him haranguing his guys for failing to "step up to the plate." His new central strategy to enroll their commitment and participation more stringently was to establish "the program."

## Envisioning the Program

Toward the end of AHAD's first month of operation, Malik began to write a program prospectus. This would not only provide clients with a definitive "contract for living," but also help to establish the legitimacy of AHAD to external referral sources. At first, the prospectus was slow in the making because of the elusive nature of the program's core tenets, not to mention a nasty case of writer's block.

MALIK: [showing me his typewriter] Bilal gave me that. I am trying to come up with a format for my program, my mission, my approach, you know, get some paper somewhere and try and get something together. I can't get it yet, I usually can sit down and [slapping his hands together three times] something will come, ain't nothing coming though, man. It's locked. I help everybody else do things, and now I'm stuck with mine, and mine don't have to say that much; I just want, like, a brief summary.

Malik began to have frequent discussions with me about what he wanted to say about the recovery house program. There was something about his experience at the 42 House that was crucial to his own success. He wanted to recreate this not only in the Genoa Street house, but also down the road when he acquired his own independent living space.

MALIK: For real, for real, I don't think that I can do what I want to do without this house. Being a part of this house is my fucking strength, man,
even though I struggle with it. When I leave this house to go into my
own house, this same structure and discipline I am going to have to take
there. This is my practice ground, this is what I do, and this is what I will
continue to do in the future.

Deciding to build his program in this realm of "structure and discipline,"
Malik enlisted my help in writing down some goals and objectives, which
we eventually typed up together. Our conversations provided an outlet
otherwise absent in his life. I learned this about six weeks into my fieldwork, after checking in to make sure he was okay with my incessant hanging around.

MALIK: Yo, check this out, let me explain this to you, I ain't asking you for
nothing, I ain't looking for nothing, man, you know, like . . . basically
you givin' me what I need, you help me, you know what I'm saying, and
I'm able to help you. Because, see, like, believe it or not, these men keep
me busy, man [and I don't get enough time to think]. That's important,
because this is my dream, and my dream is to have a program that is not a
flophouse, all right, so I need something or someone outside of this here
to like let things out, or to think things through. I need to know that
somebody else is going to just listen to me, so it's okay, man, with you
being around here; I even get a kick out of it.

The official demarcation of "the program" would come with the advent
of weekly house meetings on Sunday nights, where the director and staff
would have a chance to take an inventory on the house, and residents would
have a chance to check in on their own progress and to voice any "house issues." At the very first house meeting of AHAD, Malik began to define the
program—initially, at least, by pointing precisely to what it was not:

MALIK: We been going through some shit during all these original days,
these "test days" I'm going to call them, really the thirty original days
we been here. This program has not really been active as a *program* yet,
because we didn't have a phone and we didn't have this [weekly house
meeting], but now it is an official program. We are not running a flophouse. Everybody knows what a flophouse is; everybody knows what a
boardinghouse is; everybody knows what a transitional house is; we ain't
none of those things, we a *recovery* house. I'm going to give you a perfect

example of what I am talking about: if I'm not doing a thing in here but laying my head down, getting up in the fucking morning, what kind of house is this?

INFINITE: A boardinghouse . . .

MALIK: All right, there is a boardinghouse down the street, there is a boardinghouse on every fucking block; if you want that you can go there, but this is a *recovery* house.

As a way of pressing on and clarifying what he meant, Malik drew on the notes he had compiled to disseminate at the meeting. He announced some of his founding principles and ideals for the program, carefully pointing out that while the recovery house was not a boardinghouse, it was not a facility either:

MALIK: What I'm saying is, we are pretty much laid back, because this is a house of recovery. The only difference about this house, is like this [*starts flipping through his notes*] . . . what is about this house . . . OK, here it is [*reading*], "Program goals and objectives: to help residents maintain a healthy and positive lifestyle and achieve their goals through support provided both within AHAD as well as in the recovering community." On number six it says, "To ensure that we admit recovering men who are most likely to gain from our unique program. It is not our intention to enroll those persons that we are unable to serve."

So what I'm saying is, the people that I'm bringing into this house are the people that fit the mode of this house. The purpose is to give you a unique living condition, so that no person seeking recovery or health should have to worry about having a roof over their head. You know that is being supplied for you, we all know that recovery doesn't just come from being in a recovery house; it comes from going out and getting it. But there is some things that you get from being in the recovery house that enable you to *get* recovery, and that's the only thing that I am trying to do here. This is not what we call a facility, like . . . [*to Jack*] what do you call them joints, where you come from?

JACK: A rehab?

MALIK: Yeah, it ain't one of them joints, man, it's supportive living, that's what this is basically.

Although he characterized his own program as "unique," Malik mapped out a number of core functions typical of recovery houses. He referred to overlapping definitions, from the simple concept of a "roof over your head,"

to the more complex notion of "supportive living" to "help residents maintain a healthy and positive lifestyle and achieve their goals." These types of
statements express the interests of recovery house owners in staying "right-
sized" to protect their own jurisdiction, or turf, in the continuum of recovery technologies. In saying that "recovery doesn't just come from a recovery
house," Malik expressed respect for (and deference to) the professional and
the 12-step communities while establishing the complementary role of the
recovery house. Part of being right-sized also has to do with recognizing
the strengths that the house contributes, and in this sense he was careful to
note the importance of "the mode of the house;" a structural milieu that
sets it apart from the flophouse.

In some ways expounding on this elusive mode, Infinite worked in tandem with Malik at the house meeting to entice the clients into what he
called the "atmosphere" of the program:

> INFINITE: I heard something today that really hit home with me. The re-
> covery house for me [*pauses*] . . . what it is, it's like an *atmosphere*. We learn
> how to live a different way in here, and in order to do that we must put
> ourselves in a different atmosphere. *This* is the place to do that. We set our
> own atmosphere in this house: we can have an atmosphere of negative, we
> can have an atmosphere of positive, there is so many different atmospheres
> that we can have. But we in here, we can set an atmosphere of responsibil-
> ity, we been told so many times, dictated to for so long in our addiction
> on what to do and how to do . . . If we weren't in jail it was the drug man
> telling us to wait on the corner. For so long we lived like this, but *now
> we're free, we're in liberty, we have freedom today.*

Infinite extolled the "atmosphere" of the recovery house, a quasi-institu-
tionalized space he distinguished from previous forms of state-sponsored
incarceration and the more ethereal "chains of addiction" spoken about in
12-step groups. His opening salvo illustrated the crucial importance of freedom and the open possibilities for the house's governance structure at the
house's inception. Certainly, the idea of freedom in this context is quite
compelling and seductive, particularly where the programmatic architecture of the house is concerned. Yet just as quickly as Infinite invoked the
powers of freedom to organize a new way of living, he vividly described
the dangers of anomie and the need for self-discipline:

> INFINITE: Just because we free, doesn't mean, like, we have to act like a
> child or somebody who just got out of prison who ain't seen a woman in

seven years run around trying to fuck everything. We're free, up in here, in order to [build and practice] an atmosphere of being, because we not going to be in here forever, so in here we practice to go out there and live a productive way of life. It's about being able to say, I'm sitting at home with my woman, I know how to sit in the living room and enjoy a conversation, a positive conversation. It's not like, just because I'm alone in the house I'll run through the house all buck naked, you know what I mean? It's a learning process, this is our basic training, our training camp, and what we put forth here is *an atmosphere of discipline, for disciplining ourselves, not somebody else disciplining us.*

The concept of autonomy is crucial here ("there is so many different atmospheres that we can have"), as it casts the men as engineers of their own fate, or at the very least their own recovery house "atmosphere." There is *atmosphere of discipline* much for the men to celebrate in the absence of overt forms of suppression or force, as they will no longer be "dictated to . . . on what to do and how to do." (To illustrate this point further, when I asked how things were going in the recovery house, Infinite typically responded, "It's all good—ain't no hack callin' out, 'lockin' down on Floor two!'") Yet there was also a power vacuum for the men to address, one that threatened security with irrationality, disorder, and chaos. The antidote that Infinite referred to, which they themselves must create, is "an atmosphere of discipline." This is known *& autonomy* more commonly in the recovery house vernacular as "working a program"; or, the implementation of a broadly conceived set of activities meant to set out clear channels for prudent conduct in everyday life. Program logic holds that so long as the addict is able to engage in activities organized around notions of self-discipline, self-regulation, and self-surveillance, he will enlarge the sphere of individual liberty. Here Infinite set forth the notion of a "training camp," where one develops the capacity of the will to regulate drives, desires, and impulses.

He articulated the rewards of doing so in compelling terms:

INFINITE: There is a format to everything in life, and there is a format to this program, and if you allow yourself to become a part of something that's positive, then we got to be open-minded and we got to start putting forth and doing little things in this house, to say, "This is mine, this is my place, my safe haven, my place of learning how to rehabilitate, to make something new, a new creature, a new way of living." Believe it or not, you have more space to yourself in a house this size, than a house bigger than this, you understand what I'm saying, *if* you have the respect of each other. We're going to have to set that atmosphere not just for ourselves but for other people that come through the door. So they will see this, and see how we doing this, being that insample [*sic*], not an example but an insample, because this is what we living, we live here, so we an insample. All of us together need to step up to the plate and do what we need to do, with no questions asked. We asked enough questions when we was out there [using] and none of them got answered. Now we have an answer to be something that's greater than what we was.

The conditions under which this is possible, to become "something . . . greater than what we was," are highly complex. As Marianna Valverde notes, there is a paradox created when trafficking the "will" as a mechanism to encompass both desire and its regulation.[7] In the recovery house setting, this paradox requires—at the very least—that the men participate in, and get with, "the program."

In Malik's and Infinite's sometimes maladroit (and often convoluted) speeches in which they tried to articulate just what the program *does*, as well as what "doing" the program means, we can begin to tease out two separate technical strands operating in the recovery house: (1) a disciplinary structure—that is, a format or a mode—that helps to sustain the living environment and the "recovery atmosphere" itself; and (2) a technological structure or therapeutic milieu that facilitates the recovery process in concert with other recovering technologies (for example, professional treatment and 12-step meetings). Further elaboration on these points is warranted, for it is here that we can locate the inner workings of abstract programmatic space in recovery houses—an almost ontological space that, as Infinite poignantly articulated, can even transcend the cramped quarters of a two-story row house based on its emancipatory valence. The potential for liberation rests in a very carefully calculated formula that balances discipline and freedom. The complexity of this balance can be sketched out using Malik's innovative concept of "the advanced recovery house."

## "Blackout is forever in some joints!": The Making of an "Advanced" Recovery House and a Carefully Calculated Freedom

The most successful recovery house operators are able to forge skillful programmatic linkages between the concept of freedom, the manufacture of consent, the designation of rule structures, and the mandates of economic pragmatism. Malik's initial strategy to sell AHAD as an "advanced" recovery house encompassed all four points. In fact, Malik invented the advanced category to set his program apart from the more tightly controlled ones, including houses with extended blackout periods, or managers and directors who arbitrarily put their houses on lockdown. Some even went so far as to dictate what their residents could or could not say in 12-step meetings. He explained that in his house, while there was certainly a rule structure, his program would not impinge on the "personal lives" of clients:

> MALIK: You can't tell nobody how to run their personal lives. What you can tell them is, like, the rules and regulations in your program, but you can't just be making shit up, like, "Uh, no spitting on the sidewalk today," or "Walk like a lady"—you know, all that shit. Every time Blanche's manager goes through some shit, it's like, "Oh-oh, here it comes, we getting ready to get it." And that's not fair. I be pissed off a lot of the time, but I can't take it out on people like that. I might kick some shit around, but I'm not going to interfere with people's lives. We came in here to find a life and to get a life. Now that we get a life you tell us we can't have a life? No sir.

The spectrum of discipline was well known to operators and clients in Kensington's recovery house community, and Malik's critical comments about the strictness of other programs were quite commonplace. Men typically left houses that deployed mechanisms of excessive control. Garvey, for example, was one of several who found their way out of highly disciplinary programs thought to be antithetical to the principles of recovery:

> GARVEY: That Positive Attitudes and a lot of them other recovery houses, I can't do that [type of program]. I can't be like a prisoner. I got a bad personality and I can't take people lordin' over me. I got to deal with people that treat me like a man, because I can't recover like that. I mean, you can't leave, or get nothing to eat, you supposed to sit there and starve from 6:30 in the morning 'til 7:00 at night. That's crazy, man, that's not a part of recovery. I didn't even do that getting high, I ate! I ain't going to sit there and die, and I'm not trying to, like, hit my bottom *in* recovery. So I left there after two days, and it's by chance and prayer that I ran into Malik.

Garvey's statement about hitting bottom in recovery articulates client perceptions of recovery houses as potentially impoverishing spaces that are perhaps even more punitive than the travails of active addiction. As many addicts say, recovery must become something better than what they had. Following this premise, liberation is a crucial part of staying on the path. Malik and Clarence recognized this, at least in theory, and made attempts to maximize freedom and minimize discipline in their programmatic structures.

Operators use the ratio of freedom to discipline much as they use other forms of categorization: as a tool of differentiation, primarily to establish legitimacy and to attract clients in a competitive market. Yet their logic here exceeds that of economic pragmatism alone. Malik's previous statement, that the recovering subject comes in to "find a life and to get a life," indicates that recovery house operators actively privilege the concept of emancipation. To actualize and cultivate this appreciation, operators formulate a deliberate "local knowledge" of their client. Clarence, riffing on the difference between imprisonment and recovery, insisted that an over-reliance on direct control was ineffective for the rebellious nature of the addict:

> CLARENCE: If you go to a CODAAP-funded facility, the whole thing is run off of control, controlling the client. Some of those people are there because they don't want to go to jail, but you put them in that environment and they feel like they in jail anyway. If I know one thing about drug addicts, [it's] that they some rebellious people, man. You can't believe that if you just keep them locked up and keep them away from [drugs] that they not going to do it. If they going to use, they going to use no matter how long you leave them locked up. So, like, it is kind of a situation where you want to offset that by allowing them some freedom. And the point is, we don't want to chase them, you want them to be comfortable enough to *want* to stay clean, so you give them some space to allow them to become the men and women that they want to become. I mean, you don't need to punish these people more than they already punished themselves. Plus, if you start to try and control us, [you lose us].

Clarence highlighted several points that are essential to recovery house technologies. First, addicts are presupposed to be, and actively constituted as, rebellious people whose unyielding (if misguided) agency has already produced requisite levels of punishment for acquiescence and surrender through the trials of active addiction.[8] Overly strict programming is therefore not only unnecessary, it is also ineffective, since the house "loses" the client as he or she perceives personal "freedom" to be compromised under controlling conditions. Always holding out the AA principle of "attraction rather than promotion," the knowing recovery house operator functions on the logic of consent, and the manufacture of desire.[9] The strategy is to "offset" the recalcitrant will and the failings of the strictly disciplinary framework by "allowing them some freedom," so that addicts can "become the men and women they want to become."

Following this logic, Malik's advanced recovery house concept sought to activate and expand the sphere of liberty for his clients by cultivating their volition, consent, and voluntarism through egalitarian means. Again, he compared this to the restrictions in other houses:

> MALIK: In other houses you ain't going in and out the fucking door, you ain't going in the kitchen or none of that, am I right or wrong [*asking Tessio*]?
> TESSIO: [*concurring*] They got signs up, no one is allowed in there . . .
> MALIK: No going in the kitchen, no touching the icebox, no sir.

That is, it was important to Malik to deinstitutionalize his setting as much as possible, not only experientially but physically. He avoided "shelterlike" rules such as locked refrigerators or signage meant to separate clients from staff, and openly referred to himself as both "director and client" to set a "familylike" atmosphere. Malik also tried to take pride in the small things, such as keeping his house immaculate and providing the men with special extras like Blockbuster movie nights and Monday night football. Perhaps the most conspicuous marker designating his program as "advanced" was the absence of a blackout period, a sizeable advantage for the client in search of more freedom.

> MALIK: Blackout is forever in some joints. And when you off blackout, all you can do is march to a meeting and march back. Ain't no going to Center City and all that shit, you understand what I'm saying? They'd rather you just sit the fuck there, and start fighting and aggravating, all that old bullshit.

Malik's strategy of distancing his program from the stricter houses was simple enough, but the disciplinary spectrum in question is much more complicated. His contention that "blackout is forever in some joints" marks one end of it, where many operators have no qualms about embracing a more disciplinary framework. In particular, several of the Christian recovery house operators openly touted their extended blackout periods and strict curfews as necessary elements for controlling their otherwise uncontrollable populations. Some even insisted that the more lax programs gave the industry a bad name, giving excessive freedoms that allowed addicts to "run the streets" at will. Even Malik recognized that for all of its accolades, his advanced program had potentially negative consequences:

> MALIK: You see, this house right here can do two things for you: this house can help you, or it can hurt you. If you really don't want to recover, or if you really don't want to stop drinking, this house will hurt you, because of the freedom, you know what I'm saying? The freedom that you have to come and go in here, if you using it to do something for yourself you all right, but otherwise you in trouble. So you got to look at it like this here: do I take advantage of the opportunity to be able to have the freedom, to go as I please, and do something with my life? Or do I *not* take advantage and go fuck shit up.

The inherent risk in Malik's programmatic philosophy is located in perhaps its most generative and powerful asset: his belief that transformation depends on the willful choices of recovering subjects. Clients can resist the punishing "choices" of addiction, which served as a-priori disciplinary force (as Clarence stated, "you don't need to punish these people more than they already punished themselves"), only by freely choosing something else. Choice was also central to the notion of a client "tak[ing] advantage of the opportunity to be able to have the freedom . . . and do something with my life" or choosing instead to abuse freedom by simply going to "fuck shit up."

Yet Malik's taxonomy—one type of freedom operating in service of recovery, and one type in service of ongoing self-destruction—also invites reflection on the crucially significant concept of *intervention* in the recovery house. Even though Malik highlighted the issue of choice as a matter of client free will, he also factored into his calculations the recovery house operator's influence in swinging the client toward the path of recovery. So an operator with an excessively liberal program risks going the way of the flophouse. This risk fortified Malik's belief that a client's temporary surrender of freedom is paradoxically a necessary part of his accessing true autonomy. The key to a successful, humane, and "advanced" recovery house is to find a balance between excessive discipline and the relative anarchy of the flophouse.

It is in light of these calculations that operators craft and put into place rule structures and systems of governmentality, calibrated in many respects by the degree to which one leans more toward despotism or liberalism. Malik's keen appreciation of this spectrum illustrates his skillful hand in the art of governance, and his invention of the advanced category was clearly meant to tip the balance toward liberalism—both as his best hope for his clients' recovery and as a canny, pragmatic move to make the concept of liberty a marketable commodity. Freedom of choice meant something else to his clients, however.

## Working a Program "on the Daily"

> Precepts governing everyday life are organized around the care of the self in order to help every member of the group with the common task of salvation.
> —MICHEL FOUCAULT, "TECHNOLOGIES OF THE SELF"

For a client, "working a program" means active participation in the different aspects of recovery: (1) performing daily chores with others to maintain the recovery house; (2) attending appointments in the formalized treatment sector as well as 12-step meetings (each of which operators consider a supplement or complement to recovery house living); and (3) adhering to a regimented daily schedule that encompasses all of these activities. Mandatory client enrollment in all three realms sets recovery houses apart from mere flophouses or boardinghouses.

*[margin note: Working a Program]*

Malik admitted his first white client, Jack, a self-proclaimed "old beatnik from South Street," under the condition that he work a program. Jack was only in his late fifties, but his failing health—which he attributed to many years of hard drinking and drugging—and use of a cane made him look much more like a man in his seventies. When Malik took him into the program, Milton and Frank protested. They believed Jack had come from a psychiatric ward, and assumed his health would preclude his going to meetings.

FRANK: Listen, this is the problem I have: he is not going to go to meetings, he's not going to make meetings.
MALIK: He'll make 'em.
FRANK: He'll make meetings?
MALIK: Damn right he'll make 'em, he got to make 'em. Listen, you can't stay here and don't make meetings. You know what I did for him, right, I cut the meetings down for him, but he has to make the mandatory meetings. I talked to his case manager too, and he is in therapy now also. You know you can't come into this house and not work a program, no sir, uh uh . . . This is a *program*, and if I'm going to get my ass out here and make meetings, you got to make yours too. And even with running this I haven't stopped doing what I've been doing . . . I can't afford to!

This was the only instance that I knew of where Milton and Frank attempted to have input on a client at AHAD, and in fact it only occurred in this situation since they happened to be there on the day that Jack came in to interview with his SSI payee. But Malik always insisted that each man work a program involving mandatory 12-step meetings and some form of counseling in order to remain in residence. He began to lay down the law quite heavily in AHAD's second month, when it became clear that some of the men (Albert, for example) were not only failing to attend counseling, but also shirking their responsibilities to the house.

In his initial periods of frustration as the house opened, Malik had watched his men closely to evaluate how disciplined they would be on their own before he would step up to adopt a more authoritarian strategy. The opening weeks of his program were "test days," to "see how far the client would go, see what kind of house the client is going to take this for." He knew his clients would act as if they were testing an invisible fence.

> MALIK: I don't want this to turn into an institution or nothing like that; what I expected was for guys to step up to the plate, like, "I ain't doing nothing today, do you need some help?" or something like that. Because that's how I was thinking this thing was going to work. Basically, this first month, right, has been like a learning lesson for me; I wanted to see how much I can do without changing this or without changing that, and see how far the client would go, see what kind of house the client is going to take this for.

Dissatisfied with his initial assessments, he called a meeting at which he invoked a vague set of rules to ensure resident compliance on the grounds of guaranteeing sobriety and freedom.

> I watch what you all are doing, I watch and I listen [and] I let little things go by. But now when it starts affecting me, I'm going to start saying some things, because look, it's getting cold out there, this house will fill up, with or without you this house will fill up. I'm not trying to make this thing like some of the other programs that we've been in, because we want some freedom.

Over time, he also began to threaten the men with expulsion if they failed to fall in line:

If you don't like what I am saying, you know where you can go, you know what you can do. The work of this house has got to be done. The freedom is there because the rules are here, and they are easy rules. But you have to follow them, because the only consequence in this house is, you got to go, ain't no taking your weekends or nothing like that, if you don't comply you got to go, that's it.

At Malik's advanced recovery house, freedom and its enjoyment was contingent on client adherence to a disciplinary structure that ensured the proper functioning of the house. The advanced formula operated on a zero-tolerance strategy in the absence of consequences such as revoking leaves, and Malik retained ultimate authority to eject any man who was "noncompliant."

The ability to pull the eviction trigger was important. Yet on the flip side of Malik's zero-tolerance strategy, he typically meted out freedoms, as opposed to revoking them, based on a client's level of participation in the house and his track record in working a program. So Malik most often pitched compliance by appealing to the addict's self-interest. At other times, he based the notion of compliance on the well-being of the collective as a whole, a premise directly in line with another 12-step tradition, that of placing the interests of the group above any one individual. Alternatively, Malik and other operators in Kensington sometimes justified rules on the simple grounds that there are always rules operating in any field of social relationship. In each case, Malik tied the concept of freedom directly to an individual's choices—as well as to his *conduct*—by linking personal development (under the broad rubric of recovery) to AHAD's rule structure.

## The Daily Schedule

But Malik needed to concretize the notion of compliance in ideal form. Having watched and determined how his clients acted on liberty—choosing to move toward recovery, or regress—he used his own expertise to tailor his program. His institution of the daily schedule was the most tangible framework for designating legitimate daily activities and husbanding malfeasance. Malik sketched out the daily schedule and the boundaries of fair programmatic play at his first weekly recovery house meeting:

MALIK: All right, now, breakfast is at seven o'clock, every morning. Meditation begins at seven thirty. After meditation, you got your chores to do, and at 9:25 the house shuts down. The only person left in this house after

9:25 is either the house watcher or a person that has to take care of some
business. I'm not talking about Mickey Mouse business, but serious business, you understand what I'm saying? Unless you have phone business
pertaining to your caseworker, health, SSI, job interview, job training,
or things like that that are important, at 9:30 this house should be empty
except for the sitter.

Once you leave the house at 9:25, the only time you can get back in
is at 11:45 a.m. after the AA meeting. No clients should be in the house
while the meeting is going on. At 11:45 you can come in and do what you
have to do. Now, at 1:00 p.m. there is another AA meeting, and for those
with no work or therapy, you will make that 1:00 p.m. meeting. That
meeting is from 1 to 2:30, at New Life, so that's when the house opens
back up, at about a quarter to three. This way we are constantly doing
something. There will be no lying around the house during the day, and
the TV will not come on before 3:00 p.m.

[That is the schedule], and during the day those hours will be what
we call "Always Have a Dream" hours, they are *program* hours. We have a
full house now, and we working a program now. We was, like, working a
program before too, but now with the start of this schedule, the program
is in full effect.

Institution of a *daily schedule*, in Malik's case by fiat, was tantamount to the
institution of a "program." The daily schedule organizes a way for addicts
to "live" in recovery house space, as well as in the neighborhood of Kensington, by setting out a coherent framework with clearly defined boundaries of legitimacy and transgression. It restricted clients' use of the house
itself, which operators typically designate to certain hours in order to push
them out into the corresponding mechanisms of support. It allowed for legitimate business, which, as opposed to "Mickey Mouse" business, pertains
to matters of self-improvement, many of which fall into the formal realm
of the welfare state ("caseworker, health, SSI, job training"). By incorporat-
ing a set of legitimized activities under the rubric of "taking care of business," Malik extended his program into the realm of the welfare office, the
doctor's office, and the probation and parole office. Rules and regulations
within the house and attendance at 12-step meetings and formal outpatient
counseling complete the loop, or programmatic circuitry.

MALIK: When you come in this house, these rules and regulations apply.
Everybody has mandatory [12-step] meetings to make, nonworkers are
seven, workers are four. Daytime meetings are not counted as your man-

datory meetings [because these are at night]; however, if you don't work, have IOP [intensive outpatient treatment], OP, school or other personal business, or recovery business, the morning or daytime meeting is for you also. This is some simple shit, and I'm just trying to help us run a program here. This is a recovery house, it is not a boardinghouse, it is not a transitional house. It goes under the name of *recovery house*.

For Malik, the full picture here designated the house on Genoa Street decisively and unequivocally as a space of recovery. Indeed, the institution of a schedule to regulate daily activities, both spatially and temporally, is one of the most basic elements of the recovery house, even for an advanced program like Malik's. Operators deploy the schedule on behalf of the recovering subject to help them avert the ills of addiction and to achieve such desirable states as health, autonomy, rationality, employment, and self-governance. The daily schedule presupposes certain freedoms and levels of autonomy, such as the expectation of honesty in self-reporting, as well as the willingness to contribute to the daily operations of the house. Yet there is also a direct surveillance of daily activity through regimented time schedules and paperwork (for example, sign-out logs and meeting attendance slips). These basic elements of regulation and surveillance through scheduling had been replicated in all of the houses that I studied. As another case in point, note the similarities here between Malik's and Bilal's house in reference to the functions of the daily schedule:

BILAL: On any given day, starting from Monday through Sunday, we start with an individual coming down for morning meditation, doing chores, breakfast, and then mapping out their general day. We have morning meditation, where we read from various positive literatures, like the Daily Reflection, which gives us an inspiration to get things started. We don't do a religious thing, because it's not about religion, but we talk about, you know, "My day is great today because God has blessed me to wake up," for instance, "My day is great because I have a plan of movement today." So we talk about these things, and then we plan our activities, we make meetings in the morning and in the evening because we used drugs in the morning and in the evening, so we have to substitute or replace that negative with something positive.

We also talk in morning meditation about things such as going to the dentist, going to IOP therapy treatment, going to school, or going to work. We would like to know at least three major places where they are going, so that they got a purpose in their destination, so that they aren't

just wandering around going from place to place aimlessly, and having no
destination in mind, which might get them into trouble. So we try to help
them map these things out to keep them on a sober walk, and knowing
that they got to come back here eventually to their safe haven where they
feel protected and that they've accomplished something. At the end of the
day, we talk about "What did you do today for your recovery?" In terms
of taking care of your dental work, or other medical needs, other mental
needs, school needs, et cetera. To get your day-to-day life in order, and
to utilize the resources that are available to you not only in the safe haven
of the recovery house but also through the sources that are provided to
you through the community, such as welfare, medical insurance, therapeutic treatment, and the recovery rooms of NA/AA and CA [Cocaine
Anonymous].

Bilal spoke to the regulatory and performative functions of the schedule,
designed to instill purposefulness so as to avoid the dangers of geographical listlessness. Addicts can perform the carefully administered daily activities across time and space in the service of recovery, toward rehabilitative
ends. The public proclamation of daily intentions allows one to "map these
things out to keep them on a sober walk," in addition to highlighting connections to the broader fabric of social services in Kensington.

An integral part of this extension is captured by the phrase "walking the
walk," which works at the level of the recovering subject's lived experience
to provide legitimacy to abstract principles. "Walking the walk" is meant to
set out a coherent, performative strategy for reclaiming the self.

MALIK: Listen, when you working a program you don't have to promote the
program, you don't have to wear nothing around your neck, you don't
have to have these key chains coming down your leg. I mean, I sound
good, I look good, I write it [the program], I read it, I talk it, I walk it,
but most of all I live it. You can have all the information in the world,
man, but it don't mean shit if you ain't living it.

Walking the walk, practicing recovery behaviors, or "busting new moves"
refers to eliminating old patterns associated with "dope fiend ways." The
recitation of its merits, and more important the illustration of its effects
through daily life, works to draw in the new intake in ways that are much
more effective and tangible than leaving things up to blind faith or the recovering subject's unsupported agency. Sometimes people literally walked

particular paths in order to walk the walk. Recovering subjects spoke often of avoiding certain "people, places, and things" associated with their drug-using days in order to take up residence within new spaces associated with recovery. It is common to hear men like Garvey refer to walking "in an L shape" on the main streets around Kensington to "avoid getting jammed up on them backstreets where I don't have any business being." Similarly, Malik would refer to "never stepping outside 'the pocket'" as a way to indicate the geography of his recovery, and he too would refer to the notion of an L formation by saying, "I don't walk down, like, Indiana, or Cambria, I don't deviate, man, I walk in a L shape everywhere I go, from here to treatment, treatment and back."

The act of working a recovery house program sets out a new mode for the organization of time and space in postindustrial neighborhoods like Kensington. From the perspective of the recovery house operator, regulation ideally takes hold within the realm of self governance, or technologies of the self, whereby clients monitor their own actions and place their bodies within the boundaries of programmatic space each day as they leave the house to conduct daily business. For those yet unable to govern themselves entirely, the operators provide external mechanisms of surveillance such as treatment attendance records; informal street-level tactics such as hearsay or sight of someone hanging around where they ought not to be; or requiring new clients to acquire signatures from chairpersons at 12-step meetings.

Malik and Infinite designed and put in place their basic programmatic framework to inculcate internal evaluation systems for standards of conduct. Inside the house, notions of brotherhood, support, participation, voluntarism, and self-help buttressed a structure of rules and regulations. Outside the house, clients worked a program and a daily schedule with more formalized systems of power, which operated in concert with the recovery house structure. The daily schedule offers a view into the many strategies of governmentality that operate within recovery house networks, and it is a crucial element for the understanding of "how it works." By instituting this framework within the physical space of a previously abandoned row house in a post-working-class neighborhood, Malik had joined ranks with hundreds of recovery house owners in reappropriating blighted space for the transformation of selves. In the process, they had effectively set out to differentiate their houses from a flophouse, a boardinghouse, or a rehabilitation facility. In the constitution of programmatic space, they had set the stage for a new mode of urban subjectivity, and a new mode of poverty management.

## The Constitution of the Recovering Subject

> There is times when I want to put the gas tank on back of me, with the flame-thrower thing, and go around to all the crackheads and just burn everyone getting high. Then there is other times when I just cry, man . . . because I just don't understand. You know, why you want to just stand there when help is right down the street? It's human waste . . . that's what all these motherfuckers who relapse have become, human waste. It's time to take a look at this shit, and start saying, you know what? I'm breaking the cycle, man.
>
> —MALIK

> Citizens are not born; they are made.
>
> —BARBARA CRUIKSHANK, *THE WILL TO EMPOWER* (1999)

The concept of devolution is prevalent in contemporary welfare state theory. As a heuristic, it suggests how the post-welfare state downloads authority to street-level actors such as those in recovery houses, even if only by default. But the academy's current obsession with devolution should not lead us to think that recovery house actors, as aspiring moral authorities, have taken their positions in the informal welfare state passively. Rather, it is in large part the agency of recovery house operators that *makes* recovery markets happen. Operators are one component of a growing recovery industry comprising interrelated—yet often deeply fragmented and competitive—sets of actors. For street-level addiction experts, establishing a place at the social service table requires not only that they advance an expanded vision of reform, but also that they assert authoritative claims to a distinctive *knowledge* of the recovering subject.

Remnants of the culture-of-poverty thesis serve as a discursive platform for their efforts. From the operator's starting point of actively designating the recovering subject as one who lacks the *right kind* of agency, or, perhaps put more bluntly, as "human waste," an object of intervention begins to take shape. Recovery discourse has long had great currency in the realm of transformation, particularly when its adherents are emboldened by street-level musings on labor market reentry and the more general "responsibility" themes of the contemporary present. Consider Malik's run on the links between low self-worth, welfare, and rehabilitation, which certainly articulate with the broader "incipient regulatory logics" of the post-welfare moment:[10]

> MALIK: In most cases people stay poor because the self-worth is gone, they feel like they can't be productive, in most cases don't want to be produc-

tive, and they used to being taken care of, right. If they told them they need to be missing a limb to get on welfare, these guys would be cutting their fucking toes off, man! All because the self-worth is gone.

Being in recovery, and taking the time to practice how to get employment, how to keep employment, how to make do with what you get [from welfare], this is what we here for! This is what a recovery house will allow you to do. Most long-term programs instill that self-worth back into you, and they create, or give you a skill, or try and put you into an employment position. This is what the word *rehabilitation* derived from, to be able to enter society once again, to become a taxpaying, productive member of society and to have a skill. I'm talking about [taking] responsibility for your life, that's what recovery has taught me.

The recovery house operator's remedial linkage of low self-worth and poor employment skills to the "best practices" (vaguely conceived) of the house is a typical strategy. Operators establish the recovery house as a milieu, not only for the practice of making do with meager welfare benefits, but also for self-actualization and labor market reentry. One way for the operator to assert authority in this realm is to foreground his knowledge of the recovering subject at the local level.

> BILAL: We focus on bringing this large population of addicts into the recovering arena, as taxpaying, productive members of society who vote, so we can start making changes from the inside, instead of trying to talk change from the outside. It's the old saying, everything begins at home. Our home is the addiction world, so we have to try to create some changes there by doing what we know best.

Knowledge of the impoverished addict is paramount for the recovery house operator.[11] Bilal levied this in his contention "Our home is the addiction world," a turf claim that enables him to pitch the recovery house as an ideal space, both to expend welfare dollars prudently and to politicize poor subjects. At stake here is something beyond appropriating the welfare apparatus, and beyond the utilitarian concerns of economic subsistence. We enter here into the capacity to *constitute* the addict, first as pathological subject, then as modern citizen.

This task is no small feat. It requires a complex set of activities and processes that unfold under the tutelage of recovery actors, knowledges, and discourses. At issue in the initial stage is the operator's installment of the subject as (1) a member of a collective organized for poverty survival and

risk management; (2) the proper object of recovery house discipline; and
(3) the locus of change, or the terrain on and through which self-governance
technologies may be exercised. Of great significance to each of these objectives, operators and residents must preoccupy themselves with a subject
who fails to act in his own self-interest.[12] Central to this preoccupation is
the designation and careful articulation of the "diseased will," or the "self-
will" of the active addict, which they define in contrast to the "healthy free
will" of the recovering subject.[13]

Operators fully understand that addicts come into recovery houses with
ulterior motives, and they even expect that the newcomer approaches the
house still in the hustling mindset.

> BILAL: How many people do we have coming in here faking the funk,
> and faking recovery until they accomplish what their real hidden agenda
> was, and then they go do what they going to do? For some the hidden
> agenda was to go get that check turned on, for some it's to come in and
> get three hots and a cot. Others want to satisfy the courts and get people
> off their back. You see, the [12-step] literature tells us we've been beat up,
> arrested, locked up, hospitalized, but none of these things have caused
> us to change until we *desire* to change. But even in that situation where
> people have other motives, we have to extend the trust, and the belief and
> the encouragement. We have to offer them something, saying, "You can
> do better," by exemplifying how we live. That's the attraction to bring
> them in.

Bilal spoke to an important maxim of recovery house knowledge. It is only
when one desires change that recovering technologies of the self become
capable of producing effects. This premise engenders an appreciation for,
and presupposition of, the addict's stubborn self-will in active addiction.
Recovery house operators have come to respect this as the raw material for
the making of the flexible subject. Consider the recovery aphorism that I
encountered long ago on the door of a drunk tank in Burlington, Vermont:
"If you keep doing what you did, you'll keep getting what you got." The
general idea behind this mantra informs the expertise of the recovery house
operator, who must first create an atmosphere of trust and encouragement
conducive to self-reflection on past "doings" and choices. Only then can the
operator hold the door open to a better way (how "we live" in recovery).
The task here is to redirect an ostensibly a-priori form of agency ("if you
keep doing what you *did*"), which has exhausted its utility relative to the
subject's best interests ("you'll keep getting what you got"). For the opera-

tor, however, the will has not exhausted its utility so much as it has become ripe for conversion.

And yet, we would do well to problematize the extent to which any sort of prediscursive will is present here. Each form of the will—the diseased form and the empowered form—should be considered *achievements*, both instruments and effects of recovering technologies. The operator must actively construct the diseased will as one that ultimately evacuates the capacity for self-governance and manageability; and yet recognize and even covet this at the same time for its deliverance of access to a form of agency *sui generis*, in the compulsive state. The surrender of one form of the will is necessary to achieve a new type of autonomy and freedom, and the operator's interpellative art form to achieve this surrender should not be understated. It requires constructing the will on either side of the addiction spectrum (from active to recovering) as a *medium*. This construction entails first creating belief, in this case that the addicted will operates against "true" self interest; and second, inculcating desire for a new mode of living. Making matters more complex, the operator must frame and refract the practical possibilities for action through the prism of personal choice.

## The Manufacture of Consent, and Resolve

For the recovery house operator, manufacturing consent is a crucial part of building a "solid" census. At one end of the spectrum, the operator passively anticipates consent. As Benito explained, consenting to the disciplinary structure should be a matter of "blind faith," secured perhaps most effectively by the past suffering that the subject endured. The gifts of this consent would become clear enough to the subject in time, and it was with these rewards in mind that Benito worked directly with the men in his house.

> BENITO: It's like you just believe in something because it works. You just don't question it, you go on blind faith, man, and you buy into the process. I try to explain it to my clients like this; it's like looking at a picture. See, when I first bought into this process I could only see this [*hides most of a framed picture on the wall using a piece of paper*], and then it's like, wow [*removing the paper from the picture*], it's a mountain, man! So you just, like, keep buying into this process every day. It's like trying to give people hope and confidence where they have none.

Buying into the process, or investing in it, entails subjection to a field of knowledge/power that promises transformative effects. This plays out in daily life: from doing chores, to following routine, to opening oneself up to the help and support of fellow housemates as well as recovery house staff. The payback, or gift for doing so, was quite significant in Malik's eyes. It allows a person to reclaim his soul from the wrath of unmanageability. The objective is liberation from the "chains of addiction," connecting an addict to his "innate" capacities for autonomy, responsibility, self-worth, and freedom. It is here that recovering addicts begin to speak of the "gifts of recovery." While somewhat elusive in most discussions, these "gifts" became tangible when people in the Kensington recovery house movement spoke about no longer losing their money, no longer neglecting loved ones, or no longer forgetting where they were the night before. Many spoke about being able to hold a job, open a bank account, or keep a roof over their head for the first time in years. Others spoke about liberating themselves from having to steal, rob, or "turn tricks" under the El to get high.

Operators and 12-step members alike say that the gifts of recovery manifest not only in the material world but also in ethical and moral realms. Recovering addicts attune themselves once more to their own value system, as well as to the adoption and cultivation of "positive values" for becoming productive, trustworthy, and participatory citizens. As Malik would often say, addicts ideally become capable of "reaching their dreams" if they are willing to engage in the recovery program to its fullest extent.

Recovery is much more than simply abstinence from drugs and alcohol; it is an opportunity for self-actualization. Of great significance, this opportunity entails access to a heroic self-will, and a stoic refusal to backslide even in the face of persistent material hardship.

> MALIK: You see, being clean from drugs and alcohol just ain't enough. Now that I'm clean, I ain't sleeping with nobody's broad no more, I ain't using nobody, I ain't doing none of that shit. And now I know that I need a job, I need to use my network of people, I need to use my therapist, and try to find me some work, right, or train myself with something that I can do or that I'm willing to do. You have to build something up here [*points to his head*], you see what I'm saying, that's what I did, and I did it while I lived in the recovery house system instead of waiting 'til I got out. I learned that when I was in prison. Guys in there that don't learn anything get out and wash dishes. Fuck that shit, man; I'd rather pick up a gun [to make my money]. People who fail in this thing just don't want it; they haven't learned discipline and patience.
>
> RF: But what if you get stuck in a neighborhood where there are no opportunities?

MALIK: You have to *make* your opportunities . . .

RF: After a while, if you have enough good things going on in your life, getting high looks good, but it's not worth giving up what you got. But if I'm still living homeless with no job, it is a little more difficult, and getting high looks really good . . .

MALIK: Getting high *always* looks good, all the time. I ain't trying to get clean here in Philadelphia and go back to Newark, New Jersey, or Virginia and get [high]. I'm getting clean and preparing for something, and I'm going to carry that forward with me, that's what I am going to do. I can't get clean and go back to Newark and stand there and if there ain't no jobs say something like, "Oh man, I'm clean, but they won't hire me, Rob, I'm going to go get high, fuck it!" Uh uh, no sir!

As the teachings of recovery have it, this type of resolve is necessary to overtake the all-consuming relationship that plagues any alcoholic or addict, regardless of one's race or class. The Big Book of Alcoholics Anonymous describes this resolve as a state of being "willing to go to any lengths" to get and stay sober.

The fuel for motivation lies in the *effects* of one's prior choices. Malik articulated this quite forcefully one afternoon in the AHAD living room while discussing with housemates the hepatitis C he had contracted from using dirty needles:

MALIK: We [all] suffer from the same shit, you know what I suffer from? I suffer from *myself*, what I have done to myself. I have got to accept that everything that is wrong with Malik, Malik did. The disease that I suffer from is a disease that I voluntarily went out there and got. I know this today. My life today doesn't allow me to get caught up in some pity shit about my disease, and I don't want no one else dwelling on it for me. The energy that is being used here for us people, us sick people, should be used for one thing and one thing only—for our recovery, for carrying the message of recovery. It's about how to get better, how to be self-productive in this society that we live in, and how to be put in a position where someone can tap me on the shoulder and say, "I need you today" . . . that's what it's all about.

Malik posited the self, or perhaps more specifically agency, simultaneously as the locus of failure and yet the *only* solution to change. Indeed, he celebrated individual will even in its "unhealthy" state: he refused to be a victim, and he described hepatitis C as something that he "*voluntarily went out there and got.*" Operators designate these types of claims as channels to a form of wellspring, located in a previously misguided will that unequivocally delivered what the addict now sees, with the aid of recovering technologies, as calamitous outcomes.

In theory, this type of access alone—particularly in the light of the addict's past suffering—works as a "natural" incentive for conformity. But one can scarcely expect that speeches promising the gifts of recovery or heroic self-will are enough to draw the recalcitrant subject into working a recovery house program. Consider Garvey, who, like many of Malik's men, was highly suspicious of recovery houses. First and foremost, he saw them as a form of "ghetto business" operating in absence of government oversight. Still, even he conceded that as a client, he could exploit the business toward his own ends:

> GARVEY: I guess recovery houses might give some leaders a chance to come up and get out of the ghetto, and to gain back what they lost. But recovery houses in general? I look at it like, um, it's another form of business. It does help, but it's like a business in a catch-22. It's like putting money into people's pockets, you are getting taken advantage of in the long run, but it's not like getting raped or getting a disease or anything. You can get something from it if you know what to look for.
>
> RF: In other words, you can get over on the business yourself, even though they are making money on you?
>
> GARVEY: Exactly. It's like going in the army and they tell you get up every morning and run 20 miles and do 100 push-ups. Yeah, they are using you and telling you what to do, but you are getting big and getting healthy. So you might hurt at the time, but then you look around and say, damn, I lost a lot of weight, I know how to wash dishes now, I stopped smoking. In recovery you start learning some sort of discipline if you allow yourself to. Because it's like you got the choice, we have a choice in everything we do, you got a choice to jump off a bridge, and you got a choice to deal with your problems.

While acknowledging that the more coercive elements of the house can produce positive effects, Garvey also held tight to the concept of choice. He perceived his sense of agency at all times, even when in an exploitive situation.

The recovery house system presupposes personal choice, and operates through its notional qualities. The capacity to constitute subjects hinges on the volition of those subjects who make the crucial first step of committing to "deal(ing) with their problems." It is then, at least in ideal terms, that they become governable and amenable to recovery house regulation vis-à-vis technologies of power and technologies of the self. The telling of "war stories," a separate, free-floating practice pertinent to the constitution of the recovering subject and a central mechanism of consent, will be explored in the following section.

## War Stories and the Demarcation of "Old Behaviors"

If the "clean and sober" lifestyles of the men living at AHAD often led me to forget the suffering of their past, I was reminded of that suffering on the many occasions that they would sit around the AHAD living room telling "war stories" from "back in the day." Often, these stories considered self-betrayal, as in the addict's uncontrollable and incessant practice of needle sharing against one's will or use of river or hydrant water in syringes despite threats of bacteria. The stories carried a sense of desperation, a loss of control, and a complete sense of powerlessness in relation to one's drug of choice. The men spoke of crack as a new animal on the scene that had changed everything in the ghetto, making an already desperate ecology even more intense. They recounted stories of fully functioning persons who had become street-level prostitutes, sometimes in a matter of weeks and for no more than three dollars per sex act, due to crack's all-consuming power. Malik and Garvey spoke of its destructive force, highlighting the insanity of "the chase":

> MALIK: Check this out, wrap some crack around some fucking rat poison, and a crackhead will smoke it. They be thinking once it burns, you ain't going to get the rat poison. You could put rat shit on a rock and they'd smoke it, I've even seen a motherfucker smoke fuzz balls off the floor!
> GARVEY: Ain't nothing make you chase like crack do. You can't drink up a thousand dollars' worth of liquor, can't shoot up a thousand dollars' worth of dope, but you can smoke a thousand dollars' worth of crack in a twenty-four-hour period. Or *less*, six or seven hours even . . .

Under the aegis of recovery house knowledge, the power of addiction—particularly addiction to crack—had come to garner the respect of these men. Recounting its power served to establish this respect in the initial stages, and then to reinforce it in subsequent iterations. The AHAD residents performed this by invoking crack's all-consuming power, as in the case of Rufus's life-and-death account.

RUFUS: I used to smoke so much my heart, it hurt, it actually hurt me. And I
continued, as soon as I feel a little relief, I hit it and it start hurting again.
It hurt so much. I must have had about four or five heart attacks. When
I went to get a physical, they can tell if you have had a heart attack, and
when you going to get another heart attack. I was in the hospital a long
time for it once, but when I got out I went right back and did it again.
The only good thing about that crack, it killed my fucking heart murmur
[*laughs*]. I had it all my life, and after a couple years of smoking crack, no
more heart murmur!

In the more intimate moments at AHAD, a sense of brotherhood and
comfort facilitated the telling of war stories. My primary intention here is
to pick up on the ways in which recovering subjects cultivate and reframe
their past experiences. I want to elucidate how the prerequisites of desperation and suffering, or inner workings of amenability, are constructed by
way of this particular technology of the self. Infinite's rendition of his past
curried his potential, or readiness for change, quite well, as he moved from
self-proclaimed street roughneck to manager of AHAD:

INFINITE: I ran a whorehouse and a crack house out of an abandominium
[slang for an abandoned row house], and I was greedy, I got people to
answer the door for me and I would go down in the basement and have it
nailed shut. I had cots, and dividers, I had it hooked up and I was making
*much* money in there, ten Gs a day easy. I had in the kitchen where the
sink is, a little hole cut out with a little bucket, you put the money in and
lower it down then pull it back up. I had all my shit down in the basement, video games and shit, I was cool. But the young boys up the street
got mad. The motherfuckers set me up, they wanted like, ten bundles
or something, and I kept all my stash [in another house], so I shut down
shop to go over there and get it. When I came back, the motherfuckers
was behind the steps waiting for me, and they tied me up in the basement. That's why I got all these scars and shit on me [*showing us marks on
his arms*], they beat me with boards and nails, trying to get my stash, but I
wouldn't give them nothing.
   The house was filled with people, every room, and they took and
firebombed that motherfucker, man, two people died in that bitch. The
only way I survived was somebody called my mother. I jumped out of the
basement window, and I didn't know where I was, but I heard my mom's
voice and I just started scrappin' [fighting]. I put my thing *down*. Then I

heard cars pull up, I thought it was the police, it was my little brother and his crew. They was getting ready to light them niggers up, but my mom is a minister, and she started praying and going crazy, she stood in the middle [of the two crews] so they couldn't shoot. She sent me to Michigan after that, where I had to stay on the down-low for a couple of years.

Infinite's story established street credibility by showing the harsh realities of his past. In the recovery house, however, he told it to mark the chaos and suffering of his former life, as well as the ways in which it compelled him to change.

On one particular rainy day, the men shared stories about their experiences with utility shutoffs in their days of active addiction. The harsh irony on this particular day was that AHAD's recent utilities crises, which had left the men without heat for forty-eight hours, inspired the stories.

MALIK: I remember 'way, 'way back coming into a hallway in an apartment building, and a motherfucker got these cords running all over the hall, and they were stealing [electricity]. But when I moved into the projects, the bulbs go in this way, in a normal house, but the projects put the bitches in counterclock, so you couldn't screw that shit in there to hook it up. The motherfuckers figured it out, though, and threw some shit up there with the wires [laughing]. They had two wires on a spoon, right, and stuck the fucking spoon up in there.

RUFUS: I was in a drug house one time that had no lights in it, and a guy went upstairs with jumper cables, man, saying he could [hook up the electricity] for a hit of crack. So he went up there, and we heard it go SMACK! Aeiii! [hysterical laughter] That bitch was on the floor, [whimpering] "Help me . . ." He was fucked-up, smoke coming out of his jacket, his body was twitching . . . I couldn't smoke after that [I was laughing so hard], he was, like, "Give me a rock, I'll turn that shit back on . . ." SMACK, Aeiiii! [laughing again] When you get high, you do some insane shit.

INFINITE: I seen some shit, man, I remember this one girl, she had electric but she didn't have no heat, and no kerosene either. It was sad, she was laying up there with her kids all piled up under the covers, like a little tent with a blow-dryer under there. She was sitting there with a coat on, smoking that crack, that shit was sad, man . . . [pausing for effect, then transitioning to humor] But it had to be hot up in there, because the kids were like, "Mom, it's hot under here! It's hot! Can you turn it down?" [laughter erupts]

In a peculiar way, telling war stories provides a means for bonding in recovery houses, and it has become something of an oral tradition that establishes one's place in the continuum of poverty and addiction. The humor in these stories, while suggesting a light-heartedness borne out of a distance one feels when differently positioned to tragedy, just as readily suggests the ongoing importance of pleasure and laughter in these men's lives.[14] In another sense, the men expressed a level of pride in the stories, as they typically made references to the inherent ingenuity of addicts who could always devise "a way" to persevere no matter the circumstances. Beyond the ingenuity in various schemes to pirate electricity, many of the men spoke of a street-level intelligence that produced short-term dividends. For example, stories about learning how to become "hootch" masters while in jail (by perfecting the time-honored tradition of making alcohol from bags of fermented raisins, orange peels, bread, and pilfered sugar packets) were a testament to ingenuity, as were stories about crafting devices out of anything from lotion bottles to asthma inhalers to get high.

> MALIK: These motherfuckers got brains, man! I mean, who could take a
> fucking aspirin bottle and stick a hole in it and smoke out of it? They
> chemisteresses [mispronunciation of *chemists*], they take some fucking
> powder and turn it into a rock, putting it in ammonia and all this
> shit . . . they engineers, man!

Again, these stories celebrate the power of these men's agency, even under the darkest of circumstances and to the most misguided ends. Malik would point to their uncanny brilliance almost as if to speak of the raw materials that he had to work with in transforming their lives once they came in from out of the storm. Similarly, he conceptualized the self-destruction of addiction as a form of recovery capital. This odd form of capital imbued its subjects with a sense of desperation that made them willing, teachable, and even blessed with the capacity to access a transcendent level of consciousness. So the recounting of war stories had several purposes beyond therapy, celebration, or bonding. On one level, it served as a way for the operator to constitute a powerless subject whose life had been unmanageable in the active state of addiction (save, of course, those activities necessary to stay high). On another, it served to remind the men of their capacities and strengths, indeed even their yearnings for autonomy and freedom. Malik would often try to mine the incessant war stories for these aspirations. He often intervened in daily conversations and activities in his house to teach and admonish his men.

MALIK: I mean, when you telling stories, I know you was getting high, right, but I want to know did you have any kind of life, or did you ever want to have a life. Was there something in you that wanted more, you know what I'm saying? You know we talking about some young men that really haven't lived a fucking life, man, a meaningful life anyhow, and I say that's human waste.

One great selling point for self-help recovery is its appeal to a "healthy free will" that resides in the person, *in potentio*.[15] The unfolding of recovery depends on the operator's forging an alliance with the aspirations of a self whose agency is already presupposed, if not privileged. Prior levels of suffering and pain, also known as "the wreckage of the past," can thus become substantive fuel to create the desire to change.

Yet at the same time that recovery house operators and recovering addicts recognize and celebrate past forms of the will, they also need to clearly mark these off as regressive and self-defeating.

MALIK: You know, like, I hear you guys all talk, right, and you know what, there was a time in my life that the only thing that came out of my mouth was jail. I mean, any prison I could tell you about, but you motherfuckers, look at your life, man, everything comes out your mouth is shelters, jails, and recovery houses. You know you got to break that cycle, man. We get in some bad habits in the ghetto, man, but we talking about making good habits now.

Malik included recovery houses in the cycle of inertia, because he believed that the recovery house experience is ideally a transitory process. It can, however, enable regression and another form of dependency for the addict just as easily as it can lead to true recovery. The key to avoid regression is to use the temporary space of the recovery house actively, to address old behaviors, patterns, and habits, en route to becoming "something that's greater than what we was."

Under the auspices of recovery knowledge, operators and housemates aggressively target the "old behaviors" recited in war stories as loci of change. They broadly conceive of these as offending personal choices and traits that stand egregiously and stubbornly in the way of progress. Framing one's plight under the rubric of individual choice and behaviors produces a relatively (and seemingly) manageable course of action, one that certainly becomes more tangible than, say, a focus on notions of class and racial apartheid under American capitalism. Malik, for example, often claimed that recovery was simply about making wise decisions, changing old behaviors, and doing the necessary maintenance to stay clean. He quickly dismissed his relapsing peers for "not wanting it badly enough." Recovery for Malik was a curious blend of street pride infused with personal responsibility bravado. This combination generated a lens through which he made sense of the impoverished landscape around him. In many respects, the strategy produced brilliant effects. It allowed him to extract light from darkness, hope from hopelessness, and vitality from stolid mediocrity.

Sometimes those in recovery tell war stories to pathologize even trivial behaviors from their past. Malik, for example, confidently posed self-responsibility as a solution to issues ranging from family crisis to unemployment and social inequality, and he always defined his fierce individualism in stark opposition to old behaviors and the old "dope fiend ways."

> MALIK: I try to do everything I say I'm going to do, you know; we have a million fucking ideas of what you going to do before payday, like, "I'm getting that cell phone, I'm getting you one, and I'm getting me one." Friday comes and it's like, "Yo, check this out, I thought about that shit; we don't need two cell phones, in fact we don't need one . . . let's go get high." [*laughs*] Those are the things I try not to do in here, I try to do everything I say I'm going to do. I do it with myself first and I do it with my woman next, and I do it with the men in the house. If I tell her we going to the movies, I try not to take it back like I used to, you know, "Why we going to the movies, we got tapes at home?"
>
> The [job] application I have submitted is one that I can stand on. I used to say in the application, "Yeah, I can drive the high-low," and didn't know how to drive the high-low. I couldn't stand on the application, but this one I can. I'm not going to say nothing I ain't going to do. I talk this program, and the reason is I live it.

Public repudiations also include more important activities, such as hustling.

> INFINITE: I can't hustle in recovery, I just can't do it, and I can't be seen doing it. It's just not my story. I know that I need to stay in the process a lot longer in order to change, and I'm not talking about just the alcohol, I'm talking about attitudes, man, and old behaviors. I have a goal, I have a plan, and I am not deviating from the plan. I don't need a crutch in my life, and I don't need nobody to hold on to. I need to let everything

run its course until my plan works. There is no ifs, ands, or buts about whether or not this plan is going to work. I know it is.

Infinite's statement leads us to a final purpose of the war story: as a vehicle to mark progress and growth. Malik would say that the men at AHAD needed to move on from incessant retellings, on to bigger and better things associated with recovery rather than the lifestyle of addiction. He differentiated between telling war stories simply as a way to show off, a strategy that reflected the opposite of change, and telling them to mark genuine transformation in the recovery process.

> MALIK: You see, some guys when [they telling stories], I look at them and the only thing I say is, "You ain't showing me nothing different from the way you was living." But on the other hand, when I look at a guy, say, like Rufus, he got a car, going to work, you know, he changing. And what he's showing me now is, he breaking that cycle. I'm willing to help everybody, but [his progress] makes me feel like this guy is struggling for this new way of life, for something *different*, rather than saying, "Well, you know, I'll fuck around with the recovery process, and if anything happen I'll go back to the shelter." You see what I'm saying?

In a similar manner, Malik often told his partner Blanche's story to illustrate the power of change:

> MALIK: Like I told the [Avenue AA] group, when my woman had about ninety days clean, and I had seen the transformation from a skeleton, a vampire, into a woman. I was sharing to the group, the miraculous change, you know, I was telling the story of me and her really, how something that nobody ever wanted, something discarded as trash, can turn into beauty and be treasured like this. You know what people called trash is now my gold. I seen the transformation. I [knew] this girl [when she] used to carry cans and all that shit, you see what I'm saying? To know her story, being homeless for seven years, and seeing how much [she's changed], that shows you how much this process should be appreciated.

In many respects, war stories illustrate how pain and suffering become the touchstone of spiritual growth in the recovery house movement. Growth begins with the personal narrative of the subject, who is encouraged to self-identify by a host of actors (house staff, fellow residents, counselors, even judges) as unequivocally and essentially alcoholic or drug addicted. The active constitution of suffering helps the subject come to believe, once again, that his life has become unmanageable and that he is afflicted with the disease of addiction. The purpose of disease attribution is to produce requisite levels of willingness, or, said differently, to establish the subject as the "proper object" of recovery house discipline.

Finally, consider Infinite's poignant story about rules.

> INFINITE: Something I learned a long time ago is that there are rules. When I was born there was rules. Those nine months I had to stay in my mother I had to come out, there was rules, can't stay up in there, I had to come out. There is rules for everything, there was an authority figure over the top of me at all times. When I got drunk I had to rumble, I had to do something, I had to get in some shit—that was the number one rule. I knew that, but I continued to drink. I continued to do what I wanted to do. I knew that when I didn't have that drink in me, oh my God I was going to go through it, that was another rule. So I had to go out there and do whatever I had to do. There was a rule that I was eventually going to get caught and have to pay the consequences.
>
> The first thing that came out my mouth when you ask me, "Infinite, how you living?" I'd say, "Day by day." Some old Rambo shit, I lived for the day. I take whatever comes that day—if I make it past that day I'm cool, I done won. No matter what the suffering, if I got busted with a cap and I ended up in the hospital, if I lived it was a good day. There was rules and consequences behind the rules, and I knew it before I stepped out there, so who is there to blame?

Even in addiction, people live by rules, and these rules produce certain effects in their own right. Infinite understood that he was subservient to a code, and he knew the consequences of a life of active addiction. One way to think about this is represented by the question, In a field of choices with rules, who is there to blame? (It is perhaps in this sense that Jamie Peck speaks of freedom as the new insecurity, or "neoliberal snakeoil.")[16] But we might also think of free subjects as *entitled* to struggle within a field of rules (while pre-scripted, these rules are conveyed as analogous to natural laws), much as they might be entitled to a motivating force like hunger.[17] Part of the transformative process in recovery entails a certain "coming to believe" that this code of active addiction actually renders one powerless, beset by a lifestyle that is totally unmanageable. It follows that subscription to a new set of rules or disciplinary structure for living entails a new set of consequences—in this case unprecedented levels of personal autonomy and freedom. It is important to recognize that the addict's acknowledgment of disease also sets the ground for freedom, in the sense that the "morally superior state of sobriety can only be achieved by those who struggle against their own determinations."[18] This form of agonism is the linchpin of freedom, and the substance with which free subjects are made by way of individual struggle.

## Learning from the Intake Ritual

Neither lofty speeches nor bodies alone have the capacity to transmute existential questions about suffering, sobriety, virtue, and productivity into technical questions about the most effective ways of transforming/regulating poor subjects. It is here that tactics such as the intake ritual become important. Each time Malik took in new recruits, he required them to speak for five minutes on what they could bring to the house, as well as on what the house could do for them. He hoped that the public articulation of hopes and dreams would link the self-interests of the new client to the transformative capacity of the program. When Brilliante came into the house, for example, Infinite led him through the intake ritual at the weekly house meeting:

> INFINITE: OK, in five minutes or less, you know the drill, what can you offer to this house, and what can we offer you to help you reach your dream?
>
> BRILLIANTE: What you can offer me is my sobriety, and your open arms, which you're offering right now. I am just trying to follow everything to the letter, trying to do something different, trying to do what you all are doing, because it seems to be working. I know I can't do it exactly the way that you all are doing it, but if I can get it I need to grab on and hold on. I look at you guys and see your dreams coming true, so I can't sit up here and say [all this is bullshit]. I'm just trying to get back into some double digits with clean time [in days]. It's great to be a part of this, and I hope that I can be an asset to this house. I mean, there are people that still love me, and care about me. I am the one that took myself back out there [using], and that tells me right there what I need to work on.

Brilliante was a special case at AHAD. He had previously lived with Infinite, Malik, Albert, and Delmar at Bilal's 42 House, where he had accumulated some clean time before relapsing yet again. Malik and Infinite had seen him disappear for weeks on end at the 42 House, only to return in desperation and destitution. Brilliante had become notorious for his signature crack "missions" subsidized by his infamous hustle, pumping gas and "squeegee-ing" for tips with other "crackheads" at the BP station on Lehigh Avenue. (As Brilliante told it, he and other "crack gas-pumpers" had an elaborate cuing system that required waiting one's turn and then "calling" the next incoming vehicle: "I got the blue truck!") Malik joked that he was going to build a miniature BP station for Brilliante so that he would stay away from the actual setting. His relapse pattern cast him as a risky client for the AHAD house, prompting Malik to put down restrictions at the outset. In his initial few weeks on Genoa Street, Malik did not permit Brilliante to leave the house without an "escort."

But the varied responses to Brilliante's intake "share" from Albert, Malik, and Infinite suggested that the program, and the men in it, could accommodate his inherent hopes, desires, and dreams for recovery—provided, of course, that he was willing to work.

> ALBERT: Brilliante, welcome to AHAD, you come at a good time, you come in at ground zero on something that I believe will be pretty nice. I don't agree with what you say, you can't do it like we did—you can do it *exactly* like we did. Not like how we *did*, how we *doing*, it's still an ongoing thing how we doing this thing, just like getting another day [clean]. I am witness to these guys working in my life. I don't know what I'd do without them, I get in some moods some days and they get on my ass and straighten me out. So I'm grateful to be here, and I welcome you.

> MALIK: You coming into a special program with special people, on the ground floor. You have a chance to grow just like us and with us, but you gotta tolerate some stuff, like, you can't run by yourself, man, you even said that. You going to have to walk with someone even to the Avenue for a while . . . but I know you can make it, because anyone can if they want to. This is your shot, right here, right now, this is your shot, and we're giving it to you. You come in to reach a dream, we reaching for our shit, we go through some stuff in here but as a whole we got a family going on. I know there are things you can do, and you have a lot of things to offer this program.

> INFINITE: I remember when I came over to the 42 House, when I first met Malik as my sponsor, I seen you sitting there . . . I seen all of this, I'm saying I want this, I want to do this, I want to look like that, I want to be a part of that crew, I want this thing. That was the attraction, that was what I seen. I got attached to you, man, and it hurt when you went out, but

you did it to yourself. I want you to share in this thing again, man, I can't force you, but if I have to give you restraint until you can attain what you want to attain, that's what I'll do. We see something in you that you don't see in yourself, like, it says we going to love you until you can love yourself, we showing you that love. I know that once you get a little ground under you, and you see what God has blessed you with, and see what this program can offer you, and what you can offer this program, that will give you motivation to stay. I'm still in this process too, I'm still learning, and we need to learn this thing together, we share information in here. So I welcome you, man, with open arms.

All three men expressed the more substantive elements of the program. These are the fruits, if you will, of programmatic space, which have not yet been given their proper due in this space. By making reference to notions of family, love, information sharing, and togetherness, the sentiments of the men in many ways evince the essence of self-help recovery, which operates on a model of collective solidarity and support. In the great complexity of the recovery house matrix, these ideals represent the true gold that the program has to offer.

But the efficacy of the program resided within the realm of Brilliante's willingness, his volition, his yearnings, desires, and dreams. If he would be able to privilege these notions, even if only by initially restraining his more destructive drives, he would thrive and help others to do the same, or so goes the promise and the hope. Albert declared, "you can do it *exactly* like we did . . . how we *still* doing this thing," while Malik averred, "This is your shot, right here, right now, this is your shot, and we're giving it to you," and Infinite assured him, "We see something in you that you don't see in yourself." All three extolled the merits of the program in terms of the *opportunity* it had to offer Brilliante—the chance to reclaim his power from addiction, to transform his life, and to reach his dreams. In turn, Brilliante expressed his desire to "keep it to the letter," to adhere to the programmatic structure of the house while aligning what he has to offer to its basic tenets.

From a Foucauldian perspective, the confessional intake ritual rendered Brilliante as calculable, in that his proclamation of goals made him amenable not only to having things done to him (restraints, escorts) in the name of program, but also amenable to doing things to himself in the name of his subjective capacities. The ritual installed him as the proper object, and subject, of recovery house discipline. This critical juncture is where Nikolas Rose locates the mechanisms of "governing the soul," where the human psyche becomes a possible domain for systematic government in the pursuit of sociopolitical (and socioeconomic) ends, namely to reform, educate, punish, and recover.[19] Rose contends that a new set of vocabularies, "provided by the sciences of the psyche," enable an articulation of the aspirations of government in terms of the "knowledgeable management of the depths of the soul."[20]

Insofar as success in the AHAD program depended on Malik's carefully calculated supervision and Brilliante's maximization of his own freedoms, recovery discourse designates the will as a locus of change and a terrain of governance. Governance operates at the level of the soul as well as at the level of the community of Kensington, as both vectors are replete with destructive threats as well as potentially liberating spaces. Knowing the subject, or knowing the census, allowed Malik to prescribe programmatic constraints appropriately, and he was able to exercise authority at a distance—not only by extending the program into the stretches of Kensington by controlling geographical trajectories ("You can't run by yourself, man"), but also by extending the program into the realm of values and ethics.

Malik's census-building principles, organized around his notion of program integrity and actualized to some extent in the intake ritual, were certainly not empty concepts. They were, however, rather utopian ideals that were in some ways decontextualized even within the intake ritual, which often defaulted into a recitation (and repetition) of abstractions for client, housemates, and operators alike. Malik's obsessions with "protecting" the integrity of his program suggest the presence of forces that constantly threatened his hermetic ideals. These forces pose great challenges to the workings of any discursive system of governmentality operating in the informal welfare state. And yet it is important to highlight Malik's programmatic intentions, for they suggest the extent to which the recovery house functions and culls its authority precisely by way of the operator's appeals to universal narratives of personal progress. Consideration of Malik's intentions also lets on to the interrelationship between the technologies of the program and the population on which it acts.

## Informal Case Management

The recovery projects of men like Infinite often include a full-scale remodeling of their lives. For example, it was not uncommon to see men plan to resolve debt, delinquent child support, past legal issues, and fines, or to work on marital problems, personal behaviors, or character defects. Recovery house operators like Malik act as informal case managers, working with their men to implement a broad range of plans, goals, and objectives related to personal responsibility. For the addict, this includes basic work on the life skills necessary to claim future independence, as well as work in the areas that the men at AHAD often referred to as "the wreckage of the past."

Malik worked individually with Delmar to help him open a bank account, for example. Malik controlled and monitored the account so that Delmar could achieve his goal of moving home to live with his brothers.

> MALIK: I just put together a plan for Steady [Delmar], that he could put aside $400 a month in a bank account. In two months that's $800, in three months that's $1,200; when he gets to $2,200 he's going out of here. I am trying to work with him so he goes back with his brothers. He can't control himself with his own bank account; I mean, the boy ran through $1,300 during his last relapse on crack in just one day. So he has agreed so far to allow me to take $100 a week and bank it for him. In the course of putting that money together, he needs to take one day off a week to see his family.

Malik explained that Delmar's history with money (and his marginal intelligence) warranted a contract to keep him "on track" with his goals.

The addict's failure to make the transition to something better renders the recovery house as yet another space to languish in the "project syndrome."

> MALIK: My thing is, I got to move him along and move him out of here, or he'll be stuck. We got a lot of examples of people getting stuck in recovery houses. You know, you fuck around in here, and sooner or later you be running around with an AHAD jacket and shit from 2002, and it's 2005! See, there is a cycle we call the project syndrome, like being caught up in the vicious cycle of the projects. Mother lived there, raised daughter there; daughter lives there, raised daughter there, et cetera. People caught up in the vicious cycle of paying cheap rent and don't want to move out, you know what I'm saying? So people misuse it, and instead of taking advantage of living in the projects and saving up to get out, [they get stuck]. Same shit happens in recovery houses.

To the extent to which the "vicious cycle" of the Keynesian era involved the housing projects (incidentally where Delmar was actually born and raised in Philly, and Malik moved with his family as a young boy in Newark), the post-Keynesian recovery house perhaps has its own analogous version of what Malik called the "project syndrome." To mitigate the cycle, Malik felt it was crucial that the men in his house had some sort of plan.

Malik had started acting as an informal case manager at the 42 House, where he would help men in the house to devise goal-oriented "treatment plans." He designed one such plan for a housemate trying to "stand up to his responsibilities" as a parent.

> MALIK: When I was over there at the 42 House, I was doing some shit like counselors do, like I was doing Johnson's treatment plan for a removal from the 42 House. He was trying to get the kids back into play, like going to parenting school, and he had two jobs. So I was telling him, listen, "They going to give you section 8 because you getting the boys back. You making X amount of dollars here. We got a big basement, right, I want you to start buying stuff to build a home, everything that you see on sale, right, you start buying it. So when it's time to move into your house, you'll have these things, because they'll give you a voucher for the other things."
>
> So I had all this set the fuck up, and he let a bitch come and take all his fucking money. He had said in a meeting, right, "I ain't had a woman in twenty-eight months, and I've got a pocket full of money." Next thing you know, there is a girl sitting next to him, and that was that.

While Malik's efforts were futile in this instance, he was committed to helping any man or woman in his house or in his recovery circle genuinely committed to a plan for change. He worked extensively with Infinite in grooming him for a staff position in his house (with the idea that the two of them would eventually live together with their respective partners). He tried several plans of action to keep Albert moving forward with his dream of reuniting with his family. At first, he tried a balanced approach that enabled Albert to maintain his business selling oils while looking for a regular job and staying in counseling. Malik worked with countless other young men who came into the AHAD program. His goal usually was to help his men get off probation, find gainful employment, and secure independent living. And when Malik felt some members of AHAD were somehow beyond the point of return, he used their penchant for backsliding once again as fodder for teaching opportunities. In other words, he held out men like Tessio as examples of what happens to those who lack a plan.

> MALIK: It amazes me, it reminds me of when I was jailing. Every time I went back, the same crew would be back: "Yo, what you bring with you this time, oh man, I got life, I got five." It is a joke to these people. I just

told Tessio the other night, I said you got to get yourself together, you're sixty-two fucking years old. And then I did my little thing on him, I said, "What if there were no more recovery houses, no more assisted living, no more none of this shit, what are you going to do? Do you have a place to go?" [*mocking Tessio*] "Uhhhhhhh." Old motherfucker wants to drink, period, and he ain't got no other plans.

Through recovery house networks, we can see an expansion of mentorship and informal supports operating in civil society. This expansion counters the claims of poverty scholars who lament the decline of voluntarism, the disappearance of community role models, and even the retreat of the state via mechanisms of devolution and retrenchment.

## Group Technologies and "the Covenant"

Beyond their own individual expertise in informal case management, managers like Malik also depend on the organic ties and support networks that develop between residents to buttress their efforts. In AHAD, Infinite explained that the diverse group of men living in the house, all coming from different walks of life and all working at different stages of recovery, formed the basis of a unique support network:

> INFINITE: I'm blessed, no matter what my aches and pains and all my ailments, and all the shit that I'm going through, I'm still blessed because of all the different guys in this house. Some people got some work in their lives, some people know what they have to do and they are willing to do it, they willing to be vigilant and they doing it. And some people, they working through some pain, they working through it and they not getting high doing it. Some people just unorthodox as a motherfucker, but that's how that story go with us, we all different, but we all after the same thing.
>
> Without all these different pieces, this thing wouldn't work. We all got to be different, we all need different parts, when you open a machine there is different parts, some smaller than the others but they all working for the same thing, to make this machine work, to get us another day. That's what I need in my life, I need all these guys, all their different afflictions and different pains and different stories. And I need to be able to share mine.

Infinite described his reliance on "the machine" to make vivid the dynamics of a self-help collective that thrives on a diverse population working on

a common goal. Each part of the AHAD machine needed to know how
the other worked, so the men could "pull each other up" in the event that
someone faltered or developed subversive plans for relapse. The men at
AHAD felt that their mutual vulnerability was something of an antidote
to shame and self-destruction. True change requires group work on major long-term projects of personal responsibility, such as parenting skills,
family reunification, and financial independence. But it also requires work
on the more modest, small-scale goals of the microhabitat, such as keeping
house and doing one's laundry. An incident with Delmar's socks reflects the
ways in which this group technology worked to instill the basic values of
personal hygiene and responsibility in each resident.

RUFUS: There is a bad smell up there, and I know that's where it is coming
    from . . .

MALIK: Let me tell you something, when I walked in that door it was so
    bad, at first I thought it was the mop upstairs, because as soon as you walk
    in the door it hits you. Let me make a point here, you got a guy walking
    around the room scratching his ass, you got to say something to him. You
    don't wait a couple of days, because by that time everybody has seen him.
    I use that as an example to say that when something is wrong, you got to
    go right to it. He can't pull this shit like "I ain't got time to do laundry";
    that shit got to be done. I'm the type that will take every thing off the
    fucking bed and throw it in the bag and tell him to take this shit to the
    laundry. Look, it can happen to me too, and then you just got to say, "Yo,
    man, you got to handle that," because I need to hear that shit. But you
    got to tell him, man . . . tomorrow he need to go to the laundry.

INFINITE: You know what, Malik ain't going to say nothing, because y'all
    [Rufus and Garvey] live up in that room too, and y'all should have that
    kind of rapport with each other to be able to pull each other up. You
    shouldn't be scared to pull that man up, that's how we work in here.

As director and manager of the house, Malik and Infinite believed that
confrontation of behavioral problems is most effective when accomplished
by one's peers. Addicts, operators, and even counselors model this premise
in the recovery houses, 12-step meetings, and in the group counseling that
the men attend. Malik and other recovery operators in the Kensington community often drew parallels between the therapeutic milieu of the formal
treatment sector and the structure of the recovery house, as each worked in
concert with one another toward similar ends. On one occasion when Bril-

liante complained about his group counseling sessions, Malik reminded him that it was his job to pull the group members up and ensure the quality of the session despite the failings of the treatment professionals.

BRILLIANTE: My group [counseling] isn't working, man, because we sitting in that group with no structure, and you should see them going crazy in there. As I look at it now as opposed to the way it was before when I was there, it's like, oh God. They running so many groups, they got us all crammed up in a little area. And then because they have the Spanish guys, there is a lot of them, they're trying to do double [loads]. It's not working. [*sighs and tries to take a more optimistic view*] But I'm going to get something out of it, they was blown away because I came in there and I hit deep and went straight in on this topic. And I thank God that he used me [to help the group]. I hit something and somebody hit something else and we rolled with it, we was able to use it and we was discussing the anger and how we deal with anger in recovery. So I guess I got to realize that it's my group too [and that I can turn it around by participating].

MALIK: That's why I used to say if y'all sit here and let this happen, you deserve for it to happen; I'm talking about in group, you got to take control, man, that's how group is supposed to work. In a working group the members start to confront each other, so if you got a guy sitting there who is full of shit, saying nothing for an hour, the group member has to call him out on the mat. I mean, when these guys start complaining about the group [therapy session], I tell them it's about what *you* can do, fuck what's going on in there, it's what can you do. I learn a way how to get the best out of everything. When I'm in a bad situation, I have to find something good in it, and then I latch on to whatever that is and stick with it.

The quality of the recovering technology—whether in the recovery house or in the formal treatment sector—depends on the members taking responsibility for its functioning. In this respect, even when systemic and structural failures are evident (as was often the case in the underfunded and overcrowded "Medicaid mills" where the men attended treatment, as well as in the fledgling or dilapidated recovery houses that they lived in), operators not only expect the active participation of the recovering addict, but they believe this to be the most effective and efficient mode of treatment. Recovery discourse becomes an able partner for the post-welfare state, as it relies on technologies that foster bootstrapping notions of responsibility, autonomy, and participation while functioning at a distance from state-centered, professionalized institutions.

The reliance on a social collective in the recovery movement is markedly distinct from neoliberal notions of autonomy. Recovery depends on a surrender of self-will to become part of a whole. Once this surrender occurs, the technological workings of the recovery house take hold as the system of knowledge/power forges in partnership with the individual. Malik and Bilal often summarized the basic principle here by saying, "We can't do this thing on the muscle," indicating that self-will alone is insufficient to achieve real change:

> BILAL: You need to recognize that you need people in your life; one of the biggest recognitions that we made early on was this: we found as addicts we couldn't do this thing alone. So we recognized that there was a group of people over here in the NA/AA rooms, and through the recovery house safe environment where we could begin to get our lives back in order. Most of us, all we needed was the support of other people.

Infinite described this support process as something like child rearing. The group nurtures the individual to become a fully functional, responsible, and autonomous being.

> INFINITE: In the beginning we are like children; when a baby is born you feeding the baby, all them blessings you just giving it to him. But as the child gets older, you are still getting blessings, but then it becomes like a covenant. The child starts cleaning the room; you don't get paid for cleaning your room, doing little things, going to the grocery store, stuff like that, because it becomes a partnership. And just like we came into this recovery, we came in here empty, with nothing, and we were being fed life, taught how to live. And now that we done came up a little bit, and we growing up in this thing, there is a covenant, a bond, a bond of recovery, a bond of helping another person and being of service to others instead of always being of service to yourself. Always remember that we are only allowed to be here through the atmosphere that we make [together] and with God. If we sit here and just think I did this and I did that, watch how quick we just get snatched out the window.

Infinite's articulation of the "covenant" marks a mutual agreement between collective and individual, designed so that the newcomer practices restraint from certain acts in order to achieve a new sense of liberation. Infinite spoke to the process of "coming in here empty," carrying a decisive sense of "lack" that will be compensated—through a divine process of transformation—by the deliverance of life itself. Again he spoke to the technical aspects of "learning how to live" through engagement with others and the maintenance of everyday tasks.

## Conclusion

As Marianna Valverde[21] contends, the centrality of freedom in recovery discourse—defined largely as self-control, manageability, and liberation from dependency—makes it an essential concept for anyone pursuing Foucault's insights about the ways our desires for freedoms and the requirements of authorities have become increasingly aligned in the modern era. Freedom can scarcely be seen as the opposite of control or regulation. Conversely, it has become the essence of twentieth-century democratic governance and the very means through which the status quo is reproduced.[22] By allowing recovery houses to persist in areas of spatially concentrated poverty, the state avails itself of a strategy of spatial governmentality spanning the full spectrum of freedom carefully calculated by operators at the street level—from the more sophisticated mechanisms of regulation through personal choice and the maximization of self-interest, to overt forms of coercion.

No matter which end of the spectrum a house may tend toward, there can be little question that the recovering subject in the Kensington recovery house movement embodies a new terrain of political action, a terrain that carries novel political possibilities for self-governance in areas of spatially concentrated poverty. New authorities in the "conduct of conduct" have emerged—notably recovery house operators—from the ashes of post-industrial decline and its concomitant social welfare impulses. Street-level recovery expertise has been afforded a particular role in the formulation of programs and in the technologies of power that seek to give them effect, operating through the particular relation that it has with the self-regulating capacities of subjects.[23] Applying the art of social conduct in the recovery house requires operators to find a way to constitute, access, and govern the minute and mundane reaches of the habits, desires, interests, and daily lives of individuals.[24]

As Eve Sedgwick notes, the concept of the free will is essential here, for as long as the free will has been "hypostatized and charged with ethical value, just as long has an equally hypostatized 'compulsion' had to be available as a counter-structure always internal to it, always requiring to be ejected from it."[25] The compulsion in question is addiction to chemicals;

and to battle it addicts are urged to accept or reject moral goals; to regulate themselves according to the moral code of recovery; and to establish precepts for conducting and judging their lives.[26] Recovery expertise plays a particular role in the shaping of a particular type of urban subject, one who is amenable to various forms of transformation by way of one's own newly achieved and constructed sense of agency.

I want to close this chapter, however, by lamenting (and confessing) a troubling and dissatisfying sense of abstraction in its empirical findings. While it is incumbent on me to honor the ways in which the abstractions of recovery "work" in the recovery house, I also witnessed the myriad ways in which the agonistic relationships between operators, clients, and state regulatory apparatuses inexorably eroded the recovery ideals explored here. Recovery discourse takes up residence within Foucauldian discussions of the ethical field, insofar as ethics are concerned with how knowledge is imparted to subjects as a mode of self-evaluation and a way of acting on and through an *open set of practical possibilities* in a given historical period.[27] We are talking therefore about a very particular type of pre-scripted agency, mobilized at a very particular time and place. Recovery is best understood not as a self-contained narrative characterized by either success or failure, but rather as a facet of a wider, quite complex process through which certain groups come to be subjected to more or less disciplinary regimes of governance.[28] It is in this sense that—as Marianna Valverde argues of alcohol—the logic of recovery only becomes fully visible when situated with other disciplinary projects and regulatory logics. Recovery provides opportunities for the study of complex and unpredictable interactions of a variety of governmental mechanisms and aims. Consideration of the recovery house's incessant failures provides an inroad to these types of questions in the chapter that follows.

# The Persistent Failures of the Recovery House System

**4**

## Low-Wage Labor, Relapse, and "the Wreckage of the Past"

Unlike those dealing with illnesses of the mind or of the body, those who have struggled with questions of the will have rarely known that there is a long history of ruined projects to seize and maximize the will's freedom.
—MARIANNA VALVERDE, *DISEASES OF THE WILL* (1998)

The vagaries of spatially concentrated poverty and the predatory nature of informal rental markets in the Kensington neighborhood acted like gravity in the recovery house industry, grinding down utopian visions of a life in recovery. Malik's house faced structural deterioration, utility shutoffs, and periodic food shortages when the census was low. Far from generating profits, AHAD barely survived at a subsistence level during the course of my fieldwork. While Frank ultimately earned back his initial investment, neither Milton nor Malik was able to draw a salary from the program during its first eighteen months (beyond the customary free room and board for Malik as his "manager's salary," which, as we will see, was more trouble than it was worth). The AHAD partnership also could not achieve their goal of opening two to three separate recovery houses. In fact, like most programs, they struggled merely to survive and could barely maintain the house

on Genoa Street. These outcomes are emblematic of an industry that is beset
by chronic, spatially concentrated poverty at every turn. Recovery house
operators, who have entered into a stringent market structure predicated on
cost-cutting measures, are led inexorably to practices such as overcrowding,
property neglect, interhouse competition, coercion, and the exploitation of
clients both in-house (volunteer labor) and externally (via day-labor subcontracting). The resultant systemic poverty takes a great toll on recovering subjects, who are often forced to endure levels of destitution even more extreme
than that which they endured while using drugs.

*[handwritten margin note: Cost cutting measures]*

## Agency in the Context of Systematic Impoverishment: The Case of Garvey

As Douglas explained, client destitution was built into the basic economic
formula of the recovery house experience.

> DOUGLAS: First of all, the program was made to keep you behind on rent.
> Because, like I said, you get $102.50 [every other week] as a single person,
> plus your stamps. I was giving them $100 out of $102.50, and I was *still*
> behind, due to their calculations of what your daily rate is. You will
> always be in the hole. Then on top of that, most of these recovery houses
> do not allow you to have a savings. Now I've applied to some places for
> some monetary assistance, like programs to help me so far as moving on
> to get my own [apartment], and they require you to have a savings. But if
> the recovery house doesn't allow you to have a savings, you stuck, because
> you ain't got nothing to save. They will *minimally* take $90 from you
> [biweekly], which leaves you $12.50, which is about $25 a month. That's
> for toiletries, washing your clothes, cigarettes, whatever, so what do you
> have to live on? I'm not knocking these recovery houses, but there needs
> to be a revamping of them.

The owner of Douglas's recovery house had an arcane payment system that
capitalized on the asymmetry between biweekly checks and thirty-one-day
months. As a result, Douglas actually went into debt to his recovery house.
The constant state of being "in the hole" had harsh consequences not only
for daily survival, but also for quality-of-life issues such as sobriety and the
ability to progress toward independent living—that is, for recovery itself.

> DOUGLAS: I mean, here you are, you've been stuck in addiction, in the abyss,
> and now you come out. You are just starting to get clean, by whatever

means, you need clothes, maybe some of your people start kicking in
to get you something to wear so you start feeling good about yourself.
There is a girl sitting beside you at a meeting, you start talking, you want
to take her to a movie, but you have no money to do so. Then it is like,
why am I getting clean? I can't *live* life!

Despite Malik's incessant claims that recovery houses are about learning *how
to live*, Douglas claimed that "being broke" prevented him from "liv[ing]
life." Several of the men would say that poverty "still sucks," clean or not,
leading many to question the project of recovery early on in the process.

Garvey's predicaments were emblematic in this respect, and his story is
worth an extended look. Prior to his arrival in Kensington, he maintained a
relatively comfortable life as a limousine driver, and even kept a modest sub-
urban home with his wife and three children for the better part of the 1990s.
As a lower-middle-class African American, he had grown up in Germantown
with great prejudice against places like Kensington and North Philadelphia.
But crack binges and regular alcohol and marijuana use, combined with domestic abuse, eventually put him in jail. After his release, he continued to
struggle with recidivism due to his inability to pay child support (leading to
two separate three-month terms beyond his initial sentence). Upon release
in the winter of 2003, Garvey landed in the Ridge Avenue shelter, where
he tried for weeks to find employment. A fellow shelter-mate pointed him
in the direction of Kensington, a place he had never set foot in, not even to
cop drugs. There, he was told, he could enter a recovery house, get on public
assistance, and have a chance to get his life back in order.

But as Garvey would often say, far from finding a period of respite, he
hit his bottom *in recovery*. He had never felt more impoverished than he had
as a Kensington recovery house client. After settling in at AHAD, he took
inventory of his status as a first-time welfare recipient on GA:

> GARVEY: This welfare thing, man, it's not really to live off, you can't live off
> that. I am used to having money, even in my addiction, but this welfare
> thing is not nothing you can really live off. You don't have any means for
> anything. You gotta basically look to churches or something for charity,
> and you can't *do* nothing, man, it's hard. I got child support payments to
> make, $159 a week, and it's adding up. I got out of jail in December, and
> they gave me a letter saying, you know, "Get that job." I could give the
> courts something to say I'm in a program trying to better myself, but then
> I'm not paying support and it's a responsibility I want to uphold because

I've got three children. But they ain't going to accept me not paying it for
a year anyway, which probably means I'm going back to jail.

Garvey thought he might get relief from paying child support based on
his decision to enter treatment, but he still wanted to do the right thing by
his kids. As a welfare recipient, however, he was restricted from working.
He tried to find work with the idea that he would drop GA if something
better came along, but it was hard to search given that welfare required IOP
three days a week (in addition to daily 12-step meetings). And even when he
did finally submit applications for restaurant jobs in Center City, he was
denied access as most places had a bias—in his assessment—toward "college
kids." Like several others caught up in the recovery house scene, he began to
pick up odd jobs "under the table," cleaning out vacant lots and doing some
painting for a recovery house owner.

Moreover, after weeks of failed attempts at finding formal employment,
Garvey turned his attention toward full-time recovery, as the matrix pre-
scribed. But he quickly grew frustrated with the quality of the mandatory
"treatment" program, as well as with the required 12-step meetings on Kensington Avenue. They left him feeling flat, listless, uninspired, and confined
spatially to a very particular set of opportunities. He complained about the
rampant hustling in the recovery scene and the hypocrisy that he perceived
to be operating throughout the industry. After two months at Malik's house,
the recovery house system was failing him and putting him in a dangerous
place.

> GARVEY: I want to get a job, finish treatment, get a bank account, meet
> positive people, do things like go to movies, but I feel like a car sit-
> ting idle and all these people up here are holding me back. I find myself
> overexasperated with boredom, and just having the same routine [every
> day] is starting to irritate me. Make the ten o'clock meeting, make the one
> o'clock meeting, then you are in by three o'clock, make the six o'clock
> meeting, and then the day is over. This is just not inspiring me, and I feel
> like I'm heading for trouble.

Apart from the precarious nature of his own employment, the tenuous
nature of the recovery house itself made him feel unstable and insecure. He
felt isolated (despite being surrounded by a supposed "recovery network"),
and began to worry about relapsing. He knew that one drug or alcohol relapse in the management of the house, or one visit from L&I (Philadelphia's
Department of Licenses and Inspections), or one more house financial crisis

could put him out on the street. Without any money in the bank, he soon found himself feeling more vulnerable than at any point in his life.

> GARVEY: These are some scared individuals up here, and a lot of these people I'm noticing they never had nothing, and if you never had nothing before, you just going to be scared. See, I know what it's like to have my own home, to come home and smell an air freshener instead of some other man's body. To thaw my own meat out on the plate and cook it, to lock my door and go to sleep with no worries about some guy coming in to steal. I know what it's like; I mean, I always worked, that was my thing, I was, like, "I work so I can drink, I work hard, ten hours a day!" I mean, I wasn't rich, but I was comfortable. I know what it's like to live in a neighborhood where you could come outside and say, "I love my neighborhood." Now that I'm down, I want that back again. I realize that I have to leave the old personality and try to gain something from this process, but at the same time I'm stuck in it. And this thing is just like one size fits all, but not everyone is the same . . . I need a program that fits my needs, I need it custom made, I can't get it over the counter, it's gotta be something that fits me.

There is little question that Garvey's lower-middle-class background made the impoverishment of the Kensington landscape highly visible to him, and in many respects this may have left him with what Malik often referred to as a "holier than thou" attitude. But his experience still illuminates important dynamics at play in the recovery house industry. While Garvey aspired to the stated goals of the recovery apparatus, that is, to make himself an independent, autonomous, productive member of society, in his assessment the recovery house apparatus actually thwarted the achievement of these goals. The "one size fits all" warehousing economy of the industry belied notions of choice; the spatial isolation of the houses limited his opportunities; and the actual welfare economy that fueled both the treatment and the recovery house sectors in many ways worked against his aspirations to achieve social mobility.

Short of a heroic reversal of fortune, Garvey was trapped between the recovery house system, the child support system, the deregulated labor market, and another run on crack. In the end, he conspired with another resident of Malik's house to get a hustle together, taking the quick route to a relapse. Garvey was immediately kicked out of AHAD, and after a crack binge that lasted almost a week, he ended up back at the Ridge Avenue shelter. He then left Philadelphia to take a job traveling across the country with a moving company. When he returned after a full year of active drug use, he was incarcerated once again for his continued failure to pay child support.

While the particulars of Garvey's story were unique, Malik explained, the basic scenario was typical. Most commonly, destitution preceded a return to "old behaviors" and old "hustles," which often led to relapse.

> MALIK: A guy living on D&A [drug and alcohol GA] never has nothing, and now you got this mind game thing. I gotta give my whole check, don't have cigarette money, don't have nothing, so now what do I do? Now I gotta hustle, or I gotta do something illegal just to have cigarettes and toiletries. And I'm gonna do this but I ain't gonna use? Shit, c'mon. Or you just gonna be, like, I'm not paying this, or I'm not gonna live like this. Either way you are prone to use.

The systematic impoverishment of recovery house living forced the hand of the addict, or cornered him with a set of hard choices. Perhaps ironically, or perhaps not, the only solutions to these problems rested in individual agency. Consider Garvey's story at a systemic level. The scenario began with a notable contradiction in the recovery house system. In the eyes of operators, recovering subjects make better consumers in the recovery market, or laborers within the recovery house system, than they did actual entrepreneurs (hustlers, workers, or competing recovery house operators). Some of the operators in Kensington struggled to keep their clients off the streets and away from their old hustles. Others tried to restrict clients from taking insecure employment, as low-paying jobs not only interfered with treatment (due to absences) but also threatened eligibility for treatment altogether (clients were often terminated from GA for working, resulting in a loss of Medicaid coverage). If successful in restricting these activities, operators were at least able to secure the conditions of subsistence by keeping the addicted body solvent as a paying welfare client. But the persistent poverty of the recovery house experience often undermined their efforts, leading recovering subjects back toward a series of resistance strategies such as hustling, low-wage work, or relapse.

## Hustling and the Allure of Low-Wage Work versus Recovery: The Case of Albert

Rarely have we seen a person fail who has thoroughly followed our path. Those who do not recover are people who cannot or will not give themselves to this simple program, usually men and women who are constitutionally incapable of being honest with themselves. There are such unfortunates. They are not at fault, they seem to have been born that way. They are naturally incapable of grasping and develop-

ing a manner of living which demands rigorous honesty. Their chances are less than
average.
**—AA'S PREAMBLE TO "HOW IT WORKS"**

See, it's not only getting addicted to the drugs and alcohol, a lot of guys started
out clocking, selling, dealing, hustling, and man, you gotta know, it's hard for an
honest brother to make ends meet, it really is! I mean, I don't know what kind of
money you make, but for these guys it can be really hard to get sober and to get
honest, especially since it means having no money.
**—MURPHY**

The opening epigraph of this section, taken from the fifth chapter of the Big
Book of Alcoholics Anonymous, is a well-known passage illustrating the essential qualities of honesty, openness, and willingness in recovery. Taken together, these qualities comprise the acronym HOW in the preamble to "How
It works." The second epigraph, quoting a recovery house operator named
Murphy, begins to suggest the ways in which the vagaries of spatially concentrated poverty inexorably erode AA's otherwise transcendent and universal
principles of honesty and willingness. Along these lines, Albert's story offers
an alternative illustration of "how it works." As one of the founding members of AHAD, Albert came over from the 42 House with Infinite, Malik,
and Delmar as an assistant manager to the program. He celebrated one year
of sobriety shortly after moving into the AHAD house, and seemed to be
making great progress with his recovery and his family. He was also making
strides with his fledgling business selling Muslim oils under the El tracks, a
practice that would ultimately cause great tension within Malik's program. As
noted briefly in chapter 1, Malik did not take issue with Albert's oil business
at first, and even encouraged his entrepreneurial activity so long as it was balanced with his responsibilities to his own recovery and to the recovery house.
On several occasions, we even helped as Albert came running into the AHAD
house to "bag up" his works and go back out to K&A, pumping oils into small
glass bottles from larger plastic ones. Albert explained that Malik introduced
him to selling oils, just as Bilal had gotten Malik started back in the day:

> ALBERT: I done made up some new names for my [oils], I got Nor'easter,
> and Zen. I had some extras, then I got the regular joints; this is Tommy
> Hilfiger, this one is Oxygen . . . My system has been working for me, and
> you know, people ask for what they usually buy, so I try to have what
> most are selling.
> RF: How long have you been selling?

ALBERT: Oh, about six months now. It keeps a couple dollars in my pocket
[*counting bottles*]. Bilal got me started, well, he was supplying, but Malik
turned me on to it, he got tired of doing it one day. I developed it into
an art form. See, he won't admit that I am better at selling than him. He
knows I am a better salesman.

MALIK: Maybe, but you know what, I did good. But I outgrew that shit,
man. Can't be a guy running a recovery house still running around selling
oils. I gotta move up, or at least act like it. Sometimes the money don't
come with the title.

RF: How much do you sell these for?

ALBERT: For you? Five dollars [*laughing*].

RF: How much do you usually sell them for?

ALBERT: Anywhere from $10 on down. It depends on how my money is:
if I'm all right I'll sell it for $5, if I'm struggling trying to get another
package, I got things to do, I'm starting at $10. It's worth it, though, they
pretty big bottles, and most people sell smaller bottles for $5. I try to sell
so I give them a bigger portion.

MALIK: Hell yeah, shit—he be killing 'em, man, he be out there yelling,
"Oils! Hey oils!" He be standing out there right under the El. You can
make $100 a day, right?

ALBERT: Not every day, [I average] $40–$50 a day. Sometimes I clear about
$500 a week, if I go seven days a week and business is good. You got to be
consistent with it though, man.

Over time, Albert would devote the bulk of his day to selling oils under
the El. Then he showed up at his outpatient treatment center one day, only
to learn that it had "gone out of business." Due in part to the growing success of his oil business, Albert dragged his feet finding a new place to attend
therapy. He also stopped attending 12-step meetings and slacked off on his
assistant manager responsibilities in the house. Infinite and Malik took notice and confronted him, claiming that his hustle was interfering with his
ability to "work a program." Malik reprimanded him at a house meeting,
recapitulating his antiflophouse themes:

MALIK: Listen, you ain't even doing your daily chore, and out of all the
men in here, you [should know better]. What I'm saying is this: if you
can't step up, step out, bottom line. No negotiating shit, because this is
a program, and this how it going to be run, like a program. This house
comes first, and if it's not your IOP, something doing with your recovery, something doing with your welfare, or something doing with your

health, it don't come before this house. If you not going to be a part of this house, then you not going to stay here. Nobody is going to stay in this house, right, and just come in this motherfucker and go to sleep and not work this program, as—of—to—day.

Malik's harsh rebuke of Albert's declining comportment addressed the two central factors of "working the program": house participation and treatment attendance. In Malik's eyes, Albert had simply spent all of his time selling Muslim oils at the corner of K&A while using the recovery house as he would any other form of shelter. In this instance, Malik presented an ultimatum: Albert would need to enter a new outpatient treatment facility, or leave the recovery house. If he stayed, he would also need to start living up to his responsibilities in the house as assistant manager, or face a demotion. When Albert protested, Malik insisted that no honest program in Kensington would tolerate such behavior:

> MALIK: Check this out, if you came over here to be a part of this, then be a part of it. And listen, don't let me or Infinite have to keep coming to you, you step the fuck up on your own, do what you got to do but then come into this house and step up.
> INFINITE: We just asking that you make yourself available . . .
> MALIK: [*interrupting*] And give the time to this house that you give to that corner, is that too much to ask from you?
> ALBERT: Well, I still got to . . .
> MALIK: [*shouting*] No, listen to what I'm saying, ain't no fucking program in Kensington that's going to allow a motherfucker to be out there 24/7 *and* not going to counseling. It ain't going to happen!

Relations between Albert, Malik, and Infinite, now strained, would continue to deteriorate. Finally, Albert was "stepped down" as assistant manager of the house, effectively stripped of his title and asked to give back his key (as previously noted, keys are provided only to house staff). He was allowed to stay in the house under the stipulation that he return to treatment, but by that point he had begun to resent those he once referred to as his recovery "family." Albert continued to defend his business, attributing his success with family and his girlfriend to the money he was making:

> ALBERT: I don't have to live on that $102.50 every two weeks, and that extra money allows me to be with my family, to do the things I have to do. Other than that I don't know how I would survive.

Eventually, selling oils became a bit too reminiscent of his old business of selling crack on the corner. Albert succumbed to old pressures in the K&A street scene and started smoking crack again. During the ensuing year of my fieldwork, I would see him panhandling or holding the door at a corner market for spare change. His addiction prevented him from operating his oil business, and he could now only work for short-term money to get his next fix. During the many times that Malik and I saw Albert panhandling during that year, Malik was ruthless in assessing his plight, arguing that he had simply "chosen" this path.

But it is important to note that several factors contributed to his return to drug use. Even before his problems with Malik and Infinite, his outpatient treatment center had closed suddenly, allegedly due to fraudulent bookkeeping practices that led to its bankruptcy. Simultaneously, Albert fell victim to "turf wars" between two programs after moving out of Positive Attitudes, which led to the termination of his welfare benefits. Although he was eventually reinstated, this left him temporarily without resources to pay for rent and food, and without health insurance for treatment at a new agency. At that time, Albert searched for formal employment opportunities to make ends meet, but to no avail. Consequently, he was forced to hustle more and more on the streets to survive, causing great tensions with the leadership of AHAD. The exigencies of street-level hustling put Albert in proximity to old dealers and crack users while alienating him from recovering peers, formal treatment, and ultimately, his recovery house.

Albert was certainly not alone in his predicament. Several of the men I knew were drawn back into hustling activities that were known to be risky but necessary amid the impoverished landscape of Kensington. Widespread unemployment and destitution in the recovery house setup pressured many into curbside car repair, sidewalk vending, incense sales, informal gas pumping and "squeegee-ing" for tips, and selling bootleg DVDs, videotapes, and CDs. Even Infinite, who had sworn off hustling, could never resist indulging in one of his old favorites—fixing flat tires on the street. The allure of these moneymaking opportunities created anxiety for recovery house operators, often provoking them into disciplinary responses. In one instance, a client at AHAD became so heavily involved in the bootleg DVD industry that Malik "kicked him to the curb" (kicked him out), only to have the man respond by calling Malik out in the street for a fight. But Malik and other recovery house operators also recognized that clients would need to make some cash to augment GA. Most operators knew as well that a strict policy prohibiting employment would result in a loss of clientele, and that work allowances gave them a market advantage. Thus, "rigorous honesty" and individual choice were only part of the complex and contradictory relationship between recovery, relapse, and low-wage employment. As poverty eroded and transformed systems of governmentality in recovery houses, informal and highly flexible policies emerged to make and remake the rules of contingent work.

## Informal, Flexible Policies on Low-Wage Work

Most of Kensington's recovery house operators did develop some sort of work policy. On one end of the spectrum were larger operators like Murphy, Wilson, and Benito, who took a hard line and prohibited employment, mainly because they preferred the financial stability of welfare clients. Stated in a more sanguine way, work was actively discouraged in the initial months of residence to enable clients to experience a period of respite and focus fully on treatment and recovery. Men like Wilson would say that once a person goes to work, the entire system, which had been calculated over years through the wisdom of the recovery community in conjunction with the professionalized treatment sector, inevitably breaks down. Work interferes with the IOP process, as spotty attendance not only means spotty treatment for the client, but also threatens revenues derived from informal feeder contracts between operators and outpatient treatment agencies. For example, during the annual Penn Relays track and field meet held by the University of Pennsylvania, Billings complained that half the clients of his outpatient treatment center were absent, as they had been hired out to work security by day-labor contractors. Due to the fee-for-service structure of the behavioral health care system, his revenues for the day were cut considerably. The irony was that Billings had an informal kickback arrangement with a recovery house operator who—in his simultaneous efforts to supply cheap labor to the University of Pennsylvania and addicted bodies to Billings's treatment center—had simply overbooked.

Quite apart from monetary concerns, Malik's policies on work were informed by his faith in the recovery process. He advocated a full focus on sobriety for his clients rather than seeking employment. Perhaps more than any other operator that I knew, he wanted his men to recover and did his best to keep their interests at heart. But even well-intended operators—those less concerned about either the stability of welfare clients or the opportunity to make extra money as middlemen for day laborers—face challenges from their own clients, many of whom continuously seek employment due to the impoverishing setup of the recovery house. Malik often pointed out that the client's immediate obsession with earning power was a distraction from the hard work of recovery:

> MALIK: People come in here and want a job right away, but you didn't have
> no job when you was out there [using]! I mean, the truth of the matter:
> you weren't taking care of the baby, taking care of your woman, none of
> that! Motherfucker, I picked you up on the basement steps with a black
> bag over your fucking back, *hobo style*. But then these guys want to make
> money right away, because they see other guys got it. You can never
> worry about the guy on the side of you; you just keep focusing on what
> *you* going to do. Because if you keep watching what this motherfucker
> got, you going to get caught up in some shit, develop some feelings of
> resentment, and you not going to be able to do what you need to do for
> yourself.

Malik had been successful in his own recovery by biding his time and waiting for the "right" opportunity while living an ascetic lifestyle on welfare for almost two years. He explained how his jump to open his own house, while hardly lucrative, was the right move at the right time:

> MALIK: I just always look at it like this here, my turn is coming. As long as
> I keep doing what I need to do, I'm gonna get it. You can't be hatin' in
> this motherfucker. Look, I had to wait eighteen fucking months, and I'm
> really not earning now [as director of the recovery house], so you can say
> two fucking years. But you know what, throughout all of that time God
> in the process has allowed me to eat, and I believed that when it was the
> right time for me I'd get something, man.

Malik was proud that he had used the recovery house "process" to build a foundation for moving up in life. In his case, his patience rewarded him with a janitorial job at the Navy Yard after two years on the recovery house scene—a coveted full-time position paying $10.50 an hour, with health insurance and other benefits.

Malik had reasons to be wary of his men seeking employment, as he had seen several of them get cut off from welfare after taking insecure jobs. Occasionally, and under the right circumstances, he believed that employment can be a positive and necessary element of personal transformation. He also welcomed workers into his house, provided that they had steady, full-time employment, not only for the sake of their relative stability but also because they paid more in rent. Ideally, the balance lies in the client's procurement of the "right" type of employment, which was always scarce in Kensington and all of Philadelphia for that matter. Of all of the men in Malik's house, Rufus was the only one whose job (as a parking lot attendant) even approached stability.

A client settling for anything less faced the regulatory logic of GA, which itself trapped the men between punitive benefits and the insecurities of the low-wage labor market.

> MALIK: See, a lot of these guys get caught up, then they get a bullshit job, and the job cuts back on the fucking hours, right, and now they fucked because welfare done cut you off as soon as they find out you working. And living in this recovery house ain't free, so you gotta be careful what you ask for. You fuck around and lose your welfare and say, "Now I got a job," but now I'm paying rent out my pocket and I ain't used to going to the store and buying food with real money. That shit hurts! . . . Bottom line, you have to get something that is worth saying, "The hell with welfare." It should be a full-time job, and not just a seasonal job neither, because there ain't no treatment or no rent coming out of that!

Summarizing the basic outlines of the work policy at Positive Attitudes, Bilal echoed Malik's ideas. He indicated that recovery is about providing a foundation for advancement, the matter of timing being essential:

> BILAL: We discourage full-time work until four months of basic IOP is completed, because a client needs to have a foundation in this recovery arena before he can go back out there. After IOP, we encourage you to continue with your OP either one day a week or sometimes two days a week. We encourage slow reintegration with society in terms of working, because a job alone is nothing if a person doesn't know and begin to understand themselves. We want to sit down with the people and talk about, "What is it you really want to do with yourself?"

Bilal articulated the utopian goal of transforming down-and-out addicts and "reintegrating" them into society. In this vision, the recovery house takes on rehabilitative agendas that are geared toward a reconnection with the prevailing economic engines of society—ideally the procurement of sustainable, nonalienating employment that pays a living wage.

Although these principles were attractive in theory, my fieldwork revealed a great deal of slippage in matters concerning work. This was true in programs both large and small. For example, despite his teachings on the virtues of patience, Malik knew that his men had to work and hustle to survive. He also knew that he could draw bodies away from the larger, stricter programs by introducing a more lenient policy concerning employment. As a result, he eventually developed a flexible strategy: (1) only take formal employment if it is steady, as it will jeopardize welfare and therefore limit one's ability to pay room, board, and treatment fees; or (2) only take work "under the table," as it would not interfere with welfare benefits in most cases; *and* (3) work must come second to IOP or outpatient counseling and recovery meetings. The coherence of this flexible strategy should not be overstated, as in practice it was constantly undermined (even Malik's policy on treatment was sometimes flexible, as Rufus was never required to attend). And even for hardliners running larger programs who decried the vagaries of work versus the virtues of treatment, it was another story when the work in question was commissioned by the recovery house owners themselves.

## Policy Slippage toward Informal, Low-Wage Labor: The Case of Delmar

Financial pressure on operators, chronic poverty for their clients, and the persistent allure of low-wage labor for both constantly reshaped the informal labor policies in Kensington's recovery houses. In practice, persistent poverty undermined not only the goals of "getting to know and understand the self," but also the idyllic time line of Malik's and Bilal's visionary labor policies. As the recovery house could not in actuality serve as a retraining ground or respite for career development, most recovering subjects (and recovery house operators) jumped at the chance to take any employment made available. Desperation led many to gravitate beyond the relatively stable part-time employment of the deregulated service sector, and toward intensely contingent day-labor markets.

Meager GA benefit allotments led operators themselves to accelerate conditions of flexibility, contingency, and vulnerability regarding work. For example, Bilal was one of the greatest critics of day labor, but in the face of chronic insecurity and the systematic impoverishment of the welfare setup, he found it almost impossible to avoid hiring his men out as day laborers.

> BILAL: You can get some work around your treatment hours, usually in the evening, or if you've got evening IOP or OP you can get some work during the week. We definitely encourage at least one day of work or tempo-

rary labor on the weekends so that you can get your necessary cosmetics, because your welfare alone does not handle that. It's not enough money after your rent and your food is taken out, so the guys have to go out here and do a little something on the side. So we have a situation where we are familiar with the temporary agencies around here in the neighborhood. They call us, and we provide the temporary labor.

Note the slippage here from his earlier policy ideals. As with several other issues in the recovery house industry, contradictions between what recovery house operators said and what they did in practice were common. For example, Malik too criticized temporary employers, as he was completely aware of their pernicious practices.

> MALIK: What I'm trying to get at is . . . I'm trying to show you what's going on in Kensington and these drug areas, or these run-down areas. These people come in, set up shop, businesses, right, and what happens is they are taking full advantage of the alcoholic and the addict. They're making money off of the alcoholic and the addict, man.
>
> TESSIO: They used to come to our program, take a couple guys, then say they needed two more guys, but they pay them garbage, man, and these guys are experienced . . .
>
> RF: What kind of work?
>
> TESSIO: Any kind, sheetrock, painting . . . like with one of my friends, the guy tried to screw him and he wouldn't pay him his money. He did a beautiful job, he's a professional, he painted and all, and he wouldn't give him the money. But that's how it goes, they try to not only pay you less, they try to get over and not pay you at all. I know guys who got brought into Jersey, and they couldn't collect their money. Plus there were guys that didn't want to go, but the house says you gotta go to work because you gotta pay your rent.
>
> MALIK: Listen, see what happens is, these directors of these fucking houses get paid, but they don't give a fuck about what the man gets. It's slave labor, you know what I mean? I'll supply you some bodies, and all that shit. So they do this work building this house or whatever, at the end of the week the guy says okay, I brought you lunch and I did this and that or whatever, here is $100. Now you get back to the recovery house, right, and I pull out my books on you, well, you eighty-five dollars in the hole. Do you see what I'm saying? You know I'm talking about people getting raped.

And yet, despite his harsh criticisms of widespread exploitation, Malik
was unable to avoid day-labor operations. He relied on these networks, and in
certain circumstances even extolled their therapeutic and economic benefits.

> MALIK: These things offering a day's pay for a day's work popped up years
> back, and they work to get a man a temporary job. You know, if you
> worked today, you are going to get paid today. I swear to God, even the
> weak clients can get through the day, because at the end of the day you
> got something to show for it.

Similarly, Clarence, director of the We Stood at the Turning Point program, disparaged employment's threat to recovery while boasting of the
informal labor networks he had established:

> CLARENCE: Not only does the owner of my recovery program own the
> building, he has a blind cleaning business, and he has a floor cleaning busi-
> ness. I have two guys that have security businesses; I have three other guys
> who have contracts cleaning office buildings. Where do you think they
> get their labor from? So now I got guys there on Tuesdays and Thursdays
> when they not in outpatient, I got guys there working for these contracts.
> They offsetting the $102 [$102.50 from welfare], and it keeps the guys
> there because now they don't feel like they are just existing. So I try to
> offer them guys a lot of options.

Throughout the history of the recovery house movement, purveyors of day
jobs have recognized an army of reserve labor in the recovering population.
In turn, recovery house operators have reciprocated by providing under-
the-table "options" to their clients, and flexible labor to a host of different
"employers." Over time, informal networks have become quite diversified.

> BILAL: Mostly my guys work for places like Diamond Furniture, and there
> is a bakery and a cheese factory that they also work for. These are big
> pluses for our guys, because they get these jobs, temporary but on a regu-
> lar temporary basis. Of course we have the neighborhood car washes that
> they can work for—they allow us to come in and work a weekend or a
> day or two here and there because they are always shorthanded. And then
> there are little moving jobs that come through. Plus, people in the neigh-
> borhood want them to come and help them move or clean out a basement
> or mow their yard.

The importance of day-labor arrangements cannot be overstated. Every operator and client I knew had worked in some capacity with security companies, moving companies, furniture companies, or electioneering jobs; for call servicing centers at companies such as Go Internet; and even for holiday fund-raising drives for insurance providers such as Americhoice. In some cases, the employer might even be the recovery house operator himself. Several operators reduced past debt or waived intake fees for clients who were willing to clean out basements or backyards, or engage in light maintenance activities like painting at the recovery house or at a church. Many recovery house programs launched small business ventures such as corner stores or delis, operated entirely on client labor (paid or unpaid). For example, Garvey worked for a deli owned by a recovery house at K&A for some time, where clients were expected to work for just thirty dollars a day regardless of hours worked (by his calculation, the deli was actually paying around four dollars an hour). He added that it really wasn't daily pay, but rather "thirty dollars whenever they felt like paying you, and that's if you don't owe back rent." Other recovery programs (such as One Day at a Time) are known to operate corner stores on the unpaid labor of their clients as a mechanism to practice the recovery maxim of "giving back."[1] In this sense, the exigencies of concentrated poverty in the recovery house industry produced a spatially contained, marginal pool of flexible labor ripe for exploitation.

It is perhaps accurate to say that, lacking the political power to change punitive GA benefit levels, recovery house operators were forced to compensate by contracting their clients out to temporary agencies in the neighborhood. In this sense, they operated—however inadvertently—as local front men or agents for the policy logics of workfare, and it was often in their best interest to do so. Operators profited by gouging clients for their role as middlemen in coordinating day-labor arrangements, and they also garnished clients' wages for payment of back (and future) rent. And, as if the system weren't arcane enough, finding temporary labor for a client was sometimes worth the risk for the recovery house owner, as it might develop into full-time work for the client, who would then become a worker and pay more rent. Malik explained the ways in which this complex and infinitely flexible "labor policy" worked:

> MALIK: You see, basically, if you working more than three days, your rent is going up $65, because if you working four days that's damn near like a permanent job. At Positive Attitudes the coordinator had a system: if

you went to work he didn't care, as long as it didn't interfere with your therapy. But he had a policy: if you did a day's work and you got $45, you come home and you break the house off. You give them $15, and that goes toward your rent. Every time you made money, you give them money, right, towards your bill.

RF: Towards the initial intake fee, right, but once that's paid off, are you expected to keep giving?

MALIK: Well listen, you can *always* contribute to your bill. Once that's paid off, what's wrong with giving $10 toward your next month's rent? It makes sense, as long as you breaking it off while you was making it, and that way you also stop the owner from saying, "Now, everyone who works ten hours, your rent is going up $65." See, you don't want him to institute policy, because once you institute policy it covers everybody, and everybody just can't do that. So instead you let him say, "Look, I let you go out today and make $45, right, give me $15 of that to put it on the books for next month." You try to make it personal, and responsible.

Again we see a flexible and strategic sensibility to the policy here, one that incentivizes low-wage or temp work for the client while assuring solvency in favor of the operator. In this way, operators maximize advantage from their clients' earning activities, dictating when they are appropriate, when they are not, and when they will result in garnished wages or an increase in categorical rent (from welfare fees to worker's fees). Thus, operators have become active agents in not only restructuring welfare norms, but also the rules and conventions of the informal low-wage labor market. They have a vested interest in pushing the envelope of both recovery and contingent labor as complexly interrelated regulatory forces.[2]

Malik's experience with Delmar reveals how the recovery house setup does nothing to ameliorate conditions of insecurity and contingency, and may in fact accelerate the instrumentality of both. Delmar took a job as a security guard after Malik had made a connection with a sketchy security company in nearby Frankford. Malik cancelled the weekly house meeting at a moment's notice to send all of his men on a job for this company: to work security at a football game in Frankford. He even ran out to purchase train fare and white shirts for each of them at the thrift store to accommodate the company's dress code. After a harried afternoon of preparation, the men arrived at the job, only to be sent home because another recovery house had beaten them to the punch. Still, the house did not take a total loss. The company hired Delmar for a security job at a 7-Eleven convenience store (and later a Foot Locker shoe store). Malik explained how he purchased a uniform for Delmar:

> MALIK: I hooked Delmar up, they told him he had to work the next day, and he had to have the pants with the stripe, and he had to have black shoes. So you know what I did, I put on my Superman outfit; I jumped in the batmobile and ran to the thrift store to get him a pair of shoes, striped pants, and a shirt. They don't supply shit for uniforms, I guess they been beaten so many times, you gotta be there for a while for them to get one. Fucking ready-made cop, man.
>
> RF: What do they pay him?
>
> MALIK: Well, to work the game that day it was $6 an hour, so he might make $6.50 or something like that. If he make $6 an hour it's okay, because it's under the table and he keeps his welfare, so that's good.
>
> RF: Do they give him any training?
>
> MALIK: The only training is, you walk around the goddam store and look at people. They feed him down there, and whatever they give him, shit, he'll eat it. Plus, he probably walks down the aisles opening shit. When I worked one of them jobs I ate out of every goddam aisle, man.

Delmar became a security guard overnight. And while Malik was optimistic at first about Delmar's chances in his new job, he soon realized that the payment setup had problems. As was quite typical in the informal employment sector, the security company withheld Delmar's pay ostensibly for tax purposes, even though the position was under the table:

> MALIK: How you going to put one check in the hole when they paying him in cash? You know the boy ain't too tight if he take a job without asking when payday is and what his salary is. But you know what? A lot of these places when they pay you cash, they take out their own taxes. They take it out just like they would if you was paying taxes, like, say you made $180, you getting $145 or $150. They do that, these companies.
>
> RF: So you are working under the table, but you don't get the benefit of working under the table?
>
> MALIK: You working under the table, but they just taking money from you, and you know they not reporting it, that's big down here, it's big all over. It's like this: "Yo, why don't you pay me under the table?" "I can't do that, but if you let me take taxes out of it I'll do it." You know what I mean. They do that shit.

Delmar was caught between a predatory temporary-labor economy and a punitive welfare system. Like many in the recovery house scene, Malik explained, Delmar had to tolerate the conditions, because he desperately needed Medicaid:

> MALIK: Delmar has to work under the table, because he using his welfare medical shit to get things done. But he ain't using the card fast enough! I'd be in the dentist, I'd be in the eye doctor, I'd be in the foot doctor. Get the shit done, because you fuck around, you end up with four teeth in your mouth like Blanche, because she didn't follow up and now she ain't got no fucking insurance, you know what I mean?

The situation only worsened over time. Delmar's temporary work hours were drastically decreased, and then eliminated after a theft in the shoe store happened on his watch. At the same time, he was terminated from welfare, because his caseworker had somehow learned of the work arrangement. In Delmar's experience, welfare operated as a regulatory mechanism in conjunction with low-wage work, first by the basic principle of "less eligibility," and second by purging bodies from the GA rolls into low-wage work through the ever-looming threat of cutoff. Indeed, the uncertainty, unevenness, and instability of deregulated low-wage labor, when combined with the contradictory and informal labor policies of the recovery house, set up just the type of conditions under which the logic of workfare thrives.[3]

And all of this despite the best intentions of the recovery house operator. Consider Bilal's final assessment of the labor situation in Kensington, which stands in utter contrast to his previously stated utopian visions on the transformational potential of respite and the training ground of the recovery house process:

> BILAL: There are a lot of underlying forces to keep people trapped in the neighborhood, and it's mostly because of greed. In a sense, this recovery house industry has become a modern-day slave plantation for lack of a better term.
>
> RF: That's a pretty strong statement.
>
> BILAL: I feel pretty strongly about it. You know, you are using people to work for sometimes less than minimum wage through the various agencies. The one that goes to the baseball, basketball, and football games, I don't know what agency they are using, but they end up with $30 to $35 after eight hours—that's less than $5.25 an hour. They might be doing security, they might be sweeping up or doing cleaning, but for all of these various

agencies they get less than minimum wage. And in a given house like Kensington Project, they have the money flow through the management, and then they give $20 and take the rest. If that ain't slavery I don't know what is. And when you abuse clients in terms of taking their food stamps and all their cash dollars, and then give them donated food, it reminds me of the days when the Spanish were working on the farms and the blacks were in the slavery huts, and gave them the scraps and all the pig guts and all that there . . . the donated parts of the pig, right. That's what it reminds me of.

## Seeking Refuge in the Recovery House Labor System

For recovering subjects like Malik, Bilal, Benjie, Clarence, and countless others seeking a way out of the depredations of low-wage labor, the recovery house industry itself presents an alternative career path. An elaborate and informal recovery house labor system has evolved since the passage of Pennsylvania's 1982 Welfare Reform Act. Through an informal apprenticeship system, recovery house operators groom the next generation of staffers by linking the promise of recovery to the potential for upward mobility. Indeed, since many directors "grow up" to own recovery houses after working as chore monitors and assistant managers in early recovery, they become the north stars of upward mobility in the imaginary of impoverished addicts. As a great marker of success, most directors eventually live independently (that is outside of the recovery house), and a select few enter the formal treatment sector as paraprofessionals or assistant counselors (as in the case of Bilal, Wilson, Clarence, Murphy, and Benito). Many directors (and managers) also market their expertise as consultants to novice investors interested in setting up recovery houses (as in the case of both Bilal and Malik). Most of these men would be hard pressed to find work in other realms of the formal and semiformal economy, let alone to become managers, counselors, or entrepreneurs. In this respect, the industry is often seen as a career path that affords informal social legitimacy in a field in which the men have undisputed expertise, as well as eventual material reward. The consequent social relations enroll individuals in alliances that combine the service of self-transformation with the formation of subsistence economies.

Yet while some have been able to gain access to the more professional route in the formal treatment sector, it is undoubtedly more typical for men like Malik to try their lot in the informal recovery house industry. And, for aspiring operators to even have this chance, they must first move through the ranks of an informal, hierarchical recovery house labor system—from client to chore monitor to assistant manager to manager—that in many respects mirrors and in some ways exceeds the predatory nature of low-wage work. In fact, recovery house "labor" is typically not referred to as labor at all, but simply regarded as participation in the activities required for self-help recovery. Nonetheless, owners and directors extract capital from the labor of their subordinates, and the amount of work performed by staff certainly begs the question of compensation when put into proper perspective.

Managers, for example, typically work seven days a week without monetary reward. Their only remuneration comes in the form of a "manager's salary," which amounts to free room and board. The word *salary* is a bit of a misnomer here. In this case, it translates to a rather ironic (and often graduated) entitlement to the sum of one's own welfare benefits. For managers on GA, this amounts to $205 a month plus food stamps, whereas managers on SSI (Supplemental Security Income) often receive in the vicinity of $300. In addition, managers receive perks (or "play") such as flexibility on curfew and overnight leave. Most houses designate only one bed space for the manager "salary." Assistant managers and chore monitors committed to advancing often work for months "paying dues" trying to get this coveted slot, but in the interim they work for free. The incentive? To learn the industry "inside and out." For example, when Malik entered Positive Attitude's 42 House, Bilal lived in the house rent free as a manager while working full time as a counselor at an outpatient treatment center. Even though the owner of Positive Attitudes refused to designate more than one slot to the in-kind salary held by Bilal, Malik saw the position as an opportunity to learn how the business worked.

> MALIK: See, normally the manager doesn't pay rent after you've been there
> for a while, but I could never be the manager, because Bilal was the
> manager. But I ran the house, so he knew that to keep me there he would
> have to make it worthwhile. He was letting me know, no matter what
> the sacrifices is, if you stick to this it's going to be worth your while. I
> know he's got some shit with his ass, you know, that little motherfucker
> is slick. But I worked eighteen months under him, and it worked for me,
> because now I know how this shit works! I watched Bilal do it, he was my
> mentor. Some stuff he didn't want me to see, but I saw it anyhow. I'd be
> like, "What did you do that for," he be like, "Aw, c'mon man, I did that
> because I wanted this guy to do this and the other guy to do that." When
> I was with him I stuck close to his ass, and I took just what I needed.

Malik saw his position as a way of "paying dues" before taking his place within the recovery house industry as a director and would-be owner. This basic scheme has institutionalized a state-subsidized labor system that all but eliminates overhead costs for recovery entrepreneurs. As a uniform practice, embedded within the system, the absence of staff payment is rarely questioned, although it is often indirectly resisted by many clients' refusing to take on staff positions.

The trials of subsistence in an impoverished industry combined with the allure of increased profits (via the suppression of overhead) often leads to coercive practice. Many owners and directors develop creative incentive structures for the dispensation of fringe benefits and monetary rewards, by delaying a manager's salary for months until he "proves himself" or "earns it" across a "probationary period." This practice may be justified by house "policy" or by the director's arbitrary discretion, which are usually one and the same.

Field examples illustrate the ways in which informal policies are diffused, transferred, and reproduced. In Malik's case, the idea of a delayed salary had achieved the status of common sense. His reproduction of the policy in his own program was justified by the precedent of his own experience, which he considered typical for the industry as a whole. Accordingly, even though he resented the "probationary period" at Positive Attitudes (to the extent that he shortened it in his own house), he transferred its basic tenets to AHAD.

> MALIK: You see, with your staff, you can train them by saying, "Listen, here is what we going to do: I can't give you money for the first six months, but after that you get your rent free," that's what you tell your manager. At most houses it's nine fucking months before you ready to go with a salary, unless you act exceptionally well. And that's as a *manager*, not an assistant manager.

Maintaining these practices allows directors to increase labor demands on the manager (often enabling the director to pursue employment on the side) for less payment. Directors also maximize house return by calibrating the manager salary to the number of beds filled in the house. Consider Malik's ingenuity when trying to enroll Garvey for the position of house manager at AHAD:

> MALIK: See, what I'll do for [Garvey], suppose I start working at a job, right, and he stays there to run the house. I'll take $100 off his rent, *as long as the house keeps a certain count*. But I won't let him know that right off; you see, you don't let him know what you doing or he'll look forward to

that; you just surprise him. When it comes time to pay the rent, you just say it then, because once you say something out your face, man, it's like damn near a written thing.

RF: So you keep it casual, that way you can do it . . .

MALIK: [*cutting me off*] When it suits you, when the money allows you to do it.

In Malik's incentive structure, the manager's salary was contingent on the house census, which of course is keyed directly to house revenues. He also ensured flexibility in his negotiations by always working on his time table, using verbal rather than written contracts. Like most directors, Malik avoided formal policies. This allowed directors to work on an experimental basis, using each new managerial relationship as a testing ground for novel ideas. In all of the houses I studied, these practices resulted in an unchecked and inexorable devaluation of labor, driven by the impulse to suppress over-head costs, offload responsibility, and maximize return.

The market ingenuity of recovery house directors is not limited to maxi-mizing house revenues on behalf of their own programs. Often the directors operate as savvy independent contractors, eschewing the longer-term com-mitments of program or property ownership in favor of freelance consult-ing opportunities. Malik demonstrated his abilities in this realm when Bilal was offered an opportunity to operate two recovery houses for an absentee owner. Malik advised taking the opportunity, but with a salary that was to be augmented by the free labor of his clients.

MALIK: I would do it for $1,000 a month for both houses . . .

RF: That's not enough, man, with all the work you guys do?

MALIK: Yes it is, because I get to hire my own staff, *and* live rent free. I won't be there on the daily running that shit, you know what I mean? X amount of hours a day, I come through there—three hours at this house, two hours at this house; it's five hours a day, *if* that. Just because you hired to do something don't really mean you got to do it or that you got to pay someone else to do it. That's what you got staff for; you just use the people in the program.

RF: But then don't you have to give them some of your salary?

MALIK: No, you don't give them shit! When they get to a certain point, then you start taking shit off, you know what I mean?

RF: Like rent . . .

MALIK: Yeah, you got to do that, you got to give them an incentetive [mis-pronunciation of *incentive*]. Say to 'em like, "Yo, you give me six months, man, and you live rent free." [*pauses*] Then every time one of them gets to six months, you fire him! [*laughs*]

Even in the instances in which directors negotiate with owners as independent contractors, struggles over meager revenues come at the expense of managers, in the form of delayed or graduated salaries. Recovery house owners hold a temporal advantage, by depriving managers of any form of payment until they burn out, relapse, or simply leave. A more common strategy is to "incentivize" by linking compensation to performance. As an example, I listened to Bilal one day as he advised a fledgling recovery house owner who was just starting out, and had found himself overwhelmed by the workload of sustaining a house:

> BILAL: If they on welfare, part of the incentive is to give them part of it back, to start with, and eventually let them keep the whole thing. You can't afford to pay them right yet, but you can afford to do that, for that type of service. Say they paying $90 every two weeks in welfare, but you using them in service, so instead of $90 in the first two weeks take $80, for the first two weeks. Then you get a chance to see what they capable of, and what they willing to do. And then the third week, give 'em another $5 deduction, *if* they've earned it. And then wait at least over a month, and talk to 'em about giving them a little bit more. But remember, they have to earn it.

While similar to Malik's incentive structure, Bilal's was a bit more nuanced. His emphasis was less on the census, per se, and more on linking compensation to informal performance measures. This strategy illustrates the ways in which the business model operating in recovery houses adjoins the basic tenets of labor management and cost cutting with the principles of voluntarism, governmentality, and "good citizenship." Another interesting factor is his use of the term *service*, an important concept used quite often in the rooms of AA and NA to denote the voluntary contributions of 12-step members to service boards and meetings. It is important to note that by definition—that is, according to the 12 traditions—service work is explicitly unpaid labor in the name of giving back to the group and fellowship of AA. And while there is great wisdom in this tradition, it can easily become a prostituted principle when co-opted by the recovery house industry. Moreover, linking the issue of payment directly to informal performance policies enables the rehabilitative process to be measured. In this sense, recovering subjects are interpellated as enterprising subjects, their liberation from addiction effectively caught up with the economic incentives of "career advancement."[4]

In this regard, directors often give primacy to qualities that ostensibly transcend money and status when recruiting new staff. The concept of willingness becomes an especially salient concept here. It is strategically invoked to test one's mettle for the pursuit of spiritual transformation, often by mining an addict's past zones of suffering and then appealing directly to that person's willingness to do whatever it takes to never go back. Clarence spoke to this strategy when asked how he went about selecting staff:

> CLARENCE: Through the process of being in a recovery house and being around recovering people, I learned to utilize [my skills in finding good people]. It is easy to see a person that's willing; the person that is willing stands out more than anybody. What I generally do is, I look for a guy like me, someone who does what I did when I came into the recovery house. When I went in for the first time I did whatever they told me, *whatever* they told me, and I didn't have a whole bunch to complain about, because I remember what it was like trying to get there. So I didn't worry about them taking my welfare check, that wasn't important. What was important for me was that I learned how to stay clean and get a job and learn how to take care of myself. I had to be willing, because how was I going to do that unless I let someone else teach me? So my general question is, like, how willing are you?

By linking upward mobility and personal transformation to notions of teachability and willingness, directors frame participation in recovery house labor as the path to salvation. It is significant to consider the absence of resistance to these tactics and policies. Most clients and managers have little or no recourse to pursue grievances, and with no contract or even a rental agreement, they lack the capacity to organize, which enables the house owner to exercise his spatial advantage by canceling tenure at any time. As Mike Davis says of other "invisible" rental populations,[5] routine evictions happen at the first sign of protest, often with little celebration or notice.

It should be noted, however, that staff salary was recognized as an issue in need of regulatory attention in the elite CODAAP programs that received city funding. While touring a CODAAP facility, Benito, director of the Fresh Start program, explained a very different salary system for staff. Although admitting that his program emulated other houses by designating a housefather, they made deliberate efforts to differentiate this person from paid staff:

BENITO: None of my staff live here. Because it's a CODAAP facility, we can't take out beds, it goes against the contract. We have a housefather, and yeah, he gets play, I give him extra time on his pass, he'll get little perks here and there, I'll give him a little reduction in his rent, you know, like ten dollars here and there, yeah why not. But, like, free room and board? No. Because he's not here to perform a job function, he's here to be a role model for the community, and to be a leader in the community and to show the newcomer.

RF: One of the guys that I watch, he is the director of the program, he deals with headaches all day long, he is running the show, it's more than a full-time job, and he doesn't have a salary. He gets nothing.

BENITO: That's insane.

RF: Except free room and board, and the guy that owns the house is making a profit while he runs it.

BENITO: Absolutely, because he can, because it's the norm. . . . and that's exploitation. If I got no place to go, and if the payoff for me is to run your facility and live rent free, and use the phone or whatever, yeah, guys are going to go for that as opposed to what they know are the realities out there. I mean, they can't afford five hundred dollars a month rent or mortgage or whatever, and you got no skills anyway. And guys hide in recovery houses like that. All of my guys earn a salary. That's the good thing, man, you know you're not going to get rich, but its gonna pay your bills. And you do it for the love of recovery, man, that's the bottom line.

In Philadelphia's CODAAP-funded houses, contractual arrangements dictate that each facility has a paid supervisor and upwards of four paid staff members. In program efforts to set professional boundaries between staff and clients, paid staff members are not allowed to live in the facility. Still, most CODAAP-funded staff came up through the ranks in a program like Fresh Start before getting hired (as Benito did). This suggests that the basic structure for career trajectories is similar to other recovery houses, albeit more formalized. And the CODAAP channel is also tightly limited, meaning that most recovery house aspirants are consigned to the margins with very little chance of a salary or mobility within a more formal structure. In this sense, we should not have illusions about the great strides of recovery entrepreneurs, as most continue to languish in relative poverty and insecurity even as they themselves become exploiters of their even more impoverished clients and staff. I conclude with a quote from Murphy, a "successful" director whose sentiments aptly reflect the complexities, contradictions, and limitations of an alternative career path in the "industry":

RF: It seems a lot of guys get bit by the recovery bug—they want to give back in a way, and they see it as a viable strategy for making a life, for making a career even.

MURPHY: Well, I'm hoping I can. But there are some unfortunate pieces to this too: at the top I don't have any medical insurance, and I have hepatitis C and I don't even know how that is right now. I can't get any services, and I'm not going down to lie to welfare and all that other kinda crap, I can't do that. I don't have anything for retirement right now, so there's things like that I have to consider. You know, they tell you live in the day, stay in today, but I also have to worry about when I'm sixty-five. So there are some problems with just making this my sole business, and I have other side things going on too.

## Relapse

Caught between the predatory forces of client destitution, low-wage work, and the recovery house labor system itself, is it any surprise when recovering subjects relapse into addiction? There were countless stories of relapse for the duration of my fieldwork, and even more stories of chronic struggle that often provoked me—against my own politics—to coax various figures to leave Kensington. Within AHAD, relapse in the client population was a weekly event, causing constant turnover. More transient types were prone to blow out quickly, but even Malik's most trusted confidants, who had established longer term sobriety, fell by the wayside. The typical scenario was for a client to gain enough strength and money to go back out on another run and miss the nightly curfew, only to call later from jail or the street, asking to pick up their belongings. Several times, clients stole money or random items from Malik's house before going back out. One such instance involved a man who spontaneously offered to do everyone's laundry in the house, ostensibly because he was on the way to do his own. Several of the men ran excitedly (and "stupidly," in Malik's assessment) to take him up on the offer. The man sold all of their belongings, plus the laundry cart he had borrowed, en route to a crack "mission."

These types of plots were feasible due to the ubiquitous black market in Kensington, which preyed on the economy of addiction. Recovering subjects could literally sell the clothes off their back and the sneakers off their feet in a matter of minutes. They could also fence items stolen from recovery houses such as the laundry from Malik's residents, appliances, videos, DVDs, and even recovery books. Typically, alliances formed within the house where groups of men would engage in surreptitious hustles to get high. Malik's only recourse was to drop random urine screens on his residents whenever he was suspicious of such activity. On one occasion, he exposed a ring of active users in his house by threatening the entire census with urine screens. After a string of confessions, Malik learned that six of the ten men in his house had been getting high under his roof, a crushing blow to both revenues (as he was forced to kick them all out) and his ego.

Other relapse stories hit even closer to home for Malik. He had made personal projects out of family members, bringing them down from Newark to get sober in Kensington. He also rescued Blanche, his love interest, who had lived homeless on the streets of Newark for seven years. Blanche stayed sober largely due to Malik's help. In the spring of 2004, they got married and moved into an apartment. But for every success story like this, Malik faced multiple failures. For example, Malik had brought a sister-in-law from Newark to Philadelphia, only to watch her cycle in and out of several recovery houses. She ended up in the Kensington prostitution market, a disturbingly common outcome for women who relapsed on crack. Malik's brother, a long-term heroin addict, also came to Kensington to get clean. With no medical insurance, he was forced to detox in Malik's house without appropriate medical assistance. He was so dope sick that he finally stole several items and left AHAD to get high. After that, Malik did not hear from his brother for over a year.

Other relapses, some already touched on throughout this chapter, involved members of Malik's inner circle. This included Garvey, who relapsed on crack and ended up back in the Philadelphia corrections system in the spring of 2004. At last report, he was trying his lot once again in the Kensington recovery house system. Tessio, a sixty-two-year-old Italian from Brooklyn who had charmed Malik's entire house (including me) during his three-month tenure in the winter of 2003, returned to his "bottle gang" at the corner of K&A. Tessio was known in the scene as a dying breed, a "garden variety drunk" from the old school who was proud to have burned out social services and detoxes in three different states (New York, Connecticut, and New Jersey). Tessio's relapse was perhaps predictable, as he was known to have been in over sixty recovery houses in Kensington. When I left Philadelphia in 2004, he could still be found staggering around drunk in Kensington at various points of the day. At our last meeting, Tessio told me that he had resolved to die drunk on the street.

Brilliante, a long-term friend of the founding members of AHAD, relapsed several times throughout my fieldwork. At last report, he could still be found pumping gas and "squeegee-ing" at the BP gas station on Lehigh Avenue. Jack, the self-proclaimed beatnik in his late fifties, relapsed and

lived on the streets before being arrested for public urination and intoxi-
cation. And Sarah, who had offered her apartment as a place of respite to
Blanche and Malik during their recovery house days, relapsed on crack after
two years and "lost everything." Albert continues to live on the streets of
Kensington as a panhandler. Delmar, who had accumulated close to fifteen
hundred dollars in a savings account that Malik helped him to set up using
income from his various temporary jobs as well as a tax refund, went on yet
another crack mission in the spring of 2004 that exhausted his savings in a
single night. At last report, he was living in the Ridge Avenue shelter and
trying to get back into a Kensington recovery house.

Even Rufus, who had successfully stayed clean for two years while becoming a manager of a parking lot in Center City, eventually embezzled
funds from his job for crack. At last report, he was collecting unemployment and living with his sister, struggling to reenter the recovering community. Perhaps most surprisingly, Infinite "fell off" in the spring of 2004
after accumulating more than eighteen months of sobriety. Infinite and his
wife, Lucia, had moved into an apartment to care for three nephews that
had been removed from the home of Lucia's crack-addicted sister. While
living on the state funds they received as the children's guardians, Infinite
began to drink 40-ounce malt liquors again, and Lucia followed suit by returning to regular crack use. During my last visit with Infinite, I found him
drunk in the middle of the day, surrounded by his three young nephews in
a chaotic and dilapidated apartment.

Of the twenty-five men that I came to know rather intimately at AHAD,
only Malik was successful in staying sober. Malik and Blanche celebrated eight
and seven years, respectively, in April of 2009. Several others had relapsed in
Malik's house, but I did not know them due to their short stays; countless
others had relapsed in Bilal's house. Moreover, apart from Rufus, Malik was
the only man to procure stable employment. Most of the men continued
to suffer from chronic unemployment and/or underemployment in the service sector and the informal day labor economy. Others remained on welfare
and/or were continuously incarcerated. None of the men that I knew were
able to leave Kensington despite stated desires to do so, barring a few that returned to live with relatives in the similarly impoverished neighborhoods of
West or North Philadelphia, or Newark or Baltimore. At first glance, these
outcomes prove Malik's claim that "[out of every] one hundred people that
come through the recovery houses, only two come for recovery."

The term *relapse* is quite common in the recovery house scene, perhaps
mirroring its prevalent usage in drug and alcohol treatment and research.
It is not my intention here to imply causality, or to advance conventional

empirical arguments about "outcomes" related to treatment intervention, or variables related to relapse, per se. What I can say is that the vast majority of recovering subjects that I encountered continued to use substances with disproportionately devastating effects (homelessness, prostitution, incarceration, untimely death). And I can say that these relapses were often borne out of the travails of persistent poverty, suggesting an overall outcome contiguous with longstanding strategies of warehousing as opposed to the actual transformation of selves.

Perhaps relapse reveals a broken contract between recovering technologies and the dreams of individual subjects. I have also conceived of relapse as a form of resistance, or a strategic alliance with a separate economy of knowledge/power—albeit a self-defeating resistance that is in some ways consistent with the basic tenets of cultural reproduction theory.[6] But what I ultimately want to argue is that a recovering subject's cycles of backsliding and relapse articulate with a new strategy of spatial containment and a new mode of regulating bodies in the post-welfare moment. In this sense, the meaning of relapse can only be made visible when considering the travails of persistent poverty, the predatory nature of recovery house markets (both client and labor), and the churning logics of warehousing strategies at the lower reaches of the labor market. Relapse and the vagaries of poor choices are inextricably linked to the pre-scripted channels of the recovery rubric—both locally, within the recovery house itself, and beyond, within the realm of state regulation.

## Relapse at the Local Level: Risk Management for the Recovery House Operator

For the operator, the risk for client abuse of the recovery house system is quite real. The issue of relapse provides a simple explanation of how this unfolds. Addicts can easily exhaust an entire month's income in just a few hours on a crack binge. Without money or a place to live, they seek refuge in another recovery house that will carry them in the interim, only to go back out again when the next welfare check arrives. As Malik explained, these abuses lead managers to devise intake policies and procedures to prevent losses:

> MALIK: After a while at Positive Attitudes, we was carrying so many of them, right, it was a thing where it was like, shit, if I fuck up my check I'll run to Positive Attitudes, because it's good for a month, and then when my check comes I'll leave again. So I came up with a thing where I said, "Fuck that, you know what? If you coming around on the fifth and

you just got your check on the third and it's gone, you need to go to a
shelter or somewhere else because you not coming in here."

The issue of relapse further illustrates how market discipline operates in
the industry. Economic risk becomes an organizing and motivating force,
as operators are subject to human factors associated with their economic
inputs (that is, clients) and the ephemeral and transitory qualities of poverty
and addiction. Getting "burned" too many times ultimately leads operators
to develop street-level cost-benefit expertise. Managers balance their desire
to help the fellow addict with the economic realities of sustaining a fragile subsistence niche. They perform this balancing act while dealing with a
population that is unstable by definition.

Consider, for example, a standard component of recovery house operator
wisdom: seasonal factors influence the relapse rate within the census, and by
extension, weather influences house revenues. The relatively steady flow of
bodies in the winter months makes things easier economically, whereas the
summer months pose a great challenge to most programs.

> MALIK: It's going to get cold soon, and that's when people go into reha-
> bilitation. They don't want to be released from rehab, so they enter the
> recovery houses, which keeps the numbers up. So in the wintertime you
> do good things with your money, you have to. You take that money you
> get in the wintertime to improve your house, because in the summertime
> people are quick to leave. Man, you should see 'em bail out in the sum-
> mer, they bail out on check day, that's why you gotta walk with your men
> [escort them]. They going to go back out there and stay in the fucking
> trees, man, or you can stay in an abandominium. They think they don't
> need the recovery house when it gets warm.

Even for successful recovery house operators like Clarence and Murphy,
maintaining the census was always a problem, especially during the warmer
months. But the risk of census instability remained year round for most
operators, albeit perhaps regarding issues of quality rather than quantity. In
winter, there were always people looking to merely come in out of the cold
for shelter, often for purposes related to getting "plugged in" to the public
welfare system rather than for recovery itself:

> MALIK: See, this time of year [winter], look what you getting, you not get-
> ting stayers [sic], you getting motherfuckers that it's just hard for them
> out there, and they come in here and they run. So if they don't come up

in here with no money, man, chances are you may not get no money from them. Because by the time you figure it out and put it all together, they know how long it takes to get plugged in. They can stuff you with the welfare man and then go somewhere else.

This kind of cyclical, persistent instability in the recovery house industry produces a conflictual relationship between recovery house operators and clients. And no matter what the season, Malik and others were constantly aware that not all subjects are embraced by—or choose to embrace—the tenets of recovering subjectivity. Those on the margins must be governed in harsher ways when they threaten fragile subsistence economies, and abandoned when they become a liability.

The absence of formal licensure in the recovery house industry creates conditions under which operators are free to design and deploy virtually any technique they see fit to maximize their interests and mitigate economic losses. As one example, Malik, Clarence, and Bilal all spoke separately of a blacklist that once existed in Kensington's recovery house community. To reduce the incessant hemorrhaging of clients, the list banned certain individuals known to be, as operators called them, "chronic relapsers."

> MALIK: When I first came down here, the community had a blacklist. If you messed up in my house, I would send the list in my circle, I would send it to New Desires, Positive Attitudes, you know, everybody in the box, telling them that this guy fucked me, and if he fucked me he'll fuck you. That list traveled, and it's still here, but it just ain't visible like it was before.

The blacklist instantiates a rare case of cooperation among operators, deployed primarily as a way to protect themselves from "taking hits." Economic losses caused several operators to deploy tactics that were more coercive. Some have even purchased ATM machines for the automatic procurement of rent payments on the days that benefits transfer. Others tried to limit client mobility by "locking" a person's welfare check to the address of the recovery house. The director of the Positive Attitudes program even proposed an amendment to welfare regulations that would require addicts to stay in *one* recovery house over their nine months of GA eligibility. While this move to change welfare regulations was both short lived and unsuccessful, other methods have been more effective as strategies to anchor clients to the address of the recovery house. The most typical is the standard practice of confiscating access cards. Client resistance to this practice becomes even more difficult when framed as a recovery issue by operators and residents alike. In Murphy's recovery house, I witnessed a man who resisted handing over his access card being called out by his peers for practicing "dope fiend behavior." In a similar vein, Clarence justified his practice of confiscating access cards in terms of how willing one was to go to any lengths for sobriety:

> CLARENCE: We keep everyone's access cards, and we have a standard form that they sign that allows us to do that.
>
> RF: Do they usually make a stink about that, or do they accept it?
>
> CLARENCE: Well, again we go back to this question: how willing are you?

Confiscation of access cards is one among many practices that ultimately constrict recovering subjects, despite the stated principles of choice, responsibility, and autonomy. Quite significantly, these tactics rework, or at the very least complicate, the welfare practice of placing discretionary funds directly into the hands of the welfare "consumer." While the policy logic of the state is partially grounded in the impulses of devolution and reduction of bureaucratic casework in order to "liberate" the welfare subject (or, rather simply, to "cut checks" by dispersing funds to the access card), we can see a form of re-regulation taking place in the coercive tactics of the informal recovery house operator.

A separate but related practice requires welfare recipients to surrender their benefits by making the manager of the house their actual payee. At the onset of my fieldwork, this practice was quite controversial. However, it later became steadily more acceptable across the industry, based on an apparent intensification of competition and an outbreak of especially resistant/abusive clients said to be chronic relapsers. This practice left clients with no control over their welfare benefits. As Bilal noted, some houses went even further:

> BILAL: See now, some houses are getting even slicker, they using this thing called power of attorney. It's a legal document that says they have the right to decide all the legal issues that would affect [your welfare benefits]. But in effect they already control this. You are forfeiting your legal rights . . .
>
> RF: To control your money?
>
> BILAL: To control *you*—they can make decisions in terms of 302-ing you [admitting a person to psychiatric hospitalization against that person's will], mainly because that document alludes to being incompetent to handle your own affairs. Therefore, you need a "payee" to handle your affairs, and that payee is the recovery house. You know, it's the house's responsibility

to do your grocery shopping, see what you eat, see that you wipe your ass. And you have no right to any money unless they dole it out to you.

I learned about the evolution of the payee practice from Malik, who had taken so many hits by the winter of 2004 that even he ultimately adopted the policy. And while it was not his preference to do so, several necessary tactics for economic survival often compromised Malik's recovery ethics:

> MALIK: I try to stay as close to the letter as I possibly can, but you can't always stay on the letter, man, because there are some things you have to do that are not written to make this [recovery house thing] work. You know you going to have to institute some things that ain't in the [12-step] recovery program.

Once again we see the systemically entrenched ethical dilemmas that recovery entrepreneurs face while operating in areas of spatially concentrated poverty. The social relations of recovery markets are permeated by tensions, antagonisms, and conflicts that continually threaten to erode utopian visions of recovery, and to destabilize the accumulation/subsistence process. In response, operators are prompted to use regulatory tactics to reinstate equilibrium. On the surface, disciplinary census tactics are perhaps contradictory to the principles of liberal governance, and contradictory to the functioning of free markets. But they also yield agonistic social relations—in this case, between addicts and recovery house operators—that have become embedded within the very structure of the recovery house system. It is this very agonism that endows the system with a marked, if constantly evolving, institutional coherence.

Tight profit margins and the pressures of subsistence entrench (and exacerbate) disciplinary and exploitive tactics, as operators move to shepherd and control the census. This is but one form—and one relatively benign form—of regulation that inheres in the recovery house industry. The structural dynamics of relapse and subsistence are part of a broader, contingent relationship between the recovery house, the post-welfare state, and the postindustrial city.

## Relapse within and beyond the Recovery House: Regulatory Consequences with the State

Whereas relapse affords the individual some measure of relief from, or even resistance to, impoverishment in Kensington, it also forces him to "roll the dice" in a game that is already fixed at multiple scales. Quite apart from the disciplinary measures of the operator per se, the stakes bear out in the rigorous urine screening protocols of various regulatory institutions, from public welfare, to the Department of Human Services, to probation/parole. In many recovery houses, clients must submit to urine tests as a residency requirement (a positive screen is grounds for immediate dismissal and a call to the caseworker or parole officer). All of the city's CBH (Community Behavioral Health)-funded outpatient treatment centers require random urine screens. In fact, most third-party payers (including Medicaid managed care and the probation and parole department) require urine screens as a matter of contract. As a result, urine screens were commonplace in the most informal of Kensington's recovery programs. While Malik typically deployed the urine screen only when he suspected drug use (this was also due to the fact that screening was expensive), he explained that in larger programs screening was part of living in a recovery house:

> MALIK: See, that's what I'm trying to tell you: Positive Attitudes had a
> hookup, they used to pee us at least twice a week, everybody in the
> program. You come in and he'd stand right there and you took a piss, the
> whole program. They used to have one company that they sent all the
> urines to, like a hundred at a time.

The concept of relapse enables us to use the house itself as a way to track the many ways in which the state reaches into the lives (indeed, the biochemistry) of recovery subjects, even as it keeps its hands off the recovery house. On several fronts, we see how a downsized and privatized state is no less governmental or regulatory. If one wanted to use the recovery house "to address old behaviors, patterns, and habits," the outcome was mutually beneficial to the addict and the state. However, if one wanted simply to use the recovery house to "go fuck shit up," as Malik often said, this too was covered by the system. Along pre-scripted channels, the game in a way was rigged before it even began. It is in this sense that the management of relapse must be conceived as a symptom of our contemporary urban condition.

## The "Wreckage of the Past"

The regulatory effects of the recovery house thrive not only on systematic impoverishment, spatial containment, and the failed choices of drug addicts and alcoholics in the unfolding present, but also on what many addicts refer to as "the wreckage of the past." In this sense, even the most successful recovering addicts—those who have accumulated long-term sobriety and even achieved social mobility at some level—continue to experience ongoing encounters with the state regulatory apparatus. While all recovering subjects must contend with the broad array of personal consequence, ostensibly stemming from years of active addiction, the consequences clearly vary across divisions of race and class. It is one thing to get sober through middle-class channels such as an Employee Assistance Program (EAP), in the context of a well-paying job that supports a family. It is an entirely different matter to find oneself sober with an eighth-grade education, failing health, a debilitating legal and credit history, and no sign of stable employment in sight.

I watched "the wreckage of the past" implode several sobriety plans during my fieldwork. The burden of addiction histories, forged along racial and class lines, became too much to bear for recovering subjects even years into sobriety, whether they were clients, operators, or counselors. Oftentimes, the wreckage of the past entered the realm of health, as past experiences of living hard on the street came back to punish the bodies of recovering subjects. For instance, Malik and Blanche both suffered from severe dental problems and had to race the Medicaid clock to have their remaining teeth pulled (their respective ages were fifty-two and thirty-nine). The couple also had chronic problems with their feet, undergoing several surgeries to relieve the pain of past abuses. Malik linked these types of problems directly to years of street addiction:

MALIK: Blanche had to go in to get her feet fixed. They cut the bone [on the side] and shaved it down. I had it done three times. Here, this is mine [*shows me how his toes went out of alignment to the point that they had to be broken and realigned*]. When you an addict or alcoholic, you develop a walk, and it's a bad walk, just like when your posture is bad. You see the methadone people [*hunches over and drags a leg*], you ever see them? All of them walk the same. You develop that walk, man, and you wear stuff out of season. Some people wear boots all fucking year round, these motherfuckers wear boots in the summer. You not treating your feet like they supposed to be treated, and your feet let you know.

While these health issues were relatively manageable, others were more serious. Like many men in the recovery house scene, Malik had constant liver complications stemming from the hepatitis C he had contracted using dirty needles in the early 1980s. He would often say that he had to deal with his hepatitis C without complaining, as it was he himself who had gone out and practiced high-risk behaviors "voluntarily" (despite the fact that access to medical care for his ongoing ailments was impossible after being cut off from welfare). Similarly, several recovering addicts in Kensington lived with HIV/AIDS contracted from intravenous drug use and/or past prostitution. One close friend of Malik and Blanche's, who was HIV-positive, remained clean for two years before succumbing to a relapse on crack due to stressors from her illness. Within a matter of days, she sold everything in her furnished apartment and returned to street life under the El. I also came to know two recovering addicts who later died in recovery houses (one in Malik's house, and one in Bilal's) due to liver complications stemming from years of poverty-stricken addiction. The devastation from the wreckage of the past continued to reflect class stratification and the uneven consequences of history.

Other pronounced complications related to the wreckage of the past stemmed from ongoing entanglements with the legal system, as well as pressures and debilitations from child support payments and debt/credit problems. Infinite, for example, was forced to return to jail three times during his sobriety due to unresolved legal fees, and probation and parole violations. Similarly, two other AHAD men in addition to Garvey were thrown into jail based on their inability to pay back child support. Blanche was suddenly cut from the Pennsylvania welfare rolls when it was discovered that she had outstanding arrest warrants and court costs in the state of New Jersey. This type of scenario was quite typical for recovering subjects, who were often forced to sit in jail for weeks without recourse due to bureaucratic red tape.

Such occurrences were not limited simply to newcomers in the recovery process. During the winter of 2003, I arrived at Malik's house to learn that Bilal had been arrested after a routine traffic stop. Bilal had a warrant out for his arrest dating back to the late 1980s, when he was charged with welfare fraud in Camden, New Jersey. Despite his status as a model citizen, assistant substance abuse counselor, and recovery house director with over six years of sobriety, Bilal spent almost a month in jail and his car was immediately impounded. Bilal explained the original charges: when he began to use heroin again after four years clean, he relapsed after being diagnosed as having cancer.

> BILAL: I thought for sure I was dying. So if I believe I am dying, I'm going to go out the way I think I should go out, and that's what I did. I started using drugs again, after four years of being clean. And that was just clean time—that wasn't no program time; I didn't know nothing about the program. So I got high every day, and I got my drugs by any means I had to. I did some shit out there, I know that . . . that's my biggest worry is I

don't know what else they are going to come up with out of my past. I always worry about that. I don't even know if they got more stuff, but this one was for welfare fraud, that's what the original warrant was for, that's what showed up on the cop's computer screen when he pulled me over. He was going to let me go for driving without a license, but when he ran a background check on me, this shit popped up. So you see, the wreckage of my past is no joke, man.

Even the most successful recovering addicts, those who were able to integrate into the formal treatment sector as assistant counselors, continued to backslide due to insufficient supports, persistent poverty, poor education, and generally low social capital. As Billings explained, there was always a risk in hiring paraprofessional counselors from the recovery house scene, as they were prone to ongoing legal problems or relapses. Moreover, due to a lack of training and a lack of adequate supervision and financial support, paraprofessionals often became overwhelmed with the rigors of paperwork under Philadelphia's fee-for-service behavioral health reimbursement structure. Tensions in these areas often resulted in termination of employment. In fact, Bilal had recently left his job working for Billings due to paperwork problems at the time of his arrest, leaving him unemployed for the duration of my fieldwork. Billings explained that three of his counselors had experienced similar fates:

RF: How is your staff holding up?
BILLINGS: Well, they are holding up as best as they can. Bilal left, though, he got in a little trouble. Well, first he left because he wasn't doing his notes, and that cost me about $3,700. When CBH [Community Behavioral Health] does their audit they take charts, and about $3,700 worth of notes weren't accounted for, so I have to pay that back. But beyond that I found out that unfortunately Bilal had some other matters pending that he hadn't taken care of, so he is incarcerated now.
    And then Benjie also, I had to let him go; Benjie couldn't keep his notes up, and for whatever reason it seems that Benjie has gone out and relapsed. Benjie was probably having some problems with drinking or whatever else, I've been working with him for a lot of years, this is the third time that I have taken him back. But when it comes to pressure, he just can't handle it. And then I told you I had to let Joe go because he relapsed and then broke into the office after hours to steal . . . well, he didn't break in because he had a key. He has come back and apologized, he apologized to the staff and he apologized to me.

Billings recounted the struggles of three of his recovering counselors, two of whom had relapsed and one of whom had been incarcerated. He explained that this was "the nature of the game," made somewhat ironic by the fact that the city encouraged hiring recovering addicts:

> BILLINGS: That's one of those things, when you hire assistant counselors you run the risk, because you know these people—Bilal, Benjie, and Joe were all assistant counselors. I spent a lot of time with them. The state and CBH wants us to be involved with recovering people in our programs, but there is always a risk because of their past and current problems. It is just a part of the business that you want to take people who are recovering, and they have an ability to relate to the clients. But sometimes you have that problem with people who are not yet fully committed to the process.

Indeed, Billings knew the score on those "not yet fully committed to the process." He himself had a torrid past, and had spent a significant part of his life in and out of prisons. He had first operated a federally funded methadone clinic in the early 1970s, but then relapsed on heroin and embezzled federal funds, subsequently running the clinic into the ground. He spent much of the 1980s in prison before coming back to open up his current treatment center. As an ex-felon, Billings could not get licensure. Like several recovery entrepreneurs that I knew, his business ventures were in either his wife's or a partner's name.

The wreckage of the past does not always lead to relapse. Yet even for those who remain sober through all its trials, social mobility is greatly limited. For example, after Bilal became unemployed, he experienced a rapid financial decline (exacerbated by legal fees) that led him back into hustling despite his senior status in the recovery industry. During the last eight months of my fieldwork, Bilal developed a movie empire in the basement of his recovery house, copying bootleg videotapes and burning DVDs to sell from his living room. He also returned to selling Muslim oils and incense, and began to market "recovery-oriented" items such as tapes of basic texts (the Big Book of AA and the Basic Text of NA), poetry, and memorabilia from the AA cofounders. All the while, he worked to put together numerous proposals to get his own recovery house program off the ground (and enlisted my help), but was unable to get under way because of his poor credit history. At one point, Bilal was hired at a separate outpatient treatment center, only to be dismissed when his criminal record check failed. He remained unemployed until the end of 2004, surviving on his position as recovery house director in addition to revenues from his various entrepreneurial pursuits. At fifty-eight years of age, the wreckage of his past was indeed no joke:

> BILAL: I got two things that are big in my life right now: I don't have a job, and I don't have a lady. Notice the order I put those things in. 'Cause for me, a job must come first. But as it stands now, I'm a broke-ass son of a bitch. I wake up in the morning and I say to myself, I need $35 to get a physical, so my first goal is, let me make $35 hustling to get a physical. Once I make that, I put it up. I can generally do that selling oils, incense, and the DVDs and cassettes. Sometimes I do other things too, sometimes I write letters for people and I charge them a dollar for my service. They think nothing of a dollar, but those dollars add up. I pick up pennies off the ground. Like my daddy used to tell me, those pennies make dollars, and I've never forgotten that. You'd be surprised, one day I brought in thirty-seven dollars' worth of pennies, man.

Following my move to Chicago, I received a phone call from Malik one night telling me that Bilal had done something drastic. After seven years clean and a five-year stint running his Positive Attitudes program, Bilal pulled a rental truck up to the recovery house in the middle of the night, filled it with stolen items from the house, sold them, purchased as much heroin as he could, and then proceeded to abandon the truck on a Kensington side street. Malik did not see or hear from him for weeks. When Bilal finally resurfaced, he moved in with his AA sponsor and began methadone treatment. He continues to take methadone at the time of this writing.

## Conclusion

At first glance, we might conclude that recovery houses fail to work as mechanisms of self-transformation. But what's in play here are a series of agonistic relationships, in this case spawned from the systemic failures of a peculiar form of marketized voluntarism. In the recovery house movement, the inexorable demise of utopian ideals pervades collective experience. Recovery house operators, often against their own best intentions, are forced to transmute risk, vulnerability, and further suffering onto recovering subjects. However, with no effective means of redress and a highly contingent state of tenure, the recovery house client and operator alike get trapped within a variegated set of disciplinary forces. Relapse and the wreckage of the past have become visible as both instrument and effect of a new mode of poverty management, trapping the subject between the predatory subsistence market of the recovery house, the deregulated low-wage service sector, and the many forms of statecraft associated with each (from probation and parole to formal treatment, to welfare administration, child support, and the behavioral health system). Within this expanded recovery matrix, the extent to which active drug and alcohol use continues seems almost irrelevant, or simply beyond the point. The system itself thrives as much, if not more, on the guarantee of failures as it does on success.

# Unruly Spaces of Managed Persistence  5

In the November 8, 2001, issue of the *Philadelphia City Paper*, the journalist Gwen Shaffer captured the weekly's cover story with perhaps the most comprehensive media exposé to date of the Philadelphia recovery house movement. Shaffer's story carried the provocative title "Silent Treatment: Hundreds of Unregulated Drug-Recovery Houses Operate in Philadelphia without Any Government Oversight."[1] While this account offered a relatively fair assessment of the many positive yet contradictory elements of recovery houses—mainly by extolling the ways in which house operators since the early 1980s had "started rebuilding abandoned houses and transforming them into places of support"—the headline is quite emblematic.[2] It reflects widespread references in the media, in political circles, and on the street to the proliferation of an "underground" and "unmonitored industry" comprising "illegally operated" recovery houses.

Throughout the 1990s in particular, the Philadelphia press put forth a story of an isolated, rogue movement said to resist regulation and "government oversight" based on its propensities for rampant exploitation and profits.[3] In many respects, the mid-1990s was the apex of community and city opposition to recovery houses, as allegations about illegal activities in several houses in the Kensington neighborhood circulated widely. The most notorious scandal dates back to 1995, when an investigation led by the State of Pennsylvania exposed an "underground system" of interstate travel operated by the New Jersey Department of Probation and Parole. In violation of the interstate compact stipulating that felons would not be relocated across state lines without notifying proper authorities, New Jersey had "quietly shipped about 1000 drug addicted felons" into Pennsylvania recovery houses. Hundreds of these had gone directly to unlicensed Kensington programs that lacked any type of professional staff or legitimate monitoring structure. State welfare officials found that the recovery houses immediately directed the parolees to acquire voter registration cards in order to get on the Pennsylvania welfare rolls, forcing Philadelphians to "literally [pay] the consequences, in welfare support, medical costs and [increasingly] blighted neighborhoods."[4] Critics contended that the system cost taxpayers at least $500 monthly per client in cash, food stamps, and medical assistance.

The scandalous nature of these events, along with the recovery house movement's historically troubled and stigmatized reputation, leads to an important question: how have recovery houses managed to survive, indeed even to thrive, given their status as "unregulated" spaces functioning under the radar of government control? For analytical guidance with this question, I rely on a growing cadre of scholars seeking to understand urban informality and the proliferation of governmentalities in slums.[5] Much of this literature is driven—either explicitly or implicitly—by the following essential premise: whereas many underground economies function by virtue of their invisibility, irregular housing settlements do not enjoy such a luxury. This premise is, perhaps, a simple truism, but one that prompts important parallel questions about the conspicuous nature of "illegally operated" and "unregulated" recovery houses in Philadelphia's urban core. What's at stake here are questions concerning the *persistence* of informal settlement space, which provides inroads to questions of how nonintervention by the city and the states manifests as a mechanism of power in its own right, as well as how informal regulatory measures are taken up on the street.

As a way to explore these questions in this chapter, I build on Alan Smart's conceptual framework for the persistence of informal settlement space. Recovery houses meet several criteria for Smart's schematic, particularly that of *market persistence*, which occurs when a continued demand for services creates subsistence opportunities; and *inertial persistence*, whereby various forms of illicit activity thrive in an ecology of state inaction. The primary issue that I want to build on is Smart's notion of *managed persistence*, which refers to cases where the government allows an activity to continue in order to reap certain benefits.[6] Using managed persistence as a heuristic, I will trace the contours of enabling relationships between recovery house actors and Philadelphia's Department of Licenses and Inspections, city government more generally, the welfare state, and the geography of the Kensington community. Recovery houses become visible not merely as a haven for either benevolent self-helpers or unscrupulous actors in the informal economy, but also as a manifestation of postindustrial decline and post-Keynesian trends in social welfare.

## An Ecology of Managed Persistence?

A number of cursory "ecological" or "conjunctural" factors enable recovery house proliferation in Philadelphia.[7] The glut of a cheap and degraded housing stock in nongentrifying urban enclosures, and the dearth of affordable housing across the city, is an obvious place to start. On the side of the recovery house operator, the presence of some thirty thousand abandoned row houses, located mostly in West Philly, North Philly, and Kensington, suppresses housing values to readily accessible (if not fire-sale) levels. On the side of the client, my fieldwork showed that perhaps equally important as the agenda of recovery itself, recovery houses provided much needed alternatives to fair-market rents. Over the past thirty years, an increasing state of housing "un-affordability" has existed in Philadelphia.[8] Earned income and public assistance have not kept pace with rising housing costs, as the value of the minimum wage has declined by 30% while the buying power of welfare payments has decreased by 60%.[9] Philadelphia has a deficit of thirty thousand affordable housing units for rental households having annual incomes below $20,000. In this context, recovery houses play a vital role in providing affordable housing for the impoverished, particularly those living on $205 per month in GA benefits. In fact, Malik and others often stated that people rarely enter recovery houses to achieve sobriety, but rather do so simply because they cannot afford a place to live. For the same reason, the lack of "transitional housing" and the unattainability of independent living often kept men trapped in recovery houses for years at a time.

Clustered around a cheap housing supply in areas of spatially concentrated poverty, the presence of recovery houses drew large numbers of addicts into one of the only *expanding* forms of affordable housing in Philadelphia. City officials also recognized this. When asked about the future of

the recovery house movement, CODAAP Housing Initiative coordinator
Marvin Levine attributed the growth of the recovery house networks to the
dearth of affordable housing in the city and its degraded housing stock:

> ML: If there were more affordable, decent housing in Philadelphia, there
> would be less need for recovery houses. They are filling a niche because
> the older, poorer housing stock really hasn't been upgraded. It's an old
> rust belt city, and as the population has fled it has left a lot of hulking
> shells and warehouses that periodically burn down. [In terms of recovery
> houses], we can see that something has filled the shell.

In addition to affordable housing, Levine alluded to another commonly
cited factor explaining the persistence of the houses. Operators contributed—however inadvertently—to former mayor John Street's antiblight
campaign by occupying abandoned or vacant properties.[10] Many operators
touted their role in fueling the economies of local businesses, since the large
consumption powers of collective living arrangements have an impact even
if driven by the pooling of food stamps. In this sense, Bilal envisioned the
houses as a revitalization strategy, because reductions in crime helped businesses return to Kensington:

> BILAL: Right now, Kensington is on the upswing, and it's just lately that
> people are beginning to understand this. It's mainly due to recovery,
> because we are taking addicts off the streets who would normally be out
> there trying to rob somebody. And if it is not safe to run a business in this
> area, your customers are at risk, your product is at risk, and anybody that
> comes in with merchandise, trucks, delivery, they at risk.

The ability to generate revenue through an informal social service market is another explanatory factor that allows recovery houses to persist,
particularly given their location in opportunity-starved environments. But
perhaps more important, and especially since profits are so rarely achieved,
most recovery entrepreneurs believe that their presence and capacity to persist stems from the social services they provide in absence of formal funding.
Informal service delivery accommodates not only the citywide mandates of
fiscal austerity, but also the contemporary obsession in social policy with
market models and the impulse to capitalize on the innovations of recovery
entrepreneurs.
The product of "recovering technologies"[11] also suggests a great confluence between recovery house knowledge/power and the contemporary

rationalities of the post-welfare state. Recovery forges alliances between the liberation of the self and the pathways to personal success, ostensibly allowing subjects to break the chains of poverty, welfare dependency, and incarceration.[12] Recovery has emerged as post-welfare antipoverty mechanism par excellence, assuring subjects that they can change, achieve self-mastery, control their own destiny, and transform themselves into the oft-repeated phrase, "productive members of society." By maximizing self-interest and empowerment in service of a recovery lifestyle, the conduct of everyday existence is recast as a series of problems to be managed in the informal realm of civil society. The ethics of recovery enterprise infuse previously unruly segments of the populace with mechanisms of self-governance by mirroring (and in some cases refracting or deflecting) state bureaucracies. Traditional forms of regulation become seemingly obsolete, no longer necessary to ensure harmony between the social objectives of the state and the personal desires of addicts. It is in this sense that the discourse of recovery, drawing on the self-steering capacities of impoverished subjects, becomes an able partner for the devolutionary welfare state.

Along more modest lines, many operators contended that their programs were necessary as a stopgap measure, a mechanism of last resort for the social residuum. In their proud assessments, operators took the dregs of society, those whom no one else would take. In addition to feeding and clothing the addict, the houses "carried" them while they awaited birth certificates and social security cards to obtain public assistance.[13] Moreover, some of the larger recovery house operators boasted of having an excess of twenty people in their programs with no means of supporting themselves. We can see, then, how social and managerial costs are deferred to Kensington recovery houses. These beliefs led Malik and Bilal to surmise that the future of the industry is hardly in jeopardy. The range of benefits provided, not the least of which was keeping people off the streets and maintaining social order, was indispensable in their eyes.

BILAL: First of all, recovery houses serve society's purpose, because we're taking homeless people, drug addicts and criminals if you will, off the street. And if we can do something three out of ten times, that's less that they got to lock up and spend over $30,000 a year on in prison. So the benefits outweigh the problems, especially when you can get the community involved, and they buy in. If we can take three out of ten and make them productive members of society again, [that's saying something]. And in the meantime we keep people off the streets, if even for a little while. So they're not in a hurry to tear this system down.

Bilal's comments on the role of the recovery house networks in reducing the prison population reflect common perceptions among Kensington's recovery house operators. Several went so far as to say that the presence of recovery houses was inversely proportional to the crime rate in the neighborhood, hailing their active role in community policing initiatives such as Operation Sunrise and Safe Streets. Clarence, the owner and operator of six recovery houses, added that the welfare dollars provided to GA clients was a small price to pay for a mechanism that facilitates societal goals such as crime control and deinstitutionalization:

> CLARENCE: Recovery houses are good for the community; for one
> thing it keeps the problems down. Because if we have less people on
> drugs we have less problems. That's not even a given: if you remove the
> people that you have on drugs, you remove a large portion of the crime
> rate, so that's making it safe. So the minute that you start to take things
> away from the recovering community, what you are asking for is a higher
> crime rate. If they took away the welfare, addicts would start robbing
> every day and nobody would have a place to live. Everybody cannot
> afford an apartment; everybody cannot afford a house. Some people are
> uneducated and unable to do it. And some people are institutionalized for
> life.
>
> [Society] said they wanted to get away from that part, saying, "Well,
> we don't want people to be institutionalized." So it's like this, either you
> allow this recovery house thing, or you build more jails, which [in turn]
> makes our taxes increase because we still gotta pay for them. So how do
> we balance this? The recovery house community is the balance. They
> don't always see that, man, but that's the balance.

Clarence offered a typical operator's rendition of the stabilizing, ancillary functions of the recovery house in Philadelphia. Billings took this logic a step further, emphasizing that the informal nature of recovery houses protected them from shifting political currents:

> BILLINGS: You know treatment budgets are always in jeopardy, but the
> recovery houses always pop up again. Because the fellas do make a few
> dollars—every guy in the house gets $205, and he pays that toward the
> recovery house for his room and board and food stamps. Sometimes in
> turn they use them for cheap labor, and there is a lot that goes on, but
> if they weren't organized like that then all these people would be on the
> streets. And then they would be at *their* houses [the city elite], breaking in

and stuff like that, and they know that. I'm just giving it to you straight as to what it's really holding together. If it wasn't for recovery houses, we'd have people running up and down the street.

Focusing on the social control functions of relief, Billings offered something of a spin on the classic regulatory perspective on social welfare.[14] It is in a similar spirit that Jacob Riis' seminal text, *How the Other Half Lives*, can be read not so much as an exercise in benevolence, but as a way of sounding the alarm to the ruling class.[15] But in the case of recovery houses, the argument extolling their function in "keeping the balance" is quite pervasive among operators, in terms of both crime control and their unique functions in an age of urban fiscal austerity. Many treatment providers agreed with this assessment, arguing that the only way to relieve overcrowded institutions and budgetary crisis is to strengthen the treatment sector and its veritable floodplain of recovery houses.

A state budget crisis in the summer of 2003 provided something of an empirical test case for these arguments. Under great time constraints, Governor Ed Rendell put a bare-bones budget in front of a Republican-controlled state House of Representatives, expecting that it would face prima-facie rejection. To everyone's surprise, the house fast-tracked the measure as a political move that would ultimately force Rendell to either veto his own budget or face cuts in social expenditure favorable to conservatives. Among the spending cuts was $104 million in statewide drug and alcohol treatment funding, about $40 million to $44 million of which was targeted for Philadelphia. Consequently, the city faced threats to several of its treatment initiatives, including Forensic Intensive Recovery (FIR), the CODAAP Housing Initiative (CHI), Treatment Court, and the Behavioral Health Special Initiative (BHSI). During the few months that the treatment industry ruminated over the gutting of its financial base, recovery house apologists came forward to champion their cause in compelling ways. Bilal commented that the budget cuts would expose the informal recovery house's irreplaceable role in filling the gaps of retrenchment:

BILAL: Without these houses, there in effect is very little being done in terms of treatment. The rehabs are playing a large part, the detoxes are playing a large part, but that's all getting ready to dry out and fall by the wayside because of lack of funding. So, what's going to be king of the hill now? The recovery houses. The recovery houses are getting ready to move up to another level whether they like it or not, because basically, it's the only institution left standing.

Bilal imagined recovery houses, however fantastically, as providing a full-
scale exit strategy for the state. Similarly, in Malik's eyes, closing doors in
the formal treatment sector meant more clients for programs like his, which
he contended were "privately funded" and therefore immune to political
crisis. Malik was not alone in this assessment, and many saw a potential
"boon" or at the very least a reinvigorated position in the social service sector. At a city hall rally to "restore the funds" for treatment funding, a key
figure in the BHSI initiative agreed.

> RF: Do you see a direct impact of these budgets cuts on recovery houses in
> Philadelphia?
> DF: Oh, yeah, without a doubt, because what's going to happen is because
> there is no D&A [drug and alcohol] treatment, most people are going to
> go into recovery houses, you know, and I think that's cool, at least that's
> there.

In the end the state dodged a bullet, restoring $102 million to the budget for
treatment funds. But in the eyes of many, the crisis revealed the benefits that
the city enjoys from recovery houses.

Thus, factors ranging from the provision of informal social services, to
crime reduction, to their elective affinities with the policy logics of the contemporary welfare moment are common explanations for the persistence
and proliferation of recovery houses in the city of Philadelphia. At first
glance, recovery houses may seem a purely functional if not logical manifestation of a particular historical juncture, following the classic ecological tenets of social disorganization and reorganization. But a more nuanced
understanding requires further exploration of the state's response to the recovery house movement. The following sections explore how regulation is
understood and experienced by recovery house actors and city officials, as
well as how the concept of "un-regulation"—when placed under critical
scrutiny—prompts us to rethink the question of regulation and the concept
of managed persistence.

## The State Response: L&I and the Generative Aspects of Inertial Persistence

> There can be a million of them so long as they are safe . . . so long as they are in
> compliance.
> —L&I UNIT SUPERVISOR STANLEY ROBINSON

Philadelphia's primary default agency for regulation of its recovery houses
is the Department of Licenses and Inspections (L&I). Information concern-

ing the ways in which L&I conceptualizes, oversees, and regulates recovery houses revealed, at least in part, how and why recovery house networks persist in the Kensington community. L&I is the institution responsible for setting minimum health, safety, and maintenance standards for all the city's houses, apartment buildings, and commercial structures. The agency assumes regulatory jurisdiction for recovery houses in the same way as it would for any other type of multiple-occupancy residential building. Unit Supervisor Stanley Robinson and Inspector David Perez explained to me the basic requirements for multiple-occupancy housing inspection licensure, carefully noting that they are concerned solely with the structure itself, not with what goes on programmatically within its walls:

> ROBINSON: First of all, zoning is the first step in order to establish the legal occupancy of the structure. If they are not properly zoned, they are illegal.
> RF: That's different from a boardinghouse license . . .
> ROBINSON: Right; you should be unable to get your license unless you have proper zoning.
> RF: Zoning basically means the land use is appropriate for the neighborhood?
> ROBINSON: That's part of it; you are registering your use with the city, you are letting us know what's going on behind the door of that address. Beyond zoning we are not so much concerned with the agency itself [that is, what the agency *does*], but we are concerned with the legality of the location, which is where licensure also comes in. All structures fall on the lap of Licenses and Inspections—whether it is commercial, industrial, or residential, it has to fall on us. Now if there was another quasi agent that dealt with the *quality* of these [recovery houses], that would fall under them. But we don't get into the quality of the programs, we simply make sure that the structures are up to code so that whoever is inside, for whatever reason, is safe, and doesn't have to worry about a fire or anything like that.
> RF: So you are concerned with space, bricks and mortar, the building, period.
> ROBINSON: The structure, right; we do not regulate the actual programs that they are running.
> PEREZ: It is what you might call life safety, the health and welfare of the person within the four walls.

L&I's jurisdiction pertains to the registration of use, and the legality of the location. Since the agency considers most recovery houses structurally "not in compliance" with zoning and licensing regulations, it classifies them en masse as an illegal form of settlement. Robinson articulated L&I's basic position on the matter:

> ROBINSON: Recovery houses became an issue for the city mainly in the 1990s, and it started because most of these programs were illegal. If we had a list of these things, we would be on it. Because as far as we're concerned, unless we are there to check and give the location a clean bill of health, these people are at risk every time they go to sleep at night. That's our position, because we believe, especially since they are being operated illegally, that there are shortcuts being taken in order to maximize profits. And not that we want to eliminate so much profits, but we want to eliminate shortcuts at the risk of health and safety.

As Robinson made clear, operator malfeasance is an important issue. From the agency's perspective, the operator's willful and financially motivated noncompliance leads inexorably to "shortcuts."

> ROBINSON: These places know what they are supposed to be doing, and they just choose not to. Everybody that has any even minimal knowledge of the city of Philadelphia knows that you need zoning and licenses. But that incurs costs, that incurs the possibility of getting turned down, that incurs a lot of things. Especially if they are receiving money from different agencies or organizations, they want to be able to grab that money up until they get caught by us, because if we get them it's going to hurt in the pocket. Basically, we want to eliminate shortcuts at the risk of health and safety. [And again] not so much that we care about profits, we just want to make sure that they are safe, period.

Specifically, L&I's regulatory attention is tuned to wiring, overcrowding, smoke detectors, use of double-key locks, "main drain" or plumbing problems, and appropriate number of bathrooms. Robinson and Perez explained the basic concerns, as well as their protocol for violations:

> PEREZ: Usually these recovery houses are illegal when we walk in; there are a lot of problems we have to proceed with. You go into some of these houses and you see that they have, like, homemade bunk beds; they establish an illegal occupancy until we get 'em. It's actually an eyesore to the neighborhood until it is properly zoned, or they have become educated in how to operate a so-called recovery house.

ROBINSON: Any of those violations may exist, and depending on how severe those violations are, that will determine our course of action. Sometimes we [give them thirty days to comply and then] come back. Then
the next inspection will send them to municipal court. Or, we might just
cease the operation immediately because we believe that something could
happen tonight that could cause a loss of life.

Despite the sense that illegally operated recovery houses pose a threat to
the safety of their residents, Perez and Robinson cited several factors that in-
hibit their efforts to get a better handle on them. For one, the agency's main
strategy for identifying the houses is only marginally effective, at best.

PEREZ: [For the most part] we rely on neighborhood complaints in order to
learn about these things.

RF: So, if a program slips itself into a neighborhood that's tolerant of the
house, they can go on for years . . .

PEREZ: For years without us knowing, that's right. Unless we go there for a
survey and they open the doors to us, and we end up going in and making
an inspection.

ROBINSON: Which has happened. We have gone there with regular program
surveys and stumbled across them.

PEREZ: But this is a problem within the department, because we don't know
about them unless we get complaints from the communities, like community groups and the neighborhoods.

ROBINSON: And in some neighborhoods, I would guess that Kensington
would be an example of this, if they have existed for a great length of
time it is a normal way of life for them. So they may not know any different, they might not know it as illegal—they just see it as *being*, because
that's what they are used to.

The agency's reactive stance has allowed hundreds of recovery houses to
elude its scrutiny—particularly since they have become so normalized in
places like Kensington. Moreover, even when it does locate noncompliant
actors, L&I faces challenges with enforcement. For one thing, the surfeit
of cheap and degraded housing in Kensington often means that when a
house comes under L&I scrutiny, operators sometimes simply abandon the
location.

ROBINSON: If we go to your location, and you're illegal and the location is
bad enough, we're shutting you down. But unfortunately, what happens

*[margin handwritten note: agency's reactive stance for inspections]*

is they can go move somewhere else, you know what I mean, [which is easy to do in Kensington]. Once they get caught, they move somewhere else, until we catch them again, and that's how we stand right now.

PEREZ: It's true, once we get them they probably try to get zoning, or go through the zoning process, but if they can't get it they just move to another location, without our knowledge of where they are moving.

The issue of abandonment is further compounded by inadequate resources and staffing at L&I. According to Robinson, his chronically underfunded agency cannot keep pace with all the demands that it faces in a postindustrial city with sixty thousand vacant lots and abandoned buildings.

ROBINSON: We do have an annual program in which we try to go out and inspect and locate all the multiple occupancies that are out there. But unfortunately, there is always the personnel issue. We have so many responsibilities in this unit, and there is only so many people allocated that can catch up to these things . . .

PEREZ: Exactly.

ROBINSON: I mean, our entire unit only has about forty-five inspectors for all of the tens of thousands of locations that there are in the city. So, we're not going to say these things [recovery houses] are a low priority, because it deals with life safety issues, but it's just a matter of resources, which is unfortunate. It's the same old song but it's true here, you know what I mean? Unfortunately, we just don't have the manpower or the resources to make going out to these places enough of a preventive measure, even though we shut down a lot of them when we come across them.

Robinson described the resource shortage explanation as admittedly the "same old song." Nonetheless, the song is important. Making matters worse, L&I inspectors have no way of even getting their heads around either the numbers of actual recovery houses in the city, or their locations. L&I inspectors doubt that anyone in the city really knows how many recovery houses—legal or illegal—actually exist.

RF: So does L&I track these, do you have some estimates of how many recovery houses there are, or would they just be categorized as boardinghouses, which could be . . .

ROBINSON: [interrupts] It could be any number of things, right . . . Again, I can't personally off the top of my head say how many illegal ones are out there. Are there a lot of illegal ones out there? Yeah, sure.

PEREZ: We got plenty of illegal ones, but we don't [have a way to really know about them].

ROBINSON: And see, even the legal ones, we don't really know if they are recovery houses, because for different reasons many different locations that fall under the category of multiple-occupancy could be considered a recovery house, but we don't use that term.

RF: Because the term really doesn't exist licensure-wise, there is no license for recovery houses as things stand?

PEREZ: Right, so we don't use that term. It's simple: we go there, they have up to five clients, it is still classifiable as an R3, which is a single-family home. You go into that sixth person, it becomes an R2, which is a multiple-occupancy, so we'll cite him for a rooming house license.

ROBINSON: And there can be any number of activities going on in that R2, but we just see it as an R2.

RF: So it is possible, I mean, they would only show up on your screen as R2s if they have gone through the proper channels. And the ones that you call illegal, we really have no way of estimating what the numbers are in this office, or perhaps even in the city.

PEREZ: Absolutely not, because they bring 'em in undercover without the knowledge of the department.

ROBINSON: I would say that is about right.

Because legal recovery houses are categorized in the same way as other forms of "multiple room occupancy" (for example, an apartment building or any other structure containing six or more unrelated persons), Philadelphia lacks the ability to track them. It is also unable to track illegal houses, since they come in "undercover." Here the impossibility of tracking moves beyond a problem of unreliable intelligence (that is, community complaints) to one of categorical legitimacy. In contrast to its recognition of personal care homes for the elderly, child care centers, and mental health residential facilities—each of which holds a separate form of licensure with the state—"recovery house" simply translates to "R-2" in the language of L&I.

ROBINSON: We have caught a lot of programs that we call multiple-occupancy programs, from surveys, and that's how we wound up getting these properties, so-called recovery houses, which to the knowledge of our code is actually just a rooming house. We don't use the term *recovery house*. That is a name that is given by *them*, not us. And all we know is that there are a lot of constituents out there that are opening these houses without Licenses and Inspections knowledge, until they get caught.

PEREZ: They started with the name halfway house and named it a halfway house, now they call it recovery houses, which is the same thing to us, a form of shelter. You are sheltering people in this structure, often without proper zoning and proper usage, and therefore you are illegal.

This set of circumstances effectively blurs the city's vision not only in terms of numbers, but, more important, in terms of legibility. L&I refuses to recognize the term *recovery house*, because to the agency no such category exists. This does not, however, stop it from holding recovery houses in contempt as *potential* objects of surveillance.

To summarize, each of these factors—the reliance on community complaints; the actions of the operators themselves; the operator's capacity for geographical mobility; the absence of any sort of list or database that could provide a sense of the numbers involved as well as their locations; the lack of resources and staffing; and the conceptual ambiguity concerning the term *recovery house* itself—produces a robust constellation of nonintervention that all but assures the persistence of informal recovery houses.

Yet even while rationalizing their own ineffectiveness, Robinson and Perez brainstormed on how simple it might be to get in control of the situation. They followed the money trail and suggested that if the agencies that indirectly fund recovery houses—such as public welfare and the treatment agencies that keep them lucrative with referrals—were to take action, the houses would become traceable. The simple failure among city officials to coordinate—which could begin with communication between welfare, the formal treatment sector, and L&I—creates regulatory loopholes.

RF: So there is no communication between public welfare and this office to say, "Look, what's up with this address, it calls itself a recovery house?"

PEREZ: There is no communication [between these departments] because we are not involved with the agencies like that. All we do is make inspections. But if an agency like welfare calls and says, "I would like to have this property inspected," yes, we will go out and do it. Also, if the treatment agency itself communicates with the city about where they are placing these people, that would alleviate the problem. I mean, who placed them there? The treatment organizations are placing these people in recovery houses when they come out; they don't go there by themselves.

RF: In other words, they come out of an inpatient treatment center and a case manager says, "I'm going to send you over here to this house."

ROBINSON: Exactly. Now you see, and along those same lines, if they were to actually do that, we would have a tighter rein on them. The illegal ones that are out there, they're hard to get a grip on because we have to stumble across them unless they are reported. However, my understanding with a recovery house is that everyone is sent by an agency of some sort, and if they notify us that they are sending someone to a location, then we can get a grip on practically every location and go out and inspect.

Robinson and Perez pointed out that with communication from the welfare office, L&I could easily verify a recovery house address as legal or illegal, while notification from treatment providers of their referrals to recovery houses could also serve the same purpose.

At the end of the day, the absence of a specific recovery house license was the most significant factor in Robinson's and Perez's eyes. Specific legislation to license recovery houses would tie their funding (and legitimacy) to a protocol requiring L&I inspection.

> ROBINSON: It's really the licensure, because with family day cares there is a
> mechanism in place, where if a person was to legalize a family day care,
> they have to contact us *and* the state. And we get inspections that way for
> legalized family day cares all the time. Same thing with, like, mental care,
> personal care, and Elwin [community residential nursing services] care
> homes. If they are getting funding from somewhere, they could tip us
> off too. CODAAP does do that, but if the Department of Public Welfare
> is giving money to any of these agencies, or to all of these agencies, they
> could easily let us know too.

A separate form of licensure with the state would require recovery houses to obtain proper zoning and their license through L&I before they received funding. These comments suggest a certain feasibility to the question of regulating recovery houses—or at the very least, getting "a tighter rein on them."

But the actual feasibility of these steps harks back to Malik's and Clarence's points about the *location* of recovery houses. It also relates to the resources it would take to create a regulatory board, formally fund recovery houses, and disrupt the city's advantageous reliance on—as one reviewer of my work put it—a form of mass-produced "lumpen NGO on the cheap." Meanwhile, in the face of bureaucratic inertia and government nonintervention, just as the welfare department abdicates responsibility by stating that it just cuts checks, L&I similarly insists that all it does is make inspections.

---

Lacking any regulatory board that might otherwise track and/or recognize them, Kensington's recovery houses continue to face a crisis of legitimacy. In effect, recovery house operators must shape their program in an informal manner. In one sense, then, for those that ascribe to the popular and much-hyped "unmonitored" and "unlicensed" monikers, they are "illegal" only on a technicality. It would take state legislation to regulate their programmatic content, which to this point does not exist. In a more accurate sense, the houses are only "illegal" in one very specific way: when they are noncompliant with L&I's zoning and licensure requirements. In either case, licensed or unlicensed, under the status quo the city's and state's nonintervention creates an elusive vector of governmentality by devolving authority to an informal entity that is denied legitimacy and kept in a constant state of fear and self-governance. At this historical juncture, the future of the informal, unlicensed recovery house seems entirely secure. Its tenure is inhibited only by a feckless and unlikely agency named L&I—which continues to stand ever at the ready in absence of any concerted regulatory effort, at least so far as the recovery *house* is concerned.

> PEREZ: The issue of recovery houses, I would say it is low on the scale of priorities for the most part. And they are going to keep opening them up, because until we have knowledge of where these locations are at, they are going to keep doing it. They have done it for years.
>
> ROBINSON: But I mean, if someone should have a list we would be more than happy to go over it.
>
> PEREZ: Oh yes.

## The Operators' Perspective

Kensington's recovery house operators believed that L&I licensure could neither stem recovery house proliferation nor minimize the phenomenon known as "warehousing." They felt that L&I was an ineffective, if not irrelevant, mechanism of regulation. One could either ignore zoning and licensure guidelines entirely (as most did), or simply deal with L&I in the unlikely event that a program came under scrutiny. L&I inspectors typically grant the operator a thirty-day period for compliance. And even in some of the most egregious cases of failure upon reevaluation, the city is often reluctant to order a "cease and desist," since it cannot afford to put people out on the street. Bilal attributed the lax standards for compliance to benefits that the city reaps from the recovery houses:

BILAL: Le Anna Washington, the state senator, has been saying for years that
she doesn't want to close recovery houses down, because it would be hard
to put so many people out on the streets, not only for society but for the
people themselves. For the time being, it is better to keep them in a poor
living environment than to make them homeless. That's the predicament
they are faced with. Even with Kensington Project, they closed down
a few of their houses through L&I, and they were still supposed to be
under investigation. But the word was even though they were a hazard-
ous operation they couldn't throw all the addicts back on the street with
nowhere to go. The city didn't have adequate facilities and they knew
they couldn't just roll 'em, because the chance of going into another place
was next to nil.

Apart from the matter of simple necessity, even in the worst-case scenario—in which operator compliance was either financially prohibitive or
structurally impossible—several recovery house operators concurred with
Robinson and Perez by explaining how they could collapse the census into
their other houses (permanently or temporarily). More typically, operators
simply ignored the regulations or devised strategies to circumvent them.

BILLINGS: You see, the trick is, you only put five people in a house, because
then you don't have to get licensed. That's what they were doing for years
at Soldiers of the Lord. Except they had five people and they had twelve
mattresses in the closet, so at night they had eighteen people sleeping in
there [laughs]. Reverend Wells started One Day at a Time with one house.
Girls were sleeping on the couch at night, there was fleas and everything
else, but you went along and went along. When Arlen Specter was running for reelection as a senator, he was losing, and he got Reverend Wells
to take about fifty or sixty guys out on the street, and he won. The next
month Reverend Wells got $250,000 in unrestricted funds, and since then
they've built up. One Day at a Time is one of the biggest in the city now.
That's just the way it is.

Any attempt to sweat the industry might run into barriers on several
fronts, including political favor. Moreover, while the boardinghouse license was an elusive document for most of Kensington's operators, it often
became a symbol of power for those who had the capital to obtain one.
The few licensed program directors that I encountered often displayed it
proudly. One case in point was Clarence, who explained the power, status,
and security that licensure afforded his program:

CLARENCE: All our buildings can pass inspection, every building we have.
I mean, they are all legally coded, we got a fire system in the place, and
we have everything that they have in a legal and legitimate business. We
have the exits mapped out; I mean, we got proper *everything* so they can't
come in and shut us down. The capacity of the building is based on what
L&I told us we could have; you know, we can have X amount of people,
so that's how many people we fit, whatever they say we can have. So we
don't run into problems with L&I, and when the turf wars start to go on
they can start calling L&I on each other, but ain't nobody can call on us.

Licensure functions in perhaps unanticipated ways in the industry, then,
beyond the conventional objectives of regulation. With L&I licensure,
Clarence recognized, his program was much more robust in the face of turf
wars between programs as well as the disgruntled client who might "drop
a dime" on him. For the operator, licensure prevented the setbacks of L&I
shutdowns, which, although rare, did occur. I knew of "cease and desist"
cases in Wilson's and Murphy's programs that interrupted operations as they
scrambled to relocate clients. In this regard, licensure provided some stability and security. It also served to deepen the distinctions between houses, as
uneven enforcement created a taxonomy of irregular settlement space. For
example, without a boardinghouse license, Malik was always susceptible to
scrutiny and forced to operate with a degree of contrition and discretion. So
rather than offering an antidote to "warehousing," licensure seemed mostly
a tool for moral supremacy and market advantage.

But despite the many clear problems with enforcement, operators like
Bilal felt that L&I licensure was important, and in some ways "better than
nothing." He believed that the program's structural quality instantiated a
vital separation between "warehousing" and therapy, flophouse and recovery house:

BILAL: Most of these places put all these people in there illegally, exceeding the living capacity. There is supposed to be two bathrooms for every
six people according to L&I. You are also supposed to have eight feet
between each bed, and you should have adequate closet space, but in most
cases these things are not being provided. Not to mention proper ventila-
tion, heating, and cooling systems. We got people in here with medical
problems, and yet none of this is done. I know that this is costly, but if
you don't invest back into the business, you'll never make money. If you
just constantly opening up more houses and warehousing people, you
are creating the very population that you say you are out to help. So it's

no wonder that clients get fed up and they go back to the same lifestyle, maybe to create more havoc on the public than what they did in the past.

Bilal explained that adherence to L&I standards accorded well with recovery, in addition to making good business sense. But along with other critics and operators, he also complained that L&I licensure pertained solely to the structure of the building itself, not the quality of the recovery program therein. Kensington's recovery house movement lacked a professional body to instill ethical principles of recovery, health, and even social welfare. Consequently, Bilal and Malik felt that the capacity of recovery houses to achieve legitimacy in the public eye was minimal, as it was contingent solely on the ethical comportment of individual operators. The struggles of these men to achieve subsistence in the informal economy required a set of practices that obviated their capacity to overcome the stigma of "unregulation."

One evening while walking me to the train (as he often did under the humorous guise of "provid[ing] an escort, because Tuesday is rob the white boy night"), Malik offered a poignant analysis. He insisted that street-level operators were "running things up here," and that things were going to stay that way. To do something about it, the state would have to design "a whole other welfare system," and it had no reason to do so as long as Kensington was nothing but ghetto dwellers. Perhaps when the system collapsed under the weight of its own contradictions, things would change. In the meantime, Malik surmised that only gentrification would bring a citywide crackdown, a point that I agreed with entirely.

## Public Welfare

My interview with Public Welfare Department Unit Manager Jeffrey Blumberg suggested that Malik may have been right in saying that the state was unmotivated to design a "whole other welfare system," given its relative indifference and the benefits it enjoyed from the presence of informal recovery houses. To begin, Blumberg spoke of several enabling loopholes that give credence to the movement's reputation as an "unmonitored" phenomenon. The Pennsylvania Welfare Reform Act of 1982 did more than merely produce pump-priming dollars for the movement; it also reconfigured the state's relationship with an ever-shifting GA population.

JB: In a lot of ways there has been a system disconnect between the Department of Public Welfare and the General Assistance population. As

we've reduced benefits, we've lost sight of a lot of them. There are a lot
of initiatives happening right now for single people, like noncustodial
fatherhood, or homeless initiatives, where we are connecting with them
more and more. But there has been a system disconnect with addicts on
GA. And even if they get cash, cash from welfare is only $205 a month;
it's better than nothing but it's not going to make anybody wealthy. I'm
thinking it's been twenty years we haven't had a welfare increase. So they
are not much of a priority, because we are not referring them to places
and we are not overseeing their income support.

RF: But if you take that $205 per month and multiply it by ten in a place like
Kensington . . .

JB: You got a nice little business, that's right. But really we just pay them, so
we're not going to oversee where they spend it and live.

RF: There isn't any case management, so you are just cutting checks.

JB: Yeah, not that they are unimportant, but they are not a priority in terms
of the agency focus. They would be aware of recovery houses in each
district, but they probably don't come up too much on the radar screen
because they are not a priority, the thinking being that the maximum
[a person] will get is nine months any way. Not that we would tolerate
abuse or anything like that, and once we found out we would act on it.
But you know, they bring us the medical forms and after that we only
have to see them once during the nine-month period, because they're not
going to have any employment or training requirements, so they receive
minimal intervention from our system. It's people with children, when
you deal with children they are always a priority. But there has been a real
disconnect for single people, and that's a major issue.

The reduction in benefits and the shift in legislation, when combined
with the absence of work and training requirements and the paltry, time-
limited allotments, further relegated the recovery house population to an
ostensibly "unmonitored" and "unregulated" sphere. Whereas other populations get "more connect" (particularly workfare populations with dependents), the addict population gets class-specific recovery houses.[16] We can
see how the state benefits from recovery houses, how they act as an ancillary
mechanism, or able partner, for the declining welfare state. Who else would
take homeless drug addicts and alcoholics in off the street, provide them
an address as required by public welfare, house them for less than $205 a
month (uninhibited by factors such as first/last month's rent and security
deposit), and feed them three times a day on $139 in food stamps? In what
other housing situation would these addicts also be monitored and *required*

to attend formal drug and alcohol treatment—a typical recovery house rule that works in concert with GA requirements—and provided informal case management? Even Blumberg acknowledged the value of these informal support mechanisms, voicing his faith that most recovery houses are providing good service in absence of oversight:

> JB: Our hope is that in Kensington the majority of houses are well run and are very conscientious. Some of them even look out for opportunities for people; it may not be case management in the traditional sense but something like, "Hey, why don't you go here for a job, here's job leads," you know, and they give them other services too. I'm sure there is more of that [type of positive activity happening], or there would be much more in the news, you'd hear much more about them.

Blumberg's reflections on the connections between public welfare and the recovery houses also suggest that market persistence—arising from bureaucratic indifference and the pump-priming dollars of public assistance—is one of the most important issues helping to explain the proliferation of the movement.[17] On this matter, it seems important to simply state that profiteering is not illegal. The welfare department does not take issue with people making money in situations of collective living, no matter how informal, *unless* there is fraud involved. This holds true whether the recipient is living in a licensed or unlicensed home.

> RF: How about the issue of, say, investigating a house owner collecting everybody's cash and stamps; that is not something that is a big priority, or something that would be reason or justification for going out to a house?
>
> JB: Not unless we suspect abuse, like any kind of fraud or anything like that. But in terms of running the operation, it's not uncommon in our system, because of the mental health houses and the halfway houses that even the prisons use. We have familiarity with that, so unless something comes up on our radar screen like abuse or food stamp fraud, we don't get involved.
>
> RF: But the issue of a for-profit house, though, mainly where that profit is coming from welfare dollars is not an issue?
>
> JB: No, they are entitled to do that as long as they are [*interrupts himself and pauses when he begins to say* licensed] . . . Actually, we don't even check to see if they are licensed, like we don't cross-reference, say, with Licenses and Inspections, unless we hear of a very obvious violation; then we would report it, but other than that we don't check.

Blumberg defaulted to L&I as the only city entity having the power to regulate the houses. His admission of the Department of Public Welfare's failure to communicate with L&I indicates another loophole, or system disconnect between city agencies.

Blumberg cited a host of other reasons that he felt precluded the possibility of new regulatory efforts on the horizon. For example, when asked how the recovery house movement was able to grow to an estimated four hundred to five hundred houses, he noted a lack of community initiative to push for regulation:

> JB: Well, the social fabric of the community tolerates recovery houses. Even the community organizers, like the Norris Square CDC and the other organized community agencies, they encourage people to get involved and to take advantage of them. Then you have the entrepreneurs, some of whom may not even be substance abusers, who open up the [recovery houses]. This is a chance to make money, and it's not standardized or regulated. I'm sure in some instances they take advantage of people; they take a lot of their checks and things like that. I'm sure there are very negative living situations, which worsens their problem. I am sure some of them are really conscientious also; I don't want to label them all . . .
>
> But I guess the community would have to be asking why they would even want to regulate them, like the Kensington community, the politicians, Norris Square CDC, they have a lot of community agencies that would have to be at the forefront to make it happen. Otherwise, nobody [in the city] is probably going to take the initiative to do it.

Not only has the community lacked initiative, but the chronically underfunded public sector has been ill equipped to get a handle on the issue. And even if Philadelphia could get organized, Blumberg was not optimistic about the results it might produce. It hasn't done well in regulating licensed operations such as mental health boardinghouses and day care centers.

> JB: The more the recovery houses are standardized and overseen, [it might] help people to not be taken advantage of. However, there are a lot of regulations for mental health boardinghouses, but a lot of those people still get taken advantage of.
> RF: Because the city is slow to respond to poor conditions?
> JB: And to inspect. That's the question: do they have the staff to go out and inspect. The city budget is tight right now, and that also influences the number of inspections that can take place. Plus, you would almost

have to be an entire agency to monitor these things. [And even then], we have child care licenses in this building here, and they rarely can get to the informal day care homes. They don't have the staff, so they focus on the licensed day care centers, the group day care centers, the family day care centers where they have a lot of children. I'm sure if there is a fire or something that would put them on the radar screen, but without that, with so many homes, they would have to have the manpower to do it.

Blumberg's statements suggest that the city lacks the financial and staffing resources to regulate recovery houses, as it would require an entire agency to do so effectively. In its absence, the city basically has been taking a "no news is good news" approach. As for the local welfare offices, they not only tolerate the recovery house networks, they cooperate with them in most instances.

In the final analysis, Blumberg conceptualized recovery house networks as a crosshatch of historical motivations. The recovery house is at first "dictated by need," and then formulated at the intersection of fiscal austerity, urban informality, and a declining welfare state:

JB: The need is there, obviously, or it wouldn't have generated that many houses. Substance abuse is, unfortunately, always going to be here, and the population is going to need [recovery houses]. That's a very large operation, four hundred houses . . . and it's kind of formed on its own, not quite underground but in an informal way. It is interesting how it has developed within the existing formal systems like the welfare system; it really is interesting. Dictated by need, and also by opportunity for the entrepreneurs, so there are a lot of motives at play. One way or another, communities pick up ways to meet single-person needs, and we pay so little, so this is one way [that the community has responded creatively] to need.

Having taken shape "not quite underground but in an informal way . . . within the existing formal systems" such as welfare, recovery houses are both historically contiguous and specific. They are consistent with earlier configurations of informally or unintentionally state-subsidized mutual aid, many of which "even at the apex of laissez-faire" evinced "pre-capitalist residues of communalism."[18] But as Gøsta Esping-Andersen notes, novel mechanisms do emerge,[19] in this case within a contextually embedded, unregulated market fueled by the miserly pittance of cash assistance that provides market opportunities for street-level "entrepreneurs." We are seeing a

historically specific redistribution of responsibility, as states devolve authority by displacing misery to cities, while cities displace misery to the streets.[20]

At first glance, it is the conjuncture of factors—uneven enforcement, an
absence of formal licensure, system disconnect—that begins to explain the
"unregulated," "unmonitored," and "unworthy" character of the recovery
house. As a low-priority population, the only event that would bring attention—or, better stated, scrutiny—to the GA recipient would be a fire,
or fraudulent practices such as food stamp abuse, undisclosed income, identity theft, or false address. Perhaps Blumberg summarized it best by saying,
"Not that they are not important, but they are not a priority in terms of
agency focus . . . Not that we would tolerate abuse or anything like that, and
once we found out we would act on it."

There is little question that the houses begin with a legislative restructuring of welfare settlements, characterized in this case by subsequent trends
of "disconnect" whereby the state "loses sight" of the GA population. But
there is a form of politics at play that is not solely an act of state disavowal
or neglect as the resettlement process becomes generative on several levels.
First, disconnect enables, or unleashes, operator mobility and entrepreneurialism, to the effect that operators develop an informal realm of social service delivery as a convenient instrument for the administration of welfare.
Second, it enables a reconstruction and re-embedding of welfare hierarchies
differentiated according to status (certain populations get "more connect,"
others get the recovery house), in addition to breeding new forms of vulnerability. And finally, while it may appear at first glance that addicts on GA
receive only minimal state surveillance in the form of address verification
(via formal/informal welfare administration) and fraud investigations (which
derive from the formal state, as well as the "eyes and ears on the street"), the
following section illustrates that the ratcheting down of social security to
austere categories of fraud and abuse is far from inconsequential.

## The Deepening of Informality: Regulatory Encounters at AHAD

Early one February morning, I arrived at AHAD to find Malik in a panic.
The state inspector general had called Milton (as he was listed in the city records as the owner) stating that there would be an inspection at his house on
Genoa Street. A phone number was given as a courtesy so that he could call
to ask questions in advance. When Malik learned of the news, he implored
Milton and Frank to get a boardinghouse license as soon as possible. Before
he could mobilize them, the inspector arrived. He interrogated Delmar, the
only man home at the time, about how many people lived in the house,

how many people paid rent, and how much they paid in rent. Delmar answered as best he could, and then the inspector left him with a card, asking Milton to phone him at 9:30 the next morning.

Later, Malik studied the card's inscription: "To report fraud, waste, abuse or serious misconduct involving state agencies, call toll free." On seeing the card, his best guess was that the man was a welfare inspector (as opposed to an L&I inspector, his first guess). If he was right, Malik surmised, the man simply wanted information on the status of all of his AHAD clients. Malik studiously compiled a list from the records he kept on each man's welfare status (active or terminated), case manager, outpatient treatment center, date of entry/departure from AHAD, and social security number. He intended to provide the list to Milton so that Milton could simply read the information to the inspector. But Milton and Frank never showed up at Genoa Street the next morning, leaving Malik to respond to the inspector's queries alone. He explained the phone call that forced him into a position of decoding cryptic clues:

MALIK: So I had all this information, right, now at 9:30 a.m., there is no Milton, no Frank, nobody, you hear me? So I stayed here until 9:30 and the man called. He asked me, "Where is Milton, I'm trying to reach Milton," and I said, "He knows that you are trying to reach him and he was supposed to have contact with you today." So he says, "Are you Malik?" I said, "Yes I am," so he says, "What are you paying over there?" I told him, I said, "$180 for myself," right, [he says,] "No, where is the lease, what is he renting that place for?" So I said, "You need to talk to Milton," you know what I'm saying, because I ain't going to say anything other than [that]. Because he's not looking at a program or nothing, he wants to know from Milton, what is this place being leased for, right . . .

RF: Why does he want all of that, so he can calculate over the top of the rental amount on the lease and figure out that you are making a profit on the space?

MALIK: Probably, which is not the problem, because I told Milton to go get the boardinghouse license, and that will cover that. What he is trying to find out, and this is the most important part, is if *I* am getting any money out of this. You see what I'm saying, was *I* getting money, out of this program, and receiving money from the clients [while receiving welfare], which I wasn't.

Malik began to piece together what was happening, again having to project into the minds of the inspectors and the welfare officials to figure out how to play his cards. When I mistakenly assumed the inspector might be trying to discern whether the *house* was making a profit off welfare dollars, Malik pointed out that this was immaterial, unless *he* was the one collecting profits or a salary. As a way of retracing steps that might have led to the inspection, he reminded me that in early January his own welfare had been cut off unexpectedly. At that time, Malik had been paying Blanche's rent after she was cut off from welfare. He had given her his access card to pay rent in her recovery house, since he was exempt from paying rent, as per his "salary" arrangement at AHAD (despite his statement to the contrary to the inspector). Again, the details are arcane but significant:

> MALIK: So Blanche going to get the money to go get her rent, and there ain't nothing on it. I said. "Bullshit! today my day!" So I call my caseworker and told her I went to take some money out to take care of my business, and I ain't got no money in there. She told me I'd been terminated as of the seventh of this month [January]. I said, "For what?" She said, "Well, you run a recovery program, AHAD. The investigation says you been getting money you shouldn't be getting." I told her, "Well, I don't know where this comes about, because I remember telling you some months ago I was getting ready do some volunteer work to set this thing up in hopes that I can get a job out of it. But as far as me getting money, I ain't got no money."

When Malik had inquired about being cut off, the rationale given was that caseworkers had "caught wind" of his having opened a recovery house program, and therefore suspected he was making money above his welfare payments.

> RF: So how did they know you were running a house?
> MALIK: People were going up there, talking to the caseworkers, like, "Yeah, Malik has this program, this guy is doing good!" Plus they went to Positive Attitudes and they said I left there and was running my own program. And, when the investigator came here for Albert, and I say Albert live here . . . So I said, "Well, at least somebody should have confronted me with it, you know" . . .

The information was not verified with pay stubs, W-2s, or any other documentation. Rather, the case was made based on hearsay from the residents of his house, along with an investigator's uncorroborated allegations.

When Malik contested the allegations, his caseworker encouraged him not to push the issue. Quite significantly, she saw his career in recovery houses as a path out of welfare dependency.

> MALIK: I told her I wasn't making no money here, and she says, [*imitating a gruff bureaucratic voice*] "Well, Mr. Bronson, the investigator said you there, Positive Attitudes said that you left there and you got your own big fucking program and you make X amount of dollars . . . what I would do, I wouldn't push this shit too far, *don't you want to work for yourself?*" So she tried to trick me into it; I said, "Yeah, I want to work for myself, right, but you think I'm going to let this go like it is and then I am going to *owe* welfare money?"

The incident revealed that it was legal to collect revenues by housing addicted bodies on GA. It was considered fraud, however, for a welfare recipient to make money beyond his cash transfer. And if getting cut off was not bad enough, Malik had also believed he might be forced to pay retribution for all the months he had been operating the program and receiving welfare. To preempt this, he sent what he called an "affidavit" to the welfare office with Frank's signature, stating he was an unpaid volunteer in the AHAD program. The affidavit also stipulated that Malik was paying $180 per month in rent to Frank as the program owner.

Keeping these details in mind, fast forward to the February inspection. Just when Malik thought he had a read on the situation, it proceeded to get more complex. First of all, when Frank and Milton had heard about the inquiry, they ran scared to their lawyer friends in the Kensington community and to a man that I had seen them go to before in other points of crisis; their old political ally, State Representative John Taylor. Both Frank and Milton were collecting disability under SSI, a program that also limited the amount of money *they* could make annually. The situation put the two men into a tailspin. They considered putting the house in the name of one of their wives or even falsifying Milton's identity by using his son's social security number. Milton and Frank avoided Malik until they could get this straightened out, and it was for this reason that they jilted him on the morning they were to speak with the welfare inspector. Making matters worse, Malik began to obsess about an unrelated event, also from months earlier, when the gas was shut off at AHAD. Recall that on this occasion, Milton had drafted a bogus lease so that Malik could get the gas turned on in his name, stating that Malik paid $350 a month in rent. Malik now surmised that Milton, if brought under scrutiny for welfare fraud, could in fact make him the fall guy simply by saying that he leased the place for $350. The bogus lease could put Malik in the inspector's crosshairs for two reasons: first, he had he written a signed affidavit (accompanied by false rent receipts) stating that he paid $180 a month in rent to Frank; second, the inspector needed only to do the math regarding the $350 bogus lease—in other words, add 10 men in the house paying $180 each in rent over Malik's $350—to discern that Malik was making money while receiving benefits.

The new investigation generated levels of confusion that are difficult to disentangle even in this space. At the very least, the nature of the recovery house industry engendered disproportionate vulnerability for Malik, the least compensated and hardest working member of the partnership. But the contradictions of it all are quite compelling. Consider that Malik was forced to falsify documents to his welfare caseworker stating that he was paying rent in the house, in order to (1) waylay suspicions that he was collecting undisclosed cash; and (2) compensate for the fact that as program director he was obligated to make a salary from his own welfare benefits. In addition, earlier he had been forced to falsify a lease that served the purpose of (1) getting an account with the gas company and (2) providing some sense of security should Milton relapse and try to throw him out. The ambiguities of the situation, and the levels of anxiety and paranoia they created in the partnership, were formidable (and endemic, perhaps, to all informal or "gray" markets). None of the men could confront the situation directly, given that AHAD was built on a foundation of contradictions and half-truths.

Part of Malik's process to get clarity on the situation involved a trip to his mentor Bilal, who helped him sort everything out. After laying out the pieces, Bilal made some conclusions:

> BILAL: They basically got him two ways. The first question is, is he paying rent or a lease for the house itself. So, if he is able to rent the house, and we surmising here, right, if he is able to rent the house, where that money coming from? That rent is more than two hundred dollars a month, you see what I'm saying? The second question is, is he taking money from the other individuals to pay off the mortgage, or the lease, or whatever you want to call it, right, and then still getting welfare. That is still fraud, if you look at it that way, because he is collecting undisclosed cash. But you need to be cleared up on how he wording that question, because it's not clear how he wording it and you might give an answer that is not pertinent to the question.

So the question is, who is collecting what, and where is the money coming from, not so much where is it going, but where it is coming from, because he is collecting welfare. So, is there fraud here? That is the bottom-line question, is there fraud here. Now the whole question comes back to, are Milton and Frank going to step up to the plate? If they are worried about social security, they might not.

By scrutinizing where the money is coming from, not where it is going to, the regulatory structure of welfare sweats the recipient-operator while absolving absentee landlords. In a classic double standard updated for the post-welfare moment, the state turns its back on informal welfare entre-preneurialism and the systemic nature of an entire unmonitored industry, unless of course the entrepreneur in question is on welfare. In this case—as something of a bizarre twist on the "welfare-to-work" mantra—the state attempts to purge the welfare recipient-cum-recovery house operator from the public assistance rolls, encouraging or forcing him into an informal welfare economy of predatory subsistence. All the while, the state preserves (and updates or remakes) its age-old regulatory practices of less eligibility, punitive deterrence, and delineation of the worthy versus unworthy poor.

I have labored (with some apology to the reader) to convey the complexities and minutiae of this encounter to illustrate once again how the vagaries of political illegitimacy, extralegality, and chronic insecurity map onto individual experience. The contradictions in this situation are multiple, and the reactions of anxiety and confusion by Malik and his partners evince the liminal status of an unregulated industry that continuously labors in fear of state scrutiny; even as it works in service of state ends. Taken together, the consequences of nonintervention and unregulation in Philadelphia—while certainly indicative of selective indifference, unevenness, negligence, and incompetence—amounted in many respects to a quite insidious matrix of regulation in their own right. Indeed, the simultaneity of illegality and normalcy puts the state in not so much a reactionary as a regulatory position, on several fronts.

## Regulation in the Kensington Imaginary

Despite operators' intermittent fears that their houses would come under state scrutiny, for the most part the state never showed its face (the previous section documents one of only two direct encounters Malik's program had with the Public Welfare Department, and he never encountered L&I during my fieldwork). There were few illusions on the street, however, that the state *could* call at any time.[21] Quite palpably, recovery house owners, managers, and residents, and even treatment providers, carry the weight of the informal recovery house's extralegal status and its troubled reputation. In this respect, my efforts to contact some of the major players in the Kensington recovery house industry provided a window onto a movement forced into a constant state of paranoia and fear.

Malik and Bilal warned that certain operators would not agree to speak with me unless there was money or "good publicity" involved. The two men even assumed the role of empirical advisor to my project, voicing great concerns that the scene's most fabled rogues would deliver nothing in the way of truth or validity. When I explained that I was interested in meeting these figures whether they lied or not, they warned of a veil of secrecy that would preclude access. Malik even said I'd be better off studying the crack trade than the recovery house business:

> MALIK: You can try to go into the bottom of the drug thing, man, go in to the crack houses, and people will tell you anything for a few dollars and shit, but when you get to this recovery house part of it, some people won't tell you nothing, man, because this shit runs deep. It's bad that it is so secretive, but you have to ask what were the intentions of the program when it started.

Street-level operators and city officials alike were hooked on the story of the well-intentioned operator gone bad. They spoke fluently of the corruptive allure of profits and power in the unregulated economy that had forced certain operators underground. Perhaps the biggest case in point was a notorious operator in Kensington whose persona as a former street pimp and gang member preceded him almost invariably. This man, whom I will refer to as Jones, operated multiple houses under separate program names. When I informed Malik that I wanted to make contact with Jones, he exploded:

> MALIK: [*shouting*] Jones ain't going to let you fucking talk to him! Jones is a fucking crook, man! Check this out, Jones don't want no outsiders in his house. I knew one cat who was trying to get his kids back, and these [social] workers wanted to go inside the house to see how he's living. Jones told the cat that if they come in the house, or any one of his houses, dude would have to just pack his shit and get the fuck out.
>
> RF: What's he so paranoid about?
>
> MALIK: He bipolar. Jones got a lot of shit, man . . . he ain't going to tell you shit, he's going to snowball your ass. It's just not in Jones's favor [to talk

with you]. Jones is real paranoid, real bad, and he'll think you investigating him. I'm just trying to tell you what to look out for. And if there ain't a buck in it for him, aw, man, you done. With him it's like, what can you do for me? And even then he ain't going to tell you how the game is played. Come to think of it, Billings ain't going to let you get too far in his shit neither!

As previously noted, Billings had made the transformation from street-level hustler to CEO of a formal outpatient recovery center after serving several years in Graterford Prison. His many successes and exploits—while often respected by other self-proclaimed former street hustlers like Malik—were sometimes held in contempt. It seemed that no matter how much ground one had covered in "going legit" in the recovery industry, he was still looked upon suspiciously.

Back to the matter of Jones, Bilal agreed with Malik: if Jones didn't see anything in it for himself, he wouldn't talk to me. According to Bilal, Jones formally demanded all of his managers to forbid strangers in any of his houses. Based on the reputation that preceded this man, I felt it might be best to approach him through a connection. I knew that Billings had dealings with Jones, and I asked if he might help with a contact. Jones was an important figure, Billings concurred, but he wouldn't broker the connection, as it was not good for his reputation to openly associate with him. I finally decided to approach Jones "cold" by making a call to one of his intake houses. To my surprise, Jones immediately agreed to meet with me—not at one of his houses but at an office that he kept in Kensington. From the outset, he approached me with suspicion, scanning over my interview schedule and consent form with a careful eye and demanding to see my credentials on a business card. He started by saying that he didn't know who the hell I was, whose side I was on, or whether I was simply there to drop a dime on him. He hadn't had time to check me out before I came, so he could not trust me to be an ally of the recovering community.

Jones assured me that he had good reason to be discreet. He had things going on with L&I, and the city had been clamping down on him hard. As a result he refused to be tape-recorded in a formal interview. He was interested in learning more about my project, however, and agreed to a conversation that would be led by his questions rather than mine. Jones saw a need for formal research on the recovery house movement, partly to dispel the myths that surrounded its reputation. Despite his suspicion of me, he claimed repeatedly to be an open book by welcoming the City of Philadelphia, L&I, public welfare, or anyone else who was interested to ask questions about his business. It soon became apparent that our meeting would be about posturing.

As an act of transparency, I exposed all of my research-related whereabouts of the previous year. Jones seemed to grasp that this story would be told with or without him, so it was in his best interest to weigh in. He then began to launch attacks on L&I. As I had heard from other operators who had run into problems with code violations, Jones insisted that the nature of the inspection depended on the arbitrary whims of the inspector. He had also been told contradictory information by separate L&I officials. Jones brashly challenged the city to simply tell him what to do and he would happily comply, insisting that other programs got away with murder relative to his high-profile houses. Quite significantly, he stated repeatedly that he was in favor of some form of recovery house regulation. In his view, regulation was badly needed to stem the epidemic of greed in the recovery house community. He cited acrimonious divisions that had emerged as a direct result of free-market competition, and called for regulation to weed out the "bad apples." I found a sense of irony in Jones's diatribes. Here was allegedly one of the most paranoid and corrupt characters in the business, known for his protective and secretive practices, extolling his own virtue as an advocate for industry regulation and reform.

Like all of the operators I studied, Jones was motivated to put forth a morally pristine image of his programs. But perhaps more important, he seemed genuinely motivated to decrease arbitrary intervention and operator vulnerability in the highly contingent recovery house industry. In many respects, his position on greed evinced anxieties about a market that was *too* free. In Jones's assessment, placing controls on the market could enhance the overall quality of the recovery house industry. The perverse conditions of an unfettered marketplace allowed greed to carry the day, because the vacuum created by a lack of oversight created space for "vultures, pirates, and poachers." I found myself identifying with Jones as the scrupulous businessman while suddenly conceptualizing men like Malik in a new light—perhaps as contaminants.

Jones insisted that he never made a move without community and political approval, unlike his less scrupulous counterparts. He had been around the Kensington recovery house industry since the 1980s, and he claimed to remember a time when one simply did not make a move to put a new house on a block before gaining political and community support. When I asked if the current state of affairs meant that the recovery houses had won the NIMBY (Not in My Backyard) battle, he replied that this was true, but only because Philadelphia now tolerated the houses through its various forms of inaction. Consequently, the Kensington recovery house market was totally saturated. In the absence of regulation, abuse prevailed.

My experience with Jones raised new questions. What causes a street-level recovery entrepreneur to yearn for formalized regulation? Is it the indifference of the state? Or is it an accelerated sense of vulnerability in the unregulated market? Based on my many unsolicited discussions about regulation with recovery house operators—as opposed to the blank and stolid stares among city officials when I brought the question to them—I further questioned which side actually enjoyed the benefits of the unlicensed and unregulated industry. If a shady character such as Jones could put forth a relatively plausible (if perhaps feigned) argument in favor of regulation, what might this mean?

Jones was not the only operator I knew of who claimed to favor regulation, and in many respects Bilal surely outpaced him as a more likely and consistent advocate. Bilal explained his rationale for favoring regulation, based on the key role recovery houses played as a mechanism of the welfare state:

> BILAL: The recovery houses play a centralized role [in this community], but
> it's unfortunate that at the present time most of the recovery house insti-
> tutions are not structured nor regulated by the government.
> RF: You think that's unfortunate?
> BILAL: Yes, I do. I'm not looking for a whole lot of government interven-
> tion into our lives, in terms of regulation, but some institutions that deal
> with the public in general as far as public health is concerned and public
> well-being should be regulated, because it affects the outside society, you
> know, and it needs to be regulated. In effect the recovery house is an off-
> shoot of a hospital, in terms of care for an individual's life and well-being,
> which affects the general public over the long term. Because if they don't
> get care and [effective] treatment, they will come out here and create
> havoc on the general public in terms of theft, deception, misappropria-
> tion, and the list goes on. So it behooves us as citizens and as taxpayers to
> look towards regulating this industry, and of course it could also create
> a tax base for the city. So why not look toward regulating this industry?
> I mean, sooner or later the government is going to have to take notice of
> what is going on, and they going to have to do something about it.

Bilal described the recovery house as "an offshoot" of a hospital, a quasi-institutional public health mechanism that was worthy of regulation for the public good. His idea of taxation—just one among of his many propositions to improve the industry—was quite novel among operators. Along similar lines, he would often speak of his vision for a unified recovery coalition in Kensington. This would provide a governing body to pull the houses up to ethical standards. By creating a body that would instill accountability, Bilal surmised, the treatment of the addict would improve and the recovery house would emerge as a legitimate social service provider. Echoing Jones somewhat, Bilal stated that the major obstacle to these types of developments was city inaction, followed by the pressures of market competition. He worked on rhetorical strategies to convince operators that regulatory measures would ultimately enhance their earning capacity. He contended, however, that his counsel fell on deaf ears, due to the allure of self-interest over recovery principles in the impoverished Kensington landscape.

State inaction, combined with the pains of the free market and the absence of legitimacy, led others to voice similar desires for industry regulation. Murphy, owner of several recovery houses, was more suspicious of the impact of regulation on operator autonomy than Bilal, but he too felt that it might help to "weed out" bad actors:

> MURPHY: I hate to say this, but I think maybe the city should regulate recovery houses to cut out some of the riffraff that's out there. And that's a double-edged sword: it's good for the one reason, but the other thing is that you are going to have to do it their way or not do it at all, and that could kinda be a drag. But I kind of would be in favor of that, as long as it was to get rid of the riffraff. The people that have their side of the street clean you leave alone, and the guys that aren't you just weed them out. As long as they are not telling you how to run your recovery house, maybe it should only be bare-bones type of stuff, you know what I mean? You know, like having a hardwire system, fire drills and stuff like that, I can understand that kind of stuff, but beside that [I'm not so sure].

Murphy's suggestions amounted to little more than that which already existed in the way of "bare-bones" L&I regulations. But his comments still suggest—quite different from the scenario of the state breathing down every operator's neck—that discussions on regulation initiated within the industry.

Perhaps deceitfully, some informants called for a regulation that they intuitively felt would never materialize in a city that had long neglected the Kensington neighborhood. Malik went so far as to pitch a strategy for how Philadelphia could go about getting the industry under control if it really wanted to. His ideas here could be well suited to the boardrooms of policy makers.

MALIK: Listen, check this out. You see what you trying to do, right [*referring to my ethnographic research*]; well, I'm going to show you exactly how if the city really wanted to do something, they could do it. The city knows about us, right, and just like you befriended me and just like you're down here, they could have someone do the same thing, on some type of *Serpico* shit. Say you're for the city, and you down here, and you meet people like me—these are the people that you would bring back to that board. Because I forgot like, what's the word . . . it's like you on a *task force*, and you gotta go speak to the board: [*mocking a researcher presenting to a board in an Anglo-fied voice*] "In the year that I was out there in this recovering community, over the one hundred houses that I had intimate contact with . . ." or, you know, whatever, "I think we have four people that with our help, can build a citywide program." Do you see what I am saying? That's how it's done.

RF: But they're not doing that.

MALIK: No they're not. [*pauses*] Hell, if I wasn't so scared of being shut down, I'd promote myself! You see what I'm saying? But the numbers would be like that, because I'm going to be honest with you, man, I haven't really met a person that's truly in this shit to help another person, and most of them ain't going to do a motherfucking thing for nobody unless there is a dollar in it.

Malik invoked the issue of profits in familiar style, suggesting that it was the primary dimension that kept the movement underground, and for that matter kept the movement alive at all. And with the status quo producing only sporadic points of crises confined to areas of spatially concentrated poverty, why should Philadelphia be motivated to wake a sleeping dog? Malik pointed out that the recovery houses provided a service to the city that was too valuable. Moreover, he insisted that regulation would mean the end of profiteering, a sure-fire death knell for the industry:

MALIK: It's like I told you, we doing them a *service*, man, so they leave us alone. And besides, even if they could regulate us they would, but they can't figure out *how*. If you regulate us, you think people would be in this thing like I'm in this? Huh? If you regulate us, then you take the money part out of it, and nobody's going to do it anymore. I'm serious.

RF: Well, you can regulate it and still allow a profit to be made.

MALIK: Yeah, but these guys, man, would ask what *kind* of profit? When you making 100% profit, and now the state is going to tell you, "No, you not going to make no 100% profit on your dollar," right, that's another issue that these guys ain't going to take.

In a similar vein, Clarence felt that the regulation of business is decidedly un-American. The entrepreneurs of the recovery movement would
not stand for this infringement on their "rights." He also assumed that
regulation would put an end to the informal market mechanism in favor of
formal funding. And besides, in the face of the state budget crisis of 2003,
he asserted that public funding was simply untenable:

> CLARENCE: They can't regulate this business, they can't do that. You can't
> come in and tell somebody how to run their business.
> RF: But if they wanted to say, like, with mental health halfway houses, they
> are state regulated, and they can say if you are going to take state funds,
> you have to comply with all of these regulations. They could do that with
> recovery houses.
> CLARENCE: They would have to give everybody money, and they not going
> to do that. They're already talking about cutting funding now.

Malik echoed these sentiments, citing the prohibitive costs of formal funding and the amount of money it would take to create a regulatory infrastructure:

> MALIK: Look, man, bottom line is this, the recovery house business is
> something the city don't want to be involved in, you know that. Check
> this out, do you know the *manpower* it would take, when you talk about
> the payroll that would require for the city if they took over? Everybody
> would have to get paid, man!

By their comments, Malik and Clarence failed to recognize that the recovery house industry is funded—at least indirectly—by public money in the
form of welfare dollars. But they correctly surmised that the allotment of
discretionary cash benefits and food stamps to individuals was something
entirely different from formal funding.

According to my interviews with L&I and the Public Welfare Department as well as with the operators themselves, Philadelphia lacks the financial and staffing resources, if not the will alone, to monitor recovery houses.
In some sense, this creates a "regulatory vacuum" enabling a peculiar form
of entrepreneurialism, characterized as it is by the accumulation of welfare
bodies in a cheap and degraded housing stock. But our analysis of barriers to
state regulation must be augmented by considering the very real obstacles
that operators face in achieving legitimacy. The data suggest that with L&I
and public welfare serving as the nominal apparatuses for governmental

oversight, recovery houses have been forced to take shape informally, extra-legally, and even "illegally." Without channels to achieve legitimacy, Bilal assured me that the industry would take shape along very particular lines:

> BILAL: Listen, if they don't legalize the system, we're going to have to help ourselves, so it is going to create a bootstrap industry. We can never to-tally clean up this industry . . . we can attempt to manage it and control it, but we can never totally clean it up.

That is, operator protagonism unfolds within a preconfigured script that is both enabling and constraining. On the enabling side, illegitimacy accom-modates the addict-cum-entrepreneur, who is prone to resist state interven-tion and institutionalization. But the denial of legitimacy also comes with an excise tax. For the state, it establishes an imaginary of disorder, which in turn facilitates a strategy of managing and controlling (rather than eradicat-ing) malfeasance. Both agencies hold out the recovery houses as unruly and prosaic, in a sense demonizing and normalizing them at the same time. In other words, L&I's Robinson assumes (somewhat correctly) that the houses are seen by residents as simply "being," or regularized as part of the urban fabric, at the same time that the agency designates them as illegal. This is a very particular type of regularization. For the operator, the setup engenders a pervasive sense of vulnerability and paranoia. Part of this stems from the illicit activities operators must resort to as a matter of survival, which Bilal alluded to in saying, "if they don't legalize the system, we're going to have to help ourselves." The constitution and acceleration of urban informality only increases dependency on these practices, thrusting operators further into a zone of illegitimacy, deepening interoperator suspicion, intensifying market competition, and creating a culture of anxiety more generally. As the houses are deemed, simultaneously, forever disordered and regularized, the "territorialized uncertainty" of state intervention is secured.[22]

## Conclusion: Reinterpreting the State's Position on Regulation; A Fortified Managed Persistence

I begin my conclusion to this chapter by reconsidering Malik's proposed strategy for how the state might easily begin a process of regulating the recovery house industry. Recall his idea of sending in a task force "on some type of *Serpico* shit" so that some imagined board could capture, formal-ize, and ultimately replicate the most virtuous and beneficial elements of the recovery house movement. Malik even suggested he would be a perfect

candidate to make a presentation to such a board, were he not so scared to
approach the state. His expression of fear is part of a constellation of factors
that make him an unlikely candidate for the task. I, on the other hand, represent something of an ideal candidate. In fact, several welfare scholars have
asked me repeatedly whether my book would argue in favor of recovery
house regulation.

My admittedly privileged reasons for opting out of this in some ways
ready-made question and ready-made position are quite separate from Malik's. Put simply, I believe that the normative question of whether recovery
houses ought to be regulated is the wrong question to ask. The discourse
on recovery houses has been driven (on both sides) by an obsession with the
absence of one type of licensure (recovery house licensure, or the broad and
amorphous notion of "government oversight"), and a concomitant obsession with one type of regulation (L&I). There is no question that the analytical framework of "regulated versus unregulated" is wholly inadequate.
Certainly, the interviews and fieldwork presented in this chapter reveal a
series of missteps, lapses, and loopholes—all of which rest implicitly on the
original sin of a regulatory *void* that enables operator mobility and recovery
house persistence. State inaction (of one form) is key here, as the absence of
regulation breeds a fear-based industry operating in areas of spatially concentrated poverty. This set of circumstances, in some respects itself created by deregulatory impulses of "system disconnect," devolution, and retrenchment, clearly creates barriers to legitimacy. But quite important, this
set of circumstances also serves as an inroad to *re*-regulation on a number
of fronts.

Shifting historical conditions of urban informality reconfigure the state's
capacity to intervene at a particular site, while still accommodating the uni-
versally constant reflexive questioning of the proper scope (and rationale)
of political power endemic to liberalism.[23] Along these lines, when we consider urban informality in the conventional sense, as part of a marginalized
sector comprising the survival mechanisms of the urban poor,[24] we search
for policy measures convenient for the eradication of malfeasance, or question why and how the state keeps its hands off the recovery house. The notion of managed persistence, in turn, leaves us with explanatory keywords
such as accordance, tolerance, able partnerships, and "ancillary" modes of
treatment. We avail ourselves of compelling and accurate descriptions of
the enjoyment of "benefits," or the "feckless" nature of failed regulation.
Otherwise, the analysis depends on a strategy of revealing "voids," "vacu-
ums," nonintervention, retrenchment, rollback, and withdrawal. These
terms are all clearly important. They explain an ecological vector, or his-

torical conjuncture, created (in part) by fiscal austerity and the rollback of
the state. Such processes have enabled mobility or room to maneuver for
the recovering addict-cum-entrepreneur.

But the utility of managed persistence as I've presented it across this chapter hinges on very particular conceptions of urban informality and regulation. I would like to add to my analysis by building toward a second conception of urban informality; that which is deeply enmeshed with the formal
sector as an essential and perhaps permanent component of the modern
economy and the modern welfare state.[25] Put another way, urban informality becomes both an effect of retrenchment logic, and an instrument of an
ever-transforming matrix of state regulatory power. The effect of managed
persistence, then, as I will conceive of it here, is to translate the "unregulated" recovery house into a troubled site of regulation, on several fronts.

The recovery house matrix enables us to discern emerging regulatory
structures, logics, and relationships (both material forms and discursive
strategies), many of which may be "creatures of crises rather than constituent elements of some (planned) resolution."[26] The affinity between the
formal welfare state and informal self-help movements has only accelerated in the post-Keynesian era, within which welfare state transformation
has been a primary engine of urban transformation and restructure. This
is what Nezar AlSayyad, in reframing the NGO notion of the quiet revo-
lution, terms the "quiet encroachment."[27] On the one hand, the shift in
analytical sensibility implied here allows us to examine the ways in which
recovering subjectivity has been induced by the operations of neoliberalism
and welfare state retrenchment, while simultaneously being configured as
a form of resistance to these trends. On the other, it allows us to push back
against received notions of retrenchment to see how the state redistributes
risk, responsibility, and regulatory functions in the post-welfare age.

Consider for example the question of licensure itself. L&I licensure was
mostly conceived of as an inadequate tool of regulation by recovery house
operators and city officials alike. At another level altogether, however,
licensing allows for the promotion of urban order and civility through measures that target spaces and activities. Rather than offend liberal sensibili-
ties with the direct presence of state authority, licensing enables policing
functions to take effect by turning the work of risk management over to
the private sector. This allows government to ensure that spaces are under
constant surveillance and subject to immediate disciplinary measures, without involving centralized state knowledges.[28] But we should be careful not
to proceed unreflexively with the stories that liberal governance tells about
itself. There are two matters that I would like to take up with respect to this

refrain. First, while licensing devolves authority to private actors, it allows the state nonetheless to continue its obsessions with the unevenness of comportment and the constant need to enframe violations within a discourse of security.[29] L&I licensure thus designates a threshold of liberal governance and an administrative matrix for the question of state intervention.

While the Keynesian state generated policies to "spread" or share risk through networks of redistribution, the neoliberal state in an era of fiscal austerity and welfare state retrenchment devolves authority to locally administered networks of experts.[30] The job of these experts, in part, is to manage the risk that emerges from urban informality and its concomitant states of "advanced marginality."[31] The population's collective sense of security from the state is ratcheted down to minimal structural safety in the form of uneven code enforcement from a hapless L&I inspector, and/or the ability of clients and operators to take revenge on a house boss or competing operator by "dropping a dime." The state responds perhaps *only to* points of crisis, but, quite significantly, *to* points of crisis. As a new mode of governance, this type of relatively austere risk management has emerged as the welfare state's last vestiges have been abandoned.

My second and much more complex point draws once again on Marianna Valverde and Michel Foucault. Knowledge about specific social spaces is central to liberal governance (for example, "You are letting us know what's going on behind the door of that address"), because the differentiation of spaces allows contradictory modes of governance to coexist.[32] It is here that fragmentation and unevenness become significant, with respect to what Valverde calls a "geographicalization of spaces." L&I licensure enables a "geographicalization" of space by establishing a different mode of governance between the multiple occupancy home (the R-2) and the single family home (R-3). Thus, it is important to note that recovery houses *are* regulated under L&I's zoning and licensure requirements. However, this is a zoning category controlled by municipalities, which is quite apart from state legislation that has the authority to regulate the delivery of social services and health care. The only level of government that could legally regulate recovery house programming would be the state—under professional licensing systems, health care statutes, or regulations issued pursuant to the welfare statute Public Act 1982-75. These factors extend the scope of critique in this chapter from city-level omission and neglect to the inaction of state-level politicians and bureaucrats.[33] At this level, the *absence* of recovery house licensure is undoubtedly more complex.

This absence is a product of multiple factors related to the practical dilemmas of regulation more generally: for one, the unlikelihood that the state would have the resources to inspect; for another, the unlikelihood that proper building standards could be maintained on the small amounts of money that operators collect from their clients. But my interest here is more in the *effects* of state inaction than in any attempt to call for state-level regulation, per se. There is a multiscalar downloading of responsibility at play here, from the state to the city to the street, which is indicative of wider trends in contemporary welfare-state restructure. State inaction enables what Ananya Roy refers to as an "unmapping" of space, which in turn guarantees a "territorialized uncertainty and flexibility" of state intervention. As Roy deploys this concept in the squatter settlements of Calcutta, the power of the state is derived from an unmapping that ensures a constant negotiability regarding land rights, property rights, and even citizenship.[34] In a similar vein, the regulatory void stemming from the absence of recovery house licensure "de-geographicalizes" the space,[35] thereby mobilizing actors (or allowing them to mobilize). It discards the "visible grid" of regulated space in favor of what Colin Gordon refers to as "the necessarily opaque, dense autonomous character of the processes of *population*. It remains, at the same time, preoccupied with the vulnerability of these same processes,"[36] in this case with the need to enframe them in mechanisms of surveillance, regulation, and security.

We have seen a peculiar logic of ratcheting down, one that engenders vulnerability and reconfigures the role of the state in devolutionary welfare partnerships. In the process, the state not only appeals to—but effectively constitutes through the logic of retrenchment—new modes of informality and new strategies of survival. There is value added in informal arrangements situated within unregulated markets, for the constellation is guaranteed to fulminate a full spectrum of ethical comportment. This brings me back to Malik's important assessment: "basically, all they want to do is stop fraud and abuse. That's it, basically." I want to add to this statement again, not only fraud and abuse, *but* fraud and abuse. In the case of recovery houses, it is the informal operators themselves who have fundamentally restructured the rules of social service provision and the ways in which individuals "take up" public assistance. It is in this sense that they act as regulatory agents, or sites of rule making and enforcement within a locally specific, informal poverty management system.[37] But questions of fraud and abuse are alive and well, highly contingent and always inflected with racial and class markers. Operators are constantly at risk of being the wrong kinds of entrepreneurs and the wrong kinds of civic actors, even in the age of devolution, voluntarism, and the growing reliance on market models for public policy. And, at the same time that operators seek autonomy from regulations and the discipline imposed by the modern state, they also somehow need the security that comes from state surveillance.[38] Consequently, the negotiation between autonomy and integration spreads across a spectrum of formality to informality, legal to extralegal. It is in this light that urban informality, operator protagonism, and even subsistence appear not only as formidable barriers to operator legitimacy and regulation of one sort, but, perhaps better stated, as post-welfare mechanisms of institutional restructure.

To say that the houses are unmonitored and unregulated is simply untenable. With no effective means of redress and a highly contingent state of tenure, recovery house actors become trapped within a series of regulatory forces that operate in concert with the formal treatment sector and the informal recovery house. Chapter 4 revealed the extent to which the recovery house experience ensures a constant negotiability concerning factors well beyond L&I or recovery house licensure: welfare eligibility, probation and parole status, child support, low-wage employment, and citizenship entitlements to behavioral health care. In this sense, recovery houses are but one element of an emergent, multifarious public/private regime of regulation. Men in recovery—operators and clients alike—are caught up within the nets of welfare administration, criminal justice, family policy, de/unregulated labor, and the predatory market structure of the houses themselves. Under chronic conditions of insecurity, the state avails itself of a new form of authority over the industry that does its bidding, as well as multiple forms of authority over the subject caught up in its nets of discipline.

Taken together, the state's variegated responses do not simply enable an informal economy to persist. In fact they also *deepen* urban informality as an engine of contemporary restructure. The experiences of the recovery house actors in this and the preceding chapter evince a kind of remapping, or a re-regulation taking place in Philadelphia. This pertains not only to the recovering self, but also to the recent efforts to formalize the recovery *house* as an emergent form of statecraft. In order to push further toward a substantiation of these arguments, the recovery house must be situated squarely within the compendium of the "workfare state" and the "carceral-assistential state."[39] The following chapter takes up this agenda, further and more explicitly establishing managed persistence as a vector of governmentality by exploring tangible mechanisms of policy transfer in postindustrial Philadelphia.

# Statecraft/Self-Craft

## Policy Transfer in the Recovery House Movement

**6**

Throughout the book, I have argued that a series of agonistic relationships between the self-organization of recovery house operators and the nature of government intervention and nonintervention drive and explain the emergence, proliferation, and persistence of recovery houses. I have also argued, following Marianna Valverde, that addiction and recovery are important sites of regulatory richness due to the multiple ways in which each is governed and used to govern several entities at a single site.[1] This chapter stitches the local manifestation of the recovery house into the broader regulatory fabric characterized by Jamie Peck's *workfare state*[2] and Loïc Wacquant's *carceral-assistential state*.[3] Taken in turn, Peck sketches the new punitive "regulatory fix" in welfare reform, highlighting the current correspondence between active workfare regimes and the burgeoning flexible labor market. Wacquant takes up the penalization of social insecurity, whereby the construction of a post-Keynesian state exacts a "deadly symbiosis" between the upsizing of the penal sector and the downsizing of the welfare state to impose deregulated/desocialized low-wage labor as a norm of citizenship. The respective works of Peck and Wacquant wed the invisible hand of the deregulated labor market to processes of urban enclosure, geographical unevenness, and punitive policies for regulating the poor. But we must also pay attention to emerging forms of poverty governance that, while in some ways buttressing these developments, operate at a different scale, and quite often by way of a different set of policy logics. To fully grasp the complexity of the recovery house as a supporting boundary institution, we must look to the interstices between formal and informal institutions, toward rationalities that cannot be reduced strictly to workfare, revanchism, discipline, or punishment.

Consider Wacquant's argument that the contemporary "ghetto" now operates as "one-dimensional machinery," its dominant social types reduced to the welfare recipient and the prisoner. He contends that state institutions of social control have replaced communal institutions, "depoliticizing" the black urban subproletariat and rendering it incapable of fighting hyperincarceration. His indictment of the "first genuine prison society of history" is equally audacious and important, but it cannot account for other, more nuanced and differentiated processes of institutional restructure. Nor can it account for the institutional contradictions, multiple dimensions, and unevenness of urban informality, or the many new political projects advancing new forms of subjectivity in poor neighborhoods. Indeed, in the Philadelphia context, it is precisely the recovering subject-cum-recovery house operator who is perhaps confronting hyperincarceration head on, if only by way of a politics of recovery and welfare administration.

To understand how the recovery house situates itself, and becomes situated, within a broader set of regulatory logics, we must understand how its unique ontology intersects with a specific form of policy transfer in postindustrial Philadelphia. My purpose in this chapter is to explore a peculiar mechanism of policy transfer. My objective is to illustrate a co-constitutive process by which operators further appropriate the welfare apparatus while the state redistributes functions of discipline, surveillance, and emancipation throughout the interstices of the recovery apparatus. What I envisage here is a kind of *third-way* boundary institution or buffer zone to the workfare state and the carceral-assistential state: recovery as a technology of citizenship.[4] I will explore how the state effectively reinvents its role by occupying congenial recovery knowledge systems due to their characteristic notions of structure, accountability, and responsibility. State extensions into the recovery house movement belie not only facile notions of a retreating state, or an unequivocally revanchist state, but also the perception of the recovery house as an underground phenomenon functioning in the dark corners of "ghetto" neighborhoods. To illustrate recovery houses' enmeshment with legitimate state systems, I will analyze relationships between the houses, the Coordinating Office of Drug and Alcohol Programs (CODAAP), and the formal treatment sector. I will then explore the criminal justice system's encroachment into recovery house networks through the Forensic Intensive Recovery (FIR) and Treatment Court programs.

## Policy Transfer in CODAAP's Housing Initiative and Training Series

As illustrated in chapter 5, the absence of recovery house licensure in Pennsylvania has enabled informal recovery houses to flourish as a cottage industry in areas of spatially concentrated poverty. Philadelphia's Department of Licenses and Inspections (L&I) operates as the nominal regulatory agency in what seems to have become an exercise in futility, if even an exercise at all. But one important city program has addressed the recovery houses directly: the CODAAP Housing Initiative (CHI). The history of CHI dates back to 1994–95, when CODAAP responded to political controversy in the Philadelphia City Council surrounding the New Jersey parolee scandal, as well to a series of community complaints more generally. The controversies prompted CODAAP officials to take action. As something of a compromise to formal state licensure and as a way to formally introduce the City of Philadelphia into the recovery house market, CODAAP Director Mark Bencivengo convinced state legislators to back an RFP (request for proposals) that would directly fund six recovery houses. Word got out on the street that the city was serious about funding recovery houses, and by CHI Director Sam Cutler's and Bencivengo's assessment, the program was an instant success. A second RFP in the late 1990s drew a large pool of proposals, resulting in the addition of seven new CODAAP-funded houses. By 2003, CODAAP was funding over 300 beds in 23 subcontracted recovery houses, mostly located in the Kensington neighborhood but also in North and West Philadelphia. Through the CHI, the city had finally offered a limited channel of legitimacy to recovery houses—albeit a tightly competitive and restricted channel relative to the numbers of houses that still exist.

According to Cutler, CODAAP estimates that beyond its 23 funded houses, an additional 400 to 500 continue to operate without any oversight or formal funding. In my interviews with him, he was quick to disavow the "illegally operated" recovery houses outside CHI's purview (he took a similar position in Gwen Shaffer's *Citypaper* exposé). Cutler would speak only about his CODAAP-funded houses, referring to them as an elite and unequivocally legitimate sect based on the rigorous RFP process. Indeed, a review of CHI rules and regulations reveals that CODAAP houses face a steep climb to legitimacy compared with their freelance counterparts. Qualifying for CODAAP funding starts with a neighborhood petition covering a two-block radius of the house, as well as the signature of the appropriate city councilperson and a pledge of support from any site-relevant community group and/or religious organization. Houses must become incorporated and have comprehensive liability insurance. In addition, they must obtain a license and zoning approval from L&I.

Meeting code requirements for L&I zoning and licensure can be financially prohibitive and even structurally impossible for many (if not most) operators. Each bedroom in the house must contain 50 square feet of floor space for each occupant. The house must have at least one bathroom for every six residents (located within one floor of the sleeping area), and every habitable space must have at least one working window or skylight of an appropriate size. In addition, CODAAP has claimed it would not fund houses with bunk beds, and that it would grant preference to houses limiting occupancy to two per room. (Cutler acknowledged, however, that some CODAAP-funded houses had room occupancies of three and even four residents.) Zoning approval also requires the house to obtain a business privilege license and a business tax number, in addition to designating a "managing agent" to receive notices, orders, and summonses from L&I. Given the typical operator's resistance to putting his name on so much as a utility bill for his recovery house for fear of credit responsibility and open association, this matter posed a formidable barrier for operators like Malik.

Once the operators meet L&I standards related to the physical structure of their recovery house, CHI requires their program to comply with strict operating guidelines. To begin, CODAAP-funded houses are staffed twenty-four hours a day, seven days a week, by *salaried employees*—none of whom are allowed to reside in the house (nor or they allowed to eat there). While a funded program could designate "housefathers" from the client population for leadership purposes and light duties such as chore monitoring, paid staff (usually one supervisor and four staff) are responsible for the bulk of operating procedures. CODAAP requires staff training in the areas of medication management; health and safety standards for food preparation; intake procedures; record keeping; urinalysis (required weekly in CODAAP houses); and collaborative case management with licensed treatment providers and parole officers. Staff learn how to design and implement agency mission statements, as well as treatment goals and objectives. They also must attend a ten-week training series, which provides a credential for recovery house management in addition to sixty credit hours toward Certified Alcohol Counselor (CAC) licensure.

CODAAP developed the training series during the planning phase of the housing initiative. At this time, the agency held focus groups across Philadelphia to glean the most pressing concerns of recovery house operators. CODAAP staff used the data to construct a set of recovery house standards, which would later inform a significant part of the training curriculum. As part of my fieldwork, I attended the ten-week training in the winter of 2003 with a cohort of twenty-eight recovery house operators. During that period we were heavily inundated with seminars led by professionals from a range of social service occupations. Topics included co-occurring disorders; forensics; medical issues such as HIV/AIDS; methadone maintenance and pharmacology; confidentiality and ethics; cultural diversity; recovery house standards and regulations; resources and referrals; and even spirituality/stress management for the prevention of burnout. Sponsored in conjunction with the CHI, the training series was a source of pride for the CODAAP office. Based on its efforts to reach out to what he called a "truly grassroots movement," Cutler described the agency as innovative and timely. He contended that Philadelphia has been the only municipality in the country to fund recovery houses, making the city something of an authority on the issue. As evidence of this fact, Cutler reported that he and Bencivengo had presented CHI as a model at several policy venues in cities along the Northeast Corridor.

The rather impressive training series served as a quasi-professionalization device. It also extended the reach of city government into an informal configuration of collective survival by introducing basic operating standards. It is in this sense that the CHI and the training series represented perhaps not so much a compromise to recovery house licensure as an opportunity to introduce a restricted channel of legitimacy. As I will show, the primary purpose was to formalize the relationship between recovery houses and the criminal justice system. Perhaps inadvertently, the initiatives articulated with the spectrum of formality across the recovery house market as a whole by deepening unevenness and differentiation among operators.[5]

## The "Cadillac" of Recovery House Programs

The organizing divide is not so much formality versus informality as the differentiation that exists within informality—that which marks off different types of

informal accumulation and informal politics. The neoliberal state deepens such
forms of differentiation, fostering some forms of informality and annihilating others. It is this uneven geography that requires us to pay renewed attention to urban
informality.

—NEZAR ALSAYYAD, "URBAN INFORMALITY AS A 'NEW' WAY OF LIFE" (2004)

In relative terms, CODAAP-funded programs (such as Fresh Start) have enjoyed a positive reputation in the city. Recovery house operators in the Kensington neighborhood often referred to them as the "Cadillac of recovery
house programs." And why not, since virtually all program costs are covered
by CODAAP's relatively lavish budget. Billable expenses include, but are not
limited to, the following: maintenance/renovation; client furniture and appliances (a bed, nightstand, and lamp for each client, communal large-screen
televisions); staff furniture and equipment (office and computer supplies,
file/medical cabinets, and fax and copier machines); utilities; annual licensure fees; recovery literature and educational supports; client travel expenses
(van budgets and/or Southeastern Pennsylvania Transportation Authority
[SEPTA] tokens); and even lease/mortgage payments for the house itself.

Listening to Cutler recount these ample provisions at the CODAAP
training series, I couldn't help but compare the CODAAP house to Malik's
chronically under-resourced operation. I had visions of Malik's makeshift
office, a desk and thrift-store typewriter crammed into a corner of Milton's
former kitchen; his shoddy appliances purchased from street vendors; his
experiences with numerous utility shutoffs; and his jerry-rigged maintenance schemes that changed would-be "clients" overnight into roofers, elec-
tricians, and appliance repairmen. No wonder the well-heeled CODAAP
houses drew envy from their struggling counterparts. As Malik implied,
CHI's stable funding even allows CODAAP houses to signify a kind of
stratification in the Kensington built environment:

> MALIK: [*pointing to a CODAAP house on Frankford Avenue*] Look, man, their
> houses are all like institutional houses. Everything is up to
> code . . . they been gutted, redone, the whole shit, because they got the
> money for that. They got fucking jetties they go out and jet-spray the
> goddam sidewalk with . . . the whole fucking program is like that, and it
> has to be like that if you under CODAAP. But they broke it down to you,
> man, you need the money to do that shit.

My trips to Benito's CODAAP-funded houses on Frankford Avenue
confirmed many distinctions between the "Cadillac" of programs and the

A CODAAP-funded house on Frankford Avenue in Kensington.
Photograph by Geoff DeVerteuil. Used by permission.

many fledgling operations like Malik's. For one, Benito had the most elaborate office space that I had ever seen in North Philadelphia or Kensington,
even in formal treatment agencies. As program supervisor, Benito had a
large office with two separate lockable doors. The office had a convincing corporate aesthetic, with a large faux-mahogany desk and a Plexiglas-
covered blotter adorned with nameplate and business card holder. On the
walls were motivational messages, framed pictures of staff and clients at rec-
reational events (such as fishing trips in Puerto Rico), and lacquered plaques
documenting recovery house training and other counseling credentials.
The office contained a locked file and medical cabinet, a fax machine, a copy
machine, posted fire code and exit placards, sign-out logs, a space for client
journals, and various office trays stocked with case management paperwork.
Of all the recovery houses that I visited, Benito's was the only one that had
a late-model computer equipped with high-speed DSL. His office was also
the only one with a surveillance monitor flashing pictures alternately from
cameras located on each floor.

The house featured a renovated dining room with a table large enough to
seat fifteen people comfortably. As we toured the fully renovated kitchen,
Benito proudly showed it off. Unlike their informal counterparts, his men
were not allowed to work on the appliances.

BENITO: Some people are in it for the money from the door, you know, exploiting the clients, and using the clients to do their dirty work, you know, fixing things in the house and stuff like that. That shit is wrong. My clients will not touch anything in this house. If there is a problem with the stove, I call the repairman. If there is a problem with the washer machine, call the repairman, period. Or just buy a new washer and dryer.

The immaculate kitchen, albeit less homey due to its institutional overtones, was fully equipped with an industrial stove and restaurant-style sink (the latter featuring an extended sprayer faucet, sponge floor mat, and antiseptic tablets for rinse water). Food inspection charts and sanitary requirements for hand and dish washing were conspicuously posted. A back room contained an enormous, locked reach-in freezer, which Benito opened to show me a stockpile of food purchased monthly at a local Sam's Club (with the use of a "company van" no less). Continuing our tour upstairs, Benito boasted that none of the bedrooms contained bunk beds, and all were in compliance with L&I requirements. Most of the rooms were occupied by four men (apart from the housefather's "privilege room," which held only three), yet each man was provided a bureau and plenty of closet space. The communal living room, while similar to the basic setup I had seen in many houses, was furnished with a perimeter of couches surrounding a monstrous Sony flat-screen TV and DVD-VCR system.

Benito's recovery house was the most organized that I encountered during my research, a product perhaps of CHI's emphasis on standards and cleanliness as much as its provision of an operating budget. However, Benito was quick to reclaim much of Fresh Start's "success" from CODAAP, extolling the initiative of founder Johnny Walls as well as the sound atmosphere of brotherhood at the program that long preceded CHI.

BENITO: See, the difference with this program that other (CHI) programs don't do, like Johnny Walls the owner, he puts in his own money. He don't care [about the grant] because he doesn't need CODAAP to survive. He has his own business, and this has always been his way of giving back. I mean, these guys got a giant TV screen upstairs, you know they live good, it's clean, and there are a lot of things that he doesn't bill CODAAP for. Plus, this house was up and running way before CODAAP came in.

RF: So if it came down to it, say, the funds did dry up from CODAAP, do you think you could maintain the level of standards that you have here and that you could run the same operation with the same philosophy . . .

BENITO: Absolutely, we've been doing it for years.

RF: So you don't feel like there are strings attached to the CODAAP money
  that infringe on your autonomy, or that get in your way or anything?
BENITO: No. Quite honestly, it is Johnny's world; I work for Johnny Walls,
  not CODAAP.

As a matter of operator pride in self-organization, Benito voiced typical
opposition to the bureaucratic trappings of state funding (some operators
feared a compromise to autonomy, others a brake on "profits"). But the
absence of a direct chronological relationship between funding and a "virtuous" program should not be surprising in and of itself. CODAAP never
intended to create the intricate configurations of self-help operating in recovery houses so much as to harness, shore up, and enlist a small subset of
preexisting programs. In this light, Benito's resistance to state involvement
was perhaps paradoxical, to the extent that street-level actors ultimately
work as able partners for the postindustrial city.[6]

  The idea behind the CHI was to accommodate operator autonomy
(within reason, of course—Cutler noted some programs had been dropped
for noncompliance) while creating new links to material and political power.
Once again a "quiet encroachment"[7] is at play, and a restructuring rather
than a termination of the relationship between state and citizen.[8] The CHI
was built on a movement of operators resistant to state discipline, yet at the
same time angling (and ailing) for the security of state surveillance, funding,
and legitimacy. But the initiative's continued tolerance of (and engagement
with) Philadelphia's much larger, informal sector of recovery houses suggests something important. In accordance with Nezar AlSayyad's quote at
the start of this section, the city has fostered recovery houses in various ways,
in this case directly courting them in order to embed quasi-institutional
mechanisms within broader matrices of the political economy. We do not see
a city- or state-driven annihilation of those programs left outside the CHI's
tightly restricted, highly competitive upper echelon of recovery houses.
Conversely, ongoing city tolerance suggests a denuded strategy of minimal
risk management for the much-needed if chronically unstable houses that
are left to languish in the informal sector.

  The range of formality and institutional variance, from flophouse to
CODAAP house, is in some ways a product of the contradictory advance of
the neoliberal project. In this respect, we might consider recovery houses of
all stripes, along with criminal justice, informal labor, and workfare, as separate institutions engaged in different moments of the continuous process
of rollback/rollout neoliberalism.[9] As in the case of workfare, local variabil-
ity and dynamism in the recovery house industry are important parts of the

story, as the volatile economy of the recovery house is a source of energy for the churning of programs and addicted bodies alike.[10] The CHI's inadvertent fostering of differentiation introduces a new vector of morality and legitimacy to further stratify the movement, while providing the city with a politically expedient solution to its overcrowded jail systems. CHI instantiates a selective logic of mapping and re-regulation, in this case primarily to round out, and shore up, the buffer zones of the "carceral mesh."[11]

## The CHI and the CODAAP Training Series

CODAAP's recovery house training series provided a mechanism for the extension and promulgation of standards within a preexisting self-help mechanism of poverty survival. As evidence of these objectives, former CODAAP program analyst and training series coordinator Lorraine Scalzo explained how the city had moved to "support" a much-needed recovery house movement in the age of managed care:

> LS: I used to work at CODAAP as a program analyst, and one of the problems we faced was that once people left the treatment programs they had no place to go. Then in the '90s we started to look at the HMO turnover, and started looking more at a continuum of care, if you will, so we started saying, "Okay, now we need to fill in the gaps [from managed-care cutbacks]." Certainly the recovery community knew long before the professionals that we needed these houses, and the recovery houses had long been filling the gaps. There was a sense that we needed to support this movement, and that's where CHI came into being.

In postindustrial Philadelphia, protected zones of legitimate urban governance are in many respects "othered" by poverty survival mechanisms taking shape in poor neighborhoods. But the era of fiscal austerity and retrenchment requires a selective rapprochement, whereby the city must descend from its lofty and sequestered zones to court informal poverty survival strategies on the ground. Yet at the same time that CODAAP recognized an able partner to "fill the gap(s)," much work would have to be done to bolster an otherwise unsightly marriage. First the city had to enumerate the recovery house's challenges in order to introduce training and a set of operating standards.

> LS: [These houses] started to really crop up in the '90s. But there were criticisms of recovery houses, they were thought to be haphazard, lacking

standards and licensure in most cases, and some of the living conditions were not great. So there was definitely recognition that there needed to be some standardization of them in order to combat some of the criticisms. Also, a lot of the people who worked in recovery houses were in recovery themselves, which in and of itself was not a problem, except that they didn't have the training in terms of clinical [knowledge], you know, outside of AA/NA. So it was thought that offering training for those in recovery houses would really help them understand some of the people they were getting. I mean, you have to take a step back to look at what else is happening in the field, and what's happening is there has been a greater recognition of co-occurring disorders. Many of these people come through recovery houses. So, we focused on putting money into some training.

In a separate interview, CODAAP Program Coordinator Marvin Levine offered a similar rendition of the city's initial assessment. Levine noted that the houses were recognized as providing a valuable social service—one that could be greatly enhanced by the advent of training and standards to combat vice and decline:

ML: Kensington was becoming a haven for recovery houses, and there was recognition that some of them were real dumps. Some of them weren't fit for human habitation, some of them were exploiting people, and nobody was regulating them. So in the mid-'90s we gathered a group of twelve different recovery houses, and they were saying that number one, they were doing stuff without any kind of public money, that they were struggling, and that they were doing a service, and that they really could benefit by doing more. We agreed and thought this was a viable group of houses, so out of this meeting we generated a set of standards. We also generated the original curriculum for the recovery house training series, and opened up the training to any recovery house. We were look[ing] to promulgate these standards to everyone.

I was able to witness the CODAAP staff's dissemination of these standards as part of my fieldwork in the recovery house training series. One particularly full day included a morning session taught by Marvin Levine, "Recovery House Standards and Rules," and an afternoon session facilitated by Sam Cutler, "Management Issues for Recovery Houses." Levine began the day by eliciting the most common criticisms of recovery houses from the trainee audience. Erstwhile pupils responded with a slew of community perceptions that they had encountered: recovery houses increased prevalence of crime, drugs, blight, prostitution, vandalism, high insurance rates, and even child molestation, along with HIV/AIDS and other sexually transmitted diseases. Participants also spoke of declines in property values, quality of life, neighborhood safety, and commercial business due to recovery house proliferation. Levine captured all of the comments on a large flip chart. Using a red marker, he then attributed all of these factors solely to *the lack of government oversight*. The silver bullet to reverse these outcomes and to quell the harshest of critics, Levine claimed, was none other than a set of standards devised by CHI.

Under the somewhat vague rubric of standards, Levine covered a range of topics: staff training, confidentiality, rent policies, protections against client exploitation, and grievance procedures. He then opened up the floor for discussion on rent collection, curfews, urinalysis, work policies, and maintenance practices. Levine used the wide range of participant responses on each issue as further evidence of a disorganized industry that was sorely in need of standardization. He identified clear policies and procedures as vital mechanisms for setting out program expectations as well as for establishing accountability.

Toward the end of the seminar, Levine used his flip chart once again—this time to elicit responses on the "positive" aspects of recovery houses. Participants trotted out a familiar range of "assets": the houses' contribution to the community; their capacity to transform addicts from "tax burdens to taxpayers"; their ability to produce community role models; their role in educating the community about addiction; and their rehabilitation and beautification effects in blighted neighborhoods. Levine then openly lamented the absence of recovery house licensure, which he felt would uplift and protect the movement. In its stead, he drove toward his finishing point in selling CODAAP standards as the best alternative. He concluded by drawing on the flip chart a large triangle containing the words *training*, *standards*, and *committed staff* on each of its constituent legs. Directly to the right of the triangle Levine inscribed the sum of these parts: "= Quality House!" By the conclusion of the talk, Levine had trained his participants to provide the one-word answer, "standards," for his many fabricated scenarios of disorder. When the crowd called it out in unison, he would exclaim half-comically in response, "Ooh, I love that word!"

In the afternoon session, Sam Cutler began his talk by extolling the virtues of orderliness, a solid program and rule structure, and an abundance of "clean and well-lit spaces conducive to recovery." Cutler then proceeded to link his vision of a "quality recovery house" to the CHI standards, covering topics such as intake procedures, zoning and licensure, community support, and personnel requirements. His talk emphasized the crucial role of the recovery house manager in carrying out "best practices" such as psychosocial, employment, and family histories. Cutler also covered treatment planning, screening for co-occurring disorders and health issues, proper record keeping, and assessment practices. He envisaged the recovery house manager as an integral member of the client's "treatment team," underlining CODAAP's requirement for a minimum of three contacts per week with case managers in the formal treatment sector as well as regular contacts with probation/parole officers.

As an alternative to direct regulation relying on institutions or state power, CODAAP's Housing Initiative and training series attempted to enlist, guide, and shape the actions of recovery house operators. The purpose was to correct deficiencies and to redistribute risk and responsibility, mainly by promoting and coupling the mutual interests of the recovery house operator and the state. In opening up the training to the entire recovery house community, CODAAP also sought to work with recovery house operators outside the CHI purview. This would allow even informal actors like Malik to forge alliances with the state. Indeed, Malik's completion of the ten-week training was one of his proudest accomplishments.

It should be noted, however, that a tangible sense of futility colored much of what Levine and Cutler offered. In many ways they were pleading for voluntary compliance with standards that were not only unrealistic for most, but also lacking any type of authoritative bite (with the exception of CHI houses, of course). Nonetheless, the CHI and the training series have been the only formal extension of government into the realm of recovery house operations. These interventions work in concert with the city's otherwise lax culture of nonintervention, at least as pertains to the house itself.

## Enmeshment with Systems of Legitimacy: Recovery Houses' Connections to the Formal Treatment Sector

Chapter 4 revealed how the recovery house matrix traps recovering subjects within the disciplinary nets of the criminal justice system, the predatory recovery house market, and the low-wage/informal labor market. Another crucially important vector of the recovery house experience must now be dealt with in regulatory terms. Chapter 5 explored, somewhat unreflexively, Public Welfare Department Unit Manager Jeffrey Blumberg's contention that the GA population had suffered from a "system disconnect."

Blumberg remarked that other welfare populations, such as persons with
children or those caught up in workfare programs, get "more connect" than
the predominantly single population on GA. But this assessment failed to
account for the expansive relationship between GA and *formal* outpatient
substance abuse treatment comprising an alternative space to workfare,
which has not yet been given its proper due in this book beyond discussions of welfare administration. It is this expansive relationship that sets the
terms for the city's policy transfer in the CHI, driven by the recovery house
operator's notable utility as an ancillary mechanism of regulation.

As previously discussed in chapter 2, while exempt from formal work
and training requirements, public welfare regulations in the City of Philadelphia require all persons receiving GA for drug and alcohol dependence
to attend intensive outpatient treatment (IOP), followed by a "step down"
to outpatient treatment (OP). The treatment requirement has allowed GA
to remain politically robust in Pennsylvania. It has also given birth to a host
of outpatient treatment providers in North Philadelphia and Kensington.
These centers serve the welfare population on a fee-for-service basis under
Community Behavioral Health (CBH) managed-care guidelines. Most of
this population lives in recovery houses out of economic necessity, which
puts the formal treatment sector in the precarious position of having to
work with its less formal counterparts as a matter of economic survival.

But the connections between recovery houses and treatment go beyond
economic motives. Welfare statutes designate addiction as a temporarily
disabling condition that necessitates treatment. In this sense, CODAAP
officials stated that the formal treatment sector provides professionalized
services, such as assessment, diagnosis, counseling, and therapy. These are
services that recovery houses—despite being acknowledged as important
"supports"—are unqualified to provide.

> LS: I know one of the requirements is that if you are in the CODAAP Hous-
> ing Initiative, the person must be in outpatient treatment. The reasoning
> behind this requirement was that the recovery house was not to be a place
> for treatment per se to happen. It is a place to live, it is a structure for
> some accountability, you have meetings to attend, but it was not to be a
> place for treatment, and treatment should not be happening in the recov-
> ery house. But the motivation was to try and help people get into recov-
> ery, and not have to repeat the cycle so many times. I mean, alcoholism is
> a chronically relapsing disease, so the thinking is, here is an opportunity
> to produce optimal outcomes. We want to make our best intervention at
> this point, and that requires plugging in as many supports as possible.

Lorraine Scalzo recognized the importance of working in concert with recovery house networks, as they deliver on valued policy concepts such as structure and accountability. Substance abuse clinicians have long respected and enlisted self-help supports and halfway houses in the treatment of addiction. As part of their professionalization efforts, however, clinicians have gone to great lengths to distinguish their expert knowledge from self-help knowledge. Correspondingly, most recovery house operators go out of their way to articulate where the recovery house ends and professionalized treatment begins. Malik was careful to denote this in all of his written program materials so as to avoid any illusions about the provisions and limitations of the recovery house setting. He did this not only to avoid regulatory scrutiny (which he felt could happen, were he to overstate the house's functions by stepping into the "clinical" realm), but perhaps even more important, to show his respect for the role that professionalized treatment plays in the recovery process.

> MALIK: This whole process of recovery goes beyond the recovery house to the treatment part, because we got to ask questions about more than just the drinking part. What about all that other shit? About how I got raped? Abused? Neglected? Or how I like to fight all the time? All this other stuff that got to be dealt with . . . I'm talking about keeping your *emotional* sobriety, because before you even drink, you locked and loaded emotionally. So this is what the IOP part is for, the treatment of these emotional issues.

The formal treatment sector is the much-needed and appropriate context for addressing unresolved "emotional issues." Attention to these matters has long been considered crucial to sobriety, and even 12-step groups actively encourage the pursuit of professional help for resolution of deep-seated psychological and emotional pain. In this way, a relationship has formed historically between the self-help realm, which claims jurisdiction over the daily structures and discipline necessary to put down the drink and/or drug so that one can *live* sober; and the professionalized treatment realm, which takes on clinical matters such as depression and "unresolved family of origin issues." CODAAP's Housing Initiative recognizes the importance of this symbiotic relationship by requiring that all its residents—whether on public assistance or not—attend outpatient treatment. As Marvin Levine claimed, mandatory enrollment in treatment sets CODAAP-funded recovery houses apart from addiction halfway houses such as the Oxford House model—as well as the informal or non-CHI-funded house:

ML: All clients in the CHI are in outpatient treatment, whereas in the traditional Oxford model they house people who are working and not going
to treatment. So one of the variations here is that we are requiring people
who, if they are going to use these slots, need to be in treatment. It's a
little more proactive approach, and much more incentive-based housing,
you know, to maintain people in treatment. If they leave treatment in one
of our houses, they have to move. I think there is a wide variation about
the treatment requirements in non-CHI houses; there might be requirements to go to 12-step meetings, but that's not formal treatment, that's
self-help stuff.

I informed Levine that in my research experience, almost all recovery
houses —CODAAP-funded or not—required residents to go to treatment,
especially since their program's finances depended on it. He suspected great
variation in practice due to the absence of standards. Still, he remarked that
even informal enforcement of this requirement was good practice. Close
connections between the recovery house and the treatment provider are
said to produce "optimal treatment outcomes."

ML: In the CODAAP Housing Initiative, the house and the treatment
centers are closely involved. There is a lot of communication between the
recovery houses and the outpatient counselor, and in general the houses
are looking to share information with the counselor and vice versa. They
discuss matters like, is the person in treatment? Are their random urines
clean? They do this mostly to be on the same page as far as the person's
recovery is concerned. So there is a lot of close communication between
the CHI houses and the outpatient clinic providing formal treatment.

Levine highlighted the mutually beneficial relationship between treatment provider and recovery house. This relationship preceded the CHI, as
the treatment requirement dated back to the original GA welfare legislation
in 1982. In CODAAP's initial focus groups and studies on recovery houses,
connections between the two sectors were seen as a vital asset to Philadelphia, not only for reasons associated with treatment best practices but
also as monitoring strategies. Levine referred to "information sharing" on
matters ranging from attendance ("Is the person in treatment?") to random
urine screens, which at first glance seem quite different from clinical matters per se. In this light, we can see some slippage between actual treatment
objectives and the coercive strategies associated with the criminal justice
and public welfare systems.

The city's Public Welfare Department has recognized the connection between the formal treatment sector and recovery houses as a crucial component of the recovery matrix.

> JB: The connection between recovery houses and formal treatment centers is crucial. Recovery houses provide the basic amenity of stable housing, but people also need to go to deal with their substance abuse and recovery issues in treatment. The really good treatment centers take it to the next level and try to help someone move on with their life with jobs and things like that, which also means working with the recovery house. So the network between the property [recovery house] and the treatment center is crucial for all those reasons. It also helps for the drug center to know where the people are, so they can in a sense *oversee* them.

Jeffrey Blumberg conveyed the importance of teamwork between the treatment center and the recovery house not only on issues related to drug and alcohol addiction, but also on broader objectives connected to the agendas of public welfare. These include employment, and perhaps more important, oversight.

This discussion clearly illustrates how the recovery house operates as an ancillary modality of treatment, but several more-complex points have been raised that warrant further discussion. To begin, there is something meaningful in Lorraine Scalzo's call to "[plug] in as many supports as possible" in order to "make our best intervention." Quite apart from Scalzo's personal motives, this contention takes on a deeper significance when we consider recovery and addiction as part of a broader regulatory project. It is the conceptual porosity of recovery—driven in part by a history of decentralization and deprofessionalization in self-help groups as well as the failure to "medicalize" addiction[12]—that has enabled recovery house actors and the state to blur the boundaries between addiction and other competing anti-poverty/regulatory industries. New forms of statecraft emerge from messy and indeterminate processes of institutional restructuring that confound received notions of functionally discrete policy areas[13] (prison and recovery, formal and informal, public sector and primitively privatized voluntary sector). Both recovery house operators and the state have capitalized on the fluidity of the recovery concept to assemble various practical and discursive fragments of professionalized treatment, 12-step programs, psychology, probation and parole, and workfare. In this sense, there is more at stake in the foregoing discussion than "turf" claims. Differentiation of services establishes specific points along a continuum—from the informal recovery house, to the formal treatment sector, to public welfare, criminal justice, and low-wage labor.

Taken together, what's at stake is a multisited system of poverty management that—while in a sense unplanned by any centralized authority—is held together by the hybrid and ambiguous nature of the recovery concept. The open-endedness and infinite flexibility of what Scalzo called a "chronically relapsing disease" opens up multiple points of intervention: from treatment to employment, welfare to surveillance, housing to independence. As Malik stated poignantly, we can also include here matters of "emotional sobriety," which extend far beyond picking up a drink or a drug (family, fighting, abuse, neglect, and even rape). As much of the evidence in this book has shown, the concept of recovery operates as a single site for multiple regulatory projects, based on its almost limitless capacity for reassembly and efficient transfer across multiple policy domains.[14] Recovery thus emerges as a kind of "third way" in an age that has known chronic insecurity, mass incarceration, and a war on dependency.

## A Marketized Mechanism of Governmentality

With CBH guidelines meting out reimbursement purely on a fee-for-service basis, treatment centers receive payment only for each session at which clients are physically present. Attendance is verified incessantly in the treatment setting by daily procurement of client signatures. I witnessed the harried and frenetic practice of "sign-in" at Billings's treatment center several times. Administrative assistants corralled and herded clients through the waiting room and even interrupted group and individual counseling sessions to obtain signatures. Given the pressures of managed-care guidelines as well as the precarious nature of recovery more generally, it is clearly in the treatment director's best interest to have a steady flow of clients brought in from recovery houses. Ideally, the houses deliver clients consistently, in addition to adding a supplementary mechanism of reinforcement for session attendance.

> JB: [The treatment centers rely on recovery houses] so they have a client pool, a participant population, or a feeder source. [This is necessary] because of the managed-care structure. Without their reimbursement from CBH, the [treatment centers] don't have money for salaries. So it's an interdependence that's crucial, but I think it's just systematic, as part of the managed-care system. I don't think it's a violation unless they are abusing it in some way, like falsification of records.

Public Welfare's Jeff Blumberg recognized an economic "interdependence" between the houses and the treatment centers. The centers' connection to recovery houses not only makes good treatment sense, but also becomes a necessary element of the managed care fee-for-service structure (indeed, even for ensuring continued payment of professional salaries). As a value-added bonus, the mechanism operates freely through a market logic that maximizes and extends each partner's economic interests *and* surveillance capacities.

Of course, where profits and finances are involved there is always a way to improve one's control over the market share. Marvin Levine acknowledged that forms of graft have emerged in the recovery matrix. As was typical of CODAAP officials, he was quick to disavow the vast majority of recovery houses operating in the unlicensed, unregulated sector, setting them apart from those funded under CHI:

> ML: Certainly these questions have come up. You know, like, are there questionable practices happening at recovery houses where they have some kind of sweet deal where everybody in the recovery house is going to some clinic and the hospital is paying the recovery house to send everybody whether or not they need it? Is it becoming some kind of Medicaid mill? You know some are and some aren't. The ones that we are funding and overseeing we can vouch for, the other ones we don't. Typically hospitals or clinics have come up with mechanisms to increase their own services; sometimes it has involved recovery houses.

Levine suggested that clinics and hospitals possibly forge relationships with recovery houses to "increase their own services." My research revealed that these types of relationships with outpatient treatment centers are not only common, but also pervasive and contractual in the recovery house industry. There is great market incentive for treatment programs to ensure attendance throughout the allotted sessions. Centers typically "incentivize" client attendance by offering prizes such as portable CD players, restaurant gift certificates, and elaborate "graduation" parties that include cakes, party favors, and certificates of completion. Treatment providers also devise fairly sophisticated economic incentives for the recovery house client and operator. As a case in point, I turn to an informal contract that existed between Bilal's Positive Attitudes recovery house program and a treatment provider called The Safety Net.

According to Bilal, his boss was able to establish this contract through his dual position as cofounder of the Positive Attitudes program and counselor at the Safety Net. The Safety Net paid $22 biweekly stipends to its clients for consistent attendance throughout four months of IOP treatment. It deposited half of this money, $11.50 every other week, into each client's escrow account, to be collected in full at the completion of IOP treatment (in most cases this "step-down" payment provided $200 to $250, depending on individual attendance). From the remaining half of the money, the Safety Net paid a $10 biweekly housing stipend to Positive Attitudes. The $1.50 left over was dispensed directly to the client for discretionary pocket money (normally used for laundry and cigarettes).

Based on this scheme, Bilal told me that Positive Attitudes clients who attended the Safety Net paid $100 every other week in rent, as opposed to his other clients, who paid only $90 ($200 versus $180 per month, respectively). Although the Safety Net appeared to be a benevolent sponsor in paying the housing stipend, the center simply offset its revenues from CBH in order to secure bodies from the recovery house contract. Bilal claimed that his boss had effectively kept the agency in business by consistently providing more than thirty clients from Positive Attitudes. In turn, by increasing the rent for Safety Net clients, the recovery house was able to double-dip into the welfare system—by extracting rent funds not only from GA cash assistance, but also from medical assistance via the kickback arrangement.

While this was one of the more sophisticated schemes that I knew of, the basic strategy is typical in recovery house networks. Bilal explained that contractual arrangements were illegal in his eyes, or at the very least unethical, because welfare access card carriers are "supposed to be entitled to their choice" of treatment provider. When a house pressures clients into one program for economic reasons, freedom of choice is compromised. As a former Positive Attitudes client, Blanche explained how she was ordered to attend the Safety Net:

> BLANCHE: All of us [in the women's house] went to the Safety Net, because if you don't go to the Safety Net three days a week the owner of Positive Attitudes don't get paid. And if you not there, the Safety Net don't get paid, so the owner don't get paid and the client don't get paid from the Safety Net. Basically, you got to be there three days a week [for everyone to get paid].

Several factors—among them the systems and channels in place to get clients "plugged in" to welfare; transportation contracts; and informal feeder source contracts—often mean that recovery house operators pipeline clients like Blanche into a treatment center against their will. But in Bilal's assessment, operators typically conceal these arrangements by offering the illusion of choice and "opportunity" for their clients:

> BILAL: The only thing recovery houses have to do is to provide *opportunities* for the client to go to their choice of treatment programs. It's the only thing they have to do.

This veil of opportunity lies in something that Malik often referred to as the "blue laws" of the recovery house industry: operator practices that were ethically suspect but logistically and financially expedient. Informal contracting with treatment centers is an integral part of this realm. Clarence explained how a treatment provider wooed him through a similar type of kickback arrangement:

> CLARENCE: I could send my guys to any outpatient treatment, but really what I want to know is what are they getting, besides just treatment. They could get treatment anywhere, but the problem is they struggle in some areas, like having to get their own soap and cigarettes and stuff like that. When they broke all the time, they are always worried about getting a job, which usually drops them out of treatment. So the incentive that they give them is the money they put in the escrow account, so that the clients know that when they finish they have some money. It gives them the incentive to want to finish. Most people who are drug and alcohol dependent never finish anything, like school, nothing. So we have a verbal agreement with the treatment center. Every week they send over a list of who has been there and how many times they've been there.

The enhanced capacities for client oversight are beneficial for both treatment provider and recovery house operator. As an added bonus in this case, the new provider was willing to provide door-to-door van service between Clarence's recovery houses and the treatment center, thus reducing the chances of anyone getting "lost or caught up where they shouldn't be." Moreover, in Clarence's assessment the provision of a financial incentive actually becomes a "treatment issue," particularly since it mitigates the dire poverty that most recovery house subjects endure (often leading them to abandon treatment in favor of work, as illustrated in chapter 4). Couched in this way, it is difficult to see any problem with the arrangements. But we can see how recovering subjects are interpellated as incentive-based consumers in their own recovery projects. We can see also how regulation drives along two fronts: (1) preferring the welfare client to the low-wage worker,

the coercive practices of the operator and the treatment provider stabilize
conditions for accumulation/subsistence by controlling clients; and (2) if
a client is "lost" to the low-wage service sector, welfare caseworkers are
poised to execute the workfare logic of purging bodies from the welfare
rolls.

From the perspective of the treatment provider, Billings claimed that the
arrangements could be beneficial in other ways. For example, he noted that
by supporting certain recovery houses informally, he could help to improve
the living conditions through informal financial support. He explained how
he had operated in this way with several of his feeder sources:

BILLINGS: The City of Philadelphia realizes that we work directly with
recovery houses. I work directly with Christian recovery houses like
Soldiers of the Lord, Fountain of Hope, Refuge in Christ, and Second
Chance. I would say I have around 35 coming from Second Chance, and
about 45 people coming from Soldiers of the Lord. Some of these programs are better than others in keeping their license up and maintaining
good living conditions. I try to help with that.

For example, Fountain of Hope probably has like 65 people, and 20
of them sleep on the floor. I am in the process of trying to help them do
the right thing, because at this point I have about 35 of their clients. They
haven't done that yet, and they have been flying by the seat of their pants,
but I try to help out in certain ways. I write them a check for the heat and
that kind of stuff, because the state has a problem with money going [di-
rectly] from us [treatment providers] to those people. There is an old law
that says as a provider you can't give kickbacks to houses. Everybody does
it, but you have to do it a certain way so that you are legally correct.

The emphasis on making these types of tactics "legally correct" refers to
Malik's notion of the "blue laws," the unwritten set of rules that allow, or
rather force, recovery entrepreneurs to flex ethical boundaries to function
effectively. Similar to the operator's paranoia over illegitimacy, the ethically
ambiguous nature of the informal recovery house setup also put Billings
in a tenuous position as a treatment provider. He was invested in changing
the shrouded and informal culture of interdependence between operator
and provider. To him, it was ridiculous to continue with some sense of
wrongdoing, given the widespread practice of centers working with recovery houses as a matter of not only survival, but also best practice. He
and his clinical director devised a proposal for CBH which argued that the
involvement of recovery houses improved treatment attendance and—by

extension—treatment outcomes. The following discussion chronicles the evolution of his thought:

BILLINGS: One of the last meetings we had at CBH was regarding the IOP, and their main problem was that many programs are being provided service dollars for IOP but are not using the funds. When people come into treatment they require authorization for IOP, they will give us authorization for four months. Their statistics have shown that over the last year and a half only 34% or 36% are being used, and the rest of the dollars are being sent back. So then the state looked at CBH and said, "We're giving you $100, and for some reason you are only using $36. What's up? That's telling us you have a big problem there." Basically they say, "Here is this money, Billings," and this is what you spend to treat those people; you give them the name, they give us the authorization. But what they are saying is that 64% of that is not being spent, because Joe Blow comes two times and he goes back out.

So what we're going to show is that because the population that we're dealing with comes from the recovery houses, our statistics are much better. In fact, ours are almost reversed, and we need to show that to them, and that's because the people that are coming from recovery houses are more stable. Especially the Christian recovery houses, which keep the guys and make sure they come to treatment, compared to some of the other programs, where they have one foot in recovery and the other foot in a crack house. But as far as outcomes are concerned, that's the kind of outcomes they are looking for, that all the dollars are [being taken up]. And it's because the recovery houses have a means to *hold* the person and to see that the person comes to treatment. That stabilizes them enough so that we can treat them.

RF: Do you feel that the city and the state will be receptive and positive about going to them and saying you want to work with this system directly like this?

BILLINGS: [*raises his voice*] Well, look, the fact is that we *are* working directly with these houses, we *are*! And it's necessary [and effective]. Out of the 190 clients that I have now, 150 of them are coming from the houses, even some of the state-funded houses where some of the guys from prison go for prerelease programs. So I don't even think we need to sell this just as an attractive selling point; I think we need to sell it as a reality.

Billings articulated the stabilizing force of the recovery house matrix (they "have a means to *hold* them"). Subjects are not only more consistent treatment attendees, but also face better odds at reintegrating as "productive members of society." Moreover, recovery houses provide a viable shadow mechanism to increase market efficiency for the outpatient treatment sector by improving the takeup of welfare dollars. Billings tried to formalize this arrangement by moving the practice of informal feeder source contracts into a zone of quasi-legal negotiation. His strategy was to move away from the "dubious whitewashing" of practices emblematized by blue laws, thereby setting a precedent that could be built on in future efforts.[15] Historically, informal welfare economies and state-subsidized underworlds have been robust in the face of state attempts to curtail corruption, in part because the economies themselves are woven together by a tangle of interests.[16] But in Billings's view, the operator (and in one sense the treatment provider) could be moved into a zone of legitimacy while also allowing the state to capitalize on the recovery house formally as a site of policy innovation. Of course, with a devolutionary matrix in place that already functioned in this manner, perhaps the status quo was perfectly sufficient.

[rec. house as site of policy innovation]

### Connections to Criminal Justice: The FIR Program and Treatment Court

The criminal justice system has long enlisted the services of the professional treatment sector in helping to rehabilitate drug-addicted clients coming directly from prisons and jails. In fact, Billings serviced two separate contracts in this regard, one that operated with the state prison system and one that worked exclusively with federal inmates. Concurrently, as the previous statements by Billings and others make clear, correctional authorities also enlisted recovery house networks as ancillary mechanisms of surveillance and rehabilitation. The most calculated and direct connection between the houses and the criminal justice system in Philadelphia is CODAAP's CHI program. CHI-funded houses have formulated exclusive contracts with the state to house parolees and Treatment Court offenders as part of the city's sentence diversion program. Consequently, according to CHI Director Sam Cutler, 80% of the clients occupying roughly 300 to 350 CODAAP-funded beds in 23 houses were Forensic Intensive Recovery (FIR) clients.[17]

In 1962, a Supreme Court decision rendered drug addiction an illness rather than a crime.[18] This decision catalyzed a movement to integrate treatment strategies into the criminal justice system, resulting in a raft of experimental programs across different states. The basic idea was to provide consistent and reliable services to addicts while controlling their offending criminal behaviors in quasi-institutional treatment milieus. While it originated much later, the FIR program of the Philadelphia Adult Probation and Parole Department is one such experiment, designed to encourage active collaboration between the treatment sector, the criminal justice system, and recovery house networks. In fact, according to Cutler the FIR program and the CHI developed in earnest after an corrections officials expressed a need to reduce the inmate population in Philadelphia. At this time, state and city officials recognized recovery houses as channels for prisoner re-entry.

While the State of New Jersey had been implementing this practice for years through its underground shipment of parolees into Kensington recovery houses, the collaboration between FIR and CHI represented a novel, above-board effort to make these connections legitimate. In terms of the basic framework, Cutler explained that to qualify for the program, FIR candidates must have committed only "low-level or city-level crimes" and undergo full drug and alcohol assessment. If appropriate, offenders can reduce their sentence by as much as 50% simply by attending three phases of treatment (inpatient, intensive outpatient, and outpatient). During the latter two phases (which can last from four months to a year), clients are mandated to live in recovery houses. FIR case managers, who work in collaboration with recovery house staff and outpatient clinicians, oversee the clients. Due to the success of the initiative, over 60 drug and alcohol programs in Philadelphia contracted for FIR and other criminal justice programs as of 2003.[19]

Cutler praised the collaborative effort between FIR and CHI, noting that his CODAAP-funded recovery houses were "the only way" to reduce the prison population. He added, "politically it works for us," particularly since judges prefer to have their FIR clients go directly to CODAAP houses, where they can be assured a "heavily monitored" living environment. In the case of Fresh Start, a CODAAP-funded recovery house program that held several correctional contracts, the presence of surveillance cameras was status quo. I noticed the cameras and monitors during my tour of Benito's house, and inquired about their origin:

RF: How did the use of cameras come about?
BENITO: Johnny [the owner] wanted it, so that clients ain't allowed to go upstairs, you know, we want to make sure they don't come up here sleeping or loungin', that's not allowed, there is no laying on the furniture.
RF: Are the clients cool with that?
BENITO: Yeah, they don't mind, there's no yellin' out the windows, no hangin' out the window, we don't want to show that to the community, so the cameras just help us [monitor] the upstairs.

Benito downplayed the cameras, attributing their presence to behavioral modification and community relations rather than criminal justice. But most of his house's residents came either directly from jail (through the FIR program) or directly from Treatment Court (where they would have avoided jail by consenting to treatment).

Given that 80% of the CHI residents are FIR clients, the only channel of legitimacy for Philadelphia recovery houses is further restricted. This sets the CHI apart even more from the estimated four-hundred-plus houses that operate more typically in the informal sector. The FIR contracts also explain the institutionalized structure of the CODAAP houses, equipped as they are with paraprofessional staff, annual budget audits, and surveillance cameras. Accordingly, the city's only effort to regulate the houses directly has been largely limited to the criminal justice population. This population, which requires more discipline and surveillance to ensure compliance, safety, and also political support, is perhaps ironically the *only* population worthy of direct recovery house intervention by the city at the programmatic level. As for the unregulated houses serving the "less-worthy" poor, the city adopts a strategy of risk management (with sporadic L&I zoning regulations and selective welfare fraud investigations), drawing optimal benefit—however inadvertently—from a spatially contained antipoverty mechanism in the shadow welfare state.

Eighty percent of FIR clients are ineligible for public assistance due to felony convictions, owing to the welfare reform statutes of 1996. To compensate for this, CODAAP worked in conjunction with the Philadelphia Behavioral System to devise a program called the Behavioral Health Special Initiative (BHSI). In effect, BHSI subsidizes FIR clients so that they can attend treatment and live in recovery houses. CODAAP is the primary contract holder and preferred provider of recovery house beds for the FIR program in Philadelphia. However, Cutler acknowledged that oftentimes CHI beds are full, putting social workers, FIR case managers, parole officers, and judges in the position of having to rely on the city's more than four hundred non-CHI houses. Such was the case with Infinite, who—after serving eight years for involuntary manslaughter—qualified for the FIR program as he continued to struggle with recidivism while on probation and parole. When Infinite entered the program, no CODAAP beds were available. He was released to the Safety Net outpatient treatment program, where he was to finish out his sentence while living at a Positive Attitudes recovery house. Infinite was brought to Positive Attitudes in handcuffs, and turned over to a "treatment team" composed of his probation officer, his counselor at the Safety Net, and his recovery house manager (in this case Bilal, and then Malik). The remainder of his sentence had been grafted onto the professionalized treatment system, which would work in conjunction with the informal recovery house sector.

> INFINITE: I had been out for some time but I violated my probation, so what they did instead of reinstating the probation, they gave the time of the probation to the treatment program, and said as long as I didn't get in any trouble with the law I would be fine. I was looking at 11½ to 23 months, so now basically it's like if I was doing 11½ to 23 at the County [jail], it's the same thing; I'm just doing it on the street and in the treatment program on this thing called a special release. I'm not supervised or nothing like that; the only supervision I have is the treatment program, that's my supervision.

Like hundreds of recovery subjects, Infinite entered the recovery house matrix through the criminal justice system. It should also be noted that while he was brought to a non-CHI house, he later moved to Malik's fledgling program without any trouble. This suggests that FIR clients are afforded the mobility to take up residence in the least formal of programs.

Cases like Infinite's have become so typical that many informal programs have gone so far as to train senior recovering residents to act as "forensics liaisons," essentially paraprofessional or "peer" case managers serving clients on probation or parole. Clarence explained his forensics liaison experience:

> CLARENCE: What I actually did there was I made regular contact with all the PO's [parole officers], and the judges and the DAs and stuff. I took the guys to court, and I represented the recovery house program in court, and went in and out of the prisons. I went down to city hall and went to the courtroom with them and talked to the judge and the DAs and the public defenders when necessary. I did that for about eighteen months.

The FIR program was not the only mechanism by which sentence diversions worked in collaboration with recovery house networks. Many of the clients Clarence worked with came from a separate initiative known as Philadelphia Treatment Court, which has become particularly popular since its inception in 1997. The program, which has served thousands of nonviolent offenders with substance abuse problems, was described in the court's participant handbook as follows:

The Philadelphia Treatment Court is a highly structured program that
combines drug rehabilitation and supportive services with court supervision. Non-violent offenders with substance abuse problems can receive the
help they need to overcome their addiction while under strict supervision of
the Treatment Court judge. Treatment Court is unique because it represents
a much closer working union between treatment and the criminal justice
system than is traditionally seen in criminal courts.

The end result is a greater likelihood that offenders will remain drug free
while avoiding further contacts with the criminal justice system and become
productive members of society.[20]

Treatment Court touted its "highly structured" program as a collaborative effort between the criminal courts and the recovery apparatus, and city
officials claimed that 85% of its successful graduates remain "arrest free."[21]
As a transformative technology said to help its participants become "productive members of society," the program promised the following benefits
in its participant handbook:

- You will be clean and sober.
- You will avoid a criminal conviction and a jail sentence.
- Your record will be expunged.
- You will have better job and education opportunities.
- You will have a better relationship with family and friends.
- You will have a better understanding of yourself.
- You will have a positive outlook on life.
- You will be a contributing member of your community.

Treatment Court represents another effort by the state to extend its reach
into professional treatment and self-help recovery. Through a transformation that maximizes the interests of the state and the individual, Treatment
Court fosters self-improvement for the addict in the realms of family, employment, education, and citizenship. The combination of "drug rehabilitation and supportive services" mentioned in the program handbook refers to the recovery house's active involvement. As a case in point, Benito
worked closely with several Treatment Court clients as along with their
case managers. A firm believer in Treatment Court, he came through the
system himself after getting caught dealing heroin in North Philadelphia's
notorious El Segundo open-air drug markets. He described the basic outlines of the program in light of his experience:

BENITO: Treatment Court really works, man. Basically, if you plead guilty
to a felony of possession with intent to deliver, then most of the time you
get sentenced with the stipulation that you stay clean for a year. If you
are successful and you complete all the five phases of Treatment Court,
they expunge the charges from your records. You have to come up to the
judge every month and they do a progress report, like how many times
do you go to counseling, how many sessions, and you can't have no dirty
urines. And as soon as you successfully complete Treatment Court, your
records are expunged. But if you mess up along the way, essentially they
can give you the sentence that you pleaded guilty to. Some clients are
looking at five to ten years if they mess up, so it's good motivation for the
addict who is living on the edge.

As Benito noted, the weight of the criminal justice system provides the incentive for recovering subjects to comply with the rules and regulations of
the recovery house. This was especially helpful in his own recovery as well
as in the first house that he supervised, where almost 100% of the clients
were court stipulated from either the FIR program or Treatment Court.

BENITO: I'm a graduate of Treatment Court, [so] I was looking at fifteen to
thirty years if I messed up. That was inspiration enough and motivation
enough. That's one good thing about criminal justice across the board, it's
good motivation. I say to my guys all the time, "Do you want the PP [pro-
bation/parole] number, or do you want to get it off? Do you want to get
through this, or do you want to report to the PO for the rest of your life?
Do you want some hack telling you when you can use the shower? Or do
you want to use your own shower?" Because basically, the choice is yours.

The criminal justice system's enlistment of recovery networks illustrates its
growing reliance on the treatment sector and its supportive services. Within
this realm, crime is defined in therapeutic terms, choice is lionized as the
way out of the ghetto, and poverty is a taboo subject.

I attended a session of Treatment Court with a friend who case-managed
several clients in the program. A succession of Treatment Court participants
came before the judge, each providing progress reports on various matters,
including treatment attendance, urine screens, recovery house residence,
employment, education, and family issues. Many clients deemed "in compliance" by the judge were advanced to the next phase of Treatment Court;
a measure of success that elicited applause from the many case managers

and participants in the courtroom. For those who had poor attendance or dirty urines, the judge took a stern disciplinary tone, often relegating them to early phases of treatment. In one case, the initial prison sentence was imposed on a man who had failed to respond to several warnings. Perhaps the most compelling aspect of all of this was to see the judge acting like a therapist, asking questions of each participant such as "And how are things going with your sobriety? Your sponsor? Your family relationships?" This cursory overview suggests the ways in which the state has redistributed the institutional functions of criminal justice throughout the interstices of the addictions treatment sector and recovery house matrix.[22]

## Conclusion

By operating through recovery channels, the state has reinvented its role in the lives of poor citizens by occupying recovery knowledge systems due to their characteristic notions of structure, accountability, responsibility, and good citizenship. These extensions belie facile notions of a retreating state, suggesting instead the ways the state infiltrates preexisting survival configurations in areas of spatially concentrated poverty in order to transfer their most virtuous functions into policies and programs. In this case, Philadelphia's CODAAP works through its CHI program and training series in conjunction with the criminal justice system's FIR and Treatment Court programs. CODAAP deploys recovery knowledge as a mechanism believed to be more efficient and effective in enacting control over the populace, primarily by maximizing the self-interests of recovering subjects through carefully calculated freedoms. In this light, we become cognizant of the ways the declining welfare state, comprising the "workfare state" and its adjoining "carceral-assistential" complex,[23] takes up part of its regulatory functions through recovery knowledge. Recovery houses are effectively transferred as policy techniques for solving problems such as overcrowded prisons, workfare imperatives, devolutionary mandates, and welfare retrenchment. Taken together, I have sketched in this chapter a new form of poverty management system, whereby citizenship is not so much widely experienced through direct encounters with the state as it is through an informal, elaborate network of surveillance and emancipation in the *recovery* house. Within its confines, information is collected on every subject via welfare administration and/or criminal administration. In essence, while the state carries out its liberal objectives with each measure of "rational choice" in the addicted population, its regulatory apparatus also waits at virtually every turn of "failed choice."

# Conclusion

Soon after completing my fieldwork in the spring of 2004, I received a phone call from Malik. He told me that suddenly and without warning, he had disbanded AHAD, literally overnight. I had been aware that the men had been struggling with the water in Milton's Genoa Street house for months in the winter of 2004, at first because of faulty plumbing, which ultimately led to problems with the city's water department. Finally, the city shut off the water at the property due to delinquent taxes and fees. Malik, who at that time had ceded all managerial authority to his partner, Blanche, in order to focus on his full-time job at the Navy Yard, decided to shut down the program immediately and permanently. He was able to make "referrals" for all of the residents within a matter of hours. Most of his former clients went to Bilal's 42 House, a couple went to one of Clarence's houses, and one went to a rival program across Broad Street in North Philly. After a run that had lasted roughly eighteen months, AHAD closed down even faster than it had opened. Milton's house remains vacant at the time of this writing.

Malik continues to live just around the corner from the AHAD house, in a small one-bedroom apartment within sight of the K&A El stop. I return to Philadelphia periodically and always make a point to have dinner with him at the Aramingo Diner in Port Richmond. "By the grace of God," as he often said, echoing his sponsor Frank, Malik and Blanche celebrated eight and seven years of sobriety, respectively, in April of 2009. The couple have pressed on in recovery, even though their home group at the Avenue AA Club finally closed because it could no longer pay rent for the small storefront it occupied on Kensington Avenue. Malik was a key player in reincarnating the club in a new space and with a new name on Lehigh Avenue. Perhaps most important, he has been promoted several times at the Navy Yard, ultimately taking a supervisory position on the custodial staff. While his proudest accomplishment is his sobriety, Malik also became the proud owner of a late-1980s-model Cadillac soon after I moved to Chicago (he received his first driver's license in 2005). In 2007, he purchased a second car, and he uses one or the other ("depends what mood I'm in") for his daily commute or the occasional weekend trip to Newark.

Malik consistently reports a deep sense of satisfaction in all areas of his life, with the exception of housing. He has wanted to move out of Kensington since at least 2005, and has spoken with me several times about how to make a move to the Greater Northeast. He has struggled with the realities of credit scores, banking, and the daunting process of mortgage application. He has been unable to afford rent elsewhere in the city, in part because of Blanche's ongoing employment woes. (Blanche is currently studying for a GED—because she lacks a high school diploma, she has suffered long spells of unemployment interrupted only by temporary stints as a mail sorter at Federal Express.) But Malik remains positive for the most part, expressing gratitude at all times for his recovery and constantly marveling at how "everything somehow takes care of itself so long as I don't pick up a drink or a drug." He continues to regard his daily commitment to recovery as the single most important factor of his life, and he stays devoted to AA by sponsoring as many as twelve people at a time. As a former recovery house operator, he continues to offer his expertise as a consultant to budding entrepreneurs in the neighborhood. During one of my visits, he even tried to enlist my help in putting together a proposal to send to the mayor of Newark. Malik hoped to get the mayor's ear in supporting his newest venture: recovery houses focused specifically on people living with HIV/AIDS (the plan was short-lived, at last check anyway).

Every time I ask Malik how he has managed to stay sober in Kensington while so many of his contemporaries relapse, cycle, and recycle in and out of hustling, dealing, welfare, recovery houses, shelters, prisons, and periods of homelessness, he provides the same simple answer: "I watch what everyone else do, and then I do the opposite." This statement is infinitely revealing. The fact that Malik has made a very particular kind of self-transformation, while those around him continue to backslide and churn in and out of any number of regulatory webs and state institutions, provides an inroad to the central points I have developed throughout the book.

Contrary to the claims of many policy scholars, the Kensington recovery house movement hardly shows an absence of civil society, good citizenship, and morality in poor neighborhoods. What we have seen is a continuous absence of material resources, and an accelerated marginalization among the men in recovery houses from the new economic regimes of accumulation. These factors, combined with my analysis of the ways in which Philadelphia's recovery houses manage to survive and persist, have led me to recast the stakes of recovery, as well as the recovery *house* itself, well beyond conventional questions of abstinence from drugs and alcohol. Driven by the imperatives of benign neglect and fiscal austerity, the power of the state in Philadelphia derives in part from a politics of devolution, retrenchment, and selective intervention. Along these lines, I have situated recovery houses within broader discussions seeking to understand urban informality and the proliferation of governmentalities in slums.[1] The simultaneous enclosure, disappearance, and criminalization of urban populations have become transnational hallmarks of neoliberalism. And yet within this broader context we are also witnessing a proliferation of informal urban movements that must be tolerated, if not cultivated, as they take up new modes of poverty survival, welfare administration, and politics in areas of spatially concentrated poverty. In this sense, I have shown throughout the book that the contemporary state not only acquiesces to but effectively fosters, constitutes, and deepens its reliance on the Kensington recovery house as a highly localized and informal poverty management system.

But while there are many points of convergence here with broader social phenomena as well as bodies of scholarly literature, the Kensington recovery house also contradicts several themes in contemporary welfare state theory. Far from a coherent, unequivocally novel mechanism of the post-welfare state, it is built on the last vestiges of General Assistance. Far from an exemplary or monolithic neoliberal form, the recovery house is overrun with contradictions: individualistic yet collective; contiguous and vestigial yet historically and spatially contingent; unregulated yet disciplinary; state subsidized and marketized yet anti-consumer-choice. Far from a seamless or even an intentional policy mechanism of retrenchment and devolution, welfare legislation in Pennsylvania has inadvertently spawned an industry shot through with operator resistance, contestation, blockages, malfeasance, and incessant failures for actors involved at every level. Indeed, while post-welfare neoliberalism might be conceived as a hegemonic project, or more fantastically a new "planetary vulgate,"[2] in the case of the recovery house we see an unstable, uneven, and in some ways anachronistic jumble of impulses rather than any sort of planned, totalizing resolution. It is the internecine and sometimes aleatory interactions between operators, subjects, and state processes that somehow crystallize into a web of urban policy and poverty management.[3] To be sure, as Partha Chatterjee contends, political institutions cannot be made to work effectively by legislating them into existence, but rather must be nested in (or distilled from) a network of norms in civil society that prevail independently of the state.[4] But in the recovery house movement we begin to see how the state, as a strategic and selective terrain, privileges some informal urban poverty strategies over others. Moreover, the state in this case actually fuels preexisting mechanisms of differentiation among operators in its selectivity by offering tightly limited channels to legitimacy. I have argued that this complexity calls for ethnographic attention to the threads of state-level, street-level, and self-level strategies of urban policy restructure.

The state's variegated responses to recovery houses do not simply enable an informal economy to persist; in fact these responses deepen urban informality while attenuating *and* accelerating the capacity of informal actors to function as agents of urban restructure. The restructuring in question here refers to public welfare provision, criminal justice, relationships between citizen and state, and the contemporary boundary institutions of the postindustrial city. I have shown how the experiences of recovering subjects evince multiple forms of regulation and re-regulation taking place in Philadelphia. At the street level, this occurs within the informal subsistence economies of recovery house markets, which are driven by the many innovations in informal welfare provision (the plug-in, the address, the feeder source, the food club, and the welfare cutoff) and in highly competitive census-building projects that illustrate how operators remake the rules of GA and SSI. In addition to the predatory markets of recovery houses themselves, processes related to relapse and "the wreckage of the past" reveal the ways in which addicts are caught up in informal and highly contingent low-wage labor markets, as well as any number of state disciplinary nets, from child support, to criminal justice, to public welfare. And while these processes pertain to the recovering self, I have also revealed nascent citywide efforts to formalize the recovery *house* as a form of statecraft. Through an exploration of these efforts in chapter 6 (CODAAP's CHI, Treatment Court, and FIR programs), I have located the recovery house, and the ex-

perience of GA/SSI programs more generally, within the compendium of
the workfare state and the prison.

Taking these points together, I have followed Jamie Peck's lead in con-
ceiving of the recovery house system as a highly localized regulatory *project*—a set of interrelated tendencies expressed through chronic unevenness,
instability, and insecurity rather than a coherent or achieved post-welfare
regulatory end state.[5] We may be seeing a rejection of the integrative, top-
down, command and control strategies of the welfarist era for the fluid,
unstable regulatory configurations of the post-welfare moment, but the co-
constitutive and multiscalar nature of policy transfer is still vitally important here. I have revealed this process by distinguishing analytically between
*structures* or technologies of power (CODAAP, the criminal justice system,
L&I, public welfare, the recovery house itself) that privilege certain actors
and identities (the recovering subject, the virtuous recovery house operator,
and even the rogue recovery house operator) and the strategies by which
street-level actors respond to, interpret, and manipulate state selectivity
at the level of *conduct*.[6] Poverty survival strategies, in this case those that
regulate and discipline subjects informally, embody the stakes in political
struggles. Local actors in the recovery house movement act through local
strongholds, capitalizing on a recovery knowledge that has both provincial
and universal appeals to morality and ethics, as well as local economic appeals to survival, subsistence, and profiteering. Through a series of agonistic
relationships between the recovering self and the state, the recovery house
operator must build on, complement, and accelerate the objectives of a variegated set of regulatory logics. It is in this sense that urban imperatives
must always develop in concert with, if not in dialectical relation to, local
strategies.[7]

These points have been developed through extensive ethnographic exploration, through which I have mobilized three primary claims concerning
the variegated functions of Kensington recovery houses. First, I have illustrated how the recovery house operates as an elaborate street-level self-help
mechanism of governmentality as operators and clients alike work toward
the salvation and transformation of impoverished subjects. In the recovery house movement, the political partially loses its spatial association with
sovereign power and the state as the soul itself becomes the object of governance and reform.[8] However, far from seeing contemporary trends of retrenchment, devolution, and deregulation as an absence of government, this
book has shown that the practical techniques and inventions through which
recovery houses operate and are brought into being are distinct from political intervention, and yet distinctly alignable with political aspirations.[9] Put

another way, I have argued that the recovery house has been induced by the depredations of welfare state retrenchment and postindustrial decline while simultaneously being configured as a form of resistance to these trends. In this regard, I have argued that recovery house networks have emerged not in a historical vacuum but rather as a survival strategy based on the exigencies of state policy and urban political economy. I have revealed a very particular way in which the state, by enacting a set of interrelated strategies of policy transfer (CHI, CODAAP's training series, FIR) but also through a long history of inaction, nonintervention, and selective intervention (L&I, public welfare), redistributes risk and responsibility in the post-welfare age. In this case, operators work to transform the soul *and* to restructure the state through an informal and highly marketized street-level mechanism of governmentality.

I have also illustrated how systems of governmentality in the Kensington recovery house movement operate on a regulatory spectrum, or a carefully calculated freedom, that is both enabling and constraining for urban subjects. The many challenges associated with spatially concentrated poverty greatly compromise the utopian agenda of operating through notions of freedom and autonomy. Accordingly, recovery house operators often default to more coercive measures, despite their best intentions. Yet in every respect, we can say that recovery houses "work" as technologies of citizenship operating in concert with the contemporary welfare state. We would be hard-pressed to find a more perfect partner in the age of devolution, personal responsibility, and increasing reliance on market models (however informal) of public policy. This becomes particularly clear when we consider the efforts of reformed street criminals who take up regulatory projects on their own volition such as urine screening; power of attorney over welfare dependents; and surveillance cameras in their own homes.

As my second claim concerning the variegated functions of Kensington recovery houses, I have revealed the recovery house movement as a decidedly political movement, driven by a particular vision of emancipation and by the deliberate efforts of informal operators to reappropriate segments of Philadelphia's welfare apparatus. My exploration of AHAD's founding in chapter 1 illustrated how operators like Malik forge essential bridges between the informal/extralegal arrangements of the recovery house and the formal welfare state. On the side of the recovery house, street-level expertise takes operators into a zone of quasi-legal negotiation, mitigating their urban invisibility and moving the impoverished recovery house population into the realm of formality.[10] And while the commodification of informal housing is not a new phenomenon, we may be looking at new actors and spaces that are consolidated through their active role in the provision of informal social services.[11] This requires a rethinking of devolution, which normally engenders visions of an offloading of responsibility to a passive public. It is here that the recovery house also extends to broader conversations chronicling the growth of innovative and increasingly complex linkages between quasi-autonomous NGOs and the state.

Third, I have argued that the recovery house movement is at once an informal collective poverty survival mechanism, a mode of predatory subsistence, and a new mechanism of urban enclosure. The primary function of the recovery house as a collective survival mechanism is clear. Given the paltry sums on which addicts on GA survive, the pooling of welfare benefits to combine food and shelter with self-help recovery is an essential component explaining the movement's survival. Put simply, recovery houses are one of the only expanding mechanisms of affordable housing in Philadelphia. Operators perform significant political economic functions in the city by taking up surplus land and labor. But I have also illustrated how the vagaries of market competition and profit seeking produce what amounts to a predatory mode of subsistence. In a manner similar to other actors in highly contingent and informal economies, recovery house operators are small-scale entrepreneurs driven to minimize costs and maximize profits. As the conventional wisdom goes, to opt for recovery principles or recovery program quality over revenues is a tall order for operators. Most are forced to work under impoverished conditions, relying on welfare transfer payments that are increasingly devalued as each year passes. The failure to adjust GA payments since 1982 puts a considerable downward pressure on costs across the industry. Moreover, the absence of licensure and professional organization deprives the recovery house movement of any conventional channel for political power, which could be vital for lobbying efforts to raise welfare transfers or to fight for a more varied and formalized landscape of funding and legitimacy. The absence of a governing body or code of ethics further assures that recovery house operators have few options beyond pushing the envelope of coercive, informal census tactics to stabilize their own conditions of subsistence.

Market competition, urban informality, and the political economy of the census operate as complexly interrelated regulatory forces. As my fieldwork has shown, the recovery house experience and the systematic impoverishment of the setup often keep men trapped in recovery houses for years at a time. And even for those most successful in recovery, the channels of social mobility and the capacity to leave Kensington, or to fully escape "the wreckage of the past," are tightly constricted. In this sense, Kensington itself often seemed a formidable obstacle to overcome for the men in this study. The managed persistence of the recovery house matrix works as a mode of spatial governmentality that conceals and displaces, rather than corrects, disorder and extralegality.[12] I have argued accordingly that we are seeing a new mode of containment that shuffles and churns the dispossessed in areas of spatially concentrated poverty.

Taking these three points together, I have argued that informal recovery house operators have become central actors in a new system of poverty management designed for the governance of insecurity in the postindustrial city. Each of these points explains the survival and persistence of recovery houses, by illustrating how an informal poverty survival mechanism articulates with the restructuring of the welfare state and the political economy of Philadelphia. We might conclude with a thought exercise that asks whether, in classic Philadelphia style of charming incompetence and chronic low self-esteem, the city is more "global" than even its beleaguered politicians are aware of. Consider, for example, the opening charge of Nezar AlSayyad and Ananya Roy: now more than ever, it is important to investigate urban informality as a socio-spatial restructuring, negotiated through elaborate legal and extralegal systems of neoliberal regulation:

> Such an examination becomes even more imperative given the recent celebration of urban informality in a whole spectrum of policy positions. From the World Bank agenda of "enabling" informal development to the new celebration of self-help strategies of the urban poor, there is a growing consensus on the benefits of harnessing the efficiencies of urban informality.[13]

According to Roy and AlSayyad, urban informality has become a permanent and essential component of the modern economy and a "new way of life" in the contemporary city. As an ideology and a practice of austerity, urban informality is redefining the role, scope, and scale of the state. City officials in Philadelphia appear to be at the vanguard of urban policy, even if practically by mistake. This is perhaps even truer given that the recovery house matrix flows in part from citywide neglect. True to the core tenets of liberalism, the city dumps responsibility to the streets, the realm within which, as welfare Unit Manager Jeff Blumberg put it, "one way or another, communities pick up ways to meet single person needs." It is in this sense that so many of the central questions concerning the history and philosophy of the welfare state—citizenship, worthiness, justifiable state intervention, state versus local responsibility—are fundamentally recurring questions, recapitulated time and time again even if the questions are taken up by particular actors at very particular times and places. The unsystematicity, informality, insecurity, and precariousness of the recovery house cast these fundamental questions in a familiar and yet decidedly different light. Indeed, the Kensington recovery house movement reveals a telling and contemporary example of how we, as a citizenry, have decided "one way or another" to provide social services to the poor.

Through the enlistment and participation of recovering subjects as a vital part of the strategy for urban reform, the city all but assures that the resistance and agency of poor people unfold along very particular lines. In many respects, then, successful recovering subjects like Malik become model citizens, operating in service of the state yet outside the "conventional" political realm of the public sphere, and opting for a politics of self over a politics of social and economic justice. But this type of binary conception of politics is no longer tenable, as the ethnographic explorations of this book have illustrated. The self has been shown as a terrain on which political agency is exercised. In fact, the recovery house experience reveals how neoliberal governmentality works, precisely by juxtaposing individual and structural solutions to problems of poverty and recovery. There is no reason why, however, the recovering self cannot be conceived as a malleable and transitory self, even though addiction is framed as an essentialized identity. In other words, to take one example, there is little reason to think that even recovery house operators themselves couldn't (or shouldn't) organize to demand higher concessions from the state, along very conventional lines of political resistance (for example, unionization).

But as this book has shown, there are several factors working against this possibility. For one, for those who "get it," recovery is such a profound and in some respects unprecedented emancipatory rupture from the immediately oppressive depredations of addiction. As Malik sees it, he has experienced a radical break in recovery that far exceeds anything he experienced as a young Black nationalist participating in the Newark riots of 1967. Perhaps, then, it is hard for conventional politics to compete (I'm thinking here of Oscar Wilde's statement, "The problem with socialism is that it takes too many evenings"). For those who don't get it, the pre-scripted "choices" of the recovery rubric keep them trapped. And yet no matter whether one gets it or not, and no matter how much one is caught up in larger structures of power, recovery discourse typically posits the self as the only political solution to poverty, even though the efficacy of recovery is contingent on the strength of the group. Perhaps this is why Marx himself  was one of the most outspoken critics of the profligacy and drunkenness of the lumpen proletariat, to incite them into action as a class. But in the recovery house context, fraught with insecurities, predatory subsistence, and informal market competition, recovery discourse has more typically defaulted to fragmentation and a "more radically individuated sense of personhood," where the personal is the primary politics of salvation.[14] To the extent that new collective aid structures are attuned to the post-welfare missives of personal responsibility and the war on dependency, they may lapse into hyperindividuated mechanisms of governmentality, and/or predatory modes of self-help. In no way, however, should this lead us to think that they are any less political. I close with a quote from Malik that illustrates this claim quite graphically:

> MALIK: Look, man, America is the greatest country in the world. You know how I know this? You have to look at it like this: I don't see the American people going across the ocean trying to get to another country floating on a fucking tire, man; you just won't see that. I am really caught up in some shit, man, but what I'm learning to do now, I am learning to deal with the immediate dangers, the immediate shit that is in my life. It tells us in this book right here I was reading the other day, you know we can't be worried about world powers, you understand what I'm saying, as alcoholics. We just can't be worried about that shit. Let me see if I can find it [*paging through the Big Book to find the section he read at morning meditation*]. Here it is, "We try not to indulge in cynicism over the state of the nation, nor do we carry the world's troubles on our shoulders." That's how it's been said, man, and I think that's right.

# Notes

**INTRODUCTION**

1. The term *Northeast Corridor* refers to the heavily populated conurbation that runs from Boston to Washington, DC. In addition to these two cities, the metropolitan areas typically included in the description are Providence, Rhode Island; New Haven, Connecticut; New York City; Newark, New Jersey; Trenton and Camden, New Jersey; Philadelphia; Wilmington, Delaware; and Baltimore.

2. While it remains unclear just how many houses exist in the city (see chapter 1 for the analysis with Department of Licensing and Inspection Unit Supervisor Stanley Robinson), these estimates come from media sources as well as the city's Coordinating Office of Drug and Alcohol Programs (CODAAP). See for example K. Haney, "Property Owners and L&I Reach Accord. Judge to Work Out Agreement on Halfway-Home Dispute in Harrowgate," *Philadelphia Daily News*, March 31, 1995; M. Graham, L. King, and T. Torok, "How NJ Freed Addicts at PA's Expense: Parolees Were Sent without Permission, They Got Aid but Little Treatment," *Philadelphia Inquirer*, October 1, 1995; and G. Shaffer, "Silent Treatment: Hundreds of Unregulated Drug-Recovery Houses Operate in Philadelphia without Any Government Oversight," *Philadelphia City Paper*, November 8, 2001.

3. See A. Hillier and D. Culhane, "Vacancy Reporter" (departmental papers, Department of City and Regional Planning, University of Pennsylvania, 2001); Available at http://cml.upenn.edu.

4. U.S. Census Bureau, *United States Census of Population and Housing* (Washington, DC: Government Printing Office, 2000).

5. See Graham, King, and Torok, "How NJ Freed Addicts at PA.'s Expense."

6. See for example Shaffer, "Silent Treatment." Recovery house operators see these arrangements as mutually beneficial, as electioneering provides moneymaking opportunities for them
and their clients. Politicians typically pay $50 per worker on election days for a 6:00 a.m. to
9:00 p.m. shift. These wages are often gouged by house managers for setting up the transaction,
or to collect back rent from their clients.

7. See R. Goldwyn and J. Sillis, "Fire Ruled Racial Incident: Recovery House Was Un-
wanted," *Philadelphia Daily News*, February 1, 1994.

8. See for example M. Graham and L. King, "NJ Appears to Be in No Hurry to Reclaim
Addicts," *Philadelphia Inquirer*, October 3, 1995; K. Haney, "Property Owners and L&I Reach
Accord"; S. Simmons, "Drug Homes under Siege," *Philadelphia Daily News*, April 6, 1992; and
M. Valbrun, "Neighbors, Rehab Houses Learn to Mesh. Not Long Ago, the Two Sides in Har-
rowgate Were Enemies, and Then Decided to Talk," *Philadelphia Inquirer*, June 13, 1995.

9. Philly's alleged "pay to play" politics prompted a full-scale FBI investigation of Mayor
John Street's city hall offices during my fieldwork.

10. By extension, the failure to apply for zoning and licensure is the sole factor explaining
their "illegality." As of 2006, the official term for the boardinghouse license is the *housing inspection license*. This book uses *boardinghouse license*, as it was the term used consistently by street-level
informants and city officials for the duration of my fieldwork. For further information, see
chapter 5.

11. Always Have a Dream is used throughout the book as a pseudonym for Malik's recovery
house. I wish to acknowledge that while the name may have been used for an actual recovery
house program at some point, I never encountered it during my fieldwork for this study.

12. With respect to the names that appear in this book, I have provided pseudonyms for all
informants living or working in the Kensington recovery house scene. I have also used pseudonyms for the actual names of their respective recovery houses, with the exception of general
references to larger, more established programs such as Fresh Start (given that these are funded by
the city). I have changed the names of treatment providers and counselors who operate collabora-
tively with recovery house operators to protect their identities. All key informants at the level of
city elite are identified by name, based on their public status as state functionaries.

13. See for example C. Cain, "Personal Stories: Identity Acquisition and Self-Understanding
in Alcoholics Anonymous," *Ethos* 19, no. 2 (1991): 210–53.

14. The term "do-it-yourself welfare state" has been deployed by scholars such as S. B. Hyatt,
"Poverty in a 'Post-Welfare' Landscape," in *Anthropology of Policy: Critical Perspectives on Governance
and Power*, ed. C. Shore and S. Wright (New York: Routledge, 1997), 217–38; and J. Wolch and
G. DeVerteuil, "New Landscapes of Urban Poverty Management," *TimeSpace: Geographies of
Temporality*, ed. J. May and N. Thrift (London: Routledge, 2001), 149–68.

15. Wolch and DeVerteuil, "New Landscapes of Urban Poverty Management."

16. M. Valverde, *Diseases of the Will: Alcohol and the Dilemmas of Freedom* (New York: Cambridge University Press, 1998).

17. J. Clarke, *Changing Welfare, Changing States: New Directions in Social Policy* (Thousand Oaks,
CA: Sage, 2004).

18. D. Harvey, *The Condition of Postmodernity: An Enquiry into the Origins of Cultural Change*
(Oxford: Blackwell Publishers, 1989); D. Harvey, *A Brief History of Neoliberalism* (New York:
Oxford University Press, 2005).

19. L. Wacquant, "Scrutinizing the Street: Poverty, Morality, and the Pitfalls of Urban Ethnography 1," *American Journal of Sociology* 107, no. 6 (2002): 1468–532; quotation is from p. 1521.

20. S. Morgen and J. Maskovsky, "The Anthropology of Welfare 'Reform': New Perspectives on US Urban Poverty in the Post-Welfare Era," *Annual Reviews in Anthropology* 32, no. 1
(2003): 315–46.

21. A. Amin, ed., *Post-Fordism: A Reader* (Oxford: Blackwell, 1994); Harvey, *The Condition of Postmodernity*. B. Jessop, "Post-Fordism and the State," in Amin, *Post-Fordism*, 251–79. L. J. D. Wacquant, *Urban Outcasts: A Comparative Sociology of Advanced Marginality* (Cambridge: Polity Press, 2008).

22. M. B. Katz, *The Price of Citizenship: Redefining the American Welfare State* (New York: Holt Paperbacks / Henry Holt and Company, 2001).

23. J. Peck, "Geography and Public Policy: Mapping the Penal State," *Progress in Human Geography* 27, no. 2 (2003): 222–32.

24. For examples of scholarly works employing this analytic sensibility, see *The Foucault Effect: Studies in Governmentality; With Two Lectures by and an Interview with Michel Foucault*, ed. G. Burchell, C. Gordon, and P. Miller (Chicago: University of Chicago Press, 1991); and Nikolas Rose's *Powers of Freedom: Reframing Political Thought* (Cambridge: Cambridge University Press, 1999) and *Governing the Soul: The Shaping of the Private Self* (London: Routledge, 1990).

25. The AA "Big Book" was written in 1939 by Bill Wilson, the organization's cofounder. As the unofficial bible of Alcoholics Anonymous, the text contains an overview of its spiritual principles, steps, and traditions in chapters such as "How It Works." The book also contains several recovery narratives of early AA members.

26. I have borrowed the term *shadow welfare state* from Jennifer Wolch and Marie Gottschalk; see J. R. Wolch, *The Shadow State: Government and Voluntary Sector in Transition* (New York: Foundation Center, 1990); and M. Gottschalk, *The Shadow Welfare State: Labor, Business, and the Politics of Health Care in the United States* (Ithaca, NY: Cornell University Press, 2000). I extend the term in order to denote the many informal assemblages of collective responsibility and self-help operating in the tradition of voluntarism in the post-welfare age. While apparently decoupled from the state apparatus at first glance, myriad configurations of the shadow welfare state have emerged to forge complex partnerships with state systems—primarily in response to devolutionary trends.

27. See J. T. Patterson, *America's Struggle against Poverty in the Twentieth Century* (Cambridge, MA: Harvard University Press); A. O'Connor, *Poverty Knowledge: Social Science, Social Policy, and the Poor in Twentieth-Century US History* (Princeton, NJ: Princeton University Press, 2001).

28. While Oscar Lewis is commonly cited as the key figure responsible for laying the foundation for the original culture-of-poverty thesis, it should be noted that several elements of his work do not support a pathological view of poverty, but rather a structuralist and historical perspective (see O. Lewis, *La Vida: A Puerto Rican Family in the Culture of Poverty—San Juan and New York* (London: Secker and Warburg, 1966). Still, while there is great debate about the extent to which the arguments of Lewis and other early researchers were taken out of context, there is general consensus among poverty scholars that ethnographies in this tradition have given academic legitimacy to various political moves to disparage the poor. See for example J. Goode and J. Maskovsky, eds., *The New Poverty Studies: The Ethnography of Power, Politics, and Impoverished People in the United States* (New York: New York University Press, 2001); Hyatt, "Poverty in A 'Post-Welfare' Landscape"; O'Connor, *Poverty Knowledge*; and R. D. G. Kelley, *Yo' mama's Disfunktional!: Fighting the Culture Wars in Urban America* (Boston: Beacon Press, 1997).

29. These debates have enumerated the ways in which ethnographic knowledge production is an inherently political project replete with power inequalities and political implications. See for example J. Clifford and G. E. Marcus, *Writing Culture: The Poetics and Politics of Ethnography* (Berkeley and Los Angeles: University of California Press, 1986); and N. K. Denzin, "Confronting Ethnography's Crisis of Representation: Review Symposium; Crisis in Representation," *Journal of Contemporary Ethnography* 31, no. 4 (2002): 482–90.

30. The complexity of these challenges has been at least partially articulated in Loïc Wacquant's well-known polemic against three particular urban ethnographies of the late 1990s: Mitchell Duneier's *Sidewalk* (2001), Elijah Anderson's *Code of the Streets* (1999), and Katherine

Newman's *No Shame in My Game* (1999). In his critique of these texts, Wacquant exposes not only the enduring legacies of the culture-of-poverty debates, but also their renewed valence under neoliberal regimes. In their efforts to "spare moral strivers among urban outcasts," Wacquant argues that all three books lapse into "compassionate sociology," which, like its counterpart compassionate conservatism, intimates that deep-seated problems of urban poverty and inequality can be effaced by an infusion of personal responsibility, self-help, and "moral boot camp" training. Consider the following indictment: "Just as the romantic ethnographies of the second Chicago school were organically tied to the liberal politics of America's semi-welfare state and its then expanding social problems complex, the neo-romantic tales spun by Anderson, Duneier and Newman at the close of the regressive nineties suggest that U.S. Sociology is now tied and party to the ongoing construction of the neoliberal state and its 'carceral-assistential complex' for the punitive management of the poor" (Wacquant, "Scrutinizing the Street," 1471).

31. In Wacquant's terms, the trap is visible in the persistently unreflexive embrace of policy clichés—most notably that of moral decline borne out of isolation from middle-class values—that has led contemporary ethnographers to forage the streets in search of "paragons of morality" (Wacquant, "Scrutinizing the Street," 1469). In response to a long history of pathological accounts, we have seen an abiding wish to articulate and even celebrate the fundamental goodness—honesty, decency, frugality—of the urban poor, either by explaining deviant behaviors as a consequence of macrostructural forces or by documenting their vibrant cultures of resistance. See for example the efforts of any number of ethnographers trying to write their way out of the trappings of urban poverty research: P. I. Bourgois, *In Search of Respect: Selling Crack in El Barrio* (Cambridge: Cambridge University Press, 2003); M. Duneier, *Slim's Table: Race, Responsibility, and Masculinity* (Chicago: University of Chicago Press, 1994); M. Duneier, O. Carter, and H. Hasan, *Sidewalk* (New York: Farrar, Straus and Giroux, 2001); Goode and Maskovsky, *The New Poverty Studies*; S. Gregory, *Black Corona: Race and the Politics of Place in an Urban Community* (Princeton, NJ: Princeton University Press, 1998); Kelley, *Yo' mama's Disfunktional!*; and S. A. Venkatesh, *American Project: The Rise and Fall of a Modern Ghetto* (Cambridge, MA: Harvard University Press, 2002).

32. Goode and Maskovsky, *The New Poverty Studies*; M. Davis, *Planet of Slums* (New York: Verso, 2006); A. Roy and N. AlSayyad, eds., *Urban Informality: Transnational Perspectives from the Middle East, Latin America, and South Asia* (Lanham, MD: Lexington Books, 2004).

33. For a complete analysis of the parallel development of these two approaches, and the potential of an integrative approach for urban policy analysis, see J. Uitermark's 2005 paper: "The Genesis and Evolution of Urban Policy: A Confrontation of Regulationist and Governmentality Approaches," *Political Geography* 24, no. 2 (2005): 137–63.

34. See M. Foucault, "Governmentality," in Burchell, Gordon, and Miller, *The Foucault Effect*, 87–104; M. Foucault, "On Governmentality," *Ideology and Consciousness* 6 (1979): 5–21.

35. C. Gordon, "Governmental Rationality: An Introduction," in Burchell, Gordon, and Miller, *The Foucault Effect*, 1–51.

36. Ibid.

37. See for example Sue Hyatt's (2001) *From Citizen to Volunteer: Neoliberal Governance and the Erasure of Poverty* (in Goode and Maskovksy's *The New Poverty Studies*, pages 201–35); Julia Paley's (2001) *Marketing Democracy: Power and Social Movements in Post-Dictatorship Chile*; Aihwa Ong's *Flexible Citizenship: The Cultural Logics of Transnationality* (1999) and *Buddha Is Hiding: Refugees, Citizenship, the New America*; Partha Chatterjee's (2004) *The Politics of the Governed: Reflections on Popular Politics in Most of the World*; and James Holston's (1999) edited volume, *Cities and Citizenship*.

38. A number of scholars are looking at the ways in which governance and democracy in the contemporary era may have more to do with provision for collective well-being (formally and informally) than with individual liberties and electoral processes; see for example P. Chatterjee,

*The Politics of the Governed: Reflections on Popular Politics in Most of the World* (New York: Columbia University Press, 2004); J. Paley, *Marketing Democracy: Power and Social Movements in Post-Dictatorship Chile* (Berkeley and Los Angeles: University of California Press 2001). As Ferguson and Gupta note, new forms of politics may not entail so much a "pressing up against the state from below," but rather the establishment of able partnerships to operate as horizontal and informal organs of the state (see Ferguson and Gupta, "Spatializing States: Toward an Ethnography of Neoliberal Governmentality," *American Ethnologist* 29, no. 4 [2002]: 981–1002). It is in this sense that the recovery house movement can tell us something about transnational movements and nongovernmental actors seeking to claim political space in the new urban enclosures. See for example A. Appadurai, "Deep Democracy: Grassroots Globalization and the Research Imagination," *Public Culture* 14, no. 1 (2002): 21–47; Peck, "Geography and Public Policy"; Katz, *The Price of Citizenship*; M. E. Keck and K. Sikkink, *Activists Beyond Borders: Advocacy Networks in International Politics* (Ithaca, NY: Cornell University Press, 1998); and Paley, *Marketing Democracy*. These entities may not necessarily replace older systems, but rather overlap as coexisting apparatuses of governmentality—sometimes as parasites, other times as servants, watchdogs, or rivals (Ferguson and Gupta, "Spatializing States").

39. The discourse of alcoholism and addiction has taken center stage in any number of contemporary social policies and interventions. See for example V. Malkin, "The End of Welfare as We Know It: What Happens When the Judge Is in Charge?" *Critique of Anthropology* 25 (2005): 361–88; R. Wilton and G. DeVerteuil, "Spaces of Sobriety/Sites of Power: Examining Social Model Alcohol Recovery Programs as Therapeutic Landscapes," *Social Science & Medicine* 63, no. 3 (2006): 649–61; E. S. Carr, "'Secrets Keep You Sick': Metalinguistic Labor in a Drug Treatment Program for Homeless Women," *Language in Society* 35, no. 5 (2006): 631–53; and P. O'Malley and M. Valverde, "Pleasure, Freedom and Drugs: The Uses of 'Pleasure' in Liberal Governance of Drug and Alcohol Consumption," *Sociology* 38, no. 1 (2004): 25.

40. A. Ong, *Flexible Citizenship: The Cultural Logics of Transnationality* (Durham, NC: Duke University Press, 1999).

41. G. Esping-Andersen, *The Three Worlds of Welfare Capitalism* (Princeton, NJ: Princeton University Press, 1990); R. M. Titmuss, *Essays on the Welfare State* (London: Allen and Unwin, 1958); M. B. Katz, *In the Shadow of the Poorhouse: A Social History of Welfare in America* (New York: Basic Books, 1996); J. S. Hacker, *The Divided Welfare State: The Battle over Public and Private Social Benefits in the United States* (Cambridge: Cambridge University Press, 2002); F. F. Piven and R. A. Cloward, *Regulating the Poor: The Functions of Public Welfare* (New York: Vintage Books, 1993).

42. Uitermark, "The Genesis and Evolution of Urban Policy."

43. See for example ibid; B. Jessop, "Post-Fordism and the State"; N. Brener, *State/Space: A Reader* (Malden, MA: Blackwell, 2003); and J. Peck., *Workfare States* (New York: Guilford Press, 2001).

44. Valverde, *Diseases of the Will*; E. K. Sedgwick, *Tendencies* (Durham, NC: Duke University Press, 1993).

45. N. Brenner and N. Theodore, eds., *Spaces of Neoliberalism: Urban Restructuring in Western Europe and North America* (Oxford: Blackwell, 2002).

## CHAPTER 1

1. The "Basic Text" of Narcotics Anonymous serves as an analogue to AA's "Big Book."

2. To clarify further, the Avenue AA Clubhouse was not a recovery house, but a rented storefront space used as a meeting hall by the Avenue AA Group.

3. The Greater Northeast is a section of Philadelphia that includes the neighborhoods of Lawncrest, Rhawnhurst, Tacony, Holmesburg, Mayfair, Bustleton, Pennypack Woods, Torresdale, Fox Chase, and others. The neighborhoods of Port Richmond and Frankford are also included sometimes by locals.

4. Davis, *Planet of Slums*, 175.

5. See J. Peck and N. Theodore, "Contingent Chicago: Restructuring the Spaces of Temporary Labor," *International Journal of Urban and Regional Research* 25, no. 3 (2001), for example p. 479.

6. For an analysis of the aphorism Honesty, Openness, and Willingness (HOW), see Carr, "'Secrets Keep You Sick,'" 635.

7. The "Wheels" check is issued by the Department of Public Welfare as an in-kind benefit for public transportation. Ostensibly, it is to be used in exchange for tokens on the Southeaster Pennsylvania Transportation Authority (SEPTA) system for traveling to and from outpatient treatment. Addicts typically walk to treatment, so they can convert the Wheels check to discretionary cash by selling subway tokens (or the check itself) in K&A's informal marketplace.

8. Following this incident, the phone line remained in working order for the duration of my fieldwork. It was never clear to me if the phone stayed on because of the hookup that the phone man had made, or because Milton had cleared the bill, although I suspect the former. Malik would eventually install a pay phone (not a public phone but one that charged twenty-five cents per call, built by a small mail-order company). In this way, he was able to make the phone pay for itself each month, and he would even make a little extra from time to time for the cable bill.

9. Based in Philadelphia, PECO is an electric and natural-gas utility subsidiary of Exelon Corporation.

10. For an exploration of this maxim as a foundational premise of Keynesian economics, see J. A. Caporaso and D. P. Levine, *Theories of Political Economy* (Cambridge: Cambridge University Press, 1992).

### CHAPTER 2

1. Chatterjee, *The Politics of the Governed*.

2. Clarke, *Changing Welfare, Changing States*.

3. Jessop, "Post-Fordism and the State," 251.

4. Peck, *Workfare States*, 3.

5. Ibid., 59.

6. President's statement on the budget, quoted in ibid., 91.

7. Katz, *The Price of Citizenship*, 58.

8. As most public assistance research has focused on Aid to Families with Dependent Children (AFDC)/Temporary Assistance to Needy Families (TANF) and SSI, GA has languished in the backwaters of scholarship. While GA distribution is chronically uneven across states and localities, it can be characterized as a residual, state and locally administered program designed for the single individual who is either ineligible for, or in the process of obtaining, federally funded assistance (ADFC/TANF or SSI). As noted by L. J. Gallagher, *A Shrinking Portion of the Safety Net: General Assistance from 1989 to 1998* (Washington, DC: Urban Institute, 1999), thirty-five states (including the District of Columbia) had "state" GA programs (broadly defined as the state having some involvement) in 1999. Twenty-four of the states (including Pennsylvania) had statewide programs with uniform eligibility rules, while nine states required all counties to provide GA (with substantial rule variation across counties); the two remaining states provided supervision for those counties that "chose" to have a program (p. 1). The rest of the country, which included nearly all of the southern states and Montana, Wyoming, and North Dakota, did not have state programs (leaving the decision to administer at the county level). In only six of these states had at least one county chosen to provide, meaning that ten had no GA coverage whatsoever (ibid.).

9. Katz, *The Price of Citizenship*, 58.

10. Esping-Andersen, *The Three Worlds of Welfare Capitalism*, 21.

11. Peck, *Workfare States*, 135.

12. Gallagher, *A Shrinking Portion of the Safety Net*, 1.

13. See ibid.; A. Halter, "Homeless in Philadelphia: A Qualitative Study of the Impact of State Welfare Reform on Individuals," *Journal of Sociology and Social Welfare* 19, no. 4 (1992): 7–20. For an analysis of Massachusetts as an equal front-runner in GA reform, see Peck, *Workfare States*, 131–67.

14. Halter, "Homeless in Philadelphia," 8–9.

15. A. Halter, "The Impact of the Welfare Reform Act of 1982 on the Transitionally Needy in Philadelphia" (Ph.D. diss., University of Pennsylvania, 1986), 33.

16. A. Butto, "Urban-Rural Migration: Race, Drugs, and Community Change in Rural Pennsylvania." (Ph.D. diss., University of Pennsylvania, 1994), 14; Halter, "Homeless in Philadelphia," 8.

17. Although Pennsylvania has uniform standards statewide for eligibility, the benefit levels vary by county due to a formula that calculates the cost of shelter. The maximum is $215 in Bucks County, while the lowest is set at $174 in Armstrong County. Philadelphia County is set at $205.

18. See D. T. Beito, *From Mutual Aid to the Welfare State: Fraternal Societies and Social Services, 1890-1967* (Chapel Hill: University of North Carolina Press, 2000). Beito claims that mutual aid societies thrived in specific historical contexts that have long since disappeared. We may, however, be seeing a modern analogue in the recovery house movement, which stands as a provider of services such as low-cost housing and a means to impart "survival values such as thrift, mutualism, and individual responsibility" (p. 4).

19. Ibid.; Katz, *In the Shadow of the Poorhouse*.

20. Esping-Andersen, *The Three Worlds of Welfare Capitalism*, 3.

21. Operators intuited the goals of the residual welfare state in the street-level imperative to help a person temporarily, "until they can help themselves." Gøsta Esping-Andersen cites Richard Titmuss's (*Essays on the Welfare State* [1958]) classical distinction between residual and institutional welfare states as follows: "[In residual welfare states], the state assumes responsibility only when the family or market fails; it seeks to limit its commitments to marginal and deserving groups. [The institutional] model addresses the entire population, is universalistic, and embodies an institutionalized commitment to welfare" (Esping-Andersen, *The Three Worlds of Welfare Capitalism*, 20).

22. K. Polanyi, *The Great Transformation: The Political and Economic Origins of Our Time* (Boston: Beacon Press, 2001).

23. See Esping-Andersen, *The Three Worlds of Welfare Capitalism*, 42.

24. Ibid., 21.

25. The principle of less eligibility, a concept dating back to the English Poor Laws, stipulates that welfare benefits are always set below the prevailing local minimum wage (making the welfare recipient "less eligible" than the worker willing to earn a living at the lowest wage in any given region). GA takes the concept of less eligibility to its extreme. Not only are benefits set far below the federal poverty line (in Pennsylvania, they are set at just under 50% of the poverty line), but they also are set well below those offered in AFDC/TANF and SSI (see for example C. Blitz, "Impact of Welfare Reform on Substance Abusers' Medicaid Eligibility and Subsequent Effect on Access to and Utilization of Behavioral Health Services in Philadelphia, 1994–1999" [Ph.D. diss., University of Pennsylvania, 2001]; Gallagher, *A Shrinking Portion of the Safety Net*; R. S. Daniels, "A Matter of Fairness: The Equity of Urban General Assistance," *Review of Policy Research* 11, no. 1 [1992]: 165–76.) As illustrated by Gallagher, *A Shrinking Portion of the Safety Net*, the average benefit nationwide for GA from 1989 to 1998 held steady at just over $200 for disabled individuals, despite real value increases in both SSI benefits and the monthly federal poverty level. GA recipients are even "less eligible" within state boundaries, as several states administer at the county and/or urban level.

26. Daniels, "A Matter of Fairness"; Peck, *Workfare States*; Wolch and DeVerteuil, "New Landscapes of Urban Poverty Management."

27. Katz, *The Price of Citizenship*. See also J. R. Hackworth, *The Neoliberal City: Governance, Ideology, and Development in American Urbanism* (Ithaca, NY: Cornell University Press, 2007); W. Sites, *Remaking New York: Primitive Globalization and the Politics of Urban Community* (Minneapolis: University of Minnesota, 2003).

28. See for example W. J. Wilson, *The Truly Disadvantaged: The Inner City, the Underclass, and Public Policy* (Chicago: University of Chicago Press, 1987); M. B. Katz, ed., *The "Underclass" Debate: Views from History* (Princeton, NJ: Princeton University Press, 1993).

29. Substance abusers had been eligible to receive disability benefits under SSI since the program's inception in 1974.

30. Blitz, "Impact of Welfare Reform on Substance Abusers' Medicaid Eligibility," 19. For further information on these debates, see C. R. Gresenz, K. Watkins, and D. Podus, "Supplemental Security Income (SSI), Disability Insurance (DI), and Substance Abusers," *Community Mental Health Journal* 34, no. 4 (1998).

31. For an extended discussion of these debates, see C. Blitz, "Impact of Welfare Reform on Substance Abusers' Medicaid Eligibility." In particular, see Blitz's extensive analysis of the following sources: D. R. Gerstein and H. J. Harwood, *Treating Drug Problems*, vol. 1, *A Study of the Evolution, Effectiveness, and Financing of Public and Private Drug Treatment Systems* (Washington, DC: National Academy Press, 1990); Gresenz, Watkins, and Podus, "Supplemental Security Income (SSI), Disability Insurance (DI), and Substance Abusers"; J. R. McKay et al., "Characteristics of Recipients of Supplemental Security Income (SSI) Benefits for Drug Addicts and Alcoholics," *Journal of Nervous and Mental Disease* 186, no. 5 (1998): 290; and R. Rosenheck and L. Fishman, "Do Public Support Payments Encourage Substance Abuse?" *Health Affairs* 15, no. 3 (1996): 192–200.

32. The result, according to Blitz ("Impact of Welfare Reform on Substance Abusers' Medical Eligibility") and Halter ("Homeless in Philadelphia"), was a host of new federal, state, and county policies designed to restrict eligibility, increase oversight, and decouple cash assistance from Medicaid.

33. Further exploration of the Pennsylvania case illustrates how GA survived subsequent retrenchment efforts in the 1990s. First, in 1994, Public Law 319 no. 49 (Act 49) restricted the GA program by reducing the eligibility period for those deemed transitionally needy, and by tightening the mandates under the chronically needy category (individuals over the age of forty-five who were not disabled were shifted into the transitional category [Blitz, "Impact of Welfare Reform on Substance Abusers' Medical Eligibility," 12]). Shortly thereafter, Pennsylvania eliminated the transitionally needy category altogether with the 1995 passage of Public Law 129 no. 20. No longer was there a place for the able-bodied individual on GA; rather, only those who met the former eligibility criteria for the chronically needy, as specified in the original Welfare Reform Act of 1982, could qualify. These were primarily individuals with some form of physical or mental disability, and/or those who agreed to seek drug and alcohol treatment under the nine-month category for the "needy substance abuser."

34. SSI payments to alcoholics more than doubled that of the Philadelphia GA recipient ($484 per month versus $205 in 1997). On average, SSI was 50% higher than GA nationwide (Blitz, "Impact of Welfare Reform on Substance Abusers' Medical Eligibility").

35. As one example, Jamie Peck describes the enduring dilemma of regulation in capitalist labor markets as follows: "A sustainable social allocation of waged work must be achieved without eroding the imperative to enter the market, while recognizing that it is impossible to force the entire population into waged employment" (Peck, *Workfare States*, 50).

36. C. Offe, *Disorganized Capitalism: Contemporary Transformations of Work and Politics* (Cambridge, MA: MIT Press, 1985), 37.

37. Stated differently by Esping-Andersen, *The Three Worlds of Welfare Capitalism*, decommodification is tantamount to deproletarianization. As later chapters will show, however, the issue of "choosing freely" is in some ways complicated by the recovery question. So too are the inherent "depoliticization" effects of labor force exemption.

38. Beito, *From Mutual Aid to the Welfare State.*

39. Peck, *Workfare States*, 38.

40. Appadurai, "Deep Democracy," 24. See also S. Sassen, "Spatialities and Temporalities of the Global: Elements for a Theorization," *Public Culture* 12, no. 1 (2000): 215–32.

41. The term *dope fiend behaviors* is commonly used as a derogatory reference to old behaviors or old ways associated with active addiction. These are set out in stark contrast to the more virtuous behaviors and tactics associated with recovering technologies, such as self-responsibility, honesty, and self-assessment. "Nodding off" refers to the common tendency among active heroin users to suddenly fall asleep in social situations. It is taken as a direct sign of continued heroin use.

42. While Malik's opinions on this subject are quite common among recovery house operators, it should be noted that his sentiments and policies are quite controversial, particularly among recovery professionals who advocate for methadone maintenance. During the 2003 CODAAP recovery house training, an entire session was devoted to debunking the many myths that surround methadone, and the Philadelphia-based advocate Sherry Tractenburg went as far as to say that recovery houses which deny access to methadone clients could face repercussions under the Americans with Disability Act for their discriminatory practices.

43. In the case of Seattle (see "Inebriated in Seattle," July 20, 2006, on ABC News Online, under the blog The Blotter), the federal government has awarded $1 million in grants to a wethouse program designed to house the community's highest consumers of public funds (as measured by jail days and ER visits). In Hamilton, Ontario, a recent innovative housing program puts chronic alcoholics on a specific regimen consisting of 5 to 8 ounces of beer or wine per hour in a licensed setting (see J. Evans, "Between Care and Control: The Hospitalization of the Chronically Homeless," paper presented at the Annual Meeting of the Association of American Geographers, Boston, April 16, 2008).

44. According to Michael Katz (*The Price of Citizenship*, 144), nonprofit institutions formally organized and operated for charitable purposes are exempt from federal taxes and local property taxes based on their tax identification number in the United States Internal Revenue Code: 501 [c] (3). In 1992, about 5,600 organizations enjoyed 501 [c] (3) status.

45. Section 8 is a federal rental assistance program operated by the Department of Housing and Urban Development (HUD). It is designed to subsidize qualified tenants in private rental markets.

46. Polanyi, *The Great Transformation*, 81–89.

47. W. J. Wilson, *When Work Disappears: The World of the New Urban Poor* (Alfred A. Knopf Inc., 1996), 25.

48. See J. Maskovsky, "Do We All 'Reek' Of the Commodity?: Consumption and the Erasure of Poverty in Lesbian and Gay Studies," in *Out in Theory: Lesbians, Gays, Cultures*, ed. E. Lewin and W. Leap (Urbana: University of Illinois Press, 2002). Maskovsky cites Wilson, "The Truly Disadvantaged," as one text that exemplifies this thesis on the detriments of nonmonogamous relations and hypersexuality among the urban poor.

49. Emergency food stamps are another mechanism used as a stopgap measure for economic risk prevention. This provision, offered by the welfare office, allows addicts to expedite receipt of their food stamps. Accordingly, in the eyes of the operator, the client can contribute to the house food club immediately.

50. IOP is defined by the City of Philadelphia's Community Behavioral Health (CBH) guidelines as nine hours of group and individual treatment per week.

51. For further reflections on welfare administration as a mode of governance, see Chatterjee, *The Politics of the Governed*.

52. V. A. Zelizer, *The Social Meaning of Money* (New York: Basic Books, 1994), 195–96; cited in Katz, *The Price of Citizenship*, 301.

53. Peck, *Workfare States*; A. Roy, *City Requiem, Calcutta: Gender and the Politics of Poverty* (Minneapolis: University of Minnesota Press, 2003).

54. As William Fisher contends, the explosive growth of NGOs, both formal and informal, is equally as significant to the late twentieth century as the rise of the nation-state in the late nineteenth. The globalization of capital has shifted interdependencies among political actors in the "post-welfare" moment, creating new circulatory channels for the documentation of citizenship and the provision of social services. See for example Appadurai, "Deep Democracy"; G. Baiocchi, *Militants and Citizens: The Politics of Participatory Democracy in Porto Alegre* (Stanford, CA: Stanford University Press, 2005); Chatterjee, *The Politics of the Governed*; Davis, *Planet of Slums*; Ferguson and Gupta, "Spatializing States"; W. F. Fisher, "Doing Good? The Politics and Antipolitics of NGO Practices," *Annual Reviews in Anthropology* 26, no. 1 (1997): 439–64; Keck and Sikkink, *Activists Beyond Borders: Advocacy Networks in International Politics* (Ithaca, NY: Cornell University Press, 1998); A. Ong, *Neoliberalism as Exception: Mutations in Citizenship and Sovereignty* (Durham, NC: Duke University Press, 2006); Paley, *Marketing Democracy*; and Roy, *City Requiem, Calcutta*.

55. Davis, *Planet of Slums*, 175.

56. Esping-Andersen, *The Three Worlds of Welfare Capitalism*.

57. I credit Nik Theodore and Jamie Peck for these insights. For an example of how similar processes work in day labor markets, see Peck and Theodore, "Contingent Chicago."

## CHAPTER 3

1. Foucault, "On Governmentality"; in M. Foucault, *The History of Sexuality*, vol. 3, *The Care of the Self*, trans. R. Hurley (London: Penguin; New York: Pantheon, 1986).

2. M. Foucault, "Technologies of the Self," in *Ethics: Subjectivity and Truth*, ed. P. Rabinow (New York: New Press, 1994), 225.

3. Ibid.

4. Cruikshank, *The Will to Empower*, 4.

5. N. Rose, "Governing the Enterprising Self," in *The Values of the Enterprise Culture: The Moral Debate*, ed. P. Heelas and P. Morris (New York: Routledge, 1992), 143.

6. In this case a full compendium of "lack" in areas such as self-worth and capacity for self-governance, the latter indicated in AA's First Step: "I am powerless over alcohol, my life has become unmanageable."

7. Marianna Valverde quotes Barry Hindess to make this point: "[This] is a profoundly political paradox that pervades liberal governance . . . the central contradiction of liberalism is that people are regarded as 'born free' (as Locke said), but, they have to be *made free* through training for autonomy. This training often relies on despotic means that stand in uneasy relationship with the ostensible ends of self-governance and freedom." See M. Valverde, " 'Slavery from within': The Invention of Alcoholism and the Question of Free Will," *Social History* 22, no. 3 (1997): 252.

8. In this respect, there are echoes of utilitarianism in the rationalities of recovery house operators. As Jeremy Bentham averred, "The force of physical sanction being sufficient, the employment of political sanction would be superfluous" (as cited by Polanyi in *The Great Transformation*, 122). Of course the conflation of profiteering and social reform in Bentham's industry houses for the indigent also instantiates a nineteenth-century predecessor to the contemporary recovery house.

9. As Sue Hyatt notes in her study of public housing tenant associations in England (see Hyatt, "Poverty in a 'Post-Welfare' Landscape") supposed beneficiaries of reform get off board

when they experience empowerment strategies as oppressive. Said differently by Shore and Wright, "where they felt manipulated, the link was lost between ideology and consciousness, or professional knowledge and private, self-interested improvement. And when people failed to identify with the policies of their rulers, the normative power of modern government lost its ideological grip" (C. Shore and S. Wright, "Policy: A New Field of Anthropology," in *Anthropology of Policy*, ed. C. Shore and S. Wright [New York: Routledge, 1997], 31). See also Althusser's extensive work on the "ideological state apparatus," in L. Althusser, "Ideology and Ideological State Apparatuses (Notes Towards an Investigation)," in *The Anthropology of the State: A Reader*, ed. A. Sharma and A. Gupta (Malden, MA: Blackwell, 2006), 86–111; and Joseph Townsend's *Dissertation on the Poor Laws*, as discussed in Polanyi, *The Great Transformation*, 116–21.

10. Peck, *Workfare States*, 11.

11. As Barbara Cruikshank notes (personal communication), just as Foucault argued that the prison has culled its authority from knowing the criminal, philanthropy in its multiple forms has always drawn its authority from knowing the poor.

12. Cruikshank, *The Will to Empower*.

13. For further discussion of this preoccupation, see Valverde, *Diseases of the Will*, and Sedgwick, *Tendencies*.

14. Lest we fall victim to Robin Kelley's apt conceptualization of the culture trap, whereby poverty scholars insist on reducing cultural practices to the status of "coping mechanism," "oppositional consciousness," or "adaptational strategy," it is important to recognize the humor in these stories as "more than a response to, or product of, oppression." This analytical stance affords acknowledgment of the "artistry, the fun, and the gamesmanship that continues to exist, if not thrive, in a world marked by survival and struggle"; see Kelley, *Yo' mama's Disfunktional!* 4.

15. Sedgwick, *Tendencies*.

16. J. Peck, "Struggling with the Creative Class," *International Journal of Urban and Regional Research* 29, no. 4 (2005): 759.

17. See Polanyi's discussion of Joseph Townsend's *Dissertation on the Poor Laws* in Polanyi, *The Great Transformation*, 116–21.

18. Valverde, *Diseases of the Will*, 15.

19. Rose, *Governing the Soul*.

20. Ibid., 7.

21. Valverde, *Diseases of the Will*.

22. Rose, *Governing the Soul*.

23. Ibid.

24. Cruikshank, *The Will to Empower*.

25. Sedgwick, *Tendencies*, 134.

26. Rose, "Governing the Enterprising Self."

27. Gordon, "Governmental Rationality"; M. Foucault, "The Birth of Biopolitics," in Rabinow, *Ethics*; Foucault, "Technologies of the Self"; Rose, "Governing the Enterprising Self."

28. Valverde, "'Slavery from within.'"

**CHAPTER 4**

1. See for example Shaffer, "Silent Treatment."

2. Peck and Theodore, "Contingent Chicago."

3. Peck, *Workfare States*.

4. Rose, "Governing the Enterprising Self."

5. Davis, *Planet of Slums*, 102–3.

6. For two exemplary texts in this analytical tradition, see Bourgois, *In Search of Respect*, and P. E. Willis, *Learning to Labor: How Working Class Kids Get Working Class Jobs* (New York: Columbia University Press, 1981). As Bourgois puts it in his analysis of resistance in East Harlem,

"Although street culture emerges out of a personal search for dignity and a rejection of racism and subjugation, it ultimately becomes an active agent in personal degradation and community ruin" (p. 9).

7. N. Brenner and N. Theodore, eds., *Spaces of Neoliberalism: Urban Restructuring in Western Europe and North America* (Malden, MA: Blackwell, 2002).

## CHAPTER 5

1. Shaffer, "Silent Treatment."

2. In relative terms, Shaffer's *Philadelphia City Paper* article was actually a rather balanced account despite its incendiary title. For example, apart from an exclusive focus on operator comportment, Shaffer explored structural factors such as welfare demography, the crack and heroin epidemics of the 1980s and 1990s, the wrath of managed care, and the lack of affordable housing in Philadelphia.

3. See for example Graham and King, "NJ Appears to Be in No Hurry to Reclaim Addicts"; Haney, "Property Owners and L&I Reach Accord"; Graham, King, and Torok, "How NJ Freed Addicts at PA's Expense"; M. Valbrun, "Neighbors, Rehab Houses Learn to Mesh. Not Long Ago, the Two Sides in Harrowgate Were Enemies, and Then Decided to Talk," *Philadelphia Inquirer*, June 13, 1995; and Simmons, "Drug Homes under Siege."

4. Graham and King, "NJ Appears to Be in No Hurry to Reclaim Addicts"; Graham, King, and Totok, "How NJ Freed Addicts at PA's Expense."

5. See for example Appadurai, "Deep Democracy"; Chatterjee, *The Politics of the Governed*; Baiocchi, *Militants and Citizens*; Davis, *Planet of Slums*; Roy and AlSayyad, *Urban Informality*; J. E. Perlman, *The Myth of Marginality: Urban Poverty and Politics in Rio De Janeiro* (Berkeley and Los Angeles: University of California Press, 1976); and A. Smart, "Unruly Places: Urban Governance and the Persistence of Illegality in Hong Kong's Urban Squatter Areas," *American Anthropologist* 103, no. 1 (2001): 30–44.

6. Smart, "Unruly Places." See also J. Heyman and A. Smart, "States and Illegal Practices: An Overview," in Heyman and Smart, *States and Illegal Practices* (Oxford: Berg, 1999), 1–24; A. Smart, "Predatory Rule and Illegal Economic Practices," in *States and Illegal Practices*, 99–128.

7. To begin my analysis, I am loosely invoking the Chicago-school ecological paradigm, which deploys a cyclical model of social organization-disorganization-reorganization to explain social phenomena (for an extensive critical analysis of this paradigm, see O'Connor, *Poverty Knowledge*). I also borrow from John Clarke's model of conjunctural analysis, which seeks to understand the present historical moment not as a simple linear narrative but rather as a conjuncture of multiple routes and conflicted possibilities (see Clarke, *Changing Welfare, Changing States*).

8. A. Hillier and D. Culhane, "Closing the Gap: Housing (Un)-Affordability in Philadelphia," departmental papers (City and Regional Planning, University of Pennsylvania, 2003); available at http://works.bepress.com_hillier/8.

9. This is especially true of General Assistance. Unlike the modest increases seen in TANF and SSI across the 1990s, GA benefits have remained constant since the 1980s.

10. See for example Shaffer, "Silent Treatment."

11. Valverde, *Diseases of the Will*.

12. For an analysis of myriad discursive regimes operating with similar objectives, see Rose, *Governing the Soul*.

13. This again reveals the scalar logic of ratcheting down via retrenchment. Whereas General Assistance once served as a temporary and residual gateway or failsafe for the welfare subject awaiting Federal Assistance (SSI or TANF), recovery houses now serve as a failsafe for those awaiting General Assistance. And, in their efforts to connect addicts to GA, the operators play a crucial function in redocumenting a very particular form of citizenship.

14. See for example Piven and Cloward, *Regulating the Poor*.

15. As Andrew Beverage avers, Riis's message was something to the effect of "If we don't do something about the social unrest breeding in the heaving tenements of the Lower East Side, they will soon come to get us on Fifth Avenue!" (personal communication, 2006).

16. Marianna Valverde's work ("'Despotism' and Ethical Liberal Governance," *Economy and Society* 25, no. 3 [1996]: 357–72) has shown the class-specific nature of alcohol treatment in Victorian England. Categories are needed to justify the facilities and the relative freedom offered in retreats, since the principle of "voluntary admission" erodes as one moves down the class ladder. Just as there was a decisive spectrum ranging from country club treatment for gentile males, to reformatories for lower-class women (even though the goal may have always been the same, the restoration of weakened willpower), in the case of treatment in contemporary Philadelphia, consignment to the unregulated recovery house is limited to addicted bodies in the lower-class strata. It should be noted once again that this restratification reflects neither neoclassical nor neoliberal tenets, at least so far as the hoary concept of choice is concerned.

17. Blumberg also acknowledged that some GA recipients continue to find ways to stay on welfare, either by procuring a co-occurring disorder or by getting on SSI/SSDI, the result being that many addicts become long-term recovery house residents.

18 Esping-Andersen, *The Three Worlds of Welfare Capitalism*, 37.

19. Ibid.

20. Katz, *The Price of Citizenship*.

21. See Ferguson and Gupta, "Spatializing States," in particular their discussion of how the state creates, through mundane and unmarked practices, a powerful impression of vertical encompassment of the local. States invest a good deal of effort in developing procedures and practices to ensure they are imagined in some ways rather than others. The mundane rituals and routines of state spatialization set out a scalar hierarchy, through either surveillance and repression or benevolence and nonintervention. These practices profoundly alter "how bodies are oriented, lives are lived, and subjectivities are formed" (p. 984). In particular, the state enjoys the privilege of a particular kind of spatial mobility in the surprise visit, and in its capacity to inspect or not inspect. The function and goal of the *potential* inspection are to regulate and discipline in ways that encompass statized and de-statized (or local) forms of power.

22. For further exploration of Ananya Roy's concept of "territorialized uncertainty," see Roy, *City Requiem, Calcutta*; Roy and AlSayyad, *Urban Informality*; and N. AlSayyad, "Urban Informality as a 'New' Way of Life," in *Urban Informality*, 20.

23. This foundational question was pithily summarized by Foucault with the ultimate query, "Why must one govern?" See Foucault, "The Birth of Biopolitics.," 75. See also Valverde, "'Despotism' and Ethical Liberal Governance."

24. AlSayyad, "Urban Informality as a 'New' Way of Life."

25. Ibid., 11.

26. Peck, *Workfare States*, 38. See also A. Tickell and J. A. Peck, "Social Regulation after Fordism: Regulation Theory, Neo-Liberalism and the Global-Local Nexus," *Economy and Society* 24, no. 3 (1995): 357–86.

27. AlSayyad, "Urban Informality as a 'New' Way of Life," 17–18.

28. M. Valverde, "Police Science, British Style: Pub Licensing and Knowledges of Urban Disorder," *Economy and Society* 32, no. 2 (2003): 236.

29. Ibid.; Gordon, "Governmental Rationality."

30. V. Malkin, "The End of Welfare as We Know It."

31. See L. Wacquant, "Urban Marginality in the Coming Millennium," *Urban Studies* 36, no. 10 (1999): 1639; L. Wacquant, "Deadly Symbiosis: When Ghetto and Prison Meet and Mesh," *Punishment & Society* 3, no. 1 (2001): 95; and Wacquant, "Urban Outcasts."

32. As Valverde notes, there are differences between home and workplace, rural and urban, public and private, that justify and are rooted in different modes of governance. For example,

we do not expect small, private businesses to uphold the same bureaucratic standards regarding issues such as affirmative action that we expect of large, public institutions. In effect, by being "geographicalized, a particular mode of governance avoids being judged by the standards of a neighboring but distinct space." See for example Valverde, "'Despotism' and Ethical Liberal Governance," 368; and Valverde, "Police Science, British Style."

33. I am indebted to an anonymous reviewer of the manuscript for these insights.

34. Roy, *City Requiem, Calcutta*, 15–21. See also Roy and AlSayyad, *Urban Informality*, 20.

35. Just as deconstruction has been illuminating with respect to denaturalization in liberal doctrine, Valverde suggests as well that "de-geographicalization" is an important analytical practice for understanding the generative aspects of licensure. See Valverde, "Police Science, British Style."

36. Gordon, "Governmental Rationality," 21. There are other effects at stake here as well. By refusing to endow the recovery house with its own social-legal category, there is a sense in which the state affords itself a strategy of de-spatializing governance, shifting regulatory focus onto the individual subject and "transferring the stigma associated with the space (the recovery house) onto some but not all of the people in it." Valverde discusses this idea using the "found in" category as a device for geographicalizing government. For example, "not every human being who is physically found in a brothel will be legally considered a 'found-in.' (The arresting officers would begin by excluding themselves and then go on to exclude others whom they regarded as not involved in the business)." See Valverde, "'Despotism' and Ethical Liberal Governance," 369.

37. Peck and Theodore, "Contingent Chicago"; Wolch and DeVerteuil, "New Landscapes of Urban Poverty Management."

38. AlSayyad, "Urban Informality as a 'New' Way of Life," 18.

39. Peck, *Workfare States*. Wacquant, "Deadly Symbiosis," 1471.

## CHAPTER 6

1. Valverde, *Diseases of the Will*.

2. Peck, *Workfare States*.

3. Wacquant, "Deadly Symbiosis."

4. Cruikshank, "Revolutions Within"; Valverde, *Diseases of the Will*.

5. As Valverde notes, one way to begin thinking about how to describe and analyze the persistent influence of nonliberal, even illiberal modes of government alongside and even inside advanced neoliberalism is to reflect on the different techniques by which contradictory modes of governance have been articulated, perhaps most successfully, through taxonomies of space. The unevenness of liberal governance is thus not an anachronism destined to disappear through globalization, but a permanent feature of the dynamics of governance. See Valverde, "'Despotism' and Ethical Liberal Governance."

6. In a similar vein, Julia Paley's trope "the paradox of participation" illustrates how democratic concepts such as responsibility and participation actually *facilitate* the exit of the state while ushering in neoliberal reforms. See chapter 5 of Paley, *Marketing Democracy*, 140–81.

7. AlSayyad, "Urban Informality as a 'New' Way of Life," 17–18.

8. Paley, *Marketing Democracy*; Cruikshank, *The Will to Empower*.

9. Special thanks to Jamie Peck for help with these insights (personal communication, 2007).

10. Peck, *Workfare States*.

11. Wacquant, "Deadly Symbiosis," 95.

12. Valverde, *Diseases of the Will*.

13. See for example Peck, "Geography and Public Policy."

14. As Eve Sedgwick illustrates with a number of cases (for example, the hapless exercise addict), the concept of addiction has been evacuated "once and for all, of any necessary specificity

of substance, bodily effect, or psychological motivation . . . addiction, under this definition, resides only in the structure of a free will that is always somehow insufficiently free, a choice whose voluntarity is insufficiently pure . . . as each assertion of will has made voluntarity itself appear problematic in a new area." See Sedgwick, *Tendencies*, 132.

15. I've adapted the concept of precedent-setting from Appadurai's analysis of similar developments in the impoverished neighborhoods of Mumbai. See Appadurai, "Deep Democracy," 34.

16. See for example Katz, *In the Shadow of the Poorhouse*; Beito, *From Mutual Aid to the Welfare State*; and Polanyi, *The Great Transformation*. There are also parallels here (albeit more distant, or less immediate) to the early formation of the private welfare state; see Hacker, *The Divided Welfare State*.

17. While CODAAP estimates a CHI utilization rate of 80% bed capacity for FIR clients (approximately 240–280 clients at any given time), there are no current estimates on the number of FIR clients living in non-CHI houses.

18. See *Robinson v. California* 370 U.S. 660 (1962).

19. For more information on the FIR program, see J. L. Osbourne's unpublished senior thesis, "The Forensic Intensive Recovery Program" (University of Pennsylvania, 2003).

20. Philadelphia Treatment Court Participant Handbook (2003).

21. See J. Soteropoulos, "Restored Funding Saves Drug Programs," *Philadelphia Inquirer*, January 3, 2004.

22. For an extensive review of New York City's Treatment Court, see Malkin, "The End of Welfare as We Know It." For information at the national scale, see Erik Echolm's *New York Times* article, "Innovative Courts Give Some Addicts Chance to Straighten Out" (October 15, 2008). Echolm documents the spread of drug courts to more than 2,100 courtrooms in every state in the country since the first began in Miami in 1989. He cites a study by Urban Institute researchers that found 55,000 people nationwide in adult drug courts, at a cost of about $500 million a year in supervision and treatment (see A. Bhati, J. Roman, and A. Chalfin, "To Treat or Not to Treat: Evidence on the Prospects of Expanding Treatment to Drug-Involved Offenders," Urban Institute Justice Policy Center Research Report [Washington, DC: Urban Institute, April 2008]). These researchers claim, however, that drug courts reap more than $1 billion in reduced law enforcement and prison costs.

23. Peck, *Workfare States*. Wacquant, "Deadly Symbiosis."

## CONCLUSION

1. See for example Appadurai, "Deep Democracy"; Chatterjee, *The Politics of the Governed*; Baiocchi, *Militants and Citizens*; Davis, *Planet of Slums*; Perlman, *The Myth of Marginality*; Roy, *City Requiem, Calcutta*; Roy and AlSayyad, *Urban Informality*; and Smart, "Unruly Places."

2. P. Bourdieu and L. Wacquant, "Neoliberal Newspeak: Notes on the New Planetary Vulgate," *Radical Philosophy* 105 (2001): 2–5.

3. For a broader theoretical discussion of similar processes in urban restructure, see Uitermark, "The Genesis and Evolution of Urban Policy."

4. Chatterjee, *The Politics of the Governed*.

5. Peck, *Workfare States*.

6. For a methodological discussion of urban analysis in this vein, see Uitermark, "The Genesis and Evolution of Urban Policy."

7. Sites, *Remaking New York*.

8. Cruikshank, *The Will to Empower*; Rose, *Governing the Soul*.

9. See the introduction to Barry, Osborne, and Rose, *Foucault and Political Reason*.

10. Appadurai, "Deep Democracy."

11. See for example Roy and AlSayyad, *Urban Informality*.

12. For a discussion of spatial governmentality, see S. E. Merry, "Spatial Govemmentality and the New Urban Social Order: Controlling Gender Violence through Law," *American Anthropologist* 103, no. 1 (2001): 16–29.

13. See introduction to Roy and AlSayyad, *Urban Informality*, 2.

14. See the editors' introduction, "Millennial Capitalism: First Thoughts on a Second Coming," in *Millennial Capitalism and the Culture of Neoliberalism.*, ed. J. Comaroff and J. Comaroff (Durham, NC: Duke University Press, 2001), 15.

# Bibliography

ABC News Online. The Blotter, "Inebriated in Seattle," July 20, 2006. http://blogs. abcnews.com/theblotter/2006/07/inebriated_in_s.html.

Alcoholics Anonymous World Services. *Alcoholics Anonymous*. New York: Alcoholics Anonymous World Services, Inc., 1939.

AlSayyad, N. "Urban Informality as a 'New' Way of Life." In Roy and AlSayyad, *Urban Informality*, 7–32.

Althusser, L. "Ideology and Ideological State Apparatuses (Notes Towards an Investigation)." In *The Anthropology of the State: A Reader*, edited by A. Sharma and A. Gupta, 86–111. Malden, MA: Blackwell, 2006.

Amin, A., ed. *Post-Fordism: A Reader*. Oxford: Blackwell, 1994.

Appadurai, A. "Deep Democracy: Grassroots Globalization and the Research Imagination." *Public Culture* 14, no. 1 (2002): 21–47.

Baiocchi, G. *Militants and Citizens: The Politics of Participatory Democracy in Porto Alegre*. Stanford, CA: Stanford University Press, 2005.

Barry, A., T. Osborne, and N. S. Rose, eds. *Foucault and Political Reason: Liberalism, Neo-Liberalism, and Rationalities of Government*. Chicago: University Of Chicago Press, 1996.

Beito, D. T. *From Mutual Aid to the Welfare State: Fraternal Societies and Social Services, 1890–1967*. Chapel Hill: University of North Carolina Press, 2000.

Bhati, A., J. Roman, and A. Chalfin. "To Treat or Not to Treat: Evidence on the Prospects of Expanding Treatment to Drug-Involved Offenders," Urban Institute Justice Policy Center Research Report. Washington, DC: Urban Institute, April 2008.

Blitz, C. "Impact of Welfare Reform on Substance Abusers' Medicaid Eligibility and Subsequent Effect on Access to and Utilization of Behavioral Health Services in Philadelphia, 1994–1999." Ph.D. diss., University of Pennsylvania, 2001.

Bourdieu, P., and L. Wacquant. "Neoliberal Newspeak: Notes on the New Planetary Vulgate." *Radical Philosophy* 105 (2001): 2–5.

Bourgois, P. I. *In Search of Respect: Selling Crack in El Barrio.* Cambridge: Cambridge University Press, 2003.

Brenner, N. *State/Space: A Reader.* Malden, MA: Blackwell, 2003.

Brenner, N., and N. Theodore, eds. *Spaces of Neoliberalism: Urban Restructuring in Western Europe and North America.* Malden, MA: Blackwell, 2002.

Burchell, G., C. Gordon, and P. Miller, eds. *The Foucault Effect: Studies in Governmentality; With Two Lectures by and an Interview with Michel Foucault.* Chicago: University of Chicago Press, 1991.

Butto, A. "Urban-Rural Migration: Race, Drugs, and Community Change in Rural Pennsylvania." Ph.D. diss., University of Pennsylvania, 1994.

Cain, C. "Personal Stories: Identity Acquisition and Self-Understanding in Alcoholics Anonymous." *Ethos* 19, no. 2 (1991): 210–53.

Caporaso, J. A., and D. P. Levine. *Theories of Political Economy.* Cambridge: Cambridge University Press, 1992.

Carr, E. S. "Secrets Keep You Sick": Metalinguistic Labor in a Drug Treatment Program for Homeless Women." *Language in Society* 35, no. 5 (2006): 631–53.

Chatterjee, P. *The Politics of the Governed: Reflections on Popular Politics in Most of the World.* New York: Columbia University Press, 2004.

Clarke, J. *Changing Welfare, Changing States: New Directions in Social Policy.* Thousand Oaks, CA: Sage, 2004.

Clifford, J., and G. E. Marcus. *Writing Culture: The Poetics and Politics of Ethnography.* Berkeley and Los Angeles: University of California Press, 1986.

Comaroff, J., and J. Comaroff. "Millennial Capitalism: First Thoughts on a Second Coming." In *Millennial Capitalism and the Culture of Neoliberalism,* edited by J. Comaroff and J. Comaroff, 1–56. Durham, NC: Duke University Press, 2001.

Cruikshank, B. "Revolutions Within: Self-Government and Self-Esteem." In Barry, Osborne, and Rose, *Foucault and Political Reason,* 231–51.

———. *The Will to Empower: Democratic Citizens and Other Subjects.* Ithaca, NY: Cornell University Press, 1999.

Daniels, R. S. "A Matter of Fairness: The Equity of Urban General Assistance." *Review of Policy Research* 11, no. 1 (1992): 165–76.

Davis, M. *Planet of Slums.* New York: Verso, 2006.

Denzin, N. K. "Confronting Ethnography's Crisis of Representation: Review Symposium; Crisis in Representation." *Journal of Contemporary Ethnography* 31, no. 4 (2002): 482–90.

Duneier, M. *Slim's Table: Race, Respectability, and Masculinity.* Chicago: University of Chicago Press, 1994.

Duneier, M., O. Carter, and H. Hasan. *Sidewalk.* New York: Farrar, Straus and Giroux, 2001.

Echolm, E. "Innovative Courts Give Some Addicts Chance to Straighten Out." *New York Times,* October 15, 2008.

Esping-Andersen, G. *The Three Worlds of Welfare Capitalism.* Princeton, NJ: Princeton University Press 1990.

Evans, J. "Between Care and Social Control: The Hospitalization of the Chronically Homeless." Paper presented at the Annual Meeting of the Association of American Geographers, Boston, April 16, 2008.

Ferguson, J., and A. Gupta. "Spatializing States: Toward an Ethnography of Neoliberal Governmentality." *American Ethnologist* 29, no. 4 (2002): 981–1002.

Fisher, W. F. "Doing Good? The Politics and Antipolitics of NGO Practices." *Annual Reviews in
Anthropology* 26, no. 1 (1997): 439–64.

Foucault, M. "The Birth of Biopolitics." In Rabinow, *Ethics*, 73–79.

———. "Governmentality." In Burchell, Gordon, and Miller, *The Foucault Effect*, 87–104.

———. *The History of Sexuality*. Vol. 3, *The Care of the Self*. Translated by R. Hurley. London:
Penguin; New York: Pantheon, 1986.

———. "On Governmentality." *Ideology and Consciousness* 6 (1979): 5–21.

———. "Technologies of the Self." In Rabinow, *Ethics*, 223–51.

Gallagher, L. J. *A Shrinking Portion of the Safety Net: General Assistance from 1989 to 1998*. Washington, DC: Urban Institute, 1999.

Gerstein, D. R., and H. J. Harwood. *Treating Drug Problems*. Vol. 1, *A Study of the Evolution, Effectiveness, and Financing of Public and Private Drug Treatment Systems*. Washington, DC: National
Academy Press, 1990.

Goode, J., and J. Maskovsky, eds. *The New Poverty Studies: The Ethnography of Power, Politics, and
Impoverished People in the United States*. New York: New York University Press, 2001.

Gordon, C. "Governmental Rationality: An Introduction." In Burchell, Gordon, and Miller,
*The Foucault Effect*, 1–51.

Gottschalk, M. *The Shadow Welfare State: Labor, Business, and the Politics of Health Care in the United
States*. Ithaca, NY: Cornell University Press, 2000.

Graham, M., and L. King. "NJ Appears to Be in No Hurry to Reclaim Addicts." *Philadelphia
Inquirer*, October 3, 1995.

Graham, M., L. King, and T. Torok. "How N.J. Freed Addicts at Pa.'s Expense: Paroles Were
Sent without Permission, They Got Aid but Little Treatment." *Philadelphia Inquirer*, October
1, 1995.

Gregory, S. *Black Corona: Race and the Politics of Place in an Urban Community*. Princeton, NJ:
Princeton University Press, 1998.

Gresenz, C. R., K. Watkins, and D. Podus. "Supplemental Security Income (SSI), Disability
Insurance (DI), and Substance Abusers." *Community Mental Health Journal* 34, no. 4 (1998):
337–50.

Hacker, J. S. *The Divided Welfare State: The Battle over Public and Private Social Benefits in the United
States*. Cambridge: Cambridge University Press, 2002.

Hackworth, J. R. *The Neoliberal City: Governance, Ideology, and Development in American Urbanism*.
Ithaca, NY: Cornell University Press, 2007.

Halter, A. "Homeless in Philadelphia: A Qualitative Study of the Impact of State Welfare Reform on Individuals." *Journal of Sociology and Social Welfare* 19, no. 4 (1992): 7–20.

———. "The Impact of the Welfare Reform Act of 1982 on the Transitionally Needy in Philadelphia." Ph.D. diss., University of Pennsylvania, 1986.

Haney, K. "Property Owners and L&I Reach Accord. Judge to Work out Agreement on
Halfway-Home Dispute in Harrowgate." *Philadelphia Daily News*, March 31 1995.

Harvey, D. *A Brief History of Neoliberalism*. New York: Oxford University Press, 2005.

———. *The Condition of Postmodernity: An Enquiry into the Origins of Cultural Change*. Oxford:
Blackwell Publishers, 1989.

Heyman, J., and A. Smart. "States and Illegal Practices: An Overview." In *States and Illegal Practices*, 1–24. Oxford: Berg, 1999.

Hillier, A., and D. P. Culhane. "Closing the Gap: Housing (Un)-Affordability in Philadelphia."
Departmental papers. Department of City and Regional Planning, University of Pennsylvania, 2003. Available at http://works.bepress.com_hillier/8.

———. "Vacancy Reporter." Departmental papers. Department of City and Regional Planning, University of Pennsylvania, 2001. Available at http://cml.upenn.edu.

Hyatt, S. B. *From Citizen to Volunteer: Neoliberal Governance and the Erasure of Poverty.* In Goode and Maskovksy, *The New Poverty Studies,* 201–35.

———. "Poverty in a 'Post-Welfare' Landscape." In Shore and Wright, *Anthropology of Policy,* 217–38.

Jessop, B. "Post-Fordism and the State." In Amin, *Post-Fordism,* 251–79.

Katz, M. B. *In the Shadow of the Poorhouse: A Social History of Welfare in America.* New York: Basic Books, 1996.

———. *The Price of Citizenship: Redefining the American Welfare State.* New York: Holt Paperbacks / Henry Holt and Company, 2001.

———, ed. *The "Underclass" Debate: Views from History.* Princeton, NJ: Princeton University Press, 1993.

Keck, M. E., and K. Sikkink. *Activists Beyond Borders: Advocacy Networks in International Politics.* Ithaca, NY: Cornell University Press, 1998.

Kelley, R. D. G. *Yo'mama's Disfunktional!: Fighting the Culture Wars in Urban America.* Boston: Beacon Press, 1997.

Lewis, O. *La Vida: A Puerto Rican Family in the Culture of Poverty—San Juan and New York.* London: Secker and Warburg, 1966.

Malkin, V. "The End of Welfare as We Know It. What Happens When the Judge Is in Charge?" *Critique of Anthropology* 25 (2005): 361–88.

Maskovsky, J. "Do We All "Reek" Of the Commodity?: Consumption and the Erasure of Poverty in Lesbian and Gay Studies." In *Out in Theory: Lesbians, Gays, Cultures,* edited by E. Lewin and W. Leap, 264–86. Urbana: University of Illinois Press, 2002.

McKay, J. R., A. T. McLellan, J. Durell, C. Ruetsch, and A. I. Alterman. "Characteristics of Recipients of Supplemental Security Income (SSI) Benefits for Drug Addicts and Alcoholics." *Journal of Nervous and Mental Disease* 186, no. 5 (1998): 290.

Merry, S. E. "Spatial Governmentality and the New Urban Social Order: Controlling Gender Violence through Law." *American Anthropologist* 103, no. 1 (2001): 16–29.

Morgen, S., and J. Maskovsky. "The Anthropology of Welfare 'Reform': New Perspectives on US Urban Poverty in the Post-Welfare Era." *Annual Reviews in Anthropology* 32, no. 1 (2003): 315–46.

O'Connor, A. *Poverty Knowledge: Social Science, Social Policy, and the Poor in Twentieth-Century US History.* Princeton, NJ: Princeton University Press, 2001.

O'Malley, P., and M. Valverde. "Pleasure, Freedom and Drugs: The Uses of 'Pleasure' in Liberal Governance of Drug and Alcohol Consumption." *Sociology* 38, no. 1 (2004): 25.

Offe, C., and J. Keane. *Disorganized Capitalism: Contemporary Transformations of Work and Politics.* Cambridge, MA: MIT Press, 1985.

Ong, A. *Flexible Citizenship: The Cultural Logics of Transnationality.* Durham, NC: Duke University Press, 1999.

———. *Neoliberalism as Exception: Mutations in Citizenship and Sovereignty.* Durham, NC: Duke University Press, 2006.

Osbourne, J. L. "The Forensic Intensive Recovery Program." B.A. senior thesis, University of Pennsylvania, 2003.

Paley, J. *Marketing Democracy: Power and Social Movements in Post-Dictatorship Chile.* Berkeley and Los Angeles: University of California Press, 2001.

Patterson, J. T. *America's Struggle against Poverty in the Twentieth Century.* Cambridge, MA: Harvard University Press, 2001.

Peck, J. "Geography and Public Policy: Mapping the Penal State." *Progress in Human Geography* 27, no. 2 (2003): 222–32.

———. "Struggling with the Creative Class." *International Journal of Urban and Regional Research* 29, no. 4 (2005): 740–70.

———. *Workfare States*. New York: Guilford Press, 2001.

Peck, J., and N. Theodore. "Contingent Chicago: Restructuring the Spaces of Temporary Labor." *International Journal of Urban and Regional Research* 25, no. 3 (2001): 471–96.

Perlman, J. E. *The Myth of Marginality: Urban Poverty and Politics in Rio De Janeiro*. Berkeley and Los Angeles: University of California Press, 1976.

Piven, F. F., and R. A. Cloward. *Regulating the Poor: The Functions of Public Welfare*. New York: Vintage Books, 1993.

Polanyi, K. *The Great Transformation: The Political and Economic Origins of Our Time*. Boston: Beacon Press, 2001.

Rabinow, P., ed. *Ethics: Subjectivity and Truth*. New York: New Press, 1994.

Rose, N. "Governing the Enterprising Self." In *The Values of the Enterprise Culture: The Moral Debate*, edited by P. Heelas and P. Morris, 141–64. New York: Routledge, 1992.

———. *Governing the Soul: The Shaping of the Private Self*. London: Routledge, 1990.

———. *Powers of Freedom: Reframing Political Thought*. Cambridge: Cambridge University Press, 1999.

Rosenheck, R., and L. Fishman. "Do Public Support Payments Encourage Substance Abuse?" *Health Affairs* 15, no. 3 (1996): 192–200.

Roy, A. *City Requiem, Calcutta: Gender and the Politics of Poverty*. Minneapolis: University of Minnesota Press, 2003.

Roy, A., and N. AlSayyad, eds. *Urban Informality: Transnational Perspectives from the Middle East, Latin America, and South Asia*. Lanham, MD: Lexington Books, 2004.

Sassen, S. "Spatialities and Temporalities of the Global: Elements for a Theorization." *Public Culture* 12, no. 1 (2000): 215–32.

Sedgwick, E. K. *Tendencies*. Durham, NC: Duke University Press, 1993.

Shaffer, G. "Silent Treatment: Hundreds of Unregulated Drug-Recovery Houses Operate in Philadelphia without Any Government Oversight." *Philadelphia City Paper*, November 8–14, 2001.

Shore, C., and S. Wright, eds. *Anthropology of Policy: Critical Perspectives on Governance and Power*. New York: Routledge, 1997.

———. "Policy: A New Field of Anthropology." In Shore and Wright, *Anthropology of Policy*, 3–42.

Simmons, S. "Drug Homes under Siege." *Philadelphia Daily News*, April 6, 1992.

Sites, W. *Remaking New York: Primitive Globalization and the Politics of Urban Community*. Minneapolis: University of Minnesota 2003.

Smart, A. "Predatory Rule and Illegal Economic Practices." *States and Illegal Practices* (1999): 99–128.

———. "Unruly Places: Urban Governance and the Persistence of Illegality in Hong Kong's Urban Squatter Areas." *American Anthropologist* 103, no. 1 (2001): 30–44.

Soteropoulos, J. "Restored Funding Saves Drug Programs." *Philadelphia Inquirer*, January 3, 2004.

Tickell, A., and J. A. Peck. "Social Regulation after Fordism: Regulation Theory, Neo-Liberalism and the Global-Local Nexus." *Economy and Society* 24, no. 3 (1995): 357–86.

Titmuss, R. *Essays on the Welfare State*. London: Allen and Unwin, 1958.

U.S. Census Bureau. *United States Census of Population and Housing*. Washington, DC: Government Printing Office, 2000.

Uitermark, J. "The Genesis and Evolution of Urban Policy: A Confrontation of Regulationist and Governmentality Approaches." *Political Geography* 24, no. 2 (2005): 137–63.

Valbrun, M. "Neighbors, Rehab Houses Learn to Mesh. Not Long Ago, the Two Sides in Harrowgate Were Enemies, and Then Decided to Talk." *Philadelphia Inquirer*, June 13, 1995.

Valverde, M. "'Despotism' and Ethical Liberal Governance." *Economy and Society* 25, no. 3 (1996): 357–72.

———. *Diseases of the Will: Alcohol and the Dilemmas of Freedom.* New York: Cambridge University Press, 1998.

———. "Police Science, British Style: Pub Licensing and Knowledges of Urban Disorder." *Economy and Society* 32, no. 2 (2003): 234–52.

———. "'Slavery from within': The Invention of Alcoholism and the Question of Free Will." *Social History* 22, no. 3 (1997): 251–68.

Venkatesh, S. A. *American Project: The Rise and Fall of a Modern Ghetto.* Cambridge, MA: Harvard University Press, 2002.

Wacquant, L. "Deadly Symbiosis: When Ghetto and Prison Meet and Mesh." *Punishment & Society* 3, no. 1 (2001): 95.

———. "Scrutinizing the Street: Poverty, Morality, and the Pitfalls of Urban Ethnography 1." *American Journal of Sociology* 107, no. 6 (2002): 1468–532.

———. "Urban Marginality in the Coming Millennium." *Urban Studies* 36, no. 10 (1999): 1639.

———. *Urban Outcasts: A Comparative Sociology of Advanced Marginality.* Cambridge: Polity Press, 2008.

Willis, P. E. *Learning to Labor: How Working Class Kids Get Working Class Jobs.* New York: Columbia University Press, 1981.

Wilson, W. J. *The Truly Disadvantaged: The Inner City, the Underclass, and Public Policy.* Chicago: University of Chicago Press, 1987.

———. *When Work Disappears: The World of the New Urban Poor.* New York: Alfred A. Knopf Inc., 1996.

Wilton, R., and G. DeVerteuil. "Spaces of Sobriety/Sites of Power: Examining Social Model Alcohol Recovery Programs as Therapeutic Landscapes." *Social Science & Medicine* 63, no. 3 (2006): 649–61.

Wolch, J. R. *The Shadow State: Government and Voluntary Sector in Transition.* New York: Foundation Center, 1990.

Wolch, J., and G. DeVerteuil. "New Landscapes of Urban Poverty Management." In *TimeSpace: Geographies of Temporality,* edited by J. May and N. Thrift, 149–68. London: Routledge, 2001.

# Index

Note: *Italicized page numbers indicate photos.*

addiction, 11–12; code of, 134; crack, 127–28; linkage to decline in life outcomes, 15; provisions under GA, 67–75, 244; provisions under SSI, 73–74; as regulatory project, 17, 146, 231, 247; street-level expertise, 120–23; as symptom of contemporary urban condition, 12; as welfare category of destitution, 69

Aid to Families with Dependent Children/ Temporary Aid to Needy Families, 67, 68, 276n8, 277n25

Alcoholics Anonymous: Big Book of, 18, 273n25; fifth chapter, 18–19; First Step, 11–12; preamble to "How it Works," 152–53

AlSayyad, Nezar, 227, 235–36, 239, 268

Appadurai, Arjun, 285n15

Baltimore, Maryland, 4, 176, 271n1

Behavioral Health Special Initiative, Philadelphia (BHSI), 195, 196, 256

Beito, David, 277n18

Bencivengo, Mark, 233, 235

Bentham, Jeremy, 280n8

Blumberg, Jeffrey, 85, 207–12, 243–44, 247, 249, 268

Bourgois, Philippe, 281n6

Brenner, Neil, 23

Cain, Carol, 272n13

Chatterjee, Partha, 264, 274n37

child support, 138, 149–52, 184, 188, 230, 264

citizenship, 18, 96, 230, 268, 280n54, 284n34 (*see also* Cruikshank, Barbara); low-wage labor as a norm of, 231; operator's perspective on, 14, 42; recovery as a new mode of, 17, 55, 171, 260, 282n13; and Treatment Court, 258

Clarke, John, 66, 272n17, 282n7

Community Behavioral Health, Philadelphia (CBH), 182, 185, 186, 244, 248, 250, 252, 253, 279n50

Coordinating Office of Drug and Alcohol Programs, Philadelphia (CODAAP), 12, 25, 233, 265; CODAAP Housing Initiative (CHI), 75–76, 92, 95, 110, 172–73, 195, 203, 233–46, 249, 254–56, 260, 264; estimates on recovery houses, 271n2; recovery house training series, 12, 235, 240–43, 266, 279n42

Corzine, John, 7

Contract with America Advancement Act of 1996, 73

Cruikshank, Barbara: on self-governance, 280n6; technologies of citizenship, 21, 99, 100, 120

culture of poverty debates, 120, 273n28

Cutler, Sam, 233–36, 239, 241–43, 254–56

criminal justice. See recovery houses and criminal justice

Davis, Mike, 96, 172, 276n4 (chap. 1). See also under subsistence, niche

devolution, 18; and governmentality, 100, 193; and outdoor relief, 67; and recovery houses, 21, 120, 141, 212, 226, 228–29, 254, 260; in SSI reform, 73

differentiation: and CODAAP Houses, 235–40; informal tactics of, 96, 235, 247–48; as mechanism of regulatory restructure, 23, 264

diseased will, 101, 122–23; attribution of, 134

ecological paradigm, Chicago school, 196, 226, 282n7 (chap. 5)

Esping-Anderson, Gøsta, 67, 96, 211; on de-commodification, 70, 279n37; on residual welfare states, 277n21

Farrakhan, Louis, 13, 14

Fattah, Chaka, 7

Ferguson, James, 274n38, 283n21

Fisher, William, 280n54

Foucault, Michel, 20, 228, 273n24, 281n11, 283n23; on governmentality, 101; technologies of power, 100; technologies of the self, 100

freedom: loss of, in addiction, 12; in post-welfare policy formation, 18, 97, 134, 260; in recovery houses, 46, 102, 106, 108–15, 117, 123, 124, 130, 135, 138, 145, 245, 250, 266

Geertz, Clifford, 23

General Assistance (GA), 6–7, 18, 263, 276n8 (chap. 2); and affordable housing, 191 (see also managed persistence); cash benefit levels in Pennsylvania, 7, 14, 267, 277n17, 282n9; disconnect with GA population, 53, 207–8, 212, 226, 243–44; eligibility for the needy substance abuser in Pennsylvania, 65–75, 88, 149, 152, 156, 209, 246, 278n33 (see also Pennsylvania Welfare Reform Act of 1982); and less eligibility, 277n25; as manager's salary, 168 (see also recovery house labor system); as mechanism of outdoor relief, 22, 67, 72, 74; policy survival in Pennsylvania, 66–75; and recovery house collective survival, 44–49, 84, 92, 179, 250, 267, 283n17 (see also recovery house census-building and recruitment); regulatory logic of, 72–75, 159, 160, 163, 166, 212, 217, 282n13; and regulatory restructuring, 22, 194, 264–65

gentrification, 191, 207

Gupta, Akhil, 274–75n38, 283n21

Harrisburg, Pennsylvania, 7

Harvey, David, 272n18

Hyatt, Susan, 272n14, 273n28, 280n9

inertial persistence, 190, 196–204. See also Smart, Alan

insecurity: chronic conditions of, 4, 57, 160, 164, 217, 265, 270; governance of, 268

Jessop, Bob, 273n21

Katz, Michael, 18, 279n44

Kelley, Robin, 273n28, 281n14

Kenny, James, 7–8

Kensington: badlands moniker, 5; community groups, 6, 210; informal/untaxed economies, 6, 11, 36, 157–67 (see also recovery house informal day labor markets); media perceptions of, 10, 78, 190; migratory channels, 4, 82; poverty rates, 5; prostitution, 6, 175; racial composition, 5, 29; as recovery house capital, 4–10; revitalization, 16, 192; row houses, 3, 3, 30, 69, 70; and spatial containment, 176, 267–68

Kensington and Allegheny (K&A), 4, 5, 6, 6, 16, 28, 29, 35

less eligibility, principle of, 217, 277n25

Lewis, Oscar, 273n28

liberalism, 268; market, 72; proper scope of
    state power, 226, 283n23; spectrum of
    freedom under, 112–13, 280n7, 284n5
Licenses and Inspections, Philadelphia Depart-
    ment of (L&I), 9, 12, 78, 150, 191, 209,
    265 (see also recovery house regulation);
    boarding house licensure and recovery
    houses, 9, 33, 34, 54, 196–207, 210, 212,
    213, 227–28, 234, 272n10; operators'
    perspective on boarding house licensure,
    204–7; uneven enforcement, 9–10, 220,
    224, 228, 233, 256, 266; zoning, 9, 33,
    197–204, 228, 234, 243, 256, 272n10

managed persistence, 11, 25, 190–91, 225–30,
    268 (see also Smart, Alan); ecology of 24,
    191–96
market persistence, 190, 192, 209. See also
    Smart, Alan
Maskovsky, Jeff, 17, 273n28, 279n48
Medicaid, 143, 152, 166, 183, 249; decoupling
    from cash assistance, 278n32
methadone, 77–78, 183, 235, 279n42
Morgen, Sandra, 17
mutual aid societies, 69, 70, 74, 211, 277n18.
    See also Beito, David

Narcotics Anonymous: Basic Text, 28
neoliberalism, 17; contradictory institutions,
    239–40; and enclosure, 263; redistribution
    of risk, 227–28 (see also risk management)
New Jersey, 4; Camden, 84; Newark 1, 2, 4,
    139, 176, 269; "NJ/PA pipeline," 4; Proba-
    tion and Parole scandal of 1995, 190, 255
New Jersey Transit, 4
New York City, 4
Northeast Corridor, 4, 235, 271n1

Offe, Claus, 74
Omnibus Reconciliation Act (OBRA), 67,
    68, 73
Ong, Aihwa, 22

Paley, Julia, 274n38, 284n6
Pennsylvania Welfare Reform Act of 1982,
    24, 66–75, 87, 95, 167, 207, 228, 246,
    278n33
Peck, Jamie, 134, 265, 278n35; on historical
    and geographical specificity, 74; on the
    regulatory fix of workfare, 231; on regula-

tory restructure, 18, 283n26; temporary
    labor markets, 44
Philadelphia: housing un-affordability,
    191–92, 282n8; lax regulatory climate, 9,
    243; loss of manufacturing jobs, 4; Navy
    Yard, 40, 261–62; political culture, 9;
    population loss, 4; postindustrial decline,
    3–6, 191, 266; row houses, 2–3, 3, 70, 95,
    191; vacant properties, 3, 5, 15, 192, 200
Philadelphia City Paper, 189, 233
Philadelphia Electric Company (PECO),
    276n9 (chap. 1)
Philadelphia neighborhoods: Fishtown, 16;
    Frankford, 7; Greater Northeast, 29, 31,
    262, 275n3; North Philadelphia, 2, 3, 69,
    176, 191, 233, 244; Port Richmond, 7, 8,
    29, 31, 275n3; Torresdale, 30, 275n3; West
    Philadelphia, 3, 191, 233
Polanyi, Karl, 22, 280n8
public welfare, Philadelphia Department of,
    202–3, 243–44 (see also General Assis-
    tance; Pennsylvania Welfare Reform Act
    of 1982); operators' relationship to, 49,
    83–92, 207–12, 247, 249 (see also recovery
    house census-building and recruitment)
Puerto Rico, 4, 32, 81–82
Putnam, Robert, 14

Reagan, Ronald, 66, 67, 68, 73. See also Omni-
    bus Reconciliation Act (OBRA)
recidivism, 7, 24, 149, 256
recovery: abstinence, 11, 14, 72, 76–78, 124,
    263; gifts of, 124, 126; 12-step, 6, 11–12,
    15, 35, 102, 106, 115, 245, 246, 247;
    utopian visions, 13–17, 23, 63, 66, 92, 138,
    147, 159, 166, 181, 187; willingness, 12, 47,
    103, 134, 153, 172; wreckage of the past,
    131, 139, 182–87, 264, 267
recovery house(s): accountability, 222, 232,
    242, 244–45, 260; and city council, 7–8,
    233, 234; community complaints and
    tensions, 6, 8–9, 33, 189–90, 202, 233,
    242; community tolerance of, 10, 199,
    210, 220; consultation, 34, 167, 170, 262;
    and crime reduction, 6, 192, 194–95, 196;
    critics, 8–9, 76, 190, 207; and deinstitu-
    tionalization, 194; entrepreneurs 12, 17,
    33, 42, 70, 88, 91, 99, 152, 167,169, 173,
    181, 192, 210, 211, 224, 252, 267; esti-
    mated numbers of, 3–4, 76, 233, 271n2;

recovery house(s) (*cont.*)
and homelessness, 6, 73, 76, 90, 193, 205, 208; house reputation, 34, 47–48, 77; illegality, 196–204, 218, 272n10; infrastructure, 3, 57–64; informal detoxification, 83–84, 175; media coverage, 8, 42, 78, 189–90; movement, 3, 4, 9, 10, 12, 13–17, 65–66, 69, 75, 96, 145, 187, 189–90, 227, 263, 266–67, 269; overcrowding, 8, 44, 148, 198; partnerships, 28–34; proliferation, 4, 7–9, 10, 11, 24–25, 69, 189–90, 191–96, 204, 209, 231; repairs, 30, 33, 57, 61, 236, 237–38; as revitalization strategy, 16, 192; site acquisition, 27, 29–34; substandard housing, 8, 44, 57–64; systematic impoverishment, 24, 148–52, 160, 182; taxation, 221, 234; utilities, 10, 57–64, 129, 236

recovery house administrative categories: advanced, 39, 103, 108–13, 115; black/white houses, 81; CODAAP, 75–76, 233–40, *237*; flophouses, 6, 7, 47, 77, 113; friendly user/meth/wet house, 76–78, 80, 83, 96; intake house, 2, 39, 83–87; mens'/womens' houses, 80; money mills, 47, 78–80; nonprofit/for-profit, 79; Spanish/Christian houses, 81–82; transitional/worker/three-quarter house, 89–92

recovery house census-building and recruitment, 44–49, 100, 123, 138, 264; admissions criteria, 47, 49, 56, 138; advertising, 45–47; blacklist, 179; carrying clients, 85–87, 177, 282n13; coercive census tactics, 177–81, 267; cost-benefit expertise, 178; economic pragmatism, 41, 108, 110; freedom as recruitment tool, 46, 111 (*see also under* recovery house categories, advanced); high-road tactics, 44–45; instability, 57, 147, 178; interhouse market competition, 16, 44, 50, 57, 85–87, 148, 177–81, 220, 222, 225, 267–70; low-road tactics, 44–45; manager incentive, 170–71; profits 8, 40–44, 62, 79–80, 147, 169, 189, 192, 198, 209, 214, 218, 223, 239, 249, 267; raids, 45; referral sources/feeder contracts, 4, 10, 44–49, 52, 103, 157, 248–54 (*see also under* treatment sector, circulatory channels with recovery houses; recovery house informal welfare administration, connec-

tions to formal treatment); screening, 45, 49, 77; seasonality, 178–79; turf wars, 44, 55, 57, 156, 206; walk-ins, 49, 52; warehousing, 10, 44, 92, 151, 177, 204, 206; worker clients, 38–39, 40, 56, 94, 163–64

recovery houses and criminal justice, 4, 16, 96, 230, 235, 239, 246, 248, 264–65; Forensic Intensive Recovery, 25, 75–76, 195, 233, 254–57, 260; probation and parole officers, 10, 35, 83, 182, 234, 243; Treatment Court, 12, 25, 76, 195, 233, 254–60, 285n21

recovery house informal day labor markets, 24, 176, 264; electioneering, 7, 163, 272n6; hustling, 24, 122, 150, 152–57, 186, 187; operator policies, 157–67; Muslim oils, 28, 35, 152–57, 186

recovery house informal welfare administration, 55, 64, 66, 96, 100, 212, 232, 260, 263, 274n38; access card, 39, 69, 180–81 (*see also under* recovery house census-building and recruitment, coercive census tactics); address verification/proof of residence, 50–55, 83–87, 208, 212, 264; blackout, 46, 83–84, 87, 108–9, 111; case management, 24, 83, 101, 138–41, 208–9; connections to formal treatment, 4, 10, 44–49, 52, 75, 87–89, 103, 157, 195, 202, 230, 243–54 (*see also under* recovery house census-building and recruitment, referral sources/feeder contracts; treatment sector, formal, circulatory channels with recovery houses); food club, 92–95, 264, 279n49; food stamps, 7, 69, 87, 192, 208, 279n38, 279n49; identification, 2, 84–85; intake, 83–87, 177; intake fee, 86; intake interview as arrival scene, 37–40; intake ritual, 24, 101, 135–38; and the landline telephone, 50–56; "plug-in," 49, 83–87, 264; rent collection, 31, 35, 38, 45–46, 86, 148, 163–64, 179, 213–17, 242, 250; welfare extensions, 89–92, 283n17; welfare fraud, 6, 8, 9, 53, 78, 184–85, 209, 212–17, 229, 256; Wheels checks, 276n7 (chap. 1)

recovery house labor system, 31, 34–37, 101, 163; absentee property owner, 24, 31, 62, 217; assistant manager, 24, 34–36, 167, 169; chore monitor/housefather, 24,

34–36, 167, 172–73, 234, 238; director-
manager, 24, 30–35, 95, 101, 142, 167,
243; house watcher, 24, 36, 116; informal
apprenticeships, 16, 34, 92, 167–74;
manager's salary, 27, 147, 168–74, 216,
234; staff turnover 36, 44, 61, 171
recovery house program: consent, 20, 101,
108, 111, 123–27, 280n9; constitution
of recovering subjects, 22, 100, 120–23,
127, 134; daily schedule, 24, 38–39, 101,
115–19; disciplinary/rule structure, 109,
115, 134, 242; legitimacy, 8, 44, 75, 76, 78,
80, 96, 103, 110, 201–4, 207, 222, 224–40;
mandatory 12-step meetings, 39, 113, 116,
150; participation/working a program,
12, 13, 24, 50, 61, 63, 101–3, 107, 113–19,
143–44, 155, 168, 172, 269, 284n6; prospectus, 103; recovering technologies,
24, 63, 101, 108, 122, 123, 141–45, 177,
192–93 (see also Valverde, Marianna); war
stories, 24, 127–35; weekly house meetings, 35, 94, 104
recovery house regulation, 4, 9 (see also
Licenses and Inspections, Philadelphia
Department of (L&I); absence of specific
licensure 4, 9, 25, 179, 197–201, 203, 226,
228–30, 233, 235, 242, 267; encounters at
AHAD, 54–55, 212–17; in the Kensington
imaginary, 217–25; loopholes, 202, 207,
210, 226; nonintervention, 18, 190, 203,
204, 217, 226, 231, 243, 276, 283n21;
unregulation, 10, 196, 217
relapse, 24, 151–52, 157, 174–77, 184, 186,
262; black market for, 174; and house
dissolution, 45; and manager burnout, 61;
regulatory tensions with the operator, 57,
86, 136, 177–81; state regulatory consequences, 181–82, 187–88, 264
Rendell, Edward: state budget crisis of 2003,
195–96
retrenchment, welfare state: and governmentality, 20, 21, 25, and GA/outdoor
relief, 18, 67–68, 73, 287n33, 282n13; and
recovery houses, 141,195, 226, 227–29,
231, 240, 263, 266
Ridge Avenue Shelter, 149, 151, 176
risk management: Keynesian, 228; neoliberal/
post-welfare, 21, 66, 227–28, 239, 243,
256, 266; for the recovery house operator,

24, 31, 48, 49, 69, 85–87, 92, 96, 112,
122, 136, 163, 177–81, 187 (see also under
recovery house census-building, carrying;
recovery house census-building, coercive
census tactics; relapse, regulatory tensions
with the operator)
Riis, Jacob, 196, 283n15
Robinson, Stanley, 196–204, 225
Rose, Nikolas, 137–38, 282n12
Roy, Ananya, 268; territorialized uncertainty,
229, 283n22; unmapping of space, 229

Sedgwick, Eve, 145, 281n15, 284n14
self-governance, 12, 107, 117, 122, 123, 145,
193, 204, 280n6, 280n7
self-help, 6, 21, 99 (see also Cruikshank,
Barbara); and outdoor relief subsidies, 69,
74, 267 (see also mutual aid societies); and
post-welfarism, 191, 227, 239, 240, 245,
268, 270, 273n26; recovery, 131, 137, 141,
168, 247, 265; and urban ethnography,
273–74n30
self-will, 14, 122, 124, 126, 144. See also
diseased will
Shaffer, Gwen, 189, 233, 282n2
Smart, Alan, 24, 190–91
social mobility, 14, 41, 44, 80, 151, 167, 172,
183, 186, 267
spatial containment, 177, 182, 223, 256,
267–68
spatially concentrated poverty, 4–6, 24, 63;
impact on recovery/recovery houses, 64,
147–67, 181, 191–92, 223–26, 233, 266,
268; state's extension into areas of, 89, 99,
145, 260, 263
Specter, Arlen, 7, 205
Street, John, 7, 272n9; Neighborhood Transformation Initiative, 15, 192
subsistence, 10, 22, 42, 44, 167, 207; niche, 80,
96, 102, 178, 192, 276n4 (chap. 1) (see also
Davis, Mike); predatory nature of, 24, 57,
92, 169, 178–81, 188, 267, 270; and regulation, 188, 230, 251–52, 264–65, 267; and
welfare administration, 74, 83–97, 152, 217
(see also recovery house informal welfare
administration)
substance abuse treatment sector, formal:
circulatory channels with recovery houses,
75, 87–89, 195, 202, 230, 243–54 (see also

substance abuse treatment sector (*cont.*)
*under* recovery house census-building and recruitment, referral sources/feeder contracts; recovery house informal welfare administration, connections to formal treatment); and criminal justice, 254–60; inpatient, 40, 45, 50, 202–3, 255; Kirk Bride, 50, 56; outpatient, 11, 12, 15–16, 45, 49, 70–71, 87–89, 117, 150, 154, 157, 182, 213, 233, 256; paraprofessional counselors,167, 185–86; providers, 4, 8, 77, 83, 195, 218, 234, 244, 249, 252
Supplemental Security Income (SSI), 15, 67; payees, 35, 114; and substance abusers, 72–75, 278n31

Taylor, John, 7, 215
Temple University Hospital, 2
Theodore, Nik, 23, 44, 280n57
Thornberg, Richard, 68. *See also* Pennsylvania Welfare Reform Act of 1982

urban decay, 4, 30, 96. *See also under* Philadelphia, postindustrial decline
urban ethnography: debates in, 19–23
urban governance: rescaling of, 19, 23, 80, 96
urban informality: conventional understandings, 226; deepening of, 96, 212–17, 225, 230, 236 (*see also* differentiation; recovery house administrative categories); gray markets, 10, 216; as a mechanism of regulation and restructure, 225–30, 232, 267, 268; new modes of, 211, 229; recovery house, 44, 57–64, 76–83, 269; shifting historical conditions of, 226
urban poverty studies, 17–20
urinalysis, 35, 175, 182, 234, 242, 246, 259–60, 266. *See also under* relapse, state regulatory consequences of

Valverde, Marianna: centrality of freedom in recovery discourse, 145, 146, 147, 280n7, 283n16; found in category, 284n36; geographicalization of space, 228, 283–84n32, 284n35; regulatory richness of addiction, 17, 146, 231; stratifying effects of alcohol treatment, 283n16; taxonomies of space, 284n5
voluntarism, 6, 10, 21, 67, 102, 111, 119, 141, 171, 187, 229, 273n26. *See also* mutual aid societies; self-help

Wacquant, Loïc, 272n19; advanced marginality, 283n31; carceral-assistential state, 230–32; on the complicity of urban ethnography with neoliberal state-building, 273–74n30, 274n31
Washington, LeAnna, 205
welfare state: Fordist-Keynesian, 17, 228; informal/shadow, 18–19, 66, 72, 91, 120, 138, 143–44, 208, 211, 221, 227, 256, 266, 268, 273n26; poor relief, 22; regime types, 22; regulation theory, 19–23; residual, 22, 71, 277n21; restructure/transformation debates, 17–23, 268
welfare settlement/resettlement, 18, 66, 68, 75, 212
Wolch, Jennifer, 272n14, 272n15, 273n26
workfare: discourses, 15; and OBRA, 27; and the Pennsylvania Welfare Reform Act of 1982, 28; and recovery houses, 2, 163, 230, 231–32, 239, 244, 247, 260, 265; regulatory logic of, 252, 163, 166 (*see also* Peck, Jamie)

Zelizer, Viviana, 93

Lightning Source UK Ltd.
Milton Keynes UK
UKOW02f1643211216

290589UK00001B/141/P